McGraw-Hill Series in Speech

CLARENCE T. SIMON, *Consulting Editor*

SPEECH: CODE, MEANING, AND COMMUNICATION

McGraw-Hill Series in Speech

CLARENCE T. SIMON, *Consulting Editor*

Baird: ARGUMENTATION, DISCUSSION, AND DEBATE

Baird: DISCUSSION: PRINCIPLES AND TYPES

Baird and Knower: ESSENTIALS OF GENERAL SPEECH

Baird and Knower: GENERAL SPEECH

Black and Moore: SPEECH: CODE, MEANING, AND COMMUNICATION

Hahn, Lomas, Hargis, and Vandraegen: BASIC VOICE TRAINING FOR SPEECH

Ogilvie: SPEECH IN THE ELEMENTARY SCHOOL

Powers: FUNDAMENTALS OF SPEECH

Van Dusen: TRAINING THE VOICE FOR SPEECH

SPEECH

CODE, MEANING, AND COMMUNICATION

JOHN W. BLACK and WILBUR E. MOORE

The Ohio State University Central Michigan College of Education

McGRAW-HILL BOOK COMPANY, INC.

New York   Toronto   London   1955

SPEECH: CODE, MEANING, AND COMMUNICATION

Library of Congress Catalog Card Number 54-12247

THE MAPLE PRESS COMPANY, YORK, PA.

PREFACE

There are many approaches to the study of speech. The rhetorically minded sometimes approach speech from the viewpoint of the theory and practice of successful public speakers. The speech scientist is interested in the mechanisms of speech, in nerves and muscles, in sound waves, and in the nature of codes. The interpreter and actor view speech as a part of the artistic expression of man's humanity or spirituality. The clinically oriented observe and report the personality growth and integration that result from speaking experiences. The social scientist studies the role of speech in social conflict or social cooperation. There need be no quarrel among the advocates of any of these approaches to speech. All are seeking to understand man's use of speech to acquire meanings and to communicate them to his fellows. Like the elephant that was touched by the blind men, speech yields many impressions. It can be heard, produced, watched, measured, and refined in numerous forms. On the platform, on the stage, before the microphone, in conversation, and in conferences—in whatever milieu speech is occurring — it is worthy of study and improvement.

The introductory approach taken in this book is that speech, which consists of audible and visible symbols, provides the principal means by which man acquires, creates, communicates, and perpetuates his meanings. Of especial relevance are the current researches and theories indicating that how one symbolizes about his symbolizing or talks about his talking or knows about his knowing has far-reaching effects, both personally and socially. The manner of talking about talking leads to bigotry or tolerance, curious inquiry or dogmatism, observing, inferring, and learning, or sterile recapitulation of generalities. Our view, therefore, is comprehensive. It includes the tradition of rhetoric and interpretation, since each has contributed significantly to current patterns of thought. It encompasses the investigations of speech science, anthropology, social psychology, and semantics, since all cast new light upon the total process of communicating meanings.

The subject matter, however, is introductory and general in nature and limited in detail. The more specific content of public address, speech science, speech correction, debate, interpretation, acting, phonetics, etc., must be left for more individualized and advanced courses.

Our effort to bridge the gap between knowledge and improved performance lies in the projects. Opportunity for application of knowledge, variety of experience, and repetition of performance are essential to developing and testing skills. The projects for practice will, we hope, provide interesting classroom performances in evaluating and in communicating meanings. We trust that they will suggest others that are still more effective.

We acknowledge gratefully the many influences that our undergraduate and graduate teachers and our professional colleagues have had upon our thinking. Their unfailing encouragement of frank and open inquiry and their high respect for humane study and living have provided a strong, impelling force, even in the usual moments of discouragement. Our debt to the labors of particular individuals is obviously great and is acknowledged, inadequately, in the footnotes. To our secretaries we owe thanks for their loyalty and skill. In this, as in all our undertakings, the personal encouragement and help of our families merit our deepest appreciation.

JOHN W. BLACK
WILBUR E. MOORE

CONTENTS

I

AN OVERVIEW

YOUR SPEECH AND YOU

Just before you opened this book you were probably talking. It may have been to a classmate, a close friend, or a teacher, or you may have been talking to yourself—not aloud, of course, but silently. You may have been reminding yourself of something or questioning yourself about a statement or an opinion. Such silent talking to oneself and overt speaking to others carry the heavy burden of getting things done, making plans for the future, persuading others to help us, and giving advice to help them. The $2\frac{1}{2}$ billion human beings in the world pour out literally trillions of words a day, both directly and over such media as the telephone, radio, and television. They speak silently to themselves still other trillions of words in preparing or "getting set" to talk aloud. Much of this talk is purposeful, efficient, productive. Much of it is pleasant and a little is entertaining. But, unfortunately, much of it is tedious and fruitless. And more than a little is "crazy talk," consisting of unconscious distortions of fact, foolish surmising, dangerous conjecturing, or deliberate misrepresentation.

This power of speaking, whether for good or for ill, belongs exclusively to Homo sapiens. No other living creature possesses this power, although some animals do develop a somewhat complex code of signals. Yet, in spite of the tremendous significance and influence of both silent and oral speech and in spite of the fact most of us have talked for years, we have much to learn about the physical, physiological, social, psychological, and linguistic processes of speech if we wish to improve.

It is the dual purpose of this book to sketch some of the facts that are known about speech and to suggest ways by which you should be able to make your own speech more effective than it is. Chapter 2 will outline some of the physiological mechanisms which function to produce speech. Your understanding of these mechanisms will govern ways of

1

thinking as well as ways of speaking. Chapters 3 and 4 will explain some of the physical characteristics of the speech code (the sounds of speech). Chapters 5, 6, 7, 8, 9, 10, and 11 will analyze some of the logical, linguistic, and psychological aspects of the very complex act of speaking, while later chapters will treat specific types of speaking. At the same time, throughout the book, projects by which you can learn to apply basic principles to your own speaking will be suggested. In all these chapters you will have opportunity to observe how speech is made up of visible and audible symbols, how these symbols are produced, and how they acquire meanings which tend to perpetuate a culture. You will have a chance to learn how our manner of talking to ourselves and to others can bring us understanding or misunderstanding, pain or pleasure, new information or the tiresome repetition of old facts and opinion, how verbal habits actually can act as blindfolds or as brilliant illuminators of the world.

In the first chapter, since speech has extensive origins and far-reaching influences, we shall concern ourselves with surveying the relationships between speech and behavior, speech and culture, speech and thinking, and speech and personality. Further, since this chapter is an introduction to a course which, we hope, will lead to the development of new and refined skills in speaking, we shall present a general plan for utilizing the material of this chapter in early speech projects and in applying some of the facts presented to your own individual problems in speaking.

SPEECH AND BEHAVIOR

Speech has been described as a form of human behavior in which words may serve both as substitute stimuli to evoke responses in others and as substitute responses. One person may shout, "Fire!" to cause others to run, and the others may cry, "Where?" instead of running. Speech, then, is both a stimulus to behavior and a behavioral response to a stimulus.

Can we learn anything about speech from a study of cats, rats, and dogs? Let us see. Jules Masserman taught hungry cats to press a switch that would flash a light or ring a bell, and then to lift a trap door over a food box. Norman Maier taught rats to jump against a card like this to get into a food box but not to jump when a card like this

was exposed. In a limited sense, the rats learned to read.

For over 50 years, ever since Ivan Pavlov, the Russian physiologist, first reported his experiments on conditioning animals to respond to signals, scientists have studied the complex relations between signals and symbols on the one hand and the behavior of experimental animals on the other. Pavlov himself discovered that dogs would respond to bells, to 1,000-cycle tones, to shadows on a screen, and to pressure on a leg.

The processes by which we learn speech symbols and attach meaning to them resemble in many ways the manner by which animals learn to respond to signals. First, there is an auditory or visual experience associated closely with an object like food. After repetition of the associated experience, the sounds or visual stimuli alone will call forth the same response as that originally produced only by the food. They have thus become conditioned signals. With human beings, the words associated with experiences become the conditioned signals or symbols and evoke physiological responses similar to those produced by the original stimulus.

Let us suppose that someone spoke the sounds suggested by the words, "Sitzen Zie in einem Sessel." Would you respond? Why not? Simply because you have never associated these symbols with any response. Now let someone say, "Sit in a chair." Would you respond? Probably. Furthermore, if the words "Sitzen Zie einem Sessel" are associated with "Sit in a chair," they, too, may become conditioned symbols capable of producing the same response as the English words.

The words we speak gain their power to set off different types and degrees of response through their association with pleasant and unpleasant experiences or with other words which are associated with pleasure or pain. Thus, people who have never seen a Russian may fear all Russians simply because the term is so generally associated with Communists, while others will fear, hate, or revile Yankees, rebels, Northerners, Southerners, "Barbs," "Greeks," and a host of other classes simply because the names have been associated with something unpleasant. Words, language, the "content" of our speech derive their power largely from the culture or social community in which they occur.

Later, in Chaps. 6 and 7, we shall treat this problem in detail since these culturally indoctrinated meanings from which we reason provide our basic assumptions. At present, let it suffice to call it to your attention so that you may observe how frequently your speech as well as that of your classmates reveals more of your cultural background and your cultural values than it does about the topic under discussion. In the next section we shall observe how our cultural assumptions, preserved through speech, govern our decisions and choices.

SPEECH AND CULTURE

Daily you are confronted with a choice between two or more value systems which you have acquired by symbols and between which, by other symbols, you must make your choice. Shall you study or go to the movie? Shall you accept the philosophy of monism or hold fast to a philosophy of dualism? "Life," writes Lewis Mumford, "even at the lowest level is a selective process: a process of choosing, restraining, promoting, taking from the environment just such sustenance as is helpful toward the creature's development, rejecting what is irrelevant."[1]

Yet, ironically in one sense and fortunately in another, many of our choices were made long ago by the society and culture in which we find ourselves.[2] You are, therefore, unless you are in revolt, considerably more restricted in your freedom of choice than you may at first realize. Many of your choices are unconsciously made simply because you wish to conform to the symbol systems of your ancestors and your fellows. Your mode of dress, your food, your attitudes toward rules, regulations, and laws are what they are largely because of the values and meanings acquired by symbols from childhood. If we should ask you over to the house for a lunch of snails and grubs, your response would be "Ugh." A Frenchman's might be, "I shall be happy to come." If we asked you seriously not to let your shadow fall on a cow, you would suspect our sanity. A Hindu would not need to be asked. In some colleges we could ask a student group representing different races and different religions to our home. In other colleges such an invitation would cause embarrassment to all. These attitudes, values, beliefs held by you and others

[1] Lewis Mumford, *The Conduct of Life*, p. 31, Harcourt, Brace and Company, Inc., New York, 1951.

[2] *Ibid.*, p. 123.

make up a culture. Our culture is based upon the symbol. Leslie White of the University of Michigan writes:[1]

All culture (civilization) depends upon the symbol. It was the exercise of the symbolic faculty that brought culture into existence and it is the use of symbols that makes the perpetuation of culture possible. Without the symbol there would be no culture, and man would be merely an animal, not a human being.

Articulate speech is the most important form of symbolic expression. Remove speech from culture and what would remain? Let us see.

Without articulate speech we would have no *human* social organization. Families we might have, but this form of organization is not peculiar to man; it is not *per se, human*. But we would have no prohibitions of incest, no rules prescribing exogamy and endogamy, polygamy or monogamy. How could marriage with a cross cousin be prescribed, marriage with a parallel cousin proscribed, without articulate speech? How could rules which prohibit plural mates possessed simultaneously but permit them if possessed one at a time, exist without speech?

Without speech we would have no political, economic, ecclesiastic, or military organization; no codes of etiquette or ethics; no laws; no science, theology, or literature; no games or music, except on an ape level. Rituals and ceremonial paraphernalia would be meaningless without articulate speech. Indeed, without articulate speech we would be all but toolless: we would have only the occasional and insignificant use of the tool such as we find today among the higher apes, for it was articulate speech that transformed the nonprogressive tool-using of the ape into the progressive, cumulative tool-using of man, the human being.

In short, without symbolic communication in some form, we would have no culture. "In the Word was the beginning" of culture—and its perpetuation also.

Although speech and its products, symbols and language, serve to fix and preserve values from one generation to the next (to some too rigidly, to others too loosely), they are also the chief means by which values are modified, altered, and replaced. In religion, in philosophy, in literature, in science, symbol systems expressing beliefs in modes of conduct, the nature of the world, and the meaning of literary masterpieces are subject to critical analysis. In free cultures each individual theoretically has the right to determine for himself what traditional

[1] Leslie White, "The Symbol," *Philosophy of Science*, vol. 7, p. 460, 1940. Reprinted by permission of the author.

meanings he will hold and what he will reject, although, of course, in actuality the cultural pressures are great.

In either case, however, whether he breaks from cultural patterns or accepts them, his choice will be at a higher human level if he understands the nature of the symbol. His first step toward freedom for himself and for the culture in which he lives will be a deeper appreciation of, and a new respect for, the symbol, a purification and a clarification of language itself. We must keep in mind that the rulers of symbols will rule mankind. Sergei Chakotin in *The Rape of the Masses* explains how the Nazis trained human beings to respond to the swastika, the heel-click, and "*Heil* Hitler" to evoke more elaborate responses of acquiescence to the Nazi philosophy and policies.[1] In this instance there was little appreciation of the nature and the function of the symbol. The examining and the evaluating processes of the human mind were paralyzed because the symbol was accepted as identical with what it was supposed to represent.

On the other hand, Albert Einstein expressed the modern scientific view that symbols are to be used in formulating pictures of the world but that their structure, their relatedness to one another, must be verified by observation. He stated in respect to his unified-field theory that the difficulty was to find out whether his symbolic formulations had to do with nature, whether they were true in the ordinary sense of the word. Here we find care in symbolic formulation and caution in accepting that formulation as a "final" explanation.

SPEECH AND THINKING

Exactly what is involved when you think hard about a problem or ponder over a passage in philosophy or in literature is itself hard to know. Authorities generally agree, however, that symbolizing is at the core of all intellectual life. The four following statements are representative of most of the expert opinion on speech symbols and thinking. "The symbol-making function is one of man's primary activities, like eating, looking, or moving about. It is the fundamental process of his mind and goes on all the time."[2] "The essential act of thought is sym-

---

[1] Sergei Chakotin, *The Rape of the Masses*, E. W. Dickens (trans.), pp. 101–137, Alliance Book Corporation, New York, 1940.

[2] Susanne Langer, *Philosophy in a New Key*, p. 32, Harvard University Press, Cambridge, Mass., 1942.

bolization."[1] "But vocal events gradually become, *in a degree to which no other physiological process is at all comparable,* the medium of interaction between individual organisms and the social environment: the means whereby society controls, 'humanizes' and educates the individual, and the individual reorganizes his social environment."[2] The relation of speech symbols to thinking may be succinctly stated as follows:

1. Words introduce a refined method of analysis into thinking.

2. They provide a basis of inference, of reaching conclusions not demonstrable to the senses.

3. They make it possible for the mind to conceive the complex relational systems of the world (science, metaphysics, logic, etc.) with their many subdivisions.

The part played by our capacity to produce and respond to symbols in thinking and in knowing can be clearly seen in the story of Helen Keller's discovery of meanings. Helen Keller, who, you will recall, lost both sight and hearing while still an infant, wrote:[3]

The morning after my teacher came she led me into her room and gave me a doll. . . . When I had played with it a little while, Miss Sullivan slowly spelled into my hand the word "d-o-l-l." I was at once interested in this finger play and tried to imitate it. . . . In the days that followed I learned to spell in this uncomprehending way a great many words, among them *pin, hat, cup* and a few verbs like *sit, stand* and *walk.* But my teacher had been with me several weeks before I understood that everything has a name.

One day, while I was playing with my new doll, Miss Sullivan put my big rag doll into my lap also, spelled "d-o-l-l" and tried to make me understand that "d-o-l-l" applied to both. . . .

I learned a great many new words that day. I do not remember what they all were; but I do know that *mother, father, sister, teacher* were among them—words that were to make the world blossom for me, "like Aaron's rod, with flowers." It would have been difficult to find a happier child than I was as I lay in my crib at the close of that eventful day and lived over the joys it had brought me, and for the first time longed for a new day to come. . . .

---

[1] Arthur David Ritchie, *The Natural History of the Mind,* p. 279, Longmans, Green & Co., Ltd., New York, 1936.

[2] Frank Lorimer, *The Growth of Reason,* p. 73, Harcourt, Brace and Company, Inc., New York, 1929.

[3] From *The Story of My Life,* pp. 21–29, by Helen Keller. Copyright 1903 by Helen Keller. Reprinted by permission of Doubleday & Company, Inc., New York.

I had now the key to all language, and I was eager to learn to use it. Children who hear acquire language without any particular effort; the words that fall from others' lips they catch on the wing, as it were, delightedly, while the little deaf child must trap them by a slow and often painful process. But whatever the process, the result is wonderful. Gradually from naming an object we advance step by step until we have traversed the vast distance between our first stammered syllable and the sweep of thought in a line of Shakespeare.

The act of thinking is thus seen to include the gradual acquisition of systems of symbols, the recall to consciousness of learned symbols, and the fitting of symbol systems into larger and satisfactorily consistent systems. Thinking is involved in the "learning," in the "remembering," and in the arranging and rearranging of systems of symbols. Likewise, the symbols learned, recalled, and arranged are basic to the thinking process.[1]

Both the symbol systems and their structure (their relations to one another) are derived from the culture in which they occur. Consequently, the more our thinking is organized in accordance with the language structure, the more likely it is to appear socially valid. The more our thinking is socially valid, the more likely it is "to lead to adequate social behavior that corresponds to the patterns of group behavior."[2]

This does not mean abject conformity to social pressure in thinking. It does mean that our use of symbols cannot, as does the young child's and the schizophrene's, differ greatly from the traditional structure of symbols. Let us look at several examples to make this somewhat abstract idea clear. A five-year-old child, responding to an ink blot test, said, "A snailing toad swimming in the road." Her language although unconventional conveyed her immature conception of a snaillike and toadlike animal combined. Such a response from an adult, seriously given, would suggest failure or breakdown of adult language and thought patterns. A schizophrenic woman in a California hospital claimed that Barbara Stanwyck had traded heads with her and that she, not Barbara Stanwyck, should be the movie star. The great disparity between her symbol system and the belief of sane persons that words must fit the events gave her no concern. If anything could be

[1] Norman Cameron, *The Psychology of Behavior Disorders*, p. 82, Houghton Mifflin Company, Boston, 1947.
[2] *Ibid.*, p. 89.

said, it could, of course, happen. In varying degrees, normal persons may suffer a loss in the ability to make their symbolic representation fit that of others.

Symbol systems become meaningless jargon when they cannot be fitted into old systems or when, for unconscious or conscious reasons, old systems which are no longer valid cannot be modified to fit into new ones. Thus, individuals in all ages have found the transition from old symbol systems to new ones fraught with tensions, anxieties, and even physical violence. The formulators of socially beneficial symbol systems like those of Christ, Copernicus, and Galileo have borne the taunts, imprecations, and assaults of thousands who could not reconcile the new formulations with the old ones. On the other hand, countless fraudulent systems have been accepted when they were made to appear consistent with the old and well-accepted ones.

SPEECH AND PERSONALITY

Personality has been defined as "the most characteristic integration of an individual's structures, modes of behavior, interests, attitudes, capacities, abilities, and aptitudes."[1] Obviously, this refers to a person as a whole—his physique, his intelligence, his moods. Naturally, too, personality is reflected in a variety of ways. Speech is the most pervasive way by which an individual acquires, modifies, and reveals his personality. Strangely enough, however, particularly since man is what he is because of his speech, this aspect of personality has been largely ignored until recent years. Now, however, numerous investigations by psychiatrists, psychologists, and anthropologists focus attention upon the interrelations of speech and personality.

Although individuals whose speech deviates markedly from that of their fellows are likely also to have great differences in personality, our concern here is with the interrelations of the speech and the personality of the so-called average or nearly average individual. In general, your insight into another's personality will be greater if your keenness in observing and evaluating speech is sharpened. More important, your knowledge of speech processes will increase your own self-understanding and performance.

The manifestations of personality through speech may be studied from many vantage points and in varying intensities. The clinical psy-

[1] Norman Munn, *Psychology*, 2d ed., p. 568, Houghton Mifflin Company, Boston, 1951.

chologist and the psychiatrist use lists of words to which the individual
being studied makes oral responses. They use ink blots about which the
subject or patient talks. What he says he sees and how he organizes
what he says become clues to his personality structure, his way of looking at the world. The specialists also use pictures about which the subject invents stories, and they use incomplete sentences about home,
parents, girls, boys, hopes, etc., which the subject completes. The
completions are organized to suggest areas of difficulty and areas of
satisfaction.

Obviously, you will not expect to use such techniques to study speech
and personality. However, if you do wish to understand your own personality a little better and if you will be cautious in making judgments
about others, your close observation of the following characteristics of
the quantity and the quality of speech will repay you:

  I. Quantity of overt speech
     A. Excessive restriction of overt speech
        1. The situations in which restriction occurs
        2. Manifestations of excessive talking to self
     B. Excessive amount of overt speech
        1. The situations in which excessive talking occurs
        2. Manifestation of little silent appraisal of content
 II. Quality of overt speech
     A. Self-contradictions
     B. Verbal slips
     C. Substitution of talking for action

Such common college slang as "He clammed up," "He's the strong,
silent type," "He talks too much," "He started his mouth going and
went off and left it" suggests that many students do judge others by
the amount of their talk. More refined scientific studies indicate that
the marked extremes in the amount of speech reveal maladjustments.[1]
Other studies show that topics which cause maladjusted persons the
most trouble are the very ones they talk about the most.[2]

The quality of speech, particularly, is likely to reveal the tensions and
frustrations of an individual. Of course, all of us have changing moods

[1] Wendell Johnson, *People in Quandaries*, pp. 244–251, Harper & Brothers, New
York, 1946.
[2] Wilbur Moore, George Soderberg, and Donna Powell, "Relations of Stuttering
in Spontaneous Speech to Speech Content and Verbal Output," *Journal of Speech
and Hearing Disorders*, vol. 17, pp. 371–376, 1952.

and changing sources of information which are reflected by inconsistent statements. Macaulay, the English historian and statesman, remarked, "Man is so inconsistent a creature that it is impossible to reason from his belief to his conduct, or from one part of his belief to another." On the other hand, internal inconsistencies of speech may reflect the segregation or compartmentalizing of values that characterize a disturbed person. A professor, long frustrated over failure to win promotion, denounced the administration for not appreciating good teaching. After being told to publish articles and after successfully doing so, he belittled his colleagues who had not published, suggesting they were entirely unworthy of promotion. The sudden change of theme suggested strongly that the professor was as frustrated as ever, even though he had the promotion. As you listen to the content of conversation, discussion, and public speeches, train yourself to detect self-contradictions, even though you must be too polite to expose them. However, it is of more importance for you to understand the frustrations that lead you to contradict yourself.[1]

Unconscious contradictions are often exposed by blunders in speech. Thus, when an individual hearing of another's misfortune remarked, "I am gla-er-er—I am sorry to hear of it," the primitive and devilish pleasure he had in hearing of the other's hurt broke through the civilized veneer. Occasionally our speech blunders strip away our social disguises and expose our comically naked thoughts.[2]

Probably speech reveals the most about personality when it is substituted for action. Hamlet's soliloquies (those long talks with himself), some of which you perhaps memorized in high school, were a delaying

[1] Edward A. Strecker and Kenneth E. Appel, *Discovering Ourselves*, 3d ed., pp. 212–273, The Macmillan Company, New York, 1943.

[2] Freud gives the following interesting incident to illustrate this kind of speech blunder: "A wealthy but not very generous host invited his friends for an evening dance. Everything went well until about 11:30 P.M., when there was an intermission, presumably for supper. To the great disappointment of most of the guests, there was no supper; instead, they were regaled with thin sandwiches and lemonade. As it was close to Election Day, the conversation centered on the different candidates; and as the discussion grew warmer, one of the guests, an ardent admirer of the Progressive Party candidate, remarked to the host: 'You may say what you please about Teddy, but there is one thing—he can always be relied upon, he always gives you a *square meal*,' wishing to say *square deal*. The assembled guests burst into a roar of laughter, to the great embarrassment of the speaker and the host, who fully understood each other." Sigmund Freud, *Basic Writings*, p. 82, Random House, Inc., New York, 1938.

action because the assassination of his father's murderer was too difficult. Using a similar delaying action, students sometimes talk a great deal about getting down to work. Then, too, there are those individuals who make resolutions on New Year's Day, at the beginning of the school term, or on taking a new job after their last dismissal, and professors who explain at length why tests are not graded.

Often when life is too stubborn or too difficult to be changed to our desires, a verbal assault may be substituted for the actual effort to alter conditions. The loneliness and unhappiness of Sara Teasdale and an understandable desire to retaliate are thus reflected in the poem "I Shall Not Care."[1]

When I am dead and over me bright April
   Shakes out her rain-drenched hair,
Though you should lean above me broken-hearted,
   I shall not care.

I shall have peace, as leafy trees are peaceful
   When rain bends down the bough;
And I shall be more silent and cold-hearted
   Than you are now.

Edwin Arlington Robinson, in his poem "Miniver Cheevy," epitomizes the decay of a character who apparently lived only for his verbal assaults. You may read it in Chap. 6. In similar vein, the "big line" may give some individuals a satisfaction because they can "talk" themselves into great "deeds" without the labor of performance.

Another substitutive function of speech can be observed in such remarks as "I'd like to get away from it all." The retreat from an unkind world to a gentler one of our own symbolic creation is a common human experience. It leads to artistic expression in poetry, novels, plays, and movies. And such creations provide for many a ready retreat. Obviously, when such devices are used persistently, they may become substitutes for constructive activity. The daydreamer, the habitual movie-goer, the persistent novel reader may live in a dream world of words and seldom move in the world of action.

[1] Sara Teasdale, *Love Songs*, p. 24, The Macmillan Company, New York, 1917. Reprinted by permission of the publishers.

> And thus the native hue of resolution
> Is sicklied o'er with the pale cast of thought,
> And enterprises of great pith and moment
> With this regard their currents turn awry,
> And lose the name of action.

Students of speech will have the opportunity to note the many ways in which the speech of an individual outlines the inner structure of his personality.

In the preceding discussions of speech and culture, speech and thinking, and speech and personality, we have merely suggested a few of the many interrelationships and factors which, in any single act of speaking, influence what is said and how it is said. Figure 1 more graphically presents these interrelated factors. From it you can outline the interrelated and complex social, physiological, psychological, and physical processes underlying speech. First, a human organism who has been responding to the symbols of his culture, which has evolved from an interweaving of folklore, myth, religion, literature, science, etc., evaluates his ideas and expresses them through highly individual neuromuscular processes. Second, these processes, which are influenced by both heredity and environment, produce sound waves which are transmitted to a listener, either directly or by means of a transmission system. Third, the sound waves set off nerve impulses which have significance to the listener because they have occurred before and because they have been given a certain commonality of meaning with similar processes in the speaker.

As Fig. 1 also indicates, we can understand the physiological, chemical, physical, social, linguistic, and psychological processes only by drawing upon the contributions of the various areas of study indicated. To neglect one area is to leave a gap in our understanding of speech. Consequently, one approaches the study of speech with humility but with an excitement born of a daring quest.

SUMMARY AND APPLICATION

At the end of this chapter you should have a new appreciation of the many influences that have led you to talk, think, and behave as you do. Although you should have humility about the task of improving your speech, you should also have determination to select those cultural factors which improve speech, thinking, and personality and to reject those which cheapen or degrade. You should be more alert to the biases of listeners and more able to understand and cope with them. You

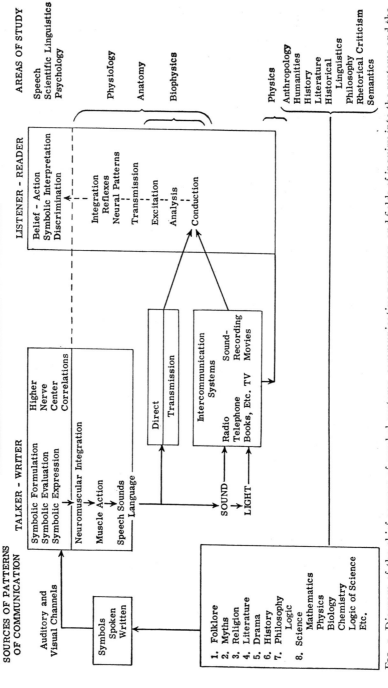

FIG. 1. Diagram of the chief sources of symbol systems, communicative processes, and fields of inquiry into the systems and the processes. (*Developed from a diagram by Hallowell Davis, M.D., in The Journal of Speech and Hearing Disorders, vol. 16, p. 3, 1951.*)

should also rightfully ask some pertinent questions: How do you propose that I start? How can I apply what I have just read?

Here are our suggestions.

1. Try to develop a truly critical and inquiring attitude about the opinions, facts, and assumptions of yourself and your associates. Do this, not with the intent of arguing, but with the desire to discover answers to the question of what led you to think and behave as you do. A spirit of friendly, cooperative inquiry will help the most.

2. Read, listen, and think creatively and imaginatively, with a view to using *new* facts, *new* opinions of your own in your speaking. Parrots can repeat sounds. Only human beings can form new combinations of sounds.

3. Relate your imaginative and creative thinking to the best values in your culture. Measure your new ideas by the most rigorous logical and ethical tests in your culture. How do you know what you say is accurate? Why do you believe it is just and important that you say it? What good will come of your saying it?

4. Develop a sense of freedom when you talk—a freedom that comes from honest inquiry and a deep appreciation of the dignity of others.

5. Try to be considerate of the time and patience of listeners.
   a. Know what you are saying.
   b. Organize it so that its main ideas are easy for the listener to grasp.
   c. Accept yourself without apology so that nervous mannerisms will not irritate or embarrass listeners.
   d. Know your purpose in talking. Is it to find relief? To make an impression? To ask for help? To share something of value? To give help?

6. Keep in mind as you try the Projects for Practice that the purpose is to bring to the level of conscious evaluation many of the speech processes which we have unconsciously learned and practiced but have never tested.

Projects for Practice[1]

1. Organize a discussion group on taboo words in your culture. Can you answer the following questions:
   a. Do you like to have certain words (*sharp, friendly, smooth*) applied to you?
   b. Do you dislike having certain words (*grind, bookworm, brain, socialist*) applied to you?

2. Organize a discussion group to consider how habitual patterns of thought affect the behavior of your class.

[1] The use of projects of some sort is, of course, essential in a speech class. The projects suggested here should be viewed not only as preparation for future speaking but as opportunity to study and to react to social groups.

3. Keep a record for three days of the value words you use. Do they reveal any particular pattern or system of values? In classes do you observe markedly different groups of value words?

4. Keep a record of your complaining for one week. Prepare a 2-minute speech on "The Fine Art of Complaining." How is complaining a symbolic attack upon symbolic restrictions?

5. Prepare a talk on "The Sincerity of Our Thanks and Our Praise." How is insincerity in compliments a use of counterfeit symbols? What is the motive behind such insincerity?

6. Prepare to discuss "The Motives for Deception."

7. Prepare to discuss "Gossip—A Means of Social Control."

8. Prepare to discuss "Advertising and Social Cohesion."

9. Prepare to discuss "Prejudice and Social Conflicts."

10. Keep a record for 1 month of the verbal slips you hear. Did they reveal any hidden motives?

11. Select one common belief held by most members of the class. Try to trace it back to its sources (a) in the members of the class, (b) in their parents, (c) in their schools, (d) in the books, pictures, conversation of their times, (e) in their associates.

12. Many topics on speech may be studied profitably. These are a few suggestions:

   a. "Rhetoric and Drama in Greece"
   b. "Oratory in Rome"
   c. "Oratory of the American Revolution"
   d. "Abolition Oratory"
   e. "Bloody-shirt Oratory"
   f. "The Broken Promises of Politics"
   g. "A Report on Campus Chatter"

Readings

Baird, A. Craig, and Franklin H. Knower, *General Speech*, chaps. 1-3, McGraw-Hill Book Company, Inc., New York, 1949.

Benedict, Ruth, *Patterns of Culture*, Houghton Mifflin Company, Boston, 1934.

Brigance, William Norwood, *Speech: Its Techniques and Disciplines in a Free Society*, chaps. 1, 2, 4, Appleton-Century-Crofts, Inc., New York, 1952.

Gray, Giles Wilkeson, and Claude Merton Wise, *The Bases of Speech*, 2d ed., chaps. 1, 9, Harper & Brothers, New York, 1946.

Johnson, Wendell, *People in Quandaries*, chaps. 1, 2, Harper & Brothers, New York, 1946.

Lee, Irving, *Language Habits in Human Affairs*, Harper & Brothers, New York, 1941.

Lumley, Frederick E., *Means of Social Control*, chaps. 1, 3, 7, 8, 12, 14, Appleton-Century-Crofts, Inc., New York, 1925.

Murray, Elwood, Raymond Barnard, and J. V. Garland, *Integrative Speech*, chaps. 1, 2, The Dryden Press, Inc., New York, 1953.

Plant, James S., *Personality and the Cultural Pattern*, The Commonwealth Fund, New York, 1937.

Stefansson, Vilhjalmur, *The Standardization of Error*, Routledge and Kegan Paul, Ltd., London, 1928.

Thonssen, Lester, and Howard Gilkinson, *Basic Training in Speech*, chap. 2, D. C. Heath and Company, Boston, 1947.

2

THE MECHANISMS OF SPEECH

In this very practical age, students are prone to ask that the utility of what they read be demonstrated. Furthermore, they demand with reason that information be given clearly and simply. As you approach the subject matter of this chapter, we should warn you that you will encounter new words and some difficult reading. To those who will not give up easily, however, we can promise definite benefits. Work with particular types of speech-handicapped persons, some as young as eight years of age, has demonstrated that a knowledge, even a little knowledge, of the speech mechanisms produces two very beneficial results. First, it leads to a more conscious and, therefore, a higher type of neural control of the muscles involved in speech, and, second, it provides the best possible kind of mental hygiene, namely, understanding and appreciation of what one is working with.

If such benefits are derived by young and handicapped students of speech, then college students who are not handicapped should benefit greatly from such knowledge.

The mechanisms which serve for speech also serve other functions, such as chewing, swallowing, breathing, sneezing, coughing, etc. As a result of the integrative action of the nervous system they serve as a unified vocalizing, resonating, and articulating instrument. The integration of functions includes the reception of sound waves by the ears, the transmission of nerve impulses from the hearing mechanism to the brain, the association of impulses of auditory origin with other meaningful experiences, and the organization of outgoing nerve impulses and their transmission to the muscle systems involved in the production of speech sounds. We shall consider briefly each aspect of this integrating process.

18

HEARING

Although, as we have observed in the story of Helen Keller, speech may be acquired by persons who never hear, good hearing is basic to the normal development of speech. In the normal development of speech, we listen to the speech sounds made by others and to our reproduction of them. We correct and refine our early inaccurate attempts. Childish speech gives way to mature speech when mechanisms and processes are normal and the speech environment is good. The mechanism of hearing, by its responsiveness to complex patterns of sounds, makes speech possible.

This responsiveness to sound waves occurs in stages as a series of delicate structures transform the sound pressure waves from the outside world into nerve impulses traveling to the brain. First, the sound waves pass through the external auditory canal and strike the tympanic membrane (eardrum), which fits somewhat like a drumhead over the inner end of the canal. The auditory canal is about 2.5 centimeters long. It is slightly bent, and larger at either end than in the middle. The column of air enclosed within the auditory canal remains at an even temperature and forms a constant fundamental mass which will transmit sound waves to the eardrum. The eardrum, which is conical in shape, sets obliquely over the inner end of the auditory canal. It thus presents a greater area to the waves than if it were set perpendicularly. It is composed of delicate fibers which run concentrically and heavier fibers which, like the ribs of an umbrella, run from the apex of the cone to the periphery. The concentric fibers, being elastic, stretch as the sound waves press inward, while the stronger riblike fibers spring inward but do not stretch. The eardrum is provided with a special protection against excessively loud sounds in that the upper segment is less taut.

Figure 2 shows how the eardrum separates the external canal from the tympanic (middle-ear) cavity. This cavity is filled with air that serves to cushion the excursions of the eardrum.

The movements of the eardrum are transmitted to the liquids within the inner ear by three tiny ossicles (bones). The first, the malleus, or hammer, is attached by a long arm to the eardrum and is suspended by ligaments from the roof of the middle-ear cavity. By studying Fig. 2, you can see that when the long arm of the hammer moves inward, the head of the hammer thrusts outward, and with it the head of the incus (anvil), which is fastened to it. At the same time, the long arm of the incus and the stapes (stirrup) are thrust inward against the membrane over the fenestra ovale (oval window). The double leverlike action of the ossicles intensifies the movements imparted to the membrane over the oval window.

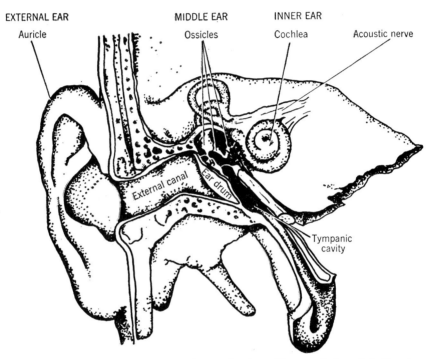

FIG. 2. Component parts of the hearing mechanism. (*By permission of the Sonotone Corporation.*)

The movements of this membrane cause the perilymph (liquid in the bony canal of the cochlea) to "vibrate." The cochlea, an intricate system of canals within the temporal bone, spirals around a conically shaped bone called the modiolus. A membranous canal, filled with endolymph, is attached to the spiral shelf and the walls of the bony cochlea and helps to separate the larger bony canal into two scalae (ladders), except at the apex or helicotrema. This membranous canal, which is approximately 30 millimeters long (less than 1¼ inches), is enclosed by Reissner's membrane and by the basilar membrane. Within the membranous canal, resting on the basilar membrane, is the organ of Corti, a delicate structure containing approximately 15,500 hair cells.[1] The hair cells projecting up into the liquid of the membranous canal connect with the nerve fibers of the auditory nerve that carry nerve impulses from the inner ear to the temporal lobe of the brain.

Whenever the liquid of the two bony cavities "vibrates," the waves compress the membranous canal. The lower end of the membranous canal apparently responds to high-frequency sounds, and the upper end responds to low frequencies. The response characteristics of the different portions of the membranous canal may be accounted for in part by the varying lengths of fibers of the basilar membrane and by the varying size of the organ of Corti. The shorter fibers and the lighter structure of the organ of Corti at the lower end may respond to high-pitched sounds, while the longer fibers and heavier construction at the apical end may respond to lower pitches.

Some popular explanations of hearing suggest that the hearing mechanism responds in much the same manner as the strings of a piano, which vibrate sympathetically when sounds of different pitches are produced in the same room. However, a more detailed study of hearing than is proper in a beginning text would lead to qualifications and additions to this concept.

CENTRAL ASSOCIATIONS

The nerve impulses set off in the inner ear travel to the auditory receptor center in the temporal lobe of the cerebral cortex. The cerebral cortex (cover), composed of roughly $9\frac{3}{4}$ billion nerve cells, is the outer layer of nerve tissue of the cerebrum. Much of the nerve tissue consists of short connecting, or association, fibers. In the human brain its complexity makes possible highly variable and modifiable behavior. Figure 3 shows the location of the hearing center. The cochlear nerve from each ear is connected with the temporal lobes of both sides of the brain and, when stimulated, sends impulses to both temporal lobes, although speech sounds are recognized only in one lobe.[2] Normally, in right-handed individuals they are recognized by the function of the left side and in left-handed individuals by the activity of the right lobe.

The terminal areas of the auditory nerve serve as distributor centers from which other areas of the brain, particularly the adjoining associa-

[1] Stephen L. Polyak, Gladys McHugh, and Delbert K. Judd, *The Human Ear,* p. 41, Sonotone Corporation, Elmsford, N.Y., 1946.

[2] Stephen Walter Ranson and Sam Lillard Clark, *The Anatomy of the Nervous System,* 8th ed., p. 322, W. B. Saunders Company, Philadelphia, 1947.

tion areas, are activated. In these areas associations between the sounds and the multitude of sights, smells, feelings, and tastes which give meaning to life and to symbols are made. Association tracts connect the important sensory and motor centers of the cortex. It is through these

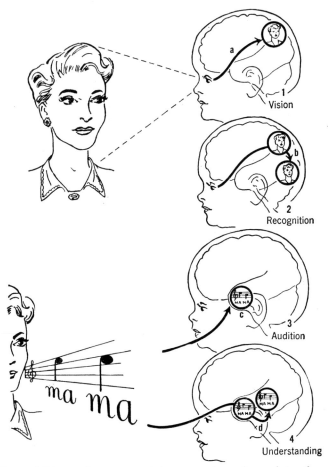

FIG. 3. How a child perceives an event, hears words, and associates them with the event. (*Reprinted from Man in Structure and Function by Fritz Kahn, by permission of Alfred A. Knopf, Inc., New York, Copyright* 1943.)

association pathways that activity in the occipital lobe (visual center) is connected with activity in the temporal lobe (hearing center). Figures 3 and 4 show how associations between visual, recognition, auditory, and speech centers lead to the voicing of meaningful words.

If the association areas fail to develop or if they are damaged, marked speech disturbances result. Blindness for printed words without other visual impairment, deafness for spoken words without other hearing loss, and loss of ability to comprehend the significance of objects,

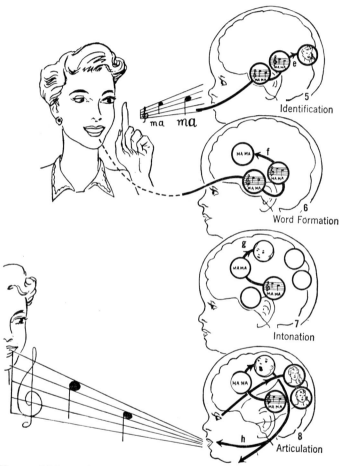

FIG. 4. How a child associates and produces words in a meaningful way. (*Reprinted from Man in Structure and Function by Fritz Kahn, by permission of Alfred A. Knopf, Inc., New York, Copyright* 1943.)

happenings, and symbols characterize the behavior of persons who have suffered from injury to these areas.

A man fifty years of age who had suffered a cerebral hemorrhage could not name an object or a picture of the object. For example, when a table was pointed to, or a picture of a table was shown, he could not say "table." If, however, the letters *ta* were shown simultaneously, he had no difficulty in saying table. A young man of thirty who had been exposed excessively to carbon tetrachloride fumes and who, after being unconscious for 3 days, had remained speechless for 3 months, telescoped the names of familiar objects when his speech did return. A station wagon became a "stagon" while a college dormitory was to him a "colmitory."

Although it would be inaccurate to pinpoint the locations of the various auditory, visual, recognition, and motor centers, still injuries to certain areas of the cortex result in rather clearly defined losses of speech function. Largely on the basis of clinical studies of specific brain damage, the speech functions of the different parts of the cortex have been inferred to be those which were indicated in Figs. 3 and 4.

It must be kept in mind, however, that the number of interconnections within the cortex runs into the billions and that damage to a specific area not only disrupts the function of the brain tissue in that area but disrupts in infinite ways the interconnections with other parts of the brain. Organic damage, therefore, interrupts the established connections and associations in ways that are peculiar to each individual and calls for the establishment of new interconnections and associations. It should also be very clear that just as the failure of these association centers to function impoverishes human experience, so the stimulation and development of the centers enrich and ennoble human living. More and more it is believed that human thought and knowledge rest upon the *association of symbols* with the raw sensory experiences more than they do upon the experiences themselves. In fact, experiments show that these symbolizing functions can reduce or increase the sensory experiences. In other words, what you see and hear is largely determined by what you "think."

MOTOR SPEECH

When the impulses of the sensory receptive centers of hearing, seeing, feeling, smelling, etc., and that of the associational areas of the cerebral cortex are channeled to the speech center (Broca's area), they are organized for the work of producing speech sounds. The speech center is in one sense not a true motor center of the brain. It is a special correlation center which receives waves of impulses and distributes them to those parts of the motor cortex serving the upper portions of the body and the tongue, mouth, and lips. These cortical areas in turn relay impulses to the motor nuclei of the cranial and spinal nerves.

The development of those areas of the motor cortex which serve the tongue, mouth, lips, and upper extremities is accompanied by the acquisition of speech and other forms of symbolic expression and by the elaboration of new and highly complex functions in the upper limbs, particularly in the hands and the fingers.[1]

MOTOR PATHWAYS

The primary motor areas of the cerebral cortex are thought to be the centers which control conscious and voluntary activity of the muscles of the body. They do so by means of projecting nerve fibers which connect them with the nuclei of the nerves that emerge from the brain stem and from the spinal cord to run to the muscles. These projecting fibers, which connect the highest portions of the brain to all nerves that activate muscles, are grouped into three main pathways.

1. THE CORTICOBULBAR PATHWAY. The first pathway we shall consider is the last to develop in the race and the latest to mature in the individual. It is called the corticobulbar-corticospinal tract (also called pyramidal tract), since its fibers run directly from the cortex to the bulb (lowest portion of the brain) and to the spinal column. This pathway crosses to the opposite side to connect with the nerves which activate the muscles. Its function is to activate the muscles for refined, precise, purposive movements. Such skills as writing, typing, playing a musical instrument, and, of course, speaking depend upon the adequate functioning of this pathway. Since this "new motor system" matures slowly, refined skills in the individual naturally are slowly acquired. This pathway functions to inhibit or check the less purposive and less organized impulses from lower brain centers. Hence, injuries to this pathway result in the release of lower centers and the overstimulation of muscles. The muscles then become overtense, or spastic. Voluntary control over the muscles diminishes or disappears completely. In some individuals injury may be so slight that only the tongue will be spastic and slow. Their *r*'s, *s*'s and *l*'s will be made laboriously or omitted. By effort and practice, voluntary control can be restored.

The normal speaker who wishes to develop superior voice and diction must practice continuously to develop refined corticobulbar control of

[1] J. E. Scarff, "Primary Cortical Centers for Movements of Upper and Lower Limbs in Man," *Archives of Neurology and Psychiatry*, vol. 44, p. 243, 1940.

the speech muscles and to make such control habitual by bringing into
activity the extrapyramidal pathway. It is for such control that the
singer, the pianist, or the acrobat spends hours daily in regular practice.

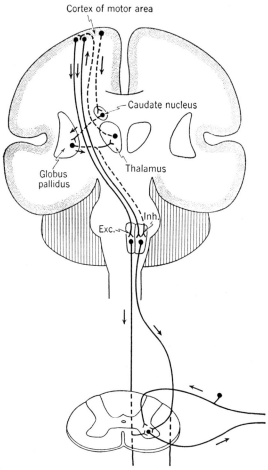

FIG. 5. Simplified representation of the extrapyramidal pathways including the
circular route from the motor cortex through the caudate nucleus and the globus
pallidus back to the cerebral cortex and thence over extrapyramidal tracts to lower
motor neurons. (*From Ernest Gardner, Fundamentals of Neurology, 2d ed., W. B.
Saunders Company, Philadelphia, 1952. By permission of the publishers.*)

2. EXTRAPYRAMIDAL MOTOR PATHS. Research has revealed that some
voluntary impulses reach the motor nerves by channels other than the
corticobulbar tract. As Fig. 5 shows, these channels involve such corre-

lation centers as the caudate nucleus (with tail), the globus pallidus (pale sphere), and the thalamus (inner chamber). One of the chief functions of this set of nerve structures is the automatic regulation and inhibition of opposing sets of muscles. For example, muscles that close the jaws can function only if the muscles that open them are inhibited. The extrapyramidal paths bring into function centers that smooth and refine movements by the reciprocal suppression of the antagonistic sets of muscles. Injury to this system results in muscle tremors or a general slowness of muscular contraction.[1]

It seems that this system, under the dominance of the caudate nucleus, contributes to normal speech in the following ways:

1. By regulating muscle tonus
2. By coordinating and connecting with the superimposed function of speech many fully developed and automatic functions
3. By maintaining required tone, depth of respiration, pitch of voice, and rhythm of utterance[2]

3. CEREBELLAR MOTOR PATHS. The third set of circuits between the motor area of the cerebral cortex and the nerves which activate the speech muscles involves the cerebellum (little brain). The cerebellum contributes tone and coordination to the different muscle structures, particularly those involved in highly skilled acts using both sides of the body. The high degree of coordination between breathing and speaking, between gestures and facial expression on the one hand and vocal inflection and speech rhythm on the other, demands the highly automatic and refined coordinations provided by the cerebellum.[3] At least when the cerebellum is badly injured, speech becomes explosive, uncoordinated, and poorly timed.[4]

FINAL COMMON PATHWAYS

As a result of the functioning of the three upper motor pathways, the nerves arising in the bulb and ending in the muscles of the tongue, lips, jaws, and larynx carry the intricate neural patterns of timing and

[1] John F. Fulton, *The Physiology of the Nervous System*, 3d ed., pp. 494–505, Oxford University Press, New York, 1949.
[2] Paul J. Zentay, "Motor Disorders of the Central Nervous System," *Journal of Speech Disorders*, vol. 2, pp. 131–138, 1937.
[3] Stanley Cobb, *Foundations of Neuropsychiatry*, 4th ed., p. 69, The Williams & Wilkins Company, Baltimore, 1948.
[4] Fulton, *op. cit.*, p. 534.

intensity to secure the rapid contractions and relaxations necessary for the utterance of words and phrases. If you will pay attention to what occurs when you say "Vladivostok" or "Leninsk Kuznetskii," you will understand that automatic control of timing and intensity is essential.

The principal motor nerves activating the speech muscles are the trigeminal (triplet), facial, glossopharyngeal (tongue-pharynx), vagus (wandering), accessory, and glossal (tongue). These nerves are the final common pathways of the neural activity which originates in the cortex, travels over the three circuits, and ultimately terminates in the coordinated muscular activity that produces voice and articulate speech.

RECIPROCAL INNERVATION

After speech is learned, it becomes, as you know from your own experience, largely automatic. This involves complicated reciprocal innervation or "feedback." Essentially, this is a process of automatic self-regulation. The principle of automatic self-regulation is similar in many respects to that involved in the thermostatic control of a gas furnace. Just as a furnace is turned on automatically when the temperature drops below a certain point and is shut off when it is raised several degrees, so the flow of messages from certain types and degrees of muscle activity tends to shut off further action, while at the same time it activates other structures for a different type or degree of activity. After one has learned to say "top" he does not need to think, "Now my tongue has touched the tooth ridge. It is time to drop it, open my jaw, and say *ah*. Now I have said *ah*. It is time to close my lips quickly to get the *p* sound." The rapid sequence of movements is partly regulated by the reciprocal innervation from muscles in action.

If you will study Fig. 6, you will observe how impulses arising from movements of the tongue feed back to the nerve center (nucleus of the hypoglossal nerve) which activates the motor nerve of the tongue. You will also observe that other nerve centers, which activate other speech muscles, also receive the feedback. Actually, this feedback mechanism is repeated in all the other nerves that serve the speech muscles. By this mechanism, centers about to be brought into action as well as those already in action receive messages that indicate the moment-to-moment state of muscular contraction in all speech structures.

These feedback mechanisms as well as the coordinating processes of the cerebellum and extrapyramidal pathways are below consciousness. Much of speech, therefore, both in respect to the meaning and the manner of production, tends to become routinized, stereotyped, automatic. At the same time, it is susceptible to antagonistic or conflictive influences from many different nerve centers. It is for this reason that speech is susceptible to all sorts of interruptions and breakdowns. Train-

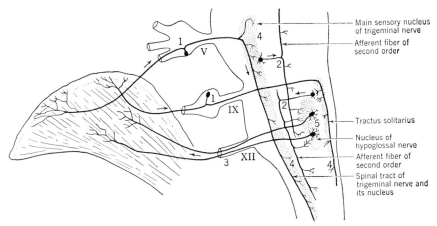

FIG. 6. The glossal nerve (cranial nerve XII) is the motor nerve of the tongue. (*From S. W. Ranson and S. L. Clark, The Anatomy of the Nervous System, 9th ed., W. B. Saunders Company, Philadelphia, 1953. [Cajal] By permission of the publishers.*)

ing in the motor control necessary for good speech and training in the symbolic aspects of speech contribute to the highest type of integration a human being can achieve.

VOICE

Thus far we have seen how sounds are transformed into neural impulses, how these neural impulses are associated with others initiated by other sense organs, and how motor impulses are organized and relayed over different circuits to impinge finally upon the cranial nerves. As a result of this extensive neural activity, muscles contract and relax to produce voice and to shape voiced and voiceless sounds into words. Let us consider now what these muscle structures are like and how they function.

If before you undertake a detailed study of the voice-producing mechanism you will try two simple experiments, you should have a better understanding of the action involved. Compress your lips tightly. Inhale. Blow against the lips without opening them, letting the cheeks puff out under the air pressure. The muscle tension of the lips is so great that the force of air exerted by the contraction of the abdominal muscles does not force them apart. Now relax the lip muscles slightly so that they "trill" as you blow through them. The muscle tension exerted is sufficient to keep the lips closed momentarily until added air pressure blows them open. With the escape of air and the consequent

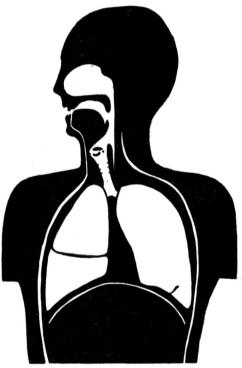

FIG. 7. A schematic representation of the processes of expiration and phonation.

reduction of pressure, they close. When the air pressure is sustained and when the tension of the lip muscles is appropriate, the cycle of opening and closing is repeated.

In a manner very similar to this, the vocal lips or folds situated at the top of the trachea (windpipe) are blown open from 70 to 275 times a second to produce voice. From Fig. 7 you can see how the air stream from the lungs passes through the vocal folds, which are the cartilaginous edges of a membrane, over the upper end of the trachea. If you will take a piece of rubber balloon, slit it, and place it over a small tube, with the slit running from front to back, and then blow through the tube, you will get a rough conception of how the vocal folds function.

The production of voice demands that the vocal folds be straight, that their inner edges be brought together, and that they be taut and vibratile. These conditions are possible because the vocal folds, which, you will remember, are the two cartilaginous edges of the folds in the membranous lining of the trachea, can be closed and tightened by the pull of laryngeal muscles. The laryngeal muscles are attached to the same cartilages that the folds are attached to. Thus, any movement of the cartilages affects the vocal folds

RESPIRATION FOR SPEECH

The vocal folds are vibrated by the outgoing breath stream. In order to talk well, it is necessary to regulate this flow of air. This control is achieved by means of the tension of the muscles of expiration. These muscles, especially those which make up the abdominal walls, are contracted firmly. As they contract, the diaphragm relaxes and the viscera, compressed by the abdominal contraction, press it upward. The vertical dimension of the chest cavity is reduced by this action and by the downward and inward movement of the ribs and sternum. This compression by the bony and muscular walls and floor of the chest cavity forces the air out of the lungs, through the trachea, between the vocal folds, and thence through the mouth or nose.

We have observed that if the vocal folds are approximated, the outgoing air is "vibrated" and "voiced" sounds are produced. If the vocal cords are not approximated, the steady stream of unvibrated air may be blocked and suddenly released to produce *p, t, k,* etc., or it may be partially blocked to produce *f, th, s, sh,* etc. Figure 7 illustrates how the outgoing breath stream may be interrupted by the vocal folds to produce voice and again shaped by the mouth and pharynx to make the individual sounds of speech.

RESONANCE

The voiced speech sounds at the level of the vocal lips are neither very loud nor distinctive. As the vibrated air passes through the cavities of the pharynx, mouth, nose, and head, it is resonated in a manner very similar to that in which the organ pipes of different length resonate the sounds produced by the vibrators of an organ. The resonators may cause a more rapid dissipation of the energy of some of the waves and thus amplify the sound, or make it louder. They may absorb more of the energy of other waves and thus damp, or attenuate, them. In this case the tones will be less loud.

The size and shape of the resonating cavities can be changed so that different, distinctive qualities of tone are emitted from the mouth. It is by the changes of the resonators that the individual vowels gain their distinctive qualities.

There are five ways in which the size, shape, and surface of the resonators may be changed.

1. The pharynx may be changed in size, shape, position, and tension of the walls.

2. The movements of the tongue, of course, may alter the oral cavity in many ways.

3. The jaws may decrease or increase the size of the oral cavity.

4. The lips affect the shape and size of the orifice of the mouth.

5. The movements of the soft palate affect the mouth, pharyngeal, and nasal resonators.

ARTICULATION

Because the muscles of the palate, tongue, lips, cheeks are numerous and complex and because they are responsive to intricate adjustments, the vibrated or nonvibrated air being forced from the lungs can be interrupted or broken up in a large number of places and in widely varying degrees. As a result of these interruptions of the breath stream, a great variety of speech sounds or phonemes may be produced, each one characterized by its own phonetic attribute. Out of the rapid and precise formation of the individual sounds emerge the larger combinations of articulate speech—words.

If you will watch yourself in a mirror as you produce the vowels, you will understand the delicate tensions and counter tensions necessary for the rapid production of speech sounds.

By the frequent recurrence of particular combinations of sounds which refer to or signify objects, events, feelings, or relations, a more or less specific meaning is acquired by each word. The words then become useful as signs or symbols to be reproduced in varying combinations and in numerous contexts or configurations of experience.

SUMMARY AND APPLICATIONS

We have indicated that the act of speaking calls upon delicate receptive mechanisms which respond to sound waves in the outside air. By undergoing chemical and electrical changes, nerve fibers transmit their response to still higher and more complex centers. These higher centers serve to correlate, associate, and direct incoming messages. Impulses to reproduce the sounds heard are relayed over motor nerves to the muscles. The facilitation and coordination of the different pathways are affected by the way we think about ourselves, our listeners, and the act of speaking. If one thinks, "I can't speak; I never could," he is talking to himself in a way that makes the unified function necessary to good speech utterly impossible. If one is talking to himself when he should be listening, he cuts off incoming messages. Or to put the matter another way, the way you are talking to yourself will govern your interpretation of incoming messages.

The far-reaching effects of our habitual ways of thinking and talking are revealed by the not infrequent occurrence of psychogenic deafness, psychosomatic ulcers, and hysterical dysphonia. They are more commonly observed in the instances of stage fright, hesitancies, and mispronunciations in an introductory speech class.

The purpose of speech training is not only to give you information about the mechanisms of speech but to shift the levels of control to the highest neurological centers and thereby to bring about a more purposive and conscious integration of those mechanisms.

Projects for Practice

1. In order to appreciate the necessity of unconscious motor activity in speech, try to pronounce the following foreign names very quickly:

Hsinghsanchen (Manchuria)
Hsiangyang (China)
Hsiachiang (China)
Kalitvenskaya (Russia)
Ustyuzhna (Russia)
Pogoryaloye Gorodishche (Russia)

Do not think these are never used by American speakers. Radio newscasters have to master quickly many words like these. With practice you can improve your neuromuscular control. Now say the following sounds at first slowly, then rapidly.

shing-shahn-juhn (Manchuria)
sh yahng yahng (China)
shyah-jyahng (China)

kah-leet'-ven-skah-yah (Russia)
oos-ty-oozh-nah (Russia)
po-go-ray'-lo-ye go-ro-dee'-shche (Russia)

By means of an atlas, locate these place names. Practice saying them until they are automatic. Try to make a factual statement to the class about one of them.

2. To show that the vocal lips are capable of forming an airtight valve over the windpipe, think the vowel *ah* and keep the muscles tense while trying to exhale.

3. To discover how resonance determines the quality of vowels, call your own telephone number to get a busy buzz. Try capping your hands over the receiver in different positions and listen carefully for the different vowel sounds produced. Practice this until you can make different vowels so that a listener can identify them.

4. Turn to page 27, and after looking up new words in the dictionary, practice them aloud several times so that you can say them easily.

5. Try saying *puh, tuh, kuh* as fast as you can. What happens? Now try *kuh, tuh, puh* as fast as you can. Again what happens? Try saying *tuh, kuh, puh*. Are there regressions to previous patterns? What is the neurological significance?

6. Try talking for 1 minute on something you know little about. Make a tape recording of this talk. Is the speech rhythm the same as your rhythm when you talk on something you know very well?

7. Try reading at sight a passage from "Slurvian Self-taught" in Chap. 4. What happens to speech rhythm and articulation? What is the significance of this occurrence.? Now try reading the passage several times. Does the humor of "Slurvian" become more apparent?

8. Practice unison pronunciation of the difficult words found in the passage used in Project 7.

9. Now read the passage, making a tape recording if possible.

Readings

Eisenson, Jon, *Basic Speech*, chap. 2, The Macmillan Company, New York, 1950.

Gray, Giles Wilkeson, and Claude Merton Wise, *The Bases of Speech*, 2d ed., chaps. 3, 4, Harper & Brothers, New York, 1946.

O'Neill, James, and others, *Foundations of Speech*, chaps. 6, 8, Prentice-Hall, Inc., New York, 1941.

Woolbert, Charles Henry, and Joseph F. Smith, *Fundamentals of Speech*, 3d ed., chap. 9, Harper & Brothers, New York, 1934.

THE SOUND OF SPEECH

Figure 8 implies a diversity both in the sound of speech and in reactions to the sound. First, we infer that unless speech has "enough" sound or, in other words, is sufficiently loud, speech fails; second, that the sound

FIG. 8. Speech is acoustic and each source of speech has unique properties. These permit listeners to describe and identify the speech of different talkers.

of speech is like a personal identification card; third, that it can arouse an unpleasant response, possibly an unnerving one like a scraping sound on a blackboard; and fourth, that the way speech sounds can get in the way of the conveying of thought efficiently, as in the instance of "too fast."

What does speech *sound* like? Our cartoon tells us that some speech sounds "squeaky," "fast," "happy," "like Jim." What does your voice sound like? The questions are disarming in their simplicity, but the answers come hard. Are you tempted to say, "Speech? Why, speech sounds like speech. That's all." We must do better than that, and one purpose of this chapter is to help you describe the sound of speech. You and your classmates, with a single set of terms among you for describing speech, will give and take meaningful statements of how you sound to each other. We can then anticipate progress toward a second and more far-reaching purpose of this chapter—a rapid and conscious alteration of the sound of our speech to make it agree with a recommended acoustic pattern. The third objective of the chapter is, we believe, contributory to this *rapid and conscious* modification—an understanding of the phenomena that determine the properties of the sounds that we hear.

These three purposes, vital to your present objectives, bear restatement. (1) We strive for an exact terminology. (2) We couch criticism in this terminology, and you efficiently focus your efforts on the single topics of the criticism. (3) The separation between the sound of your present voice and your anticipated voice is more easily bridged when a factual understanding of your voice replaces a mystical awareness that speech occurs.

Voices are not alike; they are as distinguishing as fingerprints. While only an expert can identify a person through fingerprints, anyone can match his friends' faces and voices. He can even identify voices that he hears frequently over the telephone, an instrument that erases many of the telltale traces of voice.

ATTRIBUTES OF SOUND

Sound—any sound— is a blend of four experiences. For example, as you write on a blackboard (1) you hear *loudness*, (2) you are aware of a highness or lowness of *pitch*, (3) you recognize the *quality* (timbre) of "chalk" noise, and (4) along with these you experience a *time* (duration) of the sound. The "chalk" sound is prolonged, almost continuous, if you write without interruption, and is intermittent as you cross the *t*'s and dot the *i*'s. The total "chalk" experience could never be confused with the sounds of a forest, a falling tree, rustling leaves, or the chopping of wood.

We shall treat singly loudness, pitch, quality, and time with respect to voice and emphasize a simple summative process:

$$\Sigma \text{ pitch}_{\text{Jim}} + \Sigma \text{ loudness}_{\text{Jim}} + \Sigma \text{ quality}_{\text{Jim}} + \Sigma \text{ time}_{\text{Jim}} \cong \text{Voice}_{\text{Jim}}$$

In other words, the sum of all Jim's pitch factors plus all his vocal loudness and quality and the time aspects of the voice is approximately equal to the listener's experience while hearing Jim. These are not piled on top of speech. They are the ever-present dimensions of voice, like the inevitable length, width, depth, and weight of a box.

1. THE TIME ASPECT. Even the smallest segment of speech consumes time; speech exists in time, occurs with the passing of time. In short, speech has *duration*, and we evaluate it grossly with the terms *fast* and *slow talking*. Our unit with these terms of rate is usually words—words per minute. The word itself has duration and the duration of the word includes the duration of the sounds that make up the word. These durations and the intervals between the words and between the sounds account for the time consumed in talking.

Duration in all of its aspects can be controlled by the speaker. You can make yourself talk slow or fast; indeed, consistent with our mutual interest in your improvement in speech, you can voluntarily be successively a slow and a fast talker in a single utterance. Toward this end let us examine two topics to which you can devote special effort.

a. Quantity. Your listener's notion of your rate of talking stems partly from the length of time that you permit a sound of speech to last. You might prolong some sounds throughout an exhalation, for example, [a] or [s]. You can only stretch out a preparatory phase of [d] and [g]. As you demonstrate these statements you are toying with the *quantity* of a sound, and this is a function of the rate of movement of the articulators of Chap. 2—the jaw, teeth, lips, tongue, soft palate, and so on. Each speech sound, or at most a pair of sounds, originates with a unique placement of these structures. Necessarily, then, they must be in movement during continuous speech. If the jaw and tongue are moved from one set of positions to another slowly, the individual sounds are long, have much quantity, and the rate of speech is slow. This would be the case with a school yell that begins with an *r* long enough for a dozen normal *r*'s and continues slowly: *r r r r a a a a*. When the articulators are moved rapidly, the speech sounds are short, and the rate of speech is fast. This could be the end of the yell, [ra] at top speed, and termed *staccato*. Obviously, the quantity of each sound affects the duration of the word, the phrase, the sentence, and the total speaking time. Words per minute vary as you prolong or cut short the sounds of speech.

b. Pauses. Pauses, the silent intervals between sounds and between words and phrases, are the remainder of the duration, or time aspect, of speaking. Some miniscule lapses of time are inevitable and help to set the minimum time for saying a passage. Said either fast or slow, there is a pause between the syllables of "kickback," "bookcase," "put him," "calm wind," "toy boat." You can observe them and appreciate that there are numerous short pauses throughout speech, as before the *p* of "top."

Do you see our predicament? We are treating the sound of your speech, and in the development of the first dimension, duration, we are paradoxically describing the absence of sound. This is not as unusual as it may seem. Silence is part of the sound of a clock ticking, a metronome beating out time, or a stick pulled along a picket fence. The spacings between the intermittent bursts are part of the event. A clock would not tick except for the regular intervals of silence; rather, it would produce a tone. A metronome would lose its function except for the in-between moments of silence; it, too, would yield a sustained tone. The sound of speech characteristically includes silent intervals or discontinuities between the ongoing, time-consuming sounds, syllables, and words. Our larger interest, though, is with the pauses you initiate that are beyond the elemental requirements of the language. Some of these pauses are logical, contributory to the sense of speech.

The sequence: "Would I do that? Never!" might become convincing only with a 2-second pause before "never." Likewise, pauses may occur between the major divisions of a public address. Such pauses seem to serve as the dividers of a filing cabinet—to leave related ideas together and to separate dissimilar ones. Other silences occur within words or phrases and imply a behavioral pattern that is beyond the speaker's control at the moment. The next event simply does not occur at the instant the listener expects it. These pauses may be and usually are habitual. A speaker who exhibits jerky talking one day may be expected to talk in like manner in a similar circumstance a year later unless he has undergone a systematic program of study and practice to become fluent. Both the number and length of pauses, whether voluntarily introduced or not, contribute to your listener's experience of fast talking or slow talking. Pauses are part of the sound of speech.

c. Fluency in Perspective. Fluency is not of first importance in speaking, not so important as the sense of the utterance. Some speakers, however, seem to reverse this order and to prefer an unimpeded flow of speech over exactness in either language or ideas, and some listeners use "fast talker" as a term of superlative praise. Broken rhythm occurs with stuttering; it also occurs in normal speaking. In fact, Wendell Johnson reports that observers who heard recorded speech from stutterers and nonstutterers were not highly successful in distinguishing the two groups.[1]

Johnson charges that our culture places an unrealistic premium upon fluency and sets a goal that is beyond the reach of most speakers. The beginning student of speech squirms as he hears his recorded pauses and becomes increasingly uncomfortable with voiced pauses—ones that are filled with *er, ah,* and the like. The same student may sit complacently through gross errors in reasoning—recorded again!

d. Controlling Pauses. Some clue to ridding oneself of the *er-ah-uh* pauses comes from the learning technique of negative practice, an effective procedure for overcoming habits. Knight Dunlap noticed that he was typing *hte* for *the.* He broke the habit, not by forcing himself to make *the, the, the,* but by practicing the wrong spelling, *hte, hte, hte.* In essence, he changed the involuntary wrong habit into a voluntary deliberate action. He then substituted, motion by motion, the right movements in his typing and practiced these until they became a new habit. He later used negative practice in aiding persons to rid themselves of muscular jerks and twitches. Negative practice is routine therapy with a person who stutters. He practices reproducing his blocks until his real stutter and the simulated one are indistinguishable. The real stutter, to the extent that it is a habit, is then dropped.

Our habits of vocalizing pauses, of saying "er," "ah," or "uh," yield readily to negative practice. You can apply it without supervision. Simply vocalize more pauses—say more "er's," "ah's," or "uh's" than you ever said before. Discover how it feels to say consciously *what you have been saying unconsciously.* Vocalize pauses in your speech naturally but unnecessarily, today and tomorrow, again and again for a week. Having acquainted yourself thoroughly with the occurrence, now simply refuse to let yourself say "ah," "er," or "uh"; let the pause remain

[1] Wendell Johnson, *People in Quandaries*, Chaps. 17, 18, Harper & Brothers, New York, 1946.

silent. Your listeners will probably appreciate this change, even though you do nothing to alter the rhythm or spacing of the words. The improvement is worthwhile and the experience is interesting. Next, you may reexamine recordings of your speech to find whether there are words that seem to recur in the manner that the "ah's," "er's," or "uh's" did. The word—the "well's," "and's," "very's"—can be given the same treatment that you gave the uh's.

Probably with practice, including negative practice, and careful preparation of your speeches, the illogical pauses that appear in a recording of one of your early speeches will not be so recurrent in a later recording. The sound of your speech—and at the moment our concern is with the time aspect—can be changed, but only by you.

   e. Quantification. William Norwood Brigance determined that William Jennings Bryan recorded the "Cross of Gold" speech at a rate of 150 words per minute; that actors of note read Shakesperian passages at various rates—80, 112, 135, 150, and 170 words per minute; and that prize-winning collegiate orators of the 1920's spoke 83, 90, 107, and 121 to 154 words per minute.[1]

Ten years later Jack C. Cotton listened to slowed-down recordings of radio speech and depressed a key, syllable by syllable, as he monitored the program. A stylus was deflected with each punch of the key and left a trace on smoked paper that moved at a constant rate. Cotton reported his measurements in words per minute under an assumption that an average word contains 1.5 syllables. In the instance of dramatic material, well spoken, a typical summary of the results in words per minute might be: 300 and above, 15 per cent; 200 to 299, 20 per cent; 150 to 199, 14 per cent; 100 to 148, 24 per cent; 60 to 99, 8 per cent; 49 to 59, 7 per cent; 25 to 39, 10 per cent; lower, 2 per cent.[2]

Currently, electronic devices facilitate time measurements of the units of speech. Larger samples can be handled and more analytical measurements secured. For example, J. C. Kelley and M. D. Steer obtained several aspects of rate of 24 classroom speeches by college students.[3] This analysis is summarized in Table 1.

---

[1] William Norwood Brigance, "How Fast Do We Talk?" *Quarterly Journal of Speech Education*, vol. 12, pp. 337–342, 1926.

[2] Jack C. Cotton, "Syllabic Rate: A New Concept in the Study of Speech Rate Variation," *Speech Monographs*, vol. 3, pp. 112–117, 1936.

[3] J. C. Kelly and M. D. Steer, "Revised Concept of Rate," *Journal of Speech and Hearing Disorders*, vol. 14, pp. 222–226, 1949.

TABLE I. INDEX OF RATE OF STUDENT SPEAKERS IN EXTEMPORANEOUS
SPEECHES IN SECONDS, PER CENT, AND WORDS PER MINUTE
(*Kelly and Steer*)

	Mean	Standard deviation
Mean syllable duration, sec.	0.154	0.02
Mean per cent phonation.	0.706	0.10
Mean per cent monosyllables.	0.696	0.05
Mean over-all rate, w.p.m.	159.06	23.62
Mean sentence rate, w.p.m.	208.81	30.42
Mean slowest sentence, w.p.m.	125.75	25.68
Mean fastest sentence, w.p.m.	328.42	73.13

f. Summary. Duration in speaking varies between *fast* and *slow* and includes the experiences that are named or described with words like *jerky, smooth, pause* (logical or not), *staccato, measured, legato, rhythmical, tempo,* and quantitative values of sounds, such as *long* and *short.* Duration is an experience of a listener; you are that listener. Your experience may not agree with group judgment, and physical measurements may not agree with either. Since your experience is unique, you will wish to describe it accurately.

Duration is related to the speaker's control of the breath stream and the coordination of the outgoing air with thought and with movements of the articulators. The coordination with the articulators accounts for the length of a single sound and affects rate of speaking. The coordination with the thought affects the appropriateness of the pauses. All pauses consume time and thus alter the rate of speaking. You are the speaker. You will listen to the descriptions of your rate and modify your pauses and the quantity of your sounds appropriately.

2. THE LOUDNESS ASPECT. A second experience in the sound of speech is loudness. Any sound that is perceptible, that is, exceeds our threshold or floor of hearing, has loudness or a magnitude for us. We hear this amount along a continuum from *soft* to *loud* and describe the effect freely. *Weak* is a synonym for *soft.* You can add other adjectives that signify an amount of loudness for you—*thundering, little, bellowing, gentle, big, noisy.* Adjectives are, however, of limited value in spite of the ease with which we can find them, for our verbal account is entirely subjective and every description carries with it an implicit "It seems to me."

The musician denoted loudness through a series of markings from *ppp*, for very soft, or the lower extreme of a loudness scale, to *fff*, for very loud, or the upper extreme of the range. The instrumental or orchestral interpretation of these symbols, in turn, is a matter of the director's or performer's judgment and again implies, "This is what *ppp* means to *me*."

A marked improvement has been made for indicating loudness, at least for scientific purposes, and for testing and describing such electronic equipment as voice recorders, radios, and telephones.[1]

a. The Decibel. The *decibel* is in common use as a measure of physical intensity. (The abbreviation *db* carries no period and is pronounced *deebee*.) This unit was originated by telephone engineers, and as the name implies is one-tenth of a bel. As you have guessed, the term was named for Alexander Graham Bell.

By way of orientation, the range from silence to the loudest of noises is possibly about 180 decibels. This highest level could not be withstood by the ear and could only be produced by the impact of tremendous forces, comparable to the volcanic eruptions of Krakatoa in 1883. This is higher by 10 to 15 decibels than any sound that has been measured. The relative levels of the sounds about us are suggested by Fig. 9, although such measurements to be exact would have to include an indication of the distance between the source of the sound and the point of measurement, and obviously most of the sounds that are named in Fig. 9 vary in level from moment to moment.

Now that we are using the word *decibel*, what is it? We hope that even the most squeamish nonmathematical student will not flinch at the next few sentences. The decibel is a ratio between two intensities or two pressures. Silence, or zero decibels, is technically and as a matter of convenience a power output of 10^{-16} watt or a pressure level of 0.0002 dyne per square centimeter. The ratio for computing the decibels is

$$\text{db} = 20 \log_{10} \frac{\text{pressure } A}{\text{pressure } B}$$

We now have the two principal features of the decibel. First, it is a ratio, or the number of times that one amount of sound intensity or sound pressure level is greater than another. This feature is simplified by the fact that the denominator in the instance of meters that measure

---

[1] We are using *loudness*, a psychological word, and *intensity* or *pressure*, physical terms, interchangeably. They are different but closely related.

sound levels has been set arbitrarily to lie at a pressure or power that is below the threshold of hearing. Second, the ratio is logarithmic. This is not hard to understand. Here are four numbers: 100, 1,000, 10,000,

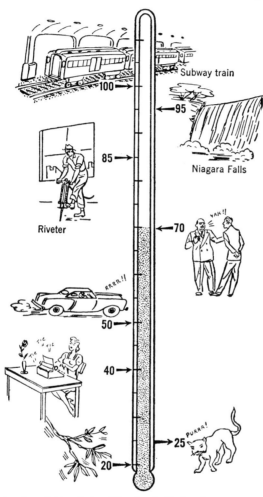

FIG. 9. Approximate relative intensities in decibels of common sounds, from the rustle of leaves to the roar of a subway train.

100,000. How many 10's have to be multiplied together to produce these numbers? Respectively: two, three, four, five. These latter four numbers are the logarithms to the base 10 of the former four. In the instance of 10,000, for example,

$$10 \times 10 \times 10 \times 10 = 10,000$$

there are four 10's—the logarithm is 4; if one sound were 10,000 times as great as another in pressure, the difference between the sounds would be 20 times 4, or 80 decibels.

An advantage of the decibel is that it tends to measure sound in terms of its magnitude to a listener, its effect. By way of analogy, let us suppose that we know the precise amount of "hammer blow" that will have the effect of denting a piece of wood as we drive a nail, that we know that ten times as great a blow will drive the nail 1 inch, one hundred times the original blow will drive the nail 2 inches, and that a single blow one thousand times that "dent blow" will push the nail 3 inches. We might conveniently, then, measure these hammer blows not by their effort but by their effectiveness in inches, thus:

$$\text{"Inch"} = \log_{10} \frac{\text{hammer blow } A}{\text{hammer blow "dent"}}$$

or, for our hardest blow,

$$\text{"Inch"} = \log_{10} \frac{1,000}{1}$$
$$= \log_{10} \text{ of } 1,000$$
$$= 3$$

In other words, our hardest blow requires 3 "inches" of drive.

The ear tends to react to sound in the manner that the wood reacted to the hammer blows. If we start with a loud sound, it takes a lot more sound energy in order to make a difference that you can notice than if we start from a soft one. Fortuitously, 1 decibel is approximately one *least* or *just noticeable difference* in loudness.[1] A rule of thumb—and a fairly accurate one—is that as the power of a sound is doubled, the level increases 3 decibels.

b. Application of the Decibel. Electronic circuits and meters replace hand computations in most applications of the decibel. A meter like the one of Fig. 10 yields values like those of Fig. 9 and turns the measurement of environmental noises into a quick, easy task that may be undertaken by anyone.

---

[1] This relationship is limited to pure tones of about 1,000 waves per second. In general, with an 80-decibel difference between two tones of this frequency, a listener is able to detect about 80 successive points, each "just noticeably louder" than the preceding. This result would be obtained, however, only with exact psychophysical procedures.

The audiogram in Fig. 11 illustrates a typical record of an individual's ability to hear several tones. The horizontal line "normal" is an average threshold of hearing, and deviations below this line indicate losses in the ability to hear specified tones. The losses are stated in decibels.

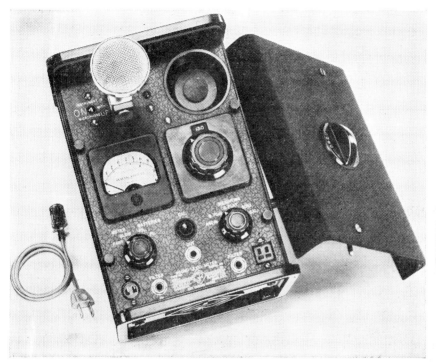

FIG. 10. Meters are available to indicate the sound pressure level of any environmental sound. These meters are especially useful for describing the level of noise in factories. Noise-abatement programs, sometimes supported by city ordinances, require sound level meters to assess the progress of the program and violations of the ordinances. (*Courtesy of General Radio Company, Cambridge, Mass.*)

Some musicians use decibel meters in directing orchestral performances. The engineer at the sending end of radio and television programs adjusts the station output in decibels. Ultimately we on the receiving end may shift the volume controls of radios and phonographs in decibels, and the unit will take its place with the cup, yard, and pound as a household unit of measurement.

If as you have talked into the microphone of a voice recorder you have been cautioned to keep the hand of the meter at *zero* and not to let it vary beyond plus 3 or minus 3, you have used the decibel on a relative scale.

Students may have noticeably soft voices and find the instruction *talk louder* difficult to follow in sustained speaking. For them, a crude meter of relative level, like the one of Fig. 12, is helpful. A series of lamps replaces a meter hand. The lamps respond differentially to sound pressure levels. The student in Fig. 12 might be working under an

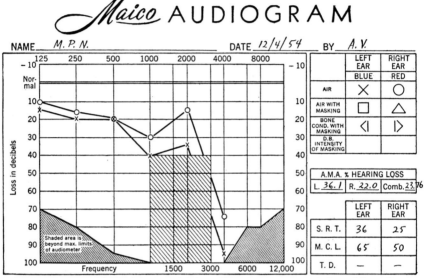

FIG. 11. The individual whose sensitivity of hearing was recorded on this audiogram had some hearing loss for tones of low pitch and was deaf to tones of high pitch. The approximate measures of sensitivity of the ear to various tones are obtained by means of an audiometer. Additional measures of the status of an individual's hearing may be secured from a word-reception test. (*Courtesy of The Maico Company, Inc., Minneapolis, Minn.*)

instruction to keep the larger lamp of the column of lamps lighted. His classmates, with both the speaker and the level indicator in view, would apprise him of his success.

c. Variety in Loudness. We stressed that variability in duration is of the essence of the sound of speech. Variety in loudness is no less important than variability in duration. Pauses, of course, afford a drastic drop in level during speech, from some to none or from much to none. There are other changes in loudness from instant to instant during talking, as when we go from an accented or loud syllable to one that is unaccented and less loud. Also the vowels of English typically differ in their relative intensities, [a] being about 4 decibels more intense than [i]. The sound of oral language is a continuously varied sequence of different loudnesses. These differences, however, are not enough to keep a listener from saying "Monotonous." We must not only be sufficiently loud to be understood, but beyond this we must talk from a reserve

FIG. 12. Engineers can build circuits that permit varying numbers of lamps to indicate different levels of vocal pressure. These indicators of relative sound pressure level can be used advantageously in large-scale classroom monitoring of a student's level.

level that accommodates continuous variety in our level of utterance, and this would be in addition to the variety that is inherent in the language.

The dependence of loudness level upon exhalation is close and can be stated simply. From an average of several talkers, it is clear that the greater the exhalatory rate, the more intense the tone. Moreover, the intensity of decibels is directly related to the outflow of the air that is used in talking. An alteration in loudness, then, is in part, possibly in major part, a matter of personal regulation of the rate of exhalation, a process that was described in Chap. 2.

d. A Role of Loudness. In 1915, James A. Winans admonished students to use conversational quality in speaking.[1] He defined this as a lively, dynamic sense of communication. The advice spread rapidly, for it provided a timely relief from the stilted posture and stereotyped vocal patterns of the last century and that continued on the Chautauqua platform and in politics up to World War I. Then came a generation that knew *conversational quality* without the definition. Practically, the word came to mean "talk as in conversation." Classroom speaking became lifeless.

Harry G. Barnes wrote of *projection* as the descriptive word that might elicit dynamic speaking.[2] Projection is an old term in speech, older than conversational quality. Its tradition lies in the theater, not with public address; the play director uses it synonymously with "get the line across the footlights. Make us believe what you are saying." Horton Talley made an analytical study of projection in the actor's voice.[3] He secured professional actors who recited and recorded lines from a play in a "projected" manner and again not "projected," and he analyzed the recordings. The principal difference that appeared between projected and nonprojected readings was in level, measured in decibels, or in the loudness of speech. Although this study was too limited in scope to permit broad generalization, the suggestion is that projection is basically related to the loudness of utterance.

Since an increase in loudness is frequently accompanied by a rise in pitch, projection may have secondary vocal aspects; indeed, nonoral characteristics of projection may show up in bodily activity. Our present interest, however, lies in the observation that loudness not only differentiates the inaudible from the audible but distinguishes animated from lifeless talking.

e. Summary. Loudness in speech varies from the faintly audible sound, even the inaudible one, to the level of screeching, piercing, or bellowing voice. This is an experience of the listener. He becomes the

---

[1] James A. Winans, *Public Speaking*, pp. 30 ff., Appleton-Century-Crofts, Inc., New York, 1915.

[2] Harry G. Barnes, *Speech Handbook*, pp. 59–62, Prentice-Hall, Inc., New York, 1941.

[3] C. Horton Talley, unpublished study relating to his article in *Archives of Speech*, vol. 2, no. 22, 28–40, 1939.

speaker's critic and requests both an adequate level for clear reception and a varied level. The gulf between your production of voice and the improved loudness that your critics suggest for you is bridged the more easily where both of you avail yourselves of the advantages of the decibel.

3. THE PITCH ASPECT. A third set of experiences that make up the sound of speech involves pitch. The musical scale provides a convenient and accurate standard for annotating vocal pitch. Any level of highness or lowness of voice can be expressed in the units of musical scores. The male speaker who might be selected to represent all male voices would have an average pitch a little higher than C below middle C, or 128 waves per second. This is approximately an octave lower than the average pitch of the representative female voice, a little lower than 256 waves per second. These measures are approximations and may seem to perpetuate old wives' tales. A reason for our being deliberately inexact is that the modal frequency varies widely among individuals and varies somewhat even with the type of speaking assignment at hand.

a. Key. Pitch varies on our subjective "to me" scale between *low* and *high*. However, there is more than one manifestation of pitch, voice being a series of high and low, and relatively high and relatively low, experiences. All the while that one is talking he varies his pitch upward and downward from a pitch that occurs most often. This representative pitch, the one that you use more frequently in talking, is *key,* and it is with respect to the typical keys that middle C and the C below middle C were applied in the preceding paragraph.

Students frequently worry that their pitch **or** key is too high or too low. Although this apprehension is usually groundless, you may easily determine your key in a manner suggested by Wilbert Pronovost.[1] He cautions that the method is not foolproof. With some reservation, then, and the aid of a partner, you may ascertain your natural key as well as your habitual one. Ask your partner to make sure that you follow the directions.

(1) Habitual Pitch. Select an easy prose passage of about 100 words and prepare to read it two or three times. During the first reading use considerable variety in pitch. Then gradually work toward a monopitch, decreasing both your upward and downward inflections. You finally

[1] Wilbert Pronovost, "An Experimental Study of Methods for Determining Natural and Habitual Pitch," *Speech Monographs,* vol. 9, pp. 111–123, 1942.

arrive at a chant. This is probably near the pitch that you use most often. Terminate the chant in a sustained *ah* and locate the pitch of the vowel on the piano keyboard.

(2) Natural Pitch. Sing from your lowest tone to your highest tone, *including the falsetto*. Repeat this singing of your range several times with the aid of a piano, making full use of the notes of the piano. Your natural pitch is probably one-fourth of the number of notes in your total range, from the lowest note that you achieved. Pronovost tried several alternative methods for determining natural pitch. None was completely successful in assigning the right natural pitches to superior speakers with whom an identity of natural and habitual pitches might be assumed. However, the method outlined here is easy and has no disadvantages over the others.

Should there be considerable discrepancy between the two keys that you have determined, you will wish to discuss appropriate exercises with your instructor.

b. Range. Variations above and below the average key or the modal point on the pitch scale define the *range of pitch*. Range is the difference between the highest and lowest pitches that a person uses while talking, and, like key, is expressed in notes, semitones, and octaves—musical terminology. Here, rather than with key, lies a more proper concern for most students who may have questions about their pitch. The *functional range*—the range that is exceeded only now and then—if limited, may again lead listeners to complain of a monotonous voice. Either *monotone* or *monopitch* describes a voice that exhibits little variation in pitch.

Usually with little effort, a speaker will demonstrate that he *can* go higher and lower, often considerably higher and lower in pitch than he customarily does. These extremes, however, not being a part of his normal vocal behavior, are only suggestive of potentialities. The ranges that are important at the moment are the one you normally use in speaking and the one you can come to use easily, the second being a slight extension of the first. With "good" voices, the range is frequently two octaves in sustained speaking and at least one octave in factual announcement comprised of 20 or 30 words.

c. Inflection. The deviations from key imply a third part of the pitch experience, *inflection*. You can use this word to denote any change in pitch that occurs either upward or downward, sudden or slow, slight or extensive, as a person talks.

d. Automatic Changes in Pitch. Some variety in pitch occurs simply as an interaction between our language and our vocal mechanism— unless the speaker deliberately sets himself to prevent it. First, pitch tends to rise with increases in loudness. This is not surprising, for certainly the vocal folds become more taut with an increase in muscular tonicity. Indeed physical effort with the hands tends to raise the frequency of the vocal-fold action.[1,2]

Second, the various sounds of speech are not of the same pitch when they are made casually. Notice that as you vocalize *hee-haw* or *see-saw*, you tend to raise the pitch with the first syllable and to lower it with the second. These positions involve different tensions in the larynx and accompany different natural pitches for the vowels.

e. Summary. Pitch in the sound of speech is the experience that the listener describes with words like *high* and *low*. More exact descriptions are possible through comparisons of the unknown pitch of the voice with the calibrated pitches of the piano. Pitch in voice is not a steady state but is a continuous variation that is achieved by inflections throughout the pitch range of the speaker.

4. THE QUALITY ASPECT. Finally, the sound of speech has *quality* or *timbre*. Let us try to get a clear notion of this vocal attribute, even though the word *quality* may seem to be the most vague of the four dimensions of sound. A saxophone and a clarinet are alike in relying on wind across reeds for making the tone. They may be alike in their pitch range. They are capable of being blown to produce the same loudness, and certainly a note can be sustained or stopped as well on one as on the other. Why have both? Answer: One sounds like a "sax" and the other like a clarinet, and the orchestra needs both kinds of sounds. A violin costing $50 and one costing $30,000 can be played with the same bow, produce the same notes, and both sound like a violin. Why invest $29,950 extra dollars? Answer: One may have better quality than the other. Two members of your class might stand at the back of the room and say a vowel with the same loudness, at the same pitch, and for the same time. Yet the vowels would not sound the same. One would be Mary's voice and the other Helen's voice. This ultimate uniqueness between voices is voice quality, and there is little point in doing more

---

[1] H. C. Taylor, "The Fundamental Pitch of English Vowels," *Journal of Experimental Psychology*, vol. 16, pp. 565–582, 1933.

[2] Donald R. Meyer, "On the Interaction of Simultaneous Responses," *Psychological Bulletin*, vol. 50, pp. 204–220, 1953.

than improving the quality that is yours. Ultimately limiting features of your voice quality are "built in." The changes that are in prospect are ones that can be wrought within your own system of resonating cavities. These resonators are more flexible than is the body of a violin, and the potentialities that they offer for improved voice quality are not likely to be exhausted. However, your system of resonators cannot be matched any place in the world, and this uniqueness precludes the possibility that your voice can sound exactly like another person's.

All the vocal attributes have been described in terms of the voice the listener hears: high-low, soft-loud, slow-fast. The terminal points on the scale for quality are subjective also: pleasant-unpleasant. You might ask, "But isn't this pleasantness attributable to my 'liking' a voice because I like the person?" Answer, "Perhaps, in part." For one reason or another you deem one quality pleasant and another unpleasant; you prefer some voices. Apart from this pleasant-unpleasant response to a voice, quality accounts in large part for the experience that leads you to say, "That's Jim's voice" or "I thought I heard Jane in here."

Words that describe voice qualities that are usually unpleasant to many people nclude *nasal, metallic, breathy, hoarse, husky, strident,* and so on. Words that seem to indicate approval of a quality include *resonant, rich, full, vibrant,* etc.

SUMMARY

At any instant in talking you are making four characteristics of voice: duration, loudness, pitch, and quality. Fortunately, there is no need to pay attention to the four separately, except when you are analyzing a voice. Such a view would tax our span of attention and cause us to lose the import of the utterance. But at one instant or another we doubtless give heed to each with, "Monopitch, don't you think?" "Talking through his nose," "Too slow for me," or "Louder, please."

AESTHETIC AND SENSE COMPONENTS

The four aspects of the sound of speech—duration, loudness, pitch, and quality—seem to serve somewhat different purposes and to elicit different reactions in speaking. (1) Every listener should have an opportunity to get the sense of an utterance. This we may term the *sense component* of speech. (2) There appears to be an inevitable aesthetic response to the sound of speech—something that we like or dislike. This we designate the *aesthetic component.*

A distinction between the *aesthetic* and *sense* components may be more complete if we look at defective speech, the domain of the speech correctionist. Children frequently undergo speech therapy for the very compelling reason that they cannot be understood in everyday talking. A child may be clearly audible but his articulation may be such that only his family can tell what he says. In this instance the sense component is lacking. Another child may be quite understandable, but his voice is so different that listeners react to it as being unpleasant. For example, some children undergo surgical repair for a cleft palate and retain a voice that is markedly nasal. Conceivably, every utterance is understandable, and still listeners label the speech *defective* and, in effect, send the child to a "repair shop for disordered speech." The object in this instance is to make the voice pleasant.

1. DIFFERENTIAL CONTRIBUTIONS OF THE ATTRIBUTES. How do the four aspects of the sound of speech relate to the sense and aesthetic components of voice respectively? The behavior of listeners contributes to the answer. They frequently ask a speaker, in one way or another, to talk louder. Obviously, his loudness is intimately related to the sense component of his speech: insufficient loudness, no sense. Occasionally, a teacher asks a student to talk more slowly, and students who are taking verbatim notes may shout in unison, "Slower!" Sense is at stake.

Requests similar to "Louder" and "Slower" are not made on the spot with respect to either pitch or quality. These two parts of the sound of speech, highness and lowness, or pitch, and pleasantness and unpleasantness, or quality, are not so vital to the listener's receiving the words of the speaker as are loudness and duration; also, from the speaker's viewpoint, pitch and quality may be more personalized, more a part of himself, than are rate and loudness. An audience would be reluctant to ask a speaker for more inflection, a lower or higher key, more *oral*, or less *muffled*, quality, less *nasality*, a more *orotund*, or *resonant*, quality.

The different reactions of the listener to the four aspects of the sound of speech are in keeping with their principal functions in speech. When the English language is adequately articulated, intelligibility, or the identification of the sounds and words, is largely dependent upon loudness and probably, within broad limits, rate. The other two attributes are correspondingly paramount in the aesthetic responses to the sound of speech. This generalization is tentatively made with respect to American English. In contrast, in many languages pitch is vital in identifying the words. Listeners, in order to identify a Chinese word, both have to hear the utterance—it too would have to be adequately loud—and identify the relative pitch. "Ma" with high pitch may mean "mother," with falling pitch, "to scold," with falling and rising pitch, "horse;" there are instances of 40 words comprised of the same group of speech sounds.

2. VOCAL SEMANTICS. We are treating *more-less* and *major-minor* relationships; not *all* or *none*. Pitch and quality certainly contribute something to sense in English, subtle meanings and innuendoes, and an actor's success may relate to his skill in imparting these extra meanings. Such meanings belie the literal definitions of the words. Said sarcastically, "Yes" can have an unmistakable meaning of "No." State officials and candidates for office may tax the ingenuity of reporters who have to "read between the spoken lines," "interpret" a statement from the way it sounds. (The human ear is the oldest of lie detectors, not infallible, of course.)

3. MULTIPLE MESSAGES. Further, we would not want you to believe that "the *sense* of the sound of speech" implies that an utterance conveys only one message. Such would never be the case. For example, let us suppose that we overhear, "I am seeing the mayor about the matter tonight at nine o'clock." Without our pretending to enumerate all the possible "messages" of this sentence in addition to the primary one, we can list several.

Message subject	*Answer*
Is the topic a civic one?	Probably
Is the talker a person who is interested in civic affairs?	Probably
Is the present time earlier than 10 P.M.?	Probably
Is the speaker a male?	Revealed by the vocal pitch
Does the speaker have a larynx?	Revealed by the vocal quality
Is the statement a threat?	Revealed by the duration-loudness pattern of the voice
Is the speaker bedridden?	Probably not
Has the speaker learned English?	Yes
Is the speaker talking with someone who understands English?	Probably

All our answers could be wrong. Possibly someone is practicing a line of a play; a demented person is soliloquizing; a speaker is telling a story; an international student is practicing his lesson in American conversational English. Even so, a single short passage of speech conveys more than a primary message; antecedent to all messages, the speech must be loud enough to be heard.

A pair of messages that are carried by the same sound are (1) your primary statement, and (2) an attitude about it. The words from the telephone might be: "Your house is on fire." You are alarmed, but your house is not on fire; a bonfire in the backyard gives the appearance that the house is burning. In recounting the story you add, "Whoever called was surely excited." The second, or overlaid, message could be more interesting than the primary one. You might have forgotten the whole incident except for recurring memories of the sound of "that voice." One difference between messages by voice and by blinking lights, telegraph, or teletype is that voice can convey multiple messages simultaneously, and the signaling devices cannot.

4. QUANTIFICATION. Emotions are our feelings about a person, event, situation, etc. Only a small number of the total range of emotions were included in a study by Grant Fairbanks and Wilbert Pronovost.[1] Students who were skilled actors read one passage with *contempt;* another to show *anger;* a third, *fear;* a fourth, *grief;* and a fifth, *indifference.* The 250-word passages were written to accommodate these interpretations readily and to include the sentences, "There is no other answer. You have asked me that question a thousand times and my reply has always been the same. It always will be the same." These sentences were edited from the recordings and played back to numbers of student listeners. Each listener had a check list of 12 emotional states, including the ones simulated by the actors, and judged, reading by reading, the emotion that was portrayed. In the instance of *contempt,* 84 per cent of the judgments were correct; *anger,* 78 per cent; *fear,* 66 per cent; *grief,* 78 per cent; *indifference,* 88 per cent. These proportions demonstrate that the sound of speech conveys meaning. This would relate to the sense of the message.

What are some of the extra meanings that you detect with certainty from time to time? Anger, fear, sarcasm, uncertainty, confidence, con-

---

[1] Grant Fairbanks and Wilbert Pronovost, "An Experimental Study of the Pitch Characteristics of the Voice during the Expression of Emotions," *Speech Monographs,* vol. 1, pp. 86–104, 1939.

descension, etc. Almost always, though, you have the advantages of the context of the message to guide your interpretation, and it is only when the words and voice are out of tune with each other that the interesting problem arises. Which message am I to believe? This dilemma is as often resolved in favor of *voice* as of *words*.

The aesthetic component of voice extends beyond the boundaries of voice quality. The preference for one voice over another is based on a reaction to all the vocal attributes, the monopitch, the jerky voice, the constant loudness, etc. Conversely, we may come to enjoy the off-color voice of the comedian or an unusual teacher.

Difficult as relevant rules may be to formulate, we have some indication about what constitutes a "good" male voice in the estimation of college students.[1] Six students read the sentence: "Tomorrow evening at this time, the famous physician, Dr. J. O. Lee, will speak to you upon a topic of vital importance." Recordings were made and played back to college students, with each reading paired twice with each of the other readings. The listeners indicated the preferred member of a pair by individual ballot. The technique permitted the six voices to be ranked according to the judgments of the group. The recordings were subsequently analyzed in terms of their duration and frequency characteristics. The preferred voices in comparison with the rejected ones demonstrated slower speaking, more pausing, longer pauses, greater functional pitch range, more upward inflections, longer downward inflections, and more instances of "altering pitch" during a pause, sometimes termed *shifts*. These measures do not take into account aspects of the vocal quality and loudness. The results agreed with those of a similar study by Lewis and Tiffin.[2]

5. SUMMARY. The four aspects of the sound of speech do not merely describe a person's speech; they provide stimuli to which the listener responds, possibly unwittingly, "This is speech that I like," or "This is 'defective-sounding' speech." Especially in the artistic speech of the stage or in interpretation, all the aspects of the sound of speech are exploited to interpret meanings, both obvious and subtle. Basic to all meaning, however, is the essential minimum loudness for the reception of speech. Until this level is achieved and with a rate of utterance that

[1] John W. Black, "A Study of Voice Merit," *Quarterly Journal of Speech*, vol. 28, pp. 67–74, 1942.

[2] Don Lewis and Joseph Tiffin, "A Psychophysical Study of Individual Differences in Speaking Ability," *Archives of Speech*, vol. 1, pp. 43–60, 1934.

permits the reception of the oral words, not even the primary message can be understood. Above this level, the full scope of the skillful voice can contribute to sense and to elicit aesthetic response.

Your voice is an instrument that you can learn to use effectively. Functionally almost none of it is *fixed*. The resonators can be used ever so differently from the way you have learned to use them, and among the potential changes there are doubtless several new experiences that can be exploited as improvements. Pitch, loudness, and duration are easily subject to your control throughout wide ranges.

The total sound of the voice, we must remember, conveys meaning. This meaning goes beyond anything that can be studied in the dictionary. The total event provides a complex auditory stimulus to your listeners who respond to the sound of speech with likes or dislikes.

SIDE-TONE: HEARING YOURSELF

We have treated the sound of speech largely from your listener's position. He, removed from you (the speaker) by some distance from inches to the greatest number of rods that your speech will carry, is the one who gets the sense or no-sense of your utterance and who reacts —aesthetically pleasant, etc. The speaker is also his own listener and this listener is utilizing the sound of speech interestingly. Each instant of it is his guide for what he produces during the next instant. *Feedback* has become almost a household word. Some part of the output of an instrument or machine operates its own regulator and maintains automatic control. The sound of the speaker's voice *feeds back* to him and causes him to modify the sound of his subsequent speech a bit, to make it softer or louder, higher or lower in pitch, faster or slower in rate; to give it one quality or another; or to resay a word or syllable—this time with another pronunciation.

The two listeners—the one who is only listening and the one who is listening to himself while talking—do not have the same experience. The speaker who is monitoring his own voice hears a sound that no other listener hears. This is dramatically demonstrated as a person listens to a high-fidelity recording of his voice. He is now an outside listener. The recordings of all his acquaintances' voices sound right, but the same apparatus when turned upon his own voice gives completely erroneous results!

If the sound the outside listener hears is to be our criterion, our self-monitoring system is not very good. It misleads us. There are good reasons for its limitations. Our sound source is directly connected with our sound receiver, the ear. We listen to ourselves as the sound of our voice is carried through (1) bone and tissue from the vocal folds and mouth to the ear, as well as through (2) air from the mouth to the ear, and again from (3) the mouth to the walls and other reflecting surfaces about us to the ears. We are the most proximate listener to our own voice, and yet we get a badly garbled reception of the sound of our speech. If we view (1), (2), and (3) above as *channels of voice transmission*, the speaker-listener hears over three channels while the listener and the microphone hear only through two channels, and it is channel 1, the bone-tissue one, that makes the difference. The full consequences of this situation upon our evaluation and control of the sound of our speech are not yet known. Apparently, though, we misjudge our own pitch, loudness, and quality, and probably our rate.

The lack of correspondence between the sound of speech that we experience and the one our listeners get requires that we accept their evaluation of our voice and believe the recording that we hear. Since the outside listener has the last word in the evaluation of the sound of our speech, we must calibrate our self-monitoring system to the voice that he recommends. This requires conscious practice, including negative practice, in order that we may acquire new habits of proper loudness, etc.

THE TECHNICAL CORRELATES

You are familiar with the quibble over whether there is any *sound* when a tree falls on a deserted island. There are sound waves but no ear to receive them. We have viewed sound as four experiences with the listener: duration, pitch, quality, and loudness. The crucial word is *experiences*. This puts us with those who say, "There is no sound of speech unless it is heard," a view that is consistent with the social environment of speech. However, our active interest in the interplay between the speaker and his listeners does not preclude an emphasis on the physical character of speech and the correlated sensory responses of the participants.

The study of speech as a social phenomenon preceded an understanding of the sound wave by centuries. Only recently has enough knowledge accumulated about the psychophysical nature of speech to make the study of its physical manifestations almost mandatory alongside the social reactions and evaluations of speech. In the mid-twentieth century, the student of speech who restricts himself to unaided subjective

judgments is simply ignoring the opportunity for an increased understanding of the speech processes, the possibility for short cuts in the
improvement of speech, and the basis for a more penetrating critical
evaluation of speech. He leaves himself unprotected against lore, myths,

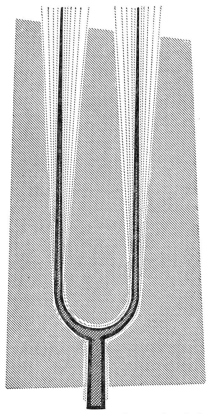

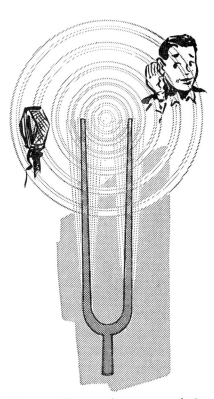

FIG. 13. The prongs of a tuning fork move *in* and *out* in a vibratory manner. The movement is not shown as affecting any transmitting medium.

FIG. 14. The moving prongs of the tuning fork in air generate waves among the molecules of the air. The waves travel through the transmitting medium to a listener's ear.

and superstitions about speech, and accepts unnecessary risks of falsely
describing what occurs in speech.

1. THE TRANSMISSION CHANNEL. Figure 13 shows a pair of prongs
that are apparently in horizontal motion. You readily identify them as a
tuning fork. The fork appears to be in isolation, possibly in a vacuum,
and thus would not be linked with you by any medium of transmission;
you would hear no sound from it. The deserted island again! Figure 14

gives us a different view. The tuning fork is in movement, this time in air, and the air forms a continuous path to the listening ear. Although there are many possible channels of sound transmission—iron, glass, water, in fact, any gas, liquid, or solid—the most common channel is the air path that lies between the speaker and the listener.

a. The Primary Channel. Sound generally travels faster in solids than in liquids and faster in liquids than in gases. The rate in air at normal temperatures at sea level is approximately 1,120 feet per second. This increases in warm air. You may have observed that speech and music apparently carry farther across a lake at night than in the daytime. The summer air at the surface of the water cools at nightfall; the sound that rises to the warm air moves faster and is bent forward and redirected downward. Any sound that is heard clearly across a lake has visited the region of warm air before arriving at the farther shore.

b. The Channel as a Secondary Source. Figure 14 suggests that the listener is in the path of a single bombardment of sound waves. We are anxious to deny this and then continue with a discussion of sound as though Fig. 14 were a true representation of the transmission of sound. Actually, we hear most sound in an environment of reflecting objects. The six sides of our rooms, the exterior surfaces of buildings, sidewalks, automobile windshields, table tops, etc., reflect sound in the manner that a mirror reflects light. The effect in a room is called *reverberation* and of discrete reflections outdoors, *echo.* The reflected sounds tend to prolong our experience with the signal, and in some instances the out-of-time bombardment causes dead spots in auditoriums. Carpets, draperies, books, rough porous plaster, wood paneling, acoustic treatments of walls, and even the presence of an audience will reduce room reverberation. Special precautions against extreme reverberation are taken in constructing broadcasting studios. The extreme effort toward achieving the ideal of Fig. 14 is in *anechoic* chambers, experimental rooms in which the six surfaces are covered with Fiberglas sound-absorbing wedges.

2. SOUND WAVES. The sound wave, the physical manifestation of sound, is the conveyor of properties that evoke pitch, quality, duration, and loudness in the listener and give rise to his aesthetic reactions to a voice. Let us note four aspects of the sound waves of Fig. 14—*wave form, condensation, rarefaction,* and *frequency.*

a. Condensation and Rarefaction. Suppose that a person were operating a pump, somewhat like a hand-type tire pump, attached to a small balloon in a manner to provide a closed system. The air initially in the chamber of the pump and the other components comprise the air of the system. With each downward stroke of the piston of the pump the balloon would become a globe and, with each upward stroke, be depressed. The downward stroke of the pump and the resistance of the balloon to expansion would produce a condensation of air molecules within the system. The upward stroke would restore the system to its original state and produce relative rarefaction of the enclosed air. This gross movement of molecules is easy to envisage.

What occurs at the exterior surface of the balloon of the preceding paragraph? It is extruded regularly into a sea of molecules, each with mass and inertia. An entire globe of molecules is pushed outward. This sphere$_1$ of minute masses hits against sphere$_2$ that lies adjacent to it and impels it outward. The molecules of sphere$_1$ soon lose their forward momentum and yield to the pull of the partial vacuum they have left in their wake. If sphere$_1$ received no further propulsion, it would retrace its course and continue backward and forward through diminishing distances. As we continue to pump, however, the balloon would expand at frequent intervals and force sphere$_1$ into continued action, etc.

Several occurrences in our analogy are noteworthy. (1) As the molecules move outward they hit other molecules and send them outward. The latter molecules hit still others. The molecules swing back through their original position and continue to swing to and fro, moving less far with each swing. A wave of *condensation* and *rarefaction* is propagated. A single molecule may not move or be displaced very far, but the *wave form* may move or be propagated for considerable distance. (2) The result of the condensation and rarefaction tends to be a globular effect extending outward from the source, not a stream like water from a faucet. (3) If air molecules were visible entities and if an onlooker might look toward the source of their movement through a field of vision 1 molecule wide, he would see no movement even if the action were reduced to slow motion. His view would be the near end of a perfectly straight string of molecules. He could observe the movement of the colliding molecules of this string only if he were privileged to view it from an angle, to look across the string. (4) The waves of condensation and rarefaction are equally spaced as they move away from the source, and the spacing is determined largely by the number of expansions of the balloon per unit of time. This rate would be the *frequency* of the wave. (5) Finally, the progress of a wave might be described at any instant by stating the relative position of the plunger of the pump. The plunger would have accompanied one complete wave through stages of condensation and rarefaction during the movement of the plunger from a position and on through its path until it was again at the original position.

b. Tuning-fork Waves. We now return to the tuning fork of Fig. 14. After the prongs are set in motion, they move outward together and inward together. Each swing is minutely less in extent than the preceding one as the prongs tend toward a state of rest. As with the balloon of our analogy, the prongs are extruded into the molecules of the air and displace them. The molecules propagate a wave of condensation, and it is trailed immediately by a wave of relative rarefaction. The frequency of the globular waves that are generated by the fork is determined by the rate of the pendulum-like swings of the prongs. The progress of the *wave front*, or the leading edge of the leading wave, is longitudinal, a straight line from the point of origin to any designated point on the periphery of the propagated sphere.

We have implied that the waves of condensation and rarefaction of a tuning fork move in a straight line, that is, are longitudinal. This action is not in keeping with the appearance of the waves we see most frequently, the ripples of water. They move outward from an origin but their feature is a vertical displacement that travels on the surface of water. Similarly, pictures of tuning-fork waves typically show a dimension that is perpendicular to the direction of propagation, like the up-and-down dimension of the right-hand side of Fig. 16. This roller-coaster contour is not to be confused with ripples, however similar in shape. The extra vertical aspect of Fig. 16 is a convenient representation of the position of a tuning-fork prong at successive movements. Merely for the measurement and examination of the wave, the amount of pressure, or the relative amount of condensation or rarefaction, is diagrammed as a dimension perpendicular to the direction of propagation.

c. Viewing the Invisible. No one is privileged to watch the molecules of air jostle about. We can, however, see the outcome of the movement in a manner summarized in Fig. 15. Here successive invisible sound waves are shown to be impinging on a diaphragm. The diaphragm yields before each impact and pushes a stylus to which it is coupled. The stylus traces its path on moving paper, and the result is the familiar perpendicular dimension of the pictures of sound waves. Obviously, the greater the force of the sound wave upon the diaphragm, the greater will be the displacement of the stylus. Thus, this record indicates the relative amount of pressure of the longitudinal sound wave. The record also permits an observer to count the successive waves, and if he knows the rate with which the paper passes the stylus, he can compute the rate of the sound waves. Portrayals of the type of Fig. 15 permit inferences about the characteristics of the invisible sound waves, but, again, such records do not depict the path through space of either a sound wave or a molecule. That path is a straight course, head on.

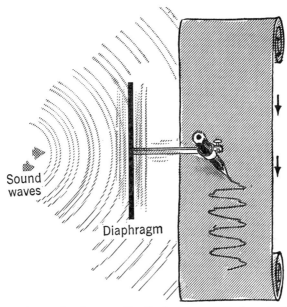

FIG. 15. The sound wave impinges on the diaphragm and displaces it. The amount of instantaneous displacement is graphed on moving paper by a stylus that is coupled to the diaphragm. Thus, the horizontal wave is represented as having a component that is perpendicular to the line of propagation.

d. Oscillation: The Circle, Pendulum, and Sine Wave in Time. Figure 16 includes portrayals of both circular motion and a wave of regular pattern, a sine wave. Trace the circle counterclockwise through one-fourth of its circumference. Now move your pencil back to the point of origin, zero degrees, and, holding your pencil as a pendulum, let it swing outward until the pencil point is between the two 90's of the figure. Prepare to do this again, but ponder what would happen if you moved your pencil upward and if Father Time insisted that passing moments neither stand still nor move backward and hence the paper on which you are making a vertical line moves to the left. You inadvertently describe the upward movement of the wave on your right instead of the circle or the path of the pendulum. Your first movement was equal to 90 degrees on the circle; your second movement was 90 degrees in the swing of a pendulum; and your conjectured form represents 90 degrees on a sine wave. The relationship among the circle, oscillatory movement, and the sine wave is close; the sine wave can be viewed as a projected circle. Already you sense that any of the movements might progress 60, 70, 180, or any other number of degrees up to 360 and then

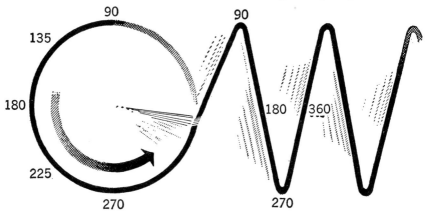

FIG. 16. Oscillatory motion may be portrayed on a time axis as a projected circle. Thus, the phase of a wave may be expressed in the terms of trigonometry, based on the circular form to which the wave corresponds. When considered alongside the frequency of a wave and the properties of the transmitting medium, the phase of a wave relates to the distance the wave travels in a specified time.

start over again. Possibly you see that at time 0.0025 second a wave that could repeat itself 100 times per second has a *phase* of 90 degrees; that at time 0.01 second this wave has a phase of 360 degrees and (on the circle) has completed one cycle; that this wave might be termed *100 cycles per second*, or 100 c.p.s.

These ideas bear restatement. The tuning fork is a fast pendulum, even as the plunger of the pump of our analogy moved as a slow pendulum. The action of the diaphragm of an earphone is like a piston, again remindful of a pendulum. This type of regular action can be described in the terminology of the circle, and, when viewed with respect to the passing of time, can be portrayed as a sine wave. Each cycle, or each wave, lasts a certain time; in other words, a measurable interval lapses between comparable points of successive waves. This amount of time is the period of the wave. How many waves of this period would occur in 1 second? This would be the *frequency* of the wave and stated in cycles per second. Here is a reciprocal relationship. Dividing 1 by the frequency of the wave yields the period of the wave, and dividing 1 by the period yields the frequency of the wave.

e. *In Space.* We have now related the sound wave to time. We traced one at phase 90 degrees. It had progressed through 0.0025 second. Let us see where it is in distance, in inches, feet, or miles. This, we now know, depends on the medium in which it is traveling. We shall assume that it is air, air of normal temperature at sea level.

The wave had a frequency of 100 cycles per second. The first of these 100 waves will be 1,120 feet removed when the last one is generated. The 100 waves will be stretched out through 1,120 feet. Each wave will be 11.2 feet long. The front edge of our 90-degree, or one-fourth of one, wave will be 11.2/4 feet, or 2.8 feet, from the source at instant 0.0025 second after its origin.

SPEECH WAVES

With this background of simple sound waves we shall proceed directly to study some of the aspects of the sound waves of speech. Principally, we move from pure tones to complex sounds or from symmetrical sine waves to wave forms of less regular contours. Figure 17 is a photograph of some of the characteristics of the successive sound waves of the word *top* as spoken once by a male speaker. We know from recent paragraphs that the sound waves were really propagated as longitudinal condensations and rarefactions. However, in the manner of Fig. 15, a meaningful perpendicular dimension has been recorded in Fig. 17. You observe the succession of similar patterns or sound waves of the vowel.

1. DURATION. We can count the successive waves of the vowel in Fig. 17; there are 20. This number relates to the time the sound lasts and to the listener's experience of duration. Were there only 12 instead of 20 and if all the other features of the two sets of waves were the same, the word would last only two-thirds as long and would sound like faster speech to the listener; or if there were more waves, the speech would sound slower. A normal rate of saying short phrases, with no interruptions other than the ones that occur between sounds and syllables as a characteristic of the sound of speech, is about five syllables per second.

2. FREQUENCY. Let us suppose that the period of wave 5 is $\frac{1}{120}$ second. The frequency of that wave is, then, 120 per second. This is the

frequency of the total wave pattern, comparable to the 100-cycle-per-second waves of our earlier example, and is *fundamental frequency;* this relates closely to the listener's experience of pitch. An average frequency for male voices cited earlier was about 128 waves per second, now cycles per second, and the corresponding average frequency of the fundamental for female voices becomes 256 cycles per second. These values correspond to the key of the pitch aspect of voice and give us no indication of

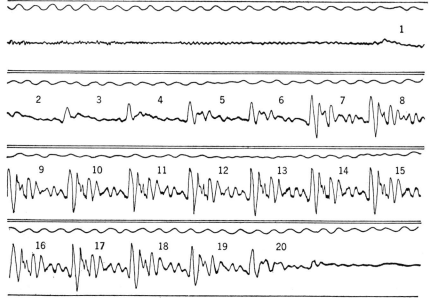

FIG. 17. A pencil tracing of a photograph of the successive sound waves of one pronunciation of *top*. The time line at the upper edge of the photograph is 440 cycles per second.

the variability of voice about these values. The frequency of the fundamental may be expected to vary slightly from wave to wave in speech. If we observe different lengths or periods among the 20 successive waves of Fig. 17, we are "seeing" a change in fundamental frequency, and on the basis of earlier paragraphs, we are seeing an inflection in pitch.

The waves of Fig. 17 correspond in time and number with the successive openings, puffings, or "vibrations" of the vocal folds that you studied in the previous chapter. Thus, the period of the sound wave is the time that lapses between successive openings of the folds.

The variability of the fundamental frequency in good speaking is illustrated in Fig. 18—three graphs of the distributions of the pitches that were employed by three professional male actors during the longest lines of their three plays. The range of the pitch of each actor is indicated by the horizontal dimension of the plots and by the accompanying musical notations (C_3 indicates middle C). The vertical dimension of the graphs indicates the relative number of instants that the actors were speaking at each frequency. Each measure was an average that extended over $\frac{1}{24}$ second; the number of measures in each distribution is shown as N.

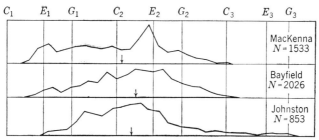

FIG. 18. A representation of the relative proportion of time three actors were at each fundamental frequency within their ranges of pitch in rendering single long speeches from plays. The vertical dimension indicates proportion of occurrences of each frequency. The horizontal dimension depicts range. C_3 represents middle C. The arrows denote median frequency. N states the number of measures that are represented by the graph. Each measure is an average covering $\frac{1}{24}$ second. (*From Milton Cowan, "Pitch and Intensity Characteristics of Stage Speech," Archives of Speech, vol. 1 [supplement], p. 64, 1935, by permission.*)

A more detailed view of the behavior of the fundamental frequency of one of the three speakers of Fig. 18 appears in Fig. 19. In this instance the frequency of the vocal-fold action of the speaker from moment to moment is plotted on the conventional musical scale. The vertical lines separate 1-second intervals. The change in fundamental frequency from instant to instant is particularly obvious.

3. AMPLITUDE. We know that the vertical dimension of each wave of Fig. 17 is directly proportional to the sound pressure level and intensity of a segment of the vowel sound. The figure, however, does not yield exact data in this regard, although it does permit two observations. (1) The word *top*, as pronounced, reached its maximum intensity only after several sound waves of the vowel had been generated. This is typical and is associated with both the movement of the mouth as [a] is in process and, less importantly, the fact that resonators, cavities of

Kenneth MacKenna

Valedictorian address from "Merrily We Roll Along" by Kaufman and Hart

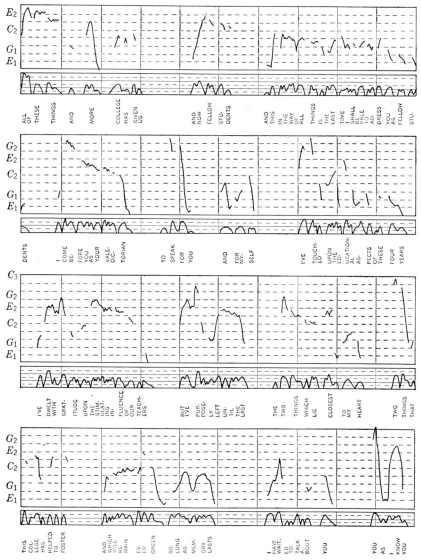

FIG. 19. A pitch graph in the manner of a musical score. Frequency is plotted as average values for each $\frac{1}{24}$ second. Intervals of silence in the actor's rendition of a passage are shown as breaks in the pitch contour. Vertical lines indicate 1-second intervals. (*From Milton Cowan, "Pitch and Intensity Characteristics of Stage Speech," Archives of Speech, vol. 1 [supplement], p. 64, 1935, by permission.*)

the head in this instance, do not attain their maximum output instantly. (2) The central portion of the figure is considerably more intense than the [p] and [t] which occur at the very beginning and end of the figure respectively. In other words, the major intensity of the word *top* is in the vowel, not the consonants. This is universally true in speech.

The sound pressure level or intensity of speech under discussion is directly related to the loudness aspect of the sound of speech. Typical measurements of sound pressure level would cite an average level for the span of time that is represented in Fig. 17. Moreover, the measure would be exact only with reference to one position, for example, "at the lip," "six inches from the mouth," etc., because sound level, in such a space as an anechoic chamber, varies inversely with the square of the distance between the points of origin and measurement. As measured 6 inches from the mouth, most of us have a range in sound pressure level of about 40 decibels, or approximately from 55 to 95 decibels in the production of a sustained vowel. Thus, we have ample resources for varying our voices considerably in level, whether we do so or not.

4. COMPLEXITY. Finally, each wave in Fig. 17 has a contour or shape that is unique. The profiles are jagged, not the smooth slopes of the pure-tone waves. These irregular, complex waves, however, can be reduced to a series of simple waves like the ones from tuning forks. And as though we were called on to check our analytical work, when the resulting series of sine waves is summated algebraically, the outcome is the same complex and irregular waves with which we started. The analytical process is exemplified in the instance of a pair of waves of small complexity in Fig. 20; the irregular waves at the top of the figure have been analyzed, somewhat in the manner of a problem in qualitative and quantitative chemistry. What elemental frequencies comprise these waves, and how much of each basic frequency is represented? The results appear in graphical solution in the representation of the pure-tone frequencies, each of a singular amplitude, shown below the complex wave of Fig. 21. The same type of analysis was applied to the several vowel waves of a pronunciation of the word *top*, like the one of Fig. 17. The vowel that was analyzed had but 17 waves. The results of the analysis are plotted in Fig. 21. The graph of Fig. 21 tells us what frequencies comprise the complex waves that one speaker uttered in *top*. The heights of the lines are to be interpreted in the same manner that one interprets the height of the pure-tone frequencies of Fig. 20,

and each diagonal line serves as a base line for portraying the components of one speech wave.

In due course, scholars will be able to extend our present limited
boundaries of knowledge and show us by an analytical process similar
to the one illustrated in Figs. 20 and 21 what frequencies are present in

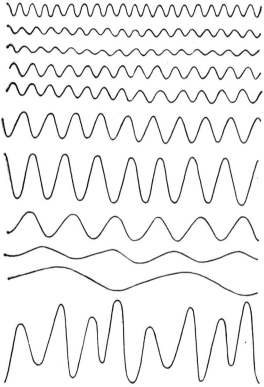

F IG . 20. The sound waves of speech may be described in terms of the unique set of
simple waves that would, if summated, reproduce the original complex pattern.
This analysis is termed *harmonic analysis* and follows a theorem proposed by the
mathematician Fourier.

the sound waves that convey to listeners the characteristics of nasality,
of hoarseness, of "talking like you have a potato in your mouth." As
we are mindful of the complex and inefficient self-monitoring system
that all of us have—channels 1, 2, and 3 of our discussion of side tone—
and the strong desire that many individuals have for a pleasant voice,
we may be struck by the need that exists for a rapid, accurate analyzer
of the complex waves of speech. We can envisage the possibility of

"seeing" our voices improve as we achieve the nonnasal voice once, twice, and again. The analyzer tells us so, and seeing is believing. Thus, the eye would supplement the speaker's deceptive ear as a monitoring instrument. The forerunners of such devices are already available. Their product is called "visible speech." Among the tasks immediately ahead is the definition of the complex waves that comprise "good"

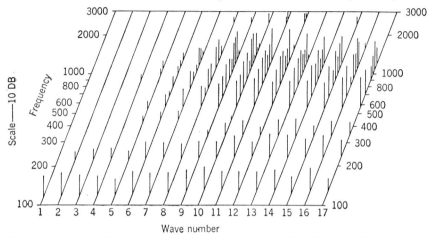

FIG. 21. An approximate analysis of successive waves like those of Fig. 17 in the manner indicated in Fig. 20. The successive waves are represented by the diagonal lines. The relative amount of sound pressure in each component of one complex wave is represented by the height of the "telephone poles" erected on a diagonal line.

speech and the segregation of the properties of the "hot-potato" voice and others.

SUMMARY

The sound of speech is a series of successive and intermittent complex tones and noises that gives an illusion of continuity. The series changes two or three times in character each fifth of a second—i.e., with each syllable, varies continuously in loudness, and in pitch seems to move upward and downward about two octaves around the middle of the piano keyboard.

The sound of speech can be controlled by the talker as he directs the processes of breathing, manages the movements of his articulators, changes the tensions of muscles that affect his resonators, and induces flexibility into the actions of the larynx—all components of the speech mechanism that we discussed in Chap. 2.

The anticipated improvement in the sound of our speech may be speeded through the acceptance of the evaluations of an outside monitor. Our own notion of the sound of our speech is distorted by the odd circumstance that we hear our speech through an extra and private channel. Our efforts may be further expedited through an appreciative awareness that our speech is an acoustic event that yields to the same analysis and description as any other sound. As engineers improve the sound of a factory through measurement, analysis, and repair, so the speaker may measure, analyze, and improve his voice.

Projects for Practice

1. Read the following lines appropriately after you have tried at least six ways of reading each line:

 a. Break,—break,—break,—
   On thy cold gray stones, O Sea! (*Alfred Lord Tennyson*)
 b. Milton! thou shouldst be living at this hour. (*William Wordsworth*)
 c. Speak the speech, I pray you, as I pronounced it to you, trippingly on the tongue. (*William Shakespeare*)
 d. Awake! for morning in the Bowl of Night
   Has flung the Stone that puts the Stars to Flight. (*Edward FitzGerald*)
 e. That age is best which is the first
   When youth and blood are warmer; (*Robert Herrick*)
 f. Roll on, thou deep and dark blue ocean, roll!
   Ten thousand fleets sweep over thee in vain. (*Lord Byron*)
 g. On with the dance! let joy be unconfined;
   No sleep till morn, when youth and pleasure meet
   To chase the glowing hours with flying feet. (*Lord Byron*)
 h. If I were an American as I am an Englishman I would never submit. Never. Never. Never. (*Lord Chatham*)
 i. It was many and many a year ago,
   In a Kingdom by the sea. (*Edgar Allan Poe*)
 j. Blessed are the meek: for they shall inherit the earth. (*Matthew*)
 k. Halt. Who goes there? (*William Shakespeare*)
 l. My name is Ozymandias, King of Kings. (*Percy Bysshe Shelley*)
 m. How do I love thee? Let me count the ways. (*Elizabeth Barrett Browning*)
 n. All the world's a stage and all the men and women merely players. (*William Shakespeare*)
 o. Flash! . . . . (You supply the line.)
 p. No more sobering announcement has been made in weeks than this:
   . . . . (You continue.)

2. The following projects relate to the description of voice:
   a. Underscore all of the adjectives that describe voice or manner of talking in an article about an individual, for example, the story accompanying the cover page of *Time* or *Newsweek*, or a featured biographical story in *The New Yorker*.
   b. Study the speech of your favorite newscaster and try to describe his four vocal attributes.
   c. Cite examples of soft-spoken and of loud characters in well-known plays or movies.
   d. Cite examples from radio, television, movies, and the stage of persons who have apparently turned unusual voice patterns into valuable assets.
   e. Most of us are surprised when we hear recordings of our voices. Enumerate under each of the four vocal attributes the aspects of your voice that sound unusual when you listen to a recording of your voice.
   f. Describe one of your teachers to a friend or your class. Do you find yourself describing his vocal attributes? Trying to reproduce his voice? Employing analogies, as "Sounds like (some widely known voice)"?
   g. Cite examples of speakers who were not loud enough. Can you add any indications that the speakers thought they were louder than they were?
   h. Report examples of English-speaking adults who were not understandable; of children; of persons whose native language was not English.
   i. Describe the speech of some hard-of-hearing adults; of children who are hard of hearing. Discuss these as examples of poor self-monitoring systems.
   j. Describe a voice that has seemed to you to be "beautiful"; another that has seemed "understandable but poor."
3. The following projects require you to analyze voice:
   a. Listen to a recording of a standard selection, as from *Hamlet*. Try to read the selection at the same rate that you have just heard. Compare the over-all times of the two readings. Moral: Do you know how fast you are talking?
   b. In teams of seven members, the class will read short passages, perhaps single identical sentences. The remaining members of the class, listeners, will rank the seven members of each team on amount of loudness. Do you fall where you belong? Probable moral: Do you know how loud you are?
   c. Listen to a recording of a speech that contains many fill-in sounds.

Tally the number of these sounds as you listen. How much variation is there in the totals of the tallies of the members of your class?

    d. Amplify, and cite examples that illustrate with respect to the time aspect of speech, "A listener's experience may not agree with group judgment, and physical measurements may not agree with either."

    e. Enumerate several disorders of speech and explain whether they relate principally or at all to quality, pitch, duration, or loudness.

4. The following projects require vocal exaggeration:

    a. Produce the voices that seem to you to go with the adult characters of some comic strips. Read the messages of several strips aloud.

    b. In pairs, students will simulate the following circumstances with both parties speaking:

        1. A patrolman gives Mrs. Van Denos III a ticket for speeding.

        2. A judge sentences a "repeater."

        3. The umpire stands by his decision.

        4. The ballad was wrong and the lamented character returns home.

    c. Pick out the softest and loudest segments from one of your recordings; the sentence that exemplifies your greatest excursion or variation in loudness; also in pitch; and in rate. Repeat the sentences, carrying further, indeed to an extreme, the characteristics that are already there.

5. This project requires factual answers.

    a. The sound in a room is 10^{-8} watt when a heating unit is not operating and 10^{-7} watt when the unit is operating. How much noise does the heating unit add to the room?

    b. Problem: An airplane is approaching its destination at 600 miles per hour. The pilot says, "Houston Tower, this is navy 737. Over." Suppose that the rate of talking is five syllables per second. How far does the plane move during this message?

    c. A block in Fig. 22 is shaded, below 40 decibels and between 1,000 and 3,000 cycles per second. Why is this area shaded? Are there some frequencies that are more precious than others?

    d. Why do hard-of-hearing people seem to hear better when they are out of doors? When they are riding a subway? Why does a person talk louder in a "dead" room than in a "live" one?

    e. There are frequencies as high as 8,000 cycles per second in speech. Where do these originate?

    f. How does a breath stream originate the sound of speech? Where is the source of the sound of speech? Do the vocal folds offer resistance to an air column? Exhaling against considerable pressure as inflating a toy balloon is *pressure breathing*. Does speech involve pressure breathing?

    g. Enumerate several sources of sound and try to classify the types of sources, for example, air columns, reeds, etc.

6. Prepare for your class and for discussion a report that treats historically an aspect of measurement in speech. (Hint: Start with the cumulative index of one of the journals cited in this chapter. After you have chosen your topic and a recent article as a point of departure, be guided by the references that you find in the article that you use.)

7. Sustained reading:

    a. Choose prose or poetry that illustrates at least three of the emotions, such as contempt, anger, fear, grief, and indifference, and practice reading to emphasize the emotional tone of the selections. Is the reading clearly different from one emotion to another? Enumerate from Chap. 2 the muscles that are used importantly in your reading.

    b. Practice reading short poems aloud with a major purpose of conveying the meaning to listeners: Milton's "On His Blindness," Shelley's "Ozymandias," one of Robert Browning's monologues, a sonnet by Shakespeare or Elizabeth Browning, and several other poems in this textbook.

    c. What are the principal vocal differences in effective readings of these two poems?

(1) From Fidelia

> Shall I, wasting in despair,
> Die because a woman's fair?
> Or make pale my cheeks with care
> 'Cause another's rosy are?
> Be she fairer than the day
> Or the flowery meads in May—
> If she think not well of me
> What care I how fair she be?

George Wither

(2) The Lost Leader

I

> Just for a handful of silver he left us,
>   Just for a riband to stick in his coat—
> Found the one gift of which fortune bereft us,
>   Lost all the others she lets us devote;
> They, with the gold to give, doled him out silver,
>   So much was theirs who so little allowed:
> How all our copper had gone for his service!
>   Rags—were they purple, his heart had been proud!

We that had loved him so, followed him, honoured him,
  Lived in his mild and magnificent eye,
Learned his great language, caught his clear accents,
  Made him our pattern to live and to die!
Shakespeare was of us, Milton was for us,
  Burns, Shelley, were with us—they watch from their
    graves!
He alone breaks from the van and the freemen,
  He alone sinks to the rear and the slaves!

II

We shall march prospering—not through his presence;
  Songs may inspirit us—not from his lyre;
Deeds will be done—while he boasts his quiescence,
  Still bidding crouch whom the rest bade aspire:
Blot out his name, then, record one lost soul more,
  One task more declined, one more footpath untrod,
One more triumph for devils and sorrow for angels,
  One wrong more to man, one more insult to God!
Life's night begins: let him never come back to us!
  There would be doubt, hesitation and pain,
Forced praise on our part—the glimmer of twilight,
  Never glad confident morning again!
Best fight on well, for we taught him,—strike gallantly,
  Menace our heart ere we master his own;
Then let him receive the new knowledge and wait us,
  Pardoned in Heaven, the first by the throne!

Robert Browning

d. Introduce into the reading of the following poems pauses of various
lengths, upward and downward inflections, and upward and downward shifts.

(1) THE AULD WIFE

The auld wife sat at her ivied door,
  (Butter and eggs and a pound of cheese)
A thing she had frequently done before;
  And her spectacles lay on her aproned knees.

The piper he piped on the hill-top high,
  (Butter and eggs and a pound of cheese)
Till the cow said "I die" and the goose asked "Why";
  And the dog said nothing, but searched for fleas.

The farmer he strode through the square farmyard;
(Butter and eggs and a pound of cheese)
His last brew of ale was a trifle hard,
The connection of which with the plot one sees.

The farmer's daughter hath frank blue eyes,
(Butter and eggs and a pound of cheese)
She hears the rooks caw in the windy skies,
As she sits at her lattice and shells her peas.

The farmer's daughter hath ripe red lips;
(Butter and eggs and a pound of cheese)
If you try to approach her, away she skips
Over tables and chairs with apparent ease.

The farmer's daughter hath soft brown hair;
(Butter and eggs and a pound of cheese)
And I met with a ballad, I can't say where,
Which wholly consisted of lines like these.

She sat with her hands 'neath her dimpled cheeks,
(Butter and eggs and a pound of cheese)
And spake not a word. While a lady speaks
There is hope, but she didn't even sneeze.

She sat with her hands 'neath her crimson cheeks;
(Butter and eggs and a pound of cheese)
She gave up mending her father's breeks,
And let the cat roll in her best chemise.

She sat with her hand 'neath her burning cheeks
(Butter and eggs and a pound of cheese)
And gazed at the piper for thirteen weeks;
Then she followed him out o'er the misty leas.

Her sheep followed her as their tails did them,
(Butter and eggs and a pound of cheese)
And this song is considered a perfect gem,
And as to the meaning, it's what you please.

Charles S. Calverly

(2) On First Looking into Chapman's Homer

Much have I travell'd in the realms of gold
And many goodly states and kingdoms seen;
Round many western islands have I been

Which bards in fealty to Apollo hold.
Oft of one wide expanse had I been told
That deep-brow'd Homer ruled as his demesne;
Yet did I never breathe its pure serene
Till I heard Chapman speak out loud and bold:
—Then felt I like some watcher of the skies
When a new planet swims into his ken;
Or like stout Cortez, when with eagle eyes
He stared at the Pacific—and all his men
Look'd at each other with a wild surmise—
Silent, upon a peak in Darien.

John Keats

Readings

Dreher, John J., "Judgments of Pitch Contours in Context," *Speech Monographs*, vol. 19, pp. 60–63, 1952.

Dunlap, K., *Habits: Their Making and Unmaking*, Liveright Publishing Corporation, New York, 1932.

Fletcher, Harvey, *Speech and Hearing in Communication*, D. Van Nostrand Company, Inc., New York, 1953.

Joos, Martin, "Acoustic Phonetics," supplement to *Language*, vol. 24, pp. 1–136, 1948.

Judson, L. S., and A. T. Weaver, *Voice Science*, Appleton-Century-Crofts, Inc., New York, 1942.

Miller, George A., *Language and Communication*, McGraw-Hill Book Company, Inc., New York, 1951.

Peterson, Gordon E., "Design of Visible Speech Devices," *Journal of the Acoustical Society of America*, vol. 26, pp. 406–413, 1954.

Pike, Kenneth L., *Tone Languages*, University of Michigan Press, Ann Arbor, Mich., 1948.

Pollack, I., J. M. Pickett, and W. H. Sumby, "On the Identification of Speakers by Voice," *Journal of the Acoustical Society of America*, vol. 26, pp. 403–406, 1954.

Potter, R. K., G. A. Kopp, and H. C. Green, *Visible Speech*, D. Van Nostrand Company, Inc., New York, 1947.

Seashore, C. E., *The Psychology of Music*, McGraw-Hill Book Company, Inc., New York, 1938.

Van Riper, Charles G., *Speech Correction*, 3d ed., Prentice-Hall, Inc., New York, 1954.

THE ACOUSTIC CODE OF SPEECH

"Did you go to the baseball game? Stay through the ninth inning? See that last out?" The first question refers to a sports event, and the third to one-third of one-half of one-ninth of a game. We can turn the questions around and start with the little unit. Three strikes make an out; three outs are half an inning. Nine innings comprise a game. One hundred fifty-four games make a season.

ANALYSIS: PARTS FROM WHOLES

Speech is a less structured quantity than *season*, but like season it is an accumulation of little events. A speaking performance is typically sustained—the classroom lecture for 50 minutes, a debate for an hour, and a conversation a succession of give and take. The performance— a play, radio program, or prepared speech—is a series of principal developments, ideas, or reasons, and they are comprised of smaller units, paragraphs, or sequences of closely knit lines. The development of this idea requires sentences, each composed of words, the words of a succession of speech sounds, and the sounds of singular combinations of frequencies.

In Chap. 3 the analysis of voice terminated with frequency. In the present chapter we treat the sounds that succeed each other to form words. Both sounds and words are considered to be symbols in our processes of oral communication. Our topics, then, are (1) the code, (2) saying the code, and (3) hearing the code. Our objectives are (1) your clear production of sounds and words and (2) your appreciation of variables that affect the reception of your clear speech.

CODE

What do you hear when you say, "Sh-sh-sh"? When you say, "Oo-oo-oo"? When you say, "Shoo, shoo"? In the first instances you heard two speech sounds, and in the final instance, speech sounds in succession and a word, "shoe" or "shoo." We are calling these small events *the code of speech*. The rationale follows. A speaker has ideas, and he renders these ideas acoustically through established symbols. He codifies his ideas in an elemental code of speech and a semantic code of words.[1]

PHONETICS

Phonetics is the science of speech sounds. If you think of science as synonymous with *laboratory*, you will wish to study the word before you accept this definition. To listen to the sounds of language discriminatingly and to classify these sounds systematically fits the methods of science, is analogous to developing a method of cataloguing books (library science), or a classification of plant life. The scientist would tentatively sort plants by one distinguishing characteristic and then another, make assumptions, and reject them, and eventually find a suitable system of classification. You may sort sounds of your language with your ear. If you listen closely you will rediscover the 50 or so distinguishable and transient acoustic experiences of English that we call speech sounds. This recognition of the sounds and the concomitant description of them is the essence of phonetics, a systematic classification of speech sounds.

1. PHONETIC SYMBOLS. The symbols that one uses to represent speech sounds are mere trappings. With all of us left to our own devices to classify sounds, a number of different alphabets would evolve, each as good as the others. It is not surprising then that a number of systems of notation have arisen, some for very special reasons. An inventor, Alexander Graham Bell, developed his system, *visible speech*, for his hard-of-hearing wife. Another was developed by an originator of a system of shorthand, and still another by a person who was interested in helping displaced persons learn English.

A system of phonetics that is to be used only by the originator can carry with it any alphabet that he understands. For him the symbols and acoustic events would have 1-to-1 correspondence, whether he

---

[1] We have no wish to argue the distinction between a "primary alphabet" or an original set of symbols and a code in the process of speaking. Presumably, a *code* replaces a primary set of symbols. If this is not the case in speaking, phonemes and words are not code but primary alphabets. Certain schools of psychology would insist that this is true. There appears to be no damage done in viewing ideas as being "coded for transmission," at least figuratively, in phonemes and words.

wrote in dots, lines, or hieroglyphics. The inventive scholar, however, probably wishes to discuss his system of phonetics or his transcribed materials with other persons of like interests. They would need to share a phonetic alphabet. Also, if phonetics is to be taught efficiently to groups, the teacher and students must have an alphabet in common. Such circumstances limit the number of alphabets that are in vogue.

The first phonetic alphabet you learned was the one employed by a dictionary to indicate the pronunciation of words. One of these systems, known as diacritical markings, originated with Benjamin Franklin's "New Alphabet."[1] Other forms of notation, sufficiently exact for their purpose, are the popular systems of shorthand.

2. THE INTERNATIONAL PHONETIC ALPHABET. The notation that is most often used among students of phonetics is excerpted from the International Phonetic Alphabet. An adequate number of these widely used characters to permit you to transcribe normal and deviate pronunciations of English appear below. You should become familiar with

Consonants

1. [p]* pee*p*	9. [ð] ei*th*er	17. [ʒ] vi*s*ion
2. [b] *bib*	10. [f]* *f*i*f*e	18. [tʃ] *ch*ur*ch*
3. [m] *m*ai*m*	11. [v] *v*al*v*e	19. [dʒ] *j*ud*g*e
4. [n] *n*oo*n*	12. [k] *c*oo*k*	20. [w] *w*ail
5. [ŋ] si*ng*	13. [g] *g*i*g*	21. [hw] *wh*ale
6. [t] *t*oo*t*	14. [s] *c*ea*s*e	22. [r] *r*ea*r*
7. [d] *d*ee*d*	15. [z] *z*one*s*	23. [l]* *l*u*ll*
8. [θ]* e*th*er	16. [ʃ] mi*ss*i*o*n	24. [h]* *h*ail
		25. [j] *y*ou

Vowels

1. [i] b*ee*t	7. [a] *a*sk (or the first sound of *aye*)	11. [o]* n*o*tation
2. [ɪ] s*i*t	8. [ə] sof*a* (this sound is called *schwa*	12. [ʌ] s*u*n (only in
3. [e] ch*a*otic	and occurs only in un-	stressed
4. [ɛ] s*e*t	stressed syllables)	sylla-
5. [æ] s*a*t	9. [u] p*oo*l	bles)
6. [ɑ] f*a*ther	10. [ʊ] p*u*ll	13. [ɔ]* *a*ll, h*o*rse

Diphthongs

1. [aɪ] *i*ce	4. [ɔɪ] b*oy*
2. [aʊ] h*ou*se	5. [eɪ] c*a*ve
3. [ou]* g*o*	6. [ɪu] m*u*te: the symbols [ju] are used when the first ele‧ment is [j] as in *u*sed.

*Sounds marked with an asterisk have been found to impair intelligibility.

[1] C. M. Wise, "Benjamin Franklin as a Phonetician," *Speech Monographs*, vol. 15, pp. 99–120, 1948.

this alphabet. Practice recording the pronunciations that you hear. Henceforth we shall rely increasingly on these symbols to indicate pronunciation.

The symbols [l̩], [m̩], [n̩], and [r̩] may represent *l*, *m*, *n*, and *r* sounds that form syllables either alone or with nonsyllabic sounds: [ˈbɑtl̩] (bottle) [ˈbɑtl̩d] (bottled), [ˈkæzm̩] (chasm), [ˈkæzm̩z] (chasms), [ˈsætn̩] (satin), [ˈsætn̩z] (satins), [ˈbʌtr̩] (butter), and [ˈbʌtr̩d] (buttered). Another convenient symbol is [ɚ], exemplified in [ˈbʌtɚ] (butter).

Practice differs in the way accent is indicated in phonetics. In this book, following the form of John S. Kenyon and Thomas A. Knott in their pronouncing dictionary,[1] primary accent is indicated by an apostrophe placed before the accented syllable.

3. REWARDS. Frequently, the reaction to a first exposure to phonetics is frustration, provoked by an odd-looking, overly long alphabet. Again, the alphabet is not the core of phonetics: the substance of phonetics lies in categorizing and describing speech sounds, not in memorizing a set of symbols.

When you can use a system of notation consistently, you can take pride in an underlying accomplishment: you can distinguish the sounds of the language. This is said to accompany a trained ear. Your skill might imply that you could learn a system of shorthand easily. Certainly you could isolate the speech sounds that a child says abnormally. You might be expected to pick up the pronunciation of a foreign language with relative ease.

The blunt fact is that an awareness of the structure of language in terms of its sounds is a convenience of inestimable value—valuable to you as a speaker and as a listener, and simply as a source of continuing satisfaction. Phonetics is part of the professional equipment of the linguist, anthropologist, telephonic engineer, actor, singer, and speech and hearing therapist.

VOWELS

In general, a vowel is a sound that can be sung. Or, a vowel is the result of an unobstructed air column that is voiced. In both statements the vowel is implicitly an acoustic event. Of course, there are vowels in spelling, five of them; but in your present study the vowels are sounds

---

[1] John S. Kenyon and Thomas A. Knott, *A Pronouncing Dictionary of American English*, G. & C. Merriam Company, Springfield, Mass., 1944.

and as a class are one of two large categories of speech sounds. Some of the vowels of English occur as you say these words: e*a*t, qu*ay*, ch*ao*tic, fr*ei*ght, *i*t, b*e*t, b*a*t, b*a*th, f*a*ther, *ou*ght, *o*bey, b*oo*t, b*u*t. The examples do not include all vowels, but they illustrate that there are more than five vowel sounds and that the relationship between vowel sounds and letters is inconsistent.

1. INITIATING THE VOWEL. In the formation of a vowel, first, the expiratory breath column keeps the vocal folds in a somewhat steady series of movements. You associate this action with pitch and cycles per second, as discussed in Chap. 3. Each burst of air through the space between the vocal folds is accompanied by a complex sound wave. We cannot know what it sounds like; it is probably about the same irrespective of the sound that is being voiced. Second, the complex vocal-fold tone is directed upward into the resonating cavities, and third, the resonators of the throat and head selectively amplify some of the frequencies of the vocal-fold tone. Depending upon which frequencies are amplified, one vowel or another is emitted and heard.

2. THE ACOUSTIC DESCRIPTION. We want our listener to hear the right vowel, of course, and not to misunderstand the word *pit* as [pɪt], [pɛt], [pæt], [pʊt], [pʌt], [pet], or [pat]; nor to hear [fiʃ] when we intend to say [fɪʃ] (fish). Such an error would occur if the resonating cavities amplified the wrong frequencies. In each vowel there are from three to five regions of resonance, or bands of predominant energy. For example, in the vowel in *top*, portrayed in Figs. 17 and 21, the frequencies that were amplified fall within the limits of 800 to 900 cycles per second, 1,000 to 1,200 cycles per second, and 2,400 to 2,800 cycles per second. These are typical although some analyses include at least one more band, approximately 3,500 to 3,600 cycles per second. This singular combination of frequencies, each band of a particular strength, results in this one vowel and no other. Another combination of frequencies would cause one of the errors above, especially if the error vowel or error word occurs in our language more frequently than the intended vowel or word, or if foreign-language listeners have in their language a vowel that approximates the error grouping of frequencies.

Some substitutions of vowels do not mar understandability. The [ɔ] in *ought* is frequently used in *father* without causing confusion. It is, nonetheless, a substitution of [ɔ] for [ɑ], and in other instances the same substitution would lead to a misunderstanding, for example, changing [kɑt] to [kɔt]. Thus, along with the descriptions above, we can add that each vowel is a singular phenomenon of resonance, to be distinguished from other vowels by cycles per second *above the fundamental.*

We know from Chap. 3 that the over-all sound pressure level of some vowels is four decibels greater than others; [ɑ] is the strongest and [i] the weakest. Some vowels consume more time on the average than other vowels; [i], [ɪ], and [ʊ] are relatively short and [ɑ], [u], and [ɔ], long. When other variables are ruled out some vowels are spoken with higher pitch than others; [i], [u], and [ʊ] are relatively high and [ɑ], [æ], and [ɔ], low. The acoustic description is obviously closely related to the physiological one that follows.

3. THE PHYSIOLOGICAL DESCRIPTION. Four physiological accompaniments are enumerated with each vowel. One of these is the relative amount of openness of the mouth when the vowel is produced. The second is the relative front-back position of the high point of the tongue when the vowel is produced. The third is the general shape of the opening of the mouth during the saying of the vowel. And the fourth is the degree of rigidity of the tongue with the production of each vowel. The first two of these traits can be read from the vowel diagram that appears in Fig. 22.

a. The Vowel Diagram. The vowel diagram of Fig. 22 is a map, a series of imaginary X-ray pictures that have been made through the left side of a speaker's face as he has sustained different vowels. The maximum excursion of the lower jaw in the production of a particular vowel relative to the others is indicated by the vertical dimension. For example, [i] is not accompanied by much jaw opening. It is called a *closed* vowel, meaning only that the mouth is nearly closed when this vowel is produced. The mouth is most *open* with the production of [ɑ]. Some authors use three classifications, *open, closed,* and *half-open,* and some phoneticians go further and set up four categories, adding *half-closed.*

The horizontal dimension of the graph indicates the relative position of the high point or uppermost bulge of the tongue when the vowel is produced. Thus, there are *front* vowels and *back* vowels. With the production of a front vowel, the tongue is typically arched somewhere near the front of the mouth, while with the back vowels the tongue tends to make a hump near the back of the mouth. Thus, [i] is a *closed front* vowel while [u] is a *closed back* vowel.

During the sustaining of a vowel the orifice of the mouth assumes a shape that is characteristic for that particular vowel. For example, in the production of [i] the opening of the mouth is a relatively flat slit. This is an *unrounded* vowel in addition to being *closed* and *front*. At the other extreme, [u] is accompanied by a rounded opening of the lips and is a *rounded* vowel. All vowels fit into one or the other category,

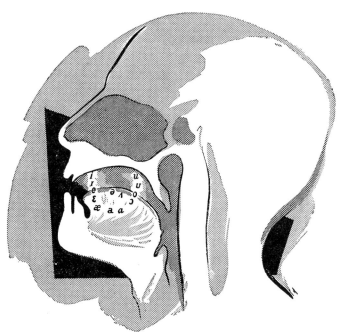

FIG. 22. Vowels have approximate physiological counterparts in the positions of the tongue. The vertical dimension of the vowel diagram indicates relative amounts of jaw opening. The horizontal dimension relates to the place along the length of the tongue at which it is "gathered" or "humped" in the production of each vowel.

although there are degrees of *rounding;* for example, the sound of German that approximates the American [i] is typically more unrounded than our sound.

Finally, as you sustain a vowel, your tongue is either *tense* or *lax*. You may not observe this difference at once. Make a few of the vowels and discover the relative amounts of tension in your tongue as you say the sounds. One of these two adjectives is typically used in a four-adjective physiological description of a vowel; for example, [i] is a *tense* vowel while [ɑ] is a *lax* vowel.

b. Perspective. You can now make a four-word description of each vowel: *open, half-open, half-closed,* or *closed; front* or *back; tense* or *lax;*

rounded or *unrounded*. These words, though, should not be taken as a generalization that will completely describe everyone's pronunciation of the vowels. The descriptive words are most appropriate when the vowels are produced in isolation, sustained. In ongoing speech the descriptions apply but to a lesser degree.

Moreover, different people do not shape their resonators alike in the production of a vowel. You may practice violations of your own four-word generalizations easily. Place a pencil between your teeth and bite on the pencil as you make the vowels. You can make them all without exercising your lower jaw at all. You *can* get by with no jaw movement, if you compensate by excessive manipulation of your tongue. Even so, Fig. 22 is a generalization, an average that was formulated by phoneticians who described their own and other people's productions of the vowel sounds when the sounds were well made. The diagram was later substantiated by investigators who used X-ray techniques, substantiated with respect to sustained sounds.

c. Application. Whether or not you are practicing the vowels as you read this material, you will be practicing them unconsciously as soon as you begin to talk. Each rendition of a vowel is practice for the next time that you say the sound and there is at least one in every word. We hope, though, that you are verifying the physiological description of vowels as you read. Conscious practice in sustaining the vowels and an analytical ear cocked to observe the acoustic properties of the vowel can markedly affect the degree with which you differentiate among the several vowels.

DIPHTHONGS

Two vowels are frequently spoken in rapid succession, or, more precisely, as a glide in which the speaker starts with one vowel and ends with another. The combination occurs within a syllable and often gives an impression of a single sound to a listener. This dual vowel sound that comes with an unimpeded flow of breath is a *diphthong*.

Many students err doubly in their notions about diphthongs. First, they hear these dual sounds as single vowels and, second, assume that diphthongs relate in some manner to two letters in spelling. Possibly a few examples will forestall these confusions. Immediately after the consonant in "boy" the speaker says the vowel [ɔ] of "ought" and then goes on to make the vowel [ɪ] or "it"; or in the word "few" he starts with the vowel [ɪ] of "it" and ends with the vowel [u] of "boot." Diphthongs, or combinations of two vowels, are not necessarily represented in writing by two, three, four, or any particular number of letters. The one-letter word *I* contains two vowels and, therefore, a diphthong.

The following words both exemplify the six common diphthongs and illustrate further some of the inconsistencies between spelling and pronunciation. The same diphthong appears throughout a row.

1. boy, soy, boil
2. I, write, pie, aye, eye
3. cow, house, bough, bow (verb) or bow wow
4. you, few, new, united, pneumatic, lute
5. a, mate, fete, wait, weight, veil
6. oh, owe, open, though, sew, roam, yeoman

CONSONANTS

The second large classification of sounds in a language is consonants. In some early cultures that used highly phonetic writing only the consonants were written, the vowels somehow falling into place when the adjacent consonants were spoken. This practice bespeaks the contribution of the consonants to intelligibility then, and in considerable measure the consonants of modern languages are the sounds that distinguish words in oral utterance.

1. INITIATING THE CONSONANTS. Consonants result from an obstructed air column, the closure being complete in some instances and slight in others. The resulting sound may be *voiced*, as in the word *bad*, or voiceless as wa*sp*; thus, the setting up of the sound may involve a dual source—action at the vocal folds and a further transfer of a wind stream to sound at the point of obstruction.

2. THE PHYSIOLOGICAL AND EFFECTIVE DESCRIPTION. The adjectives that describe the consonant are quite different from the ones we used in connection with the vowel. The classification of Fig. 23 supplies most of the adjectives. We know from the preceding paragraph that a consonant is either *voiced* or *voiceless*, a dichotomy that has a physiological foundation. Three consonants are made through the nose. This sets up a second either-or physiological dichotomy: a consonant is either *oral* or *nasal*, oral as [*lɪd*] (lid) or nasal as [*minɪŋ*] (meaning). Further, a notation can be made of the point of articulation, that is, the place at which the obstruction occurs: "back-of-tongue against roof-of-mouth" or *palatal* and *velar;* "tip-of-tongue against teeth" or *dental;* "two lips" or

bilabial; "teeth against lips" or *labiodental;* etc. Thus *b*—not [bi]—is a "voiced, oral, bilabial consonant."

Traditionally, another set of adjectives is coupled with the foregoing, and for lack of an established name we are calling them *effective.* These words both describe the sound of the consonant as the listener hears it and relate to the production of the sound. The consonant is *plosive* or *continuant* and, if the latter, is either *fricative* or *not fricative*—a plosive,

	Bi-labial	Labio-dental	Lingua-dental	Lingua-alveolar	Lingua-palatal	Lingua-velar	Glottal
Nasals	[m]			[n]		[ŋ]	
Plosives	[p], [b]			[t], [d]		[k], [g]	
Fricatives		[f], [v]	[θ], [ð]	[s], [z]	[ʃ], [ʒ]		[h]
Semivowels	[h], [w]			[l]	[r], [j]		

FIG. 23. A classification of consonants. The horizontal dimension relates to an approximate place of articulation of the consonant and extends from the frontal articulators, the lips, to the throat. The vertical dimension relates to gross aspects of the character of the consonant sounds. The voiceless consonants are placed near the left-hand side of the cells.

as [*pad*] or [*bæt*], or a continuant, as [*rol*] or [*ʃelvz*] (shelves); fricative, as [*fɪz*], or without friction, as [lɪmbɚ] (limber). A nonfricative continuant almost by definition takes on vowel characteristics. An ambiguous classification, *semivowels,* is sometimes restricted to [w] and [j] and sometimes extended beyond the ones enumerated in Fig. 23.

All the descriptive words except those relating to place of articulation can be used fairly universally in describing "all-English consonants" "all the time" as produced by "all the people."[1] The place of articula-

---

[1] The several *all*'s of our sentence are intentional, although we are acutely aware that much is yet to be learned about the formation of consonants. The following circumstance and study are indicative. Some persons who have undergone surgery for the removal of the larynx breathe through a hole in the front of the neck. Expelled air, in turn, passes by a reed and is piped into the front of the mouth. The reed vibrates all the time the air passes through the pipe. Several of these persons spoke and recorded *nonsense* syllables of the consonant-vowel-consonant type. The recordings were played back to students of phonetics who transcribed what they

tion, however, is subject to considerable individual variation. The indicated loci of articulation are generalizations and vary from person to person and from one phonetic environment to another.

3. LINGUISTIC MODIFICATION. There is variation in the way a speaker forms a consonant, depending upon the sounds that precede and follow it. These differences may be attributed to the character of the language and the special demands that unique combinations of speech sounds make upon the speech mechanism.

A consonant may have different properties, depending upon where it lies within a syllable. The consonants of [bʌt] (but) are not the same as the similar sounds in reverse order, [tʌb] (tub). The initial sound in both instances explodes and glides into the vowel. The explosion is at issue, for when the same consonants become final sounds, they are typically arrested, not permitted to explode. Indeed, when they are allowed to be plosives in the final position, the monosyllable may sound like the first and the accented syllable of a two-syllable word. Although we shall not pursue the topic, the consonant may be given still a third character when it occurs medially in a word as in [stʌb] (stub).

4. THE ACOUSTIC DESCRIPTION. Bands of frequencies are the ultimate differentiating factors among consonants. Some voiced consonants, [l], [r], [m], when sustained, have essentially the same harmonic structures as vowels. Typically, though, the consonant is accompanied by a "swishlike" noise that includes innumerable frequencies from low to high and in a context other than speech would be termed noise.[1] Some of the sounds, for example [s] and [ʃ], may be simulated by producing a noise with a stream of compressed air directed against a corner or a rough surface. The voiced sounds may be less noisy because the vocal-fold tone partially masks the noise component of the consonant.

Consonants differ from each other as much as 15 to 18 decibels, [f] and [θ] being especially weak.

---

heard. A large proportion of some of the voiceless consonants were heard right. Obviously the consonants are differentiated by more than vocal-fold action; otherwise the listeners would have heard all the reed-vibrated consonants as voiced sounds. (See Melvin Hyman, "An Experimental Study of the Relative Sound Pressure, Duration, Intelligibility and Aesthetic Aspects of the Speech of Artificial-larynx, Esophageal, and Normal Speakers," *Journal of Speech and Hearing Disorders*.)

[1] R. K. Potter, G. A. Kopp, and H. C. Green, *Visible Speech*, D. Van Nostrand Company, Inc., New York, 1947.

5. THE AFFRICATES. Figure 23 does not include two consonants, the affricates [tʃ] and [dʒ]. These sounds involve the preparatory stages for one pair of consonants, [t] and [d], and terminate in another pair of consonants, [ʃ] and [ʒ]. Moreover, the preparatory steps would seem to anticipate plosive consonants, while the ones that emerge are fricative.

6. SUMMARY. The several oral consonants of English have imperfect relationships with the English alphabet. There is adequate correspondence, however, for one who is familiar with the language to convert the printed symbols into well-established sequences of speech sounds.

Clear articulation implies that the speaker is forming consonants well. This is a motor skill that involves making and breaking firm closures, forming graduated obstructions in the path of outgoing air, and making the coordinated movements of the tongue, lips, velum, etc., rapidly. Indeed, the formation of consonants is as much a matter of muscular control as is hitting a home run or playing a Bach concerto. The task lies with the speaker. He has habits of consonant formation. He will change these only with deliberate practice.

PRONUNCIATION

The formation of the sounds of speech is called either *articulation* or *enunciation*. Pronunciation is a more comprehensive process in oral language and includes at least (1) the articulation of the sounds, (2) the saying of all of the sounds in the prescribed order and without extra ones, and (3) an emphasis on a portion of the multisyllable word, the *accented* syllable. Thus, pronunciation involves several motor skills. Your excellence in these skills may relate to the size of your vocabulary, your sensitivity to definitions, your exactness in using words—the many components of a vaguely defined *language function*.

Good pronunciation is always desirable, and the "success" of some speakers who do not have good pronunciation hardly warrants a generalization that it is a mere refinement. In some forms of speaking, as interpretation of literature, acting, and radio speech, excellence in pronunciation is presumed, and, even in conversation, habits of clear, inconspicuous pronunciation are desirable.

1. THE PRONOUNCEMENT VIEW. We digress for an analogy. The rules of spelling have become so unyielding that an unusual spelling is an error, a mistake, a sign of incompetence or illiteracy. The reader who evaluates writing by this standard of *correctness* loses track of an argument as he glares at the telltale evidence that the writer is not de-

pendable: he has misspelled a word! That the reader may have to get a dictionary to support his suspicion is beside the point. The spelling is *right* or *wrong*. This behavior has its analogue in pronunciation. Many listeners give great weight to pronunciation that follows the rule books. The missaying of a word reflects upon the speaker adversely, while correct pronunciation stimulates confidence in him.

2. A RELATIVE STANDARD OF PRONUNCIATION. The *correct* and *wrong* pronunciations of the preceding paragraph are difficult, if not impossible, to define, other than superficially. A popular dictionary explains, "The standard of English pronunciation, so far as a standard may be said to exist, is the usage that now prevails among the educated and cultured people to whom the language is vernacular."[1] A dictionary, then, tries to describe what people say, not dictate what they should say. Obviously, if a standard of American pronunciation is indefinite, a critic is ill advised who speaks with the certainty that is implied by *right* and *wrong* pronunciation. Degrees of merit, not absolutes, are at issue, and the appropriate adjectives may be *good-poor* or *acceptable-substandard*.

Good pronunciation is inconspicuous. Since a new pronunciation is rarely inconspicuous and since the attainment of good pronunciation involves new experiences in saying words, it behooves us to establish our new habits in a congenial environment. Your present class provides this rare opportunity to contribute new pronunciations to a natural, habitual flow of speech. The exercises of this chapter are intentionally lengthy and loaded. We hope that you will exploit your present opportunity to become accustomed to new pronunciations of many words and to lose your consciousness of their newness.

Good pronunciation varies with the occasion on which the words are said. Degrees of formality of the occasion correspond with the extent to which relatively *strong* or *weak* pronunciation is appropriate. The former is natural among formal surroundings and the latter equally so in informal discussions and conversations. Alternative pronunciations that some speakers might use in keeping with the occasion include [mɛ'morɪəl] and [mə'morɪəl] (memorial), ['krean] and [krɛn] (crayon), ['protɪən] and ['protin] (protein).

Pronunciation is further affected by assimilation. One sound in a word may affect the sound that precedes or follows it, and successive

---

[1] Webster's *New Collegiate Dictionary*, G. & C. Merriam Company, Springfield, Mass., copyright 1949, 1951, 1953. Used by permission.

words may be said differently from the way either would be said alone. For example, when *horse* and *shoe* are combined into *horseshoe*, the last sound of *horse* is assimilated with the first sound of *shoe* and the result approaches [hɔrʃu]. This assimilation gives easy and natural pronunciation. Similarly, "passed Stanley's store" said as individual words might be distracting. In combination the phrase approaches [pæstænlıstor]. Pronounce the words *general electric* alone and in combination. Does assimilation cause you to omit a sound?

Some assimilations have been stamped *disapproved: would* and *you* as [wʊdʒə]; *won't* and *you*, [wontʃə]; etc. Some provoke mirth: *old* and *Yale*, [oldʒel]. In the formal reading of poetry, assimilation is usually avoided. Shakespeare's Sonnet 29 has the joyous line "Like to the lark at break of day arising from sullen earth . . . !" Through assimilation, [d] is frequently inserted between the last two words.

3. THE FOCAL POINTS OF PRONUNCIATION. We have described pronunciation as including (1) articulation, (2) the right sounds in the right order, and (3) accent. Articulation is basic. Improvement in this regard requires no study of the dictionary, simply practice—sometimes directed practice—in uttering sounds, one by one, more completely.

"The right sounds in the right order" ranges from minor deviations of dialect to the blunders of Dogberry. The *per-pre* reversals are common. Are these equally common? [ædrɪ'andæk] (Adirondack), [ʌz) (us), ['prɛspərɛʃn] (perspiration), ['nıuəsəns] (nuisance as three syllables), ['gʌvmənt] (government as two syllables), [ə'mʌrkə] (America), [fɪʃ] (fish), [ɪl'nɔɪz] (Illinois).

Accent is the saying of one syllable louder than the remaining syllables of a word. For example, in these words, the first syllable is usually designated as the accented one: *lamentable, disputable, prelate, impious, gondola, industry.* But in these words the second syllable is often accented in formal speech: *abdomen, contractor, spectator, altimeter, irrevocable, dictator, finance, irrefutable.* The examples are, of course, "borderline" words.

The louder syllable probably has a higher fundamental frequency and greater duration than the unaccented syllables, but in trying out a new pronunciation, treat loudness as the singular aspect of the accented syllable. Although oral directions and descriptions like "Accent the first syllable" or "The accent is on the second syllable" are common, you may find that you cannot easily follow the instruction. Hence, a partner who serves as an outside monitor is helpful to you as you work toward new pronunciations.

4. STEPS FOR IMPROVING YOUR PRONUNCIATION. The chances are that your pronunciation is largely good. After all, you have progressed a long way in a system of formal education. Alas, there comes the day when you suddenly need that remaining small difference that lies between *good* and *excellent*, and the only way to have it then is to work toward improvement now. This involves three stages: (1) obtaining new knowledge about how to say words, (2) mastering techniques that expedite an understanding of your own pronunciation and that of other people, and (3) establishing new habits of pronunciation.

a. Apply Phonetics. If you are concerned with superior pronunciation, you have a special reason to become at home with the phonetic alphabet. After you become proficient with phonetics, examine the articulation that you hear in recordings of your speeches. This implies playing and replaying many times short phrases from the recordings and deliberately listening to the phrases apart from content. (In this practice use old-fashioned equipment, a disk instead of a tape, and a record player with a playback arm that can be moved manually and freely.)

b. Study the Dictionary. The best guide to pronunciation is a dictionary. Study the introduction of the dictionary. Read the descriptions of the sounds and of the diacritical markings. Change the indicated pronunciations of words to phonetic symbols.

c. Listen to Established Speakers. Your desire to improve your pronunciation should lead you to listen carefully to the speech that you hear. As a student, you have opportunities daily to hear the "cultured and cultivated people to whom the language is vernacular," the ones whose pronunciations are recorded in dictionaries. Close scrutiny of pronunciation, in and out of classrooms, is a prerequisite to improving your own. You will find that you rapidly improve your skill in evaluating the pronunciation that you hear. A person's recognition of good pronunciation and his skill in saying words well are so closely related that "judgment" tests are reliable substitutes for "performance" ones.[1] If you only indicate a preference between [ˈprɛlət] (prelate) and [ˈprilet], you imply the pronunciation you customarily use and the one you believe you ordinarily hear.

[1] Helene Blattner, "An Experimental Study of the Testing of Pronunciation," *Speech Monographs*, vol. 15, pp. 181–187, 1948.

5. LIMITATIONS OF THE DICTIONARY. In spite of the inestimable value to you of the dictionary, you should know its limitations.

a. Reports of the Past. The dictionary records in the present, and by the time the ink is dry, it reports of the past. Beyond a doubt, pronunciation changes, although it changes slowly. Patrick Henry, George Washington, and John Quincy Adams would seem to us to have marked dialects. Within our generation, though, what we hear as a change is our sudden awareness of what has long been a generally accepted pronunciation. Experience in the armed services convinces many students that [æl′tɪmətər] (altimeter) is a workaday pronunciation; others insist that the pronunciation of [æltə′mitər] must have changed with their entering military service.

The dictionary reports, and in spite of the fact that pronunciation changes slowly, the dictionary must always give a historical account.

b. Dialects. Within the United States there are three major regional dialects, Eastern, Southern, and General American. The dictionary cannot take into account pronunciations that are peculiar to these gross regions, not to mention the many lesser dialects that phoneticians have isolated.

c. Weak and Strong Forms. The dictionary cannot list the weak forms of pronunciation. There are striking implications about an assumption of "correct pronunciation" in the fact that the same editors and publishers of *Webster's New International Dictionary* published separately a guide to colloquial pronunciation, "the language of well-bred ease." As you might expect, the recorded pronunciations in the two books are quite dissimilar.

d. Assimilation. The dictionary must treat the word as the unit of language and cannot record the effects of assimilation.

SUMMARY. Pronunciation is fraught with personal identifications. The desire to have "good" pronunciation is in conflict with "My way of saying the word is right." Students have no monopoly on this paradox. For example, when an agent was shown the pronunciation given for the word *secretive* in his company's definitive dictionary, he said, almost in ire, "I suppose we *do* have mistakes; I'd never think of saying the word that way!" Your awareness of this behavior pattern may help you to avoid or dispel it.

Your pronunciation tomorrow will be affected by (1) your habits of pronunciation today, (2) your attentiveness to what you hear, and (3) what you do with a dictionary. The best predictor of your pronunciation of a word tomorrow is the way you say the word today. Let us hope, then, that your present pronunciation is characteristically clear and inconspicuous.

RECEIVING THE CODE

The speaker employs the codes of sounds and words and forms the acoustic symbols. The listener receives the messages symbol by symbol. An explanation of his sensory process of hearing is beyond the scope of this book. We do have a present interest, however, in the interaction among the speaker, the listener, and their language that facilitates communication.

The listener's reception of articulated speech is aided by some characteristics of the code with which he is familiar. He has never been called upon to verbalize his knowledge of his language, and he might only be conscious of what he has learned if he were suddenly confronted with exceptions. (1) He expects no English word to begin with [ŋ] and is accustomed to hearing it only at the end of a syllable. (2) Although there are more than half a million words in formal English, the chances are one in fourteen that the next word that he hears will be "the." (3) Although there are more than 50 sounds in English, the chances are one in twelve that the next sound that he hears in continuous speech will be [t]. (4) Having heard the "the," the chances are almost nil that the next word that he hears will be "the"—in spite of the fact that this sentence contains the "the-the" combination (and more).

1. THE PROBABLE SYLLABLE. The 50 speech sounds of the code in which we say our messages are spoken in many combinations as syllables and words. One out of every three syllables in English is a vowel bounded by two consonants [pɑt]; one out of five is a consonant-vowel [no]; and one out of five, a vowel-consonant [ɪn]. The less frequent syllables are vowel-consonant-consonant [old], consonant-consonant-vowel [fli], consonant-consonant-vowel-consonant [slɪk], consonant-vowel-consonant-consonant [wɑsp], consonant-consonant-vowel-consonant-consonant [klæsp] (clasp), consonant-consonant-vowel-consonant-consonant-consonant [klæsps], and finally consonant-consonant-consonant-vowel-consonant-consonant [skreps].

2. THE WORD THAT FITS. Robert Frost, in lectures, has described the poet's "commitments." The poet has freedom in his writing only before he starts, for the first word can be followed by only a select group of words. The first metrical foot reduces the poet's choice of the

kind of feet that can follow. The number of feet in the first line constitutes a commitment with respect to later lines. If the poet allows the
second line to rhyme with the first, he makes another commitment and
limits his freedom for the remainder of his composition. By the time he
finishes a verse, he has surrounded himself with commitments that he
must live up to as he continues through his composition. These limit
the potential number of words that fit.

a. Readers Identify the Words That Fit. The typescripts of some 600
classroom speeches contained more sentences of 12 words than at any
other number. A student selected a number of these sentences and
edited them by removing one word at random from each sentence, then
two words at random, three, four, and so on through seven words.[1]
She typed the remaining words, leaving no spaces to indicate where
words had been omitted, gave the edited groups of words to numbers
of college students, and asked them to construct the probable 12-word
sentences from which the words had been selected. In the instance of
11-word groups, she received the "correct" responses, the original
words in the right place, more than 50 per cent of the time. The 9- and
10-word groups were also completed correctly more often than would be
expected by chance.

If readers are aware of the positions of the missing words in sentences,
the proportion of correct responses can be quite high:

1. In the United States the Fourth of July is a national . . . .
2. The . . . of snow is white.
3. The auditorium in our . . . has poor . . . .
4. He is a . . . carrier.

Listeners employ the probabilities of the "the words that fit" and
increase the number of correctly received symbols.

b. The Degree to Which a Word Fits. If all the events—for example,
words—of our language had the same likelihood of occurrence in speech,
each would be said to convey the same amount of *information.*[2] This
circumstance does not prevail, and the extent to which it is not present
is measureable through the techniques of information theory. The
factors that prevent all items of a code group from being unequally

[1] Helen R. Miner, "A Study of the Information Content of Groups of Words,"
unpublished M.A. thesis, The Ohio State University, Columbus, Ohio, 1952.

[2] *Information* is used here in a limited sense to denote an amount of "reduction
of uncertainty" that occurs with the saying of the word or with any other symbol.

probable as a next occurrence are said to produce *redundancy*. The speech code contains many instances of redundancy, most of which have not yet been measured. Claude Shannon estimates that in spelling redundancy amounts to approximately 50 per cent.[1] In the light of our present discussion, "the word that fits" exemplifies redundancy and conveys less than maximum information. If you are able to add the missing word "white" to the sequence "The color of snow is . . . ," the saying of "white" carries no information at all. You know with 99 or 100 per cent certainty what the speaker is going to say before he says it.

Many aspects of our language contribute to redundancy, possibly none more than the fact that the vocabulary has highly probable and improbable words.

c. Factors That Contribute to Redundancy. All of us are typically lip readers to an extent. In a noise-filled room, we make higher scores on a test of word recognition when we watch the speaker than when we do not look at him.[2] Listeners exploit this redundancy.

The grammatical rules of speech contribute some redundancy. For example, with the pair of words at the outset of an utterance "Mary has . . . ," there are rules that forbid the next word's being "see," "saw," "is," "was," and a host of other words. Of course, many words can still be used, but not *all* words. Listeners take advantage of this redundancy.

The patterns of the emotional voice that were discussed earlier as reported by Fairbanks and his students are a supplementary code of speech and reduce the opportunities for misunderstood utterances.

Of successive categories of words as determined by Thorndike, the 1,000 most frequently used words are more highly intelligible than words that are designated "2" by Thorndike. (These words are the second thousand in terms of frequency of usage.) Thorndike "2" words are more highly intelligible than Thorndike "3," and so on through his many categories of words.

Another correlate of intelligibility is *number of sounds* in a word. Words with *more* sounds have a greater likelihood of being understood

---

[1] Claude Shannon and Warren Weaver, *The Mathematical Theory of Communication*, University of Illinois Press, Urbana, Ill., 1951.

[2] John J. O'Neill, "Contributions of the Visual Components of Oral Symbols to Speech Comprehension," *Journal of Speech and Hearing Disorders*, vol. 19, pp. 429–439, 1954.

than words with fewer sounds. Thus, on the average, words of five sounds are more intelligible than ones of one, two, three, or four sounds. Similarly, words with two syllables are more intelligible than words with one syllable.[1] Here a phonetic context is operating in the manner of a word context in earlier examples. This effect does not develop from redundancy but from the fact that the increased level of the accented syllable serves to maintain an adequate sound pressure level throughout the word.

d. Do We Want Redundancy? Language engineers could give us a code vastly superior to the one we have inherited if efficiency (time of utterance) were the sole criterion: fewer sounds, fewer words (no synonyms), and a code in which each sound had an equal opportunity to appear as the next sound. This language might even be capable of being spoken. However, every single sound would have to be exactly understood if the message were to convey its proper meaning. There could be no filling in on the basis of context, grammar, etc. With every utterance perfectly heard, our time of talking and listening would be vastly reduced. The classroom lecture might last only a few minutes!

How many times in a day do you ask someone to repeat what he has said because you did not understand "the first saying"? How many times in a day are you asked to repeat? These failures in reception occur in spite of the fact that our language in both sounds and words is highly redundant and that we have lived with the language for several years and are familiar with many of its statistics. A nonredundant code would place a responsibility for *perfect*—not near-perfect—articulation upon every talker. There could be no assimilation or weak forms in pronunciation.

Possibly we are fortunate in having our present wasteful code of sounds and words. Meaning is given to us in several ways and with considerable repetition within the sentence, and as we go from what-we-think-we-heard to what-we-think-we-ought-to-have-heard a few times, we feel fairly certain that the speaker must have said "thus and so." The actor can perform before large audiences, the speaker can address a nation by radio or television, and each can feel reasonably certain that the speech code has carried his meaning to a large fraction of the viewers and listeners most of the time, even though no one had the opportunity to say, "I didn't understand you," or "Will you say that again?"

---

[1] Of the two-syllable words, those with the accent on the second syllable are more intelligible than words with the accent on the first syllable.

SUMMARY

Anyone who is saying a message, obviously, has to put his message in a language that he and his listener have in common. Talking is a process of sending and receiving and, of course, involves the use of a code, in our case the English language. The language is complicated. We can use it before we know much about it. In fact, a child has adequate functional control of the 50 sounds of the code by the time he is four, five, or six years of age. An understanding of the system, though, with its vowels, consonants, diphthongs—singular combinations of *frequencies*—awaits adulthood and collegiate study. The more we study the language, the more interesting it becomes and the more respect we hold for the code in which we phrase our ideas.

We group the little phonetic elements of the code of speech into words and forthwith set up rules about a right or wrong way to say the word. Aside from the rules, though, there remains the problem of the listener's identifying the words and the speaker's saying them intelligibly. The words sometimes present no problem, really, for the meaning is known before the word is said, as in "The color of snow is . . . " More often, the word must be identified, and in this case the inherent differences in the intelligibility of different words and sounds is of consequence. Speech sounds and the ease with which different words are recognized make a difference. The speaker cannot afford to risk being not understood. He insures good reception by using precise articulation, and he insures good will by knowing the rules of pronunciation.

Projects for Practice

1. Your instructor will supervise an intelligibility test. The class will take the test in groups of 12. Each student will read a list of 24 words, and the 11 remaining students will write what they hear. Preface each word with "Number 1 is," "Number 2 is," etc., and allow enough time between your successive sentences for your listeners to write what they hear. A good way to judge this is to write the words yourself as you say them. Pick up all the papers that have been written *of your reading* as soon as you finish. After class compute your per cent right score and report it at the next class meeting. Spelling does not count, but any omitted sound is an error. (Instructor: Place the reader about 30 feet from the listeners, keep a steady, low-level noise going in the midst of the listeners; an electric fan or a motion-picture projector will serve. Equated word lists and instructions are given in Appendix B.)

2. Transcribe a 50-word passage into phonetics, using your own pronunciation as a guide. Find from your instructor which American dialect region you represent.

3. Transcribe a 50-word passage from a phonograph record into phonetics. If possible, use a recording of an actor reading standard material slowly.

4. Discuss "Oral Language Has Limited Relationships with Spelling, Legibility, and the English Alphabet." Establish the many relationships that do exist.

5. What is a digraph? A homograph? A homophone?

6. Report to the class the importance of phonetics in George Bernard Shaw's *Pygmalion*.

7. The phonetic alphabet that is given above is somewhat abbreviated. Discover from a dictionary or a book that treats the alphabet in a specialized manner some of the omissions of the alphabet as printed here.

8. Tell a story that makes use of dialect. As you listen to the stories of your classmates, make notes in phonetics. From your notes make several statements beginning "I liked the way . . . said . . . ."

9. Figure 23 is a conventional classification of consonants. Prepare a similar classification that would be arranged as follows:

	Lower lip near or against		Tongue near or against			
	Upper lip	Upper teeth	Upper teeth	Roots of upper teeth	Palate	Velum
Continuant:						
Noisy............						
Not noisy.........						
Noncontinuant:						
Noisy............						
Not noisy.........						

Can you accommodate all the consonants? How do you handle the distinction between voiced and voiceless sounds? How do you handle the nasal sounds? Do you find some fricative sounds in Fig. 23 that seem to rely on mild explosions to provide the distinguishing feature of the sounds? Where did you put them in your classification?

10. The following pages include lists of words, selected because they are frequently pronounced badly when they are used. Some of the words are seldom spoken except in the oral reading of literature. The ones that occurred among almost a third of a million words in classroom speeches are italicized.

Study the words with a dictionary as your guide. Practice the dictionary pronunciations, remembering that they are appropriate for platform address. You will probably accomplish more if you work with a partner. Practice saying each word in the middle of a sentence. The lines are numbered to help you locate a word when you are discussing the list.

1 abdomen *abdominal* abject *absent absolute* abstemious *abstract* abstruse
2 *absurd* abysmal abyss accede *accent acceptable* accessible *accessory*
3 acclimate accompaniment *accurate* acme acorn *acoustic acquit across*
4 acumen *address* adenoid *adjective* admirable *adult advantage* adversary
5 *adverse* adversely *advertisement* advocated affluence agape aged agenda
6 aggrandizement agile ague *airplane* alias alien *allege allies* all right
7 ally alma mater almond *alternate alternative* altimeter alumnae *alumni*
8 alumnus *always* amateur *American* Amherst analogous anchovy
9 anomalous *another* ante anti *any* antique *apparatus applicable appreci-*
10 *ate approximately* apricot Arab arboreal arbutus archipelago archive
11 *area argue* argumentative aria *aristocratic armistice* arraignment arrant
12 *artisan asphalt* aspirant assuage *assume* asterisk *athlete* attaché attached
13 audacious aunt au revoir aurora borealis auspices *authoritative* autopsy
14 *aviation aviator* bade ballet banal *banquet* baptism *barbarous barrel*
15 basilar baton bayou *because been being* Belgium *beneficial* bestial bijou
16 billet-doux *binocular* blackguard blatant blouse blunderbuss bona fide
17 boulevard bouquet brigand brochure brusque buccaneer buffet bulwark
18 *bureaucracy business* cabriolet cafeteria calliope *can* candelabra canta-
19 loupe *capital* caprice *caramel carburetor casual catch* catchall catchup
20 *catsup* causal caviar cello *century* cerebrum chagrin chameleon *character-*
21 *istic* chary chaperone *chassis* chastisement chauffeur chauvinism chef
22 cherubic chic chimera chimerical *chimney* chiropodist chivalrous
23 *chocolate* choleric citrus *civilization* clandestine cleanly clematis clique
24 coercion cogency *column* coma combatant comparable complaisance
25 comptroller condolence conduit confiscate concurrent conjugal conjure
26 *constitution* consummate contemplative continuity *contract* contractor
27 contrary *contrasting* contumely conversant coquetry corporeal *corps*
28 cougar *counsel coupon* crayon courtesan *creator* credence *creek* cruel
29 crux cuckoo *culinary* cupola curator cursory cyclamen cyclorama
30 cynosure czarina daguerrotype *data deaf* debacle debut debris *decade*
31 decadence decorous *defect* deficit demise *depot* deprecate depreciate
32 *describe* despicable *detail* deteriorate Detroit *diamond* diapason *diaper*
33 diatribe *dictator* difficult *digest* dinghy diphtheria diphthong *direct*
34 *dirigible* discern *discharged discourse discourteous* discreditable discretion
35 dishabille dishevel disputable *division* docile dolorous domicile dotage
36 dour *drama draught* dromedary drought *drowned* eccentric echelon
37 *economics* eczema *education* egg egregious elite elm embalmer *embarrass-*

38 *ment emphasize* empirically *enemy energy* enervate engendered ensemble
39 enthymeme *entire envelop* epilogue epitome epoch equanimity *era* err
40 erudite *especially* essay *essentially etiquette evidently* exigency *experience*
41 *experiment expert* explicable exquisite extant *extra* facile *facsimile fac-*
42 *tories facts* falcon *familiar* faucet faux pas *fete figure* film *finally finance*
43 financier *fish* flaccid *flagrant foliage for* forehead *formidable* fortune
44 fragile frequented *furthest* gala galaxy *Gambier* gape gazetteer *genius*
45 genuine geometry germane *gesture get* gibber giblets *giraffe goal golf*
46 gondola *governor* granary gratis gratuity grievous grimace grimy *guaran-*
47 *tee guidance gum* habiliments Haiti hangar *harass* Hawaii *height* heinous
48 hemispheric herculean hiccup hilarious *history* hoax homicide hoop
49 *horizon* hospitable hostile *human hundred hurricane* hygienic *hysteria*
50 ignoramus Illinois *illustrate* imbroglio *immediately* impious impotence
51 *impractical* incalculable *incidentally* incognito incomparable incon-
52 gruous incorrectness *indictment* indigent indisputable *individuals in-*
53 *dustry* inexorable infallible infamous *inflammable influence* inherent
54 inimical inquiry insatiate intaglio *integral interest* interpretative inter-
55 stice *intricate* inveigle irascible *iron* Iroquois irreparable irrelevant
56 irrevocable isolate *issues* Italian itinerary jeopardized jocund joust
57 jugular *just juvenile* labyrinth laissez faire lamentable larynx *last latent*
58 *later latter* laudable *leisure lever library* licorice livelong longevity ludi-
59 crous lyceum macadam machination *magazine maintenance* malevolent
60 maniacal *manufacturer many* marital martial *measure* memento mes-
61 dames *milk* millinery mirage *mischievous* monarchy *monopoly municipal*
62 *museum* muskmelon *mustache* naïve nape naphtha narrator *nephew* non-
63 chalant nostalgic *novice nucleus* obese obesity obligatory *oblique opening*
64 obstinacy *often* ogre oleomargarine omnibus *once* onomatopoeia *oppor-*
65 *tunity* optimistic oracular *orchestra* orgy oriole ostrich ouija *our* owl
66 pageant *palm* panorama *parliament particularly* partner *patent* pathos
67 patronage *patronize* penalize perforate pergola perseverance perspicuity
68 *perspiration* petite pianist *picture* pilaster piquant placard placate
69 poignant *policeman poor popular* population porpoise *position* post-
70 humous Poughkeepsie *powerful* precedence precedent preface *preferable*
71 prelate prelude *premier* premiere *presentation pressure prestige* pre-
72 sumptuous *prevalent* prima donna *primary probably produce program*
73 promontory promulgate *pronunciation* proprietary *protein* psalm puerile
74 *pulpit* pumpkin puncture quaffed *quantity* quay querulous quintuplets
75 *quote* rabies ragout raillery raspberry *realize really* recess *reciprocal*
76 *recognize* recondite reconnaissance recreant redolent reduce reforestation
77 refutable regime *regular regulation* relevant remedial renaissance renas-
78 cence renege reparable repay repercussion representative *reptile* requital
79 *research* reservoir respite *response responsibility resource* revaluation

80 *revenue revolution* ribald ridiculous *rise* robust rococo rodeo *roof* Roose-
81 velt *roster* rout *route routine* rudiments ruthless *sacrifice sacrilegious*
82 salmon *sanitation* sapience satiate *satire* satyr *schedule* scherzo schism
83 scintillate scion *secretary* secular semi senile *serious series* servile
84 sherbet *silhouette similarly simultaneous sincere since sincerity* sinecure
85 singularly slake slough *society* solace solstice *soot somebody* sovereignty
86 *special spectator* spinach *squash* status statutory striated *stomach strata*
87 *strength suave* subalternate subsidization succinct *such suggest suit suite*
88 superfluous supple *suppose* surcease swastika syringe *syrup* tapestry
89 tarantula *tariff* tarpaulin taximeter tedious telephonic temerity *ten*
90 tenacious textile *theater* thresh tirade *tiresome* tomato tortoise *tourna-*
91 *ment* tourniquet tragedian transmigrate tribune trio troth troublous
92 Tuesday *typhoid* ultimatum *umbrella understand* unequivocal *uniform*
93 *university* usance use *used vacuum* vagary valet valiant *various* vase
94 vaudeville vehement vehicle velum verbosity *verbatim veteran veterinary*
95 victuals villain *violence* violoncello virile *virtually* viscount vivacious
96 Washington was whooping cough *wish with wrestle your zero* zoology
97 Zwiebach

11. Read "Slurvian Self-taught" aloud. Make a list of words that John Davenport might use if he were to write lesson 2 on the subject and were to base his reporting on your campus or home town.

SLURVIAN SELF-TAUGHT[1]

John Davenport

1   Listening to a well-known Hollywood radio commentator some time
2   back, I heard her say that she had just returned from a Yerpeen trip,
3   and had had a lovely time nittly. I at once recognized her as an accom-
4   plished Slurvian linguist and, being a student of Slurvian, readily under-
5   stood that she had just returned from a European trip and while there
6   (in Yerp) had had a lovely time in Italy.
7   Slurvian is coming into common use in the United States, but I am,
8   so far as I know, the only scholar to have made a start toward recording
9   it. There is no official written Slurvian language, but it is possible, by
10 means of phonetic spelling, for me to offer a brief course of instruction in
11 it. In a short time, the student can learn enough to add immeasurably to
12 his understanding and enjoyment of conversation wherever he travels
13 in the country.
14   I first heard pure Slurvian fluently spoken by a co-worker of mine who
15 told me that his closest friend was a man named Hard (Howard). Hard

[1] John Davenport, "Slurvian Self-taught," copyright 1949, *The New Yorker Magazine, Inc.*, vol. 25 (no. 17), p. 26.

16 was once in an automobile accident, his car, unfortunately, cliding with
17 another, causing Hard's wife Dorthy, who was with him, to claps.
18 Dorthy didn't have much stamina but was a sweet woman—sweet as
19 surp.

20   I soon discovered I had an ear for Slurvian, and since I began to
21 recognize the language, I have encountered many Slurvians. At ball-
22 parks, they keep track of hits, runs, and airs. On farms, they plow furs.
23 In florist shops, they buy flars. When hard up, they bar money from
24 banks, and spend it for everything from fewl for the furnace to grum
25 crackers for the children.

26   When Slurvians travel abroad, they go to visit farn (or forn) countries
27 to see what the farners do that's different from the way we Murcans do
28 things. While in farn countries, they refer to themselves as Murcan
29 tersts, and usually say they will be mighty glad to get back to Murca.
30 A Slurvian I once met on a train told me he had just returned from a
31 visit to Mexico. He deplored the lack of automobiles down there, and
32 said that the natives ride around on little burrs.

33   A linguistic authority of my acquaintance, much interested in my
34 work in Slurvian, has suggested to me the possibility that the language
35 may be related to, or a variation of, the one still spoken in England of
36 which such a contraction as "Chumley," for "Cholmondeley," is a
37 familiar example. However, I think the evidence insufficient for drawing
38 such a conclusion. Surnames cannot be considered subject to the ordi-
39 nary rules of pronunciation. In fact, the only one I have positively
40 identified in Slurvian is Faggot, the name of the American admiral
41 who won the Battle of Mobile Bay.

42   The name Faggot brings me to a discussion of what I designate as
43 "pure" Slurvian. This includes those Slurvian words that, when spelled
44 exactly as pronounced, also make good English words (such as "Fag-
45 got," "burr," and "claps"). The day I can add to the lexicon such
46 a word, hitherto unrecorded, is a happy day for me. Here are some ex-
47 amples of pure Slurvian, alphabetically listed:

48 bean, *n.* A living creature, as in *human bean.*
49 cactus, *n. pl.* The people in a play or story.
50 course, *n.* A group of singers.
51 fiscal, *adj.* Pertaining to the body, as opposed to the spurt.
52 form, *n.* Gathering place of the ancient Romans.
53 gnome, *n.* Contraction for *no, Ma'am. Colloq.*
54 line, *n.* The king of beasts.
55 lore, *n.* The more desirable of the two berths in a Pullman section.
56 myrrh, *n.* A looking glass.
57 par, *n.* An attribute of strength, as in *the par and the glory.*

58   plight, *adj.* Courteous.
59   sears, *adj.* Grave, intent.
60   sport, *v. t.* To hold up, to bear the weight of.
61   wreckers, *n. pl.* Discs on which music is recorded for phonographs.
62   I am presently engaged in compiling a dictionary of Slurvian words,
63   which I hope will prove to be the definitive work on the subject. The
64   help of any interested students is welcomed, but I must caution such
65   students to be certain the words are genuine Slurvian, and not merely
66   regional speech, such as that of Alabama, Texas, or New England. Where-
67   Let me close with a final example, to make my meaning clear. Where-
68   ever you may be in the United States, if you hear the word "tare,"
69   the speaker probably is not referring to a Biblical weed growing in the
70   wheat. More likely, he is describing the sensation of extreme fear
71   experienced by a movie fan watching Borse Karloff in a harr picture.

12. Make a list of confusions similar to these examples.

> *a.* WESTON, CAL., July 12. By telephone from the sheriff, Deputy
> Grant Gillogly received what he thought was an order to buy 2,000
> pigs for the county farm.
> All day he drove from farm to farm but succeeded in bargaining
> for only 120 pigs. Apologetically he reported to Sheriff Bill Knowles.
> "How many pigs did you say?" The sheriff gasped.
> "Two thousand."
> "Hell, man," the sheriff shouted, "I wanted two sows and pigs."

> *b. New roses* (heard as *neuroses*).

13. Find difficult-to-pronounce phrases in plays and poems, for example,
"You erred grievously" (Ibsen's *Ghosts*).
14. Practice reading the following passage.

Semisense: practice in pronunciation:
1   The bestial, blatant blackguard from Belgium was in a contemplative
2   mood as he listened to his aunt render an aria to the accompaniment of
3   a pianist and a cello. He was a brigand and despicable and wished, by
4   clandestine methods, to obtain the diamond worn by the prima donna.
5   With a cursory glance at the candelabra, he remembered that the prima
6   donna was capricious and was adverse to his brusque and alien manner.
7   Dictator though he was in his own domicile, he made a grimace when he
8   thought that he must, things being as they were, inveigle the bijou in
9   order that she, with discretion, might be docile. The woman was not
10   naïve and was often adept at satire. After the premiere, the audacious
11   boulevard buccaneer asked the comely prima donna to come with him
12   from the theater in his cabriolet.

13   The vehicle belonged to his valet, and he had no chauffeur as his per-
14 sonal car had soot in the carburetor. The man and the prima donna
15 stopped at a hospitable inn to slake their thirst and eat sherbet and
16 caviar. The high society of the Roosevelt regime was there. Included in
17 the number was a senile man from Hawaii who had an obese nephew.
18 Contrary to what one might expect, the nephew was an alumnus of a
19 great college, his alma mater being Harvard. The nephew made a social
20 *faux pas* by putting catsup on an anchovy. This act brought a scowl to
21 his ordinarily cherubic countenance and did not lend credence to the
22 rumor that he was an alumnus of a great school. Some said that as a
23 student he would make a better chiropodist.

24   In his discourse on Hawaii the old man used little discretion. Then,
25 too, he was not able to discern and pick out just the exquisite and various
26 attributes for which the island is famous. He made, however, a Her-
27 culean effort to "put himself over," but in so doing he made a *faux pas*,
28 for inherently his native personality was also naïve. Hence he made him-
29 self ludicrous. His abnormal height added to his awkwardness. Sud-
30 denly in the middle of his dissertation he developed the hiccups. At-
31 tempting to control this, he made such a grimace that the audience burst
32 out in hilarious laughter. About this time a grimy blackguard struck my
33 forehead with the barrel of a blunderbuss. The aurora borealis and a
34 galaxy of stars scintillated before my eyes. I was enveloped as in a coma.
35 A panorama of hilarious and heinous pictures was produced. My
36 equanimity was evidently shaken when I found myself transmigrating
37 the land of the Arab astride a formidable dromedary. A Wellesley
38 alumna confiscated my agile steed and, to my chagrin, routed me.

39   Next, in a dinghy, I sailed down the Kanawha creek to a bayou. In
40 a contemplative mood, I digested caviar while I discerned a falcon
41 satiate himself with a chameleon. A querulous ostrich in his dotage at-
42 tacked the bird and confiscated his prey. A ludicrous porpoise routed the
43 tenacious bird, who assuaged himself by making a grimace at the
44 impious animal. Then a gondola carrying an exquisite female from
45 Hawaii drew alongside. Her coquetry and docility fascinated me. A more
46 dolorous man was never seen when a bestial cougar jumped on the boat
47 and was drowned.

48   The blackguard with the despicable countenance raised his binocular
49 to observe the quay. As he did so a blatant tarantula threatened him from
50 above. Feigning virility, he routed the spider with one fell swoop.
51 Thinking a respite to be poignant, he retired to his cabin where his
52 nephew, the first mate, met him with all the sapience his position of-
53 fered. A flaccid individual, he uttered an inquiry that stunned his
54 impious uncle. "You might as well be aboard a gondola, you heinous

55 fool!" replied the old man with a grimace. At this, the first mate dis-
56 cerned trouble and began to deprecate by ordering two more sherbets.
57 Then he began to remember the night at the theater when a bona fide
58 buccaneer, the blatant blackguard, presented antique argumentative
59 material which adversely affected the address of the chic chiropodist.
60   The ballet dancer wore a blouse which hid a chassis comparable only
61 to that of Helen of Troy. The robust prima donna trio added romance to
62 the premiere. The preface to the picture showed an ostrich riding non-
63 chalantly in a vehicle half filled with pumpkins and oleomargarine. The
64 mischievous nephew was in the vaudeville act and suggested that the
65 marital relation between the premier and his aunt was the result of a
66 *faux pas*, much to the embarrassment of the docile aunt who said that
67 the point would be disputable until February.

15. How are the indicated portions of the following words vital in an
avoidance of Slurvian?

per*h*aps	gen*e*rous	horr*o*r	spir*i*t
th*e* other day	hist*o*ry	vict*o*ry	diff*e*rent
lab*o*ring	terr*o*r	num*e*rous	mis*e*ry
gen*e*ral			

Have you just performed "negative practice"? Say the words in a manner to
avoid Slurvian. If you wish to be skilled in speaking Slurvian, how would you
say the following words?
    16. Practice these words, avoiding the schwa.

near it	chimerical	torrent	varnish
fear it	corridor	miracle	applicant
graded	spaded	wounded	ordinary
sordid	apparent	hundred	inherent
faded	modest	torrid	empirical
raided	April	apricot	terrible
banqueting	candid	finish	penitent
clerical	horrid		

17. Practice these words with the full quality of [ɛ]; avoid [ɪ].

get	then	bent	twenty
again	men	scent	fence
Ben	against	many	
pent	dent	pen	
lent	ten	dentist	

18. The vocal cords are frequently permitted to "vibrate" on [t] when the sound occurs between vowels. The effect is a light [d] (voicing). Avoid voicing as you practice these words.

notice	British	caught it	fought it
blotter	sooty	butter	Brutus
Saturday	mortal	portal	bottom
rattle	mighty	naughty	flighty
planter	hit it	write it	wrote it

19. A similar variation is the substitution of what is called the glottal stop for the [nt] combination. A similar difficulty occurs with words in which the syllable [ən] follows [t]. Pronounce *tighten* in a rather slipshod manner. Is there a slight grunt instead of the clear second [t]? Avoid the glottal stop as you practice these words.

important	dentist	mountain	planting
repentant	inheritance	twenty	fountain
hunting	panting	intermittent	painting
quantity	smitten	blatant	lamentable
written	kitten	patent	bitten

20. The "retroflex [r]" frequently occurs in words like these. As you practice the words and listen to your classmates, you probably will arrive at a functional meaning for "retroflex [r]." If you will think of the word as being divided before the *r* in an unstressed syllable, you will be more likely to avoid the retroflex [r].

laurel	glories	terrible	hurry
merry	sorrel	parrots	ferry
general	carry	very	guarantee
torrent	generous	barrel	tireless
corridor	current	apparel	narrow

21. "Heavy" assimilation occurs in certain combinations of sounds. Some assimilations have become acceptable. For example, *picture, feature, procedure, nature, literature* are acceptable with [tʃər] as the final sounds. Possibly you should be more careful with *education, educable, individual, individualize, pendulum,* and *modulate.* Practice the following pairs of words with minimum assimilation:

could you	fought you	won't you	wrote you
did you	set you	get you	taught you
told you	would you	had you	
can't you	should you	paid you	

22. Can you say the triple-consonant [sts] easily?

insists	consists	persists	lisps
desists	resists	wasps	wisps

23. Practice these words, trying not to omit a vowel.

ordinary	ordinance	rode in
inordinate	stayed in	played in
hid in	ordination	reared in

24. Discuss the point of view of the following letter:[1]

The stutterer, and indeed all people who speak, are troubled or frustrated by the interrupting answer to their unfinished questions. We all attempt, more or less, to ignore these interruptions and to maintain our speaking and emotional equilibrium. A search for the answer or partial answer to these interruptions, however, has been carried on for years.

A common entry in the list of complaints of people who stutter is the anticipating answer or the anticipated question. We who stutter dislike the teacher, girl friend, or teammate who engages in this mind reading. We have aired our views often enough that a rule of thumb in clinical practice is: *Don't interrupt the stutterer.* Why not? Is the use of language to show off the ego of the stutterer (or anyone else), or to get an idea across?

It took very few hours to change my attitude toward the anticipating answer. I listened to Dr. Harvey Fletcher lecture on "Information Theory" and got the idea of redundancy in language. Then I read Wiener's *Cybernetics* and Shannon and Weaver's *The Mathematical Theory of Communication.* Part of the interrupting that had been bothering me became clear and quite understandable. It was due to the redundancy of our language. All of us are familiar with the simplest example of redundancy: the u's after q's in writing; q is always followed by u. Speech abounds with similar examples. Some of them we call context. "Where are you g . . . ?" This beginning conveys a pretty certain idea, whether the final sequence of sounds is masked by noise, distorted by stuttering (or any other speech anomaly), or missing altogether. Other examples may fall short of context in the sense of a connected sequence of words. The analogue within the word makes up a large part of redundancy. Language is only a coding system, and all

[1] Keith K. Neely, *The Journal of Speech and Hearing Disorders*, vol. 16, pp. 165–166, 1951. Used by permission.

we need in the communicating process is enough of the code to permit the listener to decode the transmission.

In speech therapy we teach the person with the speech defect to practice objectivity. This word *objectivity* is all too often a piece of verbal advice without a referent. We can supply one in the "anticipating" instance by helping the stutterer gain insight into the redundancy of language as a partial explanation of the interruptions that he receives daily. We who stutter can learn to accept the interruptions more readily and in the spirit in which they are often given if the language of our society is clear to us. This understanding of redundancy is fostered somewhat in the study of speechreading, in which one decodes spoken language through identifying key words. The repetition of key words is itself convincing evidence of the redundancy in our language.

Finally, the stutterer should note that "being cut off" is a general experience, not reserved for the person with a speech defect. People with normal speech have the same experience and they may be frustrated or not, depending on whether their language is ego-oriented or not.

True, it is considered more polite to wait for the person to finish talking before we answer, but this social rule does not contain our thinking, and frequently, the expression of that thinking. Why get upset then? We have learned a redundant language. As we learn more and more about the extent of its redundancy we may be able to accept more and more the unintentional ellipses that our listeners carve from what we had intended as sentences.

25. Study the manuscript (in the *New York Times*) of a radio speech that you have recently heard. Underline the portions, possibly isolated words, that you do not remember having heard. Try to explain why you missed these parts.

26. Listen to a recorded speech for the first time with the volume control of the phonograph adjusted to a level that interferes with intelligibility. Listen several times to the same portion of the speech. Make a best guess about what is being said. Then increase the volume and check your accuracy.

27. Discuss: (*a*) errors that I have made in speech reception and corrected immediately, (*b*) errors that I must have made in speech reception but never knew about, (*c*) errors that I may have made in speech reception but never thought about.

28. Cryptographers have deciphered some remnants of ancient languages in which no vowels were written. (*a*) Why might such writing be a normal stage in the development of a written language? (*b*) How would the scientists be able to decode the writing?

Readings

Black, John W., "Accompaniments of Word Intelligibility," *Journal of Speech and Hearing Disorders*, vol. 17, pp. 409–418, 1952.

———, "Natural Frequency, Duration and Intensity of Vowels in Reading," *Journal of Speech and Hearing Disorders*, vol. 14, pp. 216–221, 1949.

Fairbanks, Grant, *Voice and Articulation Drill Book*, Harper & Brothers, New York, 1940.

———, Arthur S. House, and Eugene L. Stevens, "Experimental Study of Vowel Intensities," *Journal of the Acoustical Society of America*, vol. 2, pp. 457–459, 1950.

Heffner, R-M. S., *General Phonetics*, University of Wisconsin Press, Madison, Wis., 1949.

Hibbitt, G. W., *Diphthongs in American Speech*, Columbia College, Columbia University, New York, 1948.

Kantner, Claude E., and Robert West, *Phonetics*, Harper & Brothers, New York, 1941.

Kelly, J. P., and L. B. Higley, "A Contribution to the X-ray Study of Tongue Position in Certain Vowels," *Archives of Speech*, vol. 1, pp. 84–95, 1934.

Kenyon, John S., *American Pronunciation: A Textbook of Phonetics for Students of English*, George Wahr Publishing Co., Ann Arbor, Mich., 1944.

———, and T. A. Knott, *A Pronouncing Dictionary of American English*, G. & C. Merriam Company, Springfield, Mass., 1944.

Kurath, Hans, *Linguistic Atlas* of *New England*, Brown University, Providence, R.I., 1939.

Pratt, Fletcher, *Secret and Urgent*, The Bobbs-Merrill Company, Inc., Indianapolis, 1939.

Russell, G. Oscar, *Speech and Voice*, The Macmillan Company, New York, 1931.

Shaw, George Bernard, *Pygmalion*, Brentano's, New York, 1916.

Thorndike, E. L., *Teacher's Wordbook*, Bureau of Publications, Teachers College, Columbia University, New York, 1931.

———, and Irving Lorge, *The Teacher's Wordbook of 30,000 Words*, Bureau of Publications, Teachers College, Columbia University, New York, 1944.

Van Riper, Charles G., and Dorothy E. Smith, *An Introduction to General American Phonetics*, Harper & Brothers, New York, 1954.

Zimmerman, Jane Dorsey, *Radio Pronunciations*, King's Crown Press, New York, 1946.

5

THE VOCABULARY OF SPEECH

The present discussion is transitional. In Chap. 4 we treated sounds as a set of symbols that comprise words, and both sounds and words as available code symbols. In Chaps. 6 and 7 we shall discuss the meaning that the words acquire for us. In the present chapter we focus our attention on words as a personal resource, one that we should develop deliberately.

How human races and nationalities happened to arrive at languages has provoked much study and conjecture. Some anthropologists have proposed that the similarities among languages point to a mother language from which our modern ones have evolved. Some theorists look at the effects we achieve with language and discuss both the function and genesis of language in terms of controlling social behavior. The function of the whole language extends to its ancillary components, and thus English words become the symbols with which we control behavior within our culture.

YOUR VOCABULARY: ITS SIZE

We have somewhat more than 600,000 word symbols in English that can be used in formal communication and countless others that are used with limited social approval. No individual can ever master all the available meaningful symbols; each knows segments of the total vocabulary of his culture. Possibly a college student has *some* familiarity with 30,000 to 35,000 words. However, the doubtful reliability of such values is indicated by the fact that some estimates extend the number as high as 200,000.[1] Our listening vocabulary, or the words that we recognize

[1] G. W. Hartmann, "A Critique of the Common Method of Estimating Vocabulary Size, Together with Some Data on the Absolute Word Knowledge of Educated Adults," *Journal of Educational Psychology*, vol. 32, pp. 351–364, 1941.

when we hear language, is more limited, perhaps totaling 10,000 to 12,000 words that are understood, and our speaking vocabulary is smallest of all. E. C. Fossum and M. Ausherman individually studied, with similar results, the verbal output of speakers like you, college students, to find the size of their classroom vocabulary.[1,2] In one instance 270 students gave a total of more than 600 speeches, each of approximately 5 minutes. The speakers, in keeping with their interests, spoke on unassigned topics. Over all, the group in saying about a third of a million words used only a few more than 6,000 different words.

1. THE SOURCE OF YOUR VOCABULARY. Your vocabulary of *name* words, *action* words, and *descriptive* words develops as a result of many influences that fall under the general headings of *listening* and *reading*. You acquired most of your words unconsciously, some through necessity and others through curiosity.

a. Language Communities of Location. Your preschool vocabulary, the one from which your present and larger vocabulary emerged, was learned through imitation of heard speech at home. The symbols, their meaning and pronunciation, were thus acquired under circumstances that would lead to words that are regionalisms and pronunciations that are dialect. The potency of the environmental influences upon vocabulary led Leonard Bloomfield to include them under a special name, *language community*.[3]

A language community is a group of people who are unique in that for some special reason they use the same words unusually often. The special reason in the context of this paragraph is *location*, your home locale. On a larger scale, the *Linguistic Atlas of New England* enumerates words that are peculiar to old American communities.[4] These symbols, common usages among the inhabitants of one community, may be unfamiliar to other hearers. Your primary vocabulary, acquired by listening, probably included words that are peculiar to a language community of location.

[1] E. C. Fossum, "An Analysis of the Dynamic Vocabulary of Junior College Students," *Speech Monographs*, vol. 11, pp. 88–96, 1944.

[2] M. Ausherman, "Formal Spoken Vocabulary of College Students," unpublished M.A. thesis, The Ohio State University, Columbus, Ohio, 1950.

[3] Leonard Bloomfield, *Language*, rev. ed., Henry Holt and Company, Inc., New York, 1953.

[4] Hans Kurath (ed.), *Linguistic Atlas of New England*, Brown University, Providence, R.I., 1939.

b. Language Communities of Interest. Your youthful vocabulary was also learned in the context of your parents' special interests. Thus, you learned some more-special words that other children and adults may never learn.

Later, you developed your own interests in vocations and hobbies, and with each came a special vocabulary, the words of chemistry, football, cooking, fishing, or the college campus.

You continue to develop your vocabulary through listening and reading and to develop it largely in the light of your interests and your location.

2. A DIFFERENTIAL IN YOUR VOCABULARY. Up to this point we have treated vocabulary as an all-or-none entity; you have a word or you do not have it. This is a fallacy and the remainder of this chapter will describe and treat the implications of the disparity between the much-used and little-used portions of your vocabulary. Among the ⅓ million words of classroom speeches, were the 6,000 different words spoken an equal number of times? Not at all; "the" occurred 16,000 times, while each of 2,000 words was said but 1 time. Only 3,000 words were used more than 2 times. Nine words made up more than one-fifth, 22 per cent, of the total vocabulary: "the," "and," "of," "to," "a," "in," "that," "is," "it." As we project this vocabulary into the future, the chances are one in five that the next word we hear will be one of these words with little specific meaning. The vital vocabulary of speech lies in the remaining four-fifths of the words that we say and hear.

a. The Relativity of Your Vocabulary. You are saying and hearing different words in the ratio 16,000 to 1—the extreme value in the words of classroom speeches—and this ratio affects your skill in detecting words. We should know more about the various word frequencies between these extremes. G. K. Zipf has developed a formula that describes our use of our vocabulary: For English, the probability of a particular word is equal to 0.1 divided by the rank order of the word among the words that we use.[1] Thus, the probability of "it" among the nine words enumerated in the preceding paragraph would be $0.1/9$ or 0.012. We would expect it to occur 12 times in 1,000 words; the obtained value was 14 times per 1,000 words.

Extend this calculation to the rare words of your vocabulary instead of applying it to the ninth-most-frequent word and you may be impressed

[1] G. K. Zipf, *Human Behavior and the Principle of Least Effort,* Addison-Wesley Publishing Company, Cambridge, Mass., 1949.

with the slight exercise that you have in saying and hearing these words. Exercise in this instance is akin to familiarity. Your rare words exist on a borderline between the known and unknown vocabulary.

b. *Predicting the Weak End of Your Vocabulary.* C. E. Shannon applied the Zipf prediction formula to Godfrey Dewey's enumeration of 1,000 most frequently used English words in a manner that has relevance to all of us.[1,2] You would agree with Shannon's reasoning that the summated probabilities of the words of a vocabulary could not exceed unity. He computed the *rank* of the word that, when added to all words of higher rank or greater probability, would turn the balance to *one*. The rank of this word turned out to be 8,727. This value constitutes an estimate of a size of a vocabulary, a generalized vocabulary of the many professional writers whose works were sampled by Dewey. You might expect to exercise your familiarity with a rare word only one time in 100,000 words *on the average.*

The same procedure was applied to the vocabulary of the student speakers and yielded a predicted vocabulary of approximately 5,000 words. Obviously the weak end of your vocabulary gets almost negligible exercise.

c. *Your Handling of Probable Words.* The end of your vocabulary with which you are most familiar you handle ably. As mentioned in the preceding chapter, these words are more intelligible; you hear them readily and accurately. Also, when these words are flashed on a screen, you recognize them swiftly.

The degrees of your familiarity with words are subtle. For example, students sorted materials into interesting and dull categories.[3] These preferences would tend to separate familiar and unfamiliar materials, although the same items would not be of interest to all students. Word-reception tests were constructed over the combined lot of materials. Result? Students tended to hear the words that fell in their scope of interest and not to identify the words from dull articles.

Again, students were categorized with respect to their major interest:

[1] C. E. Shannon, "Prediction and Entropy of Printed English," *Bell System Technical Journal*, vol. 30, pp. 50–64, 1951.

[2] Godfrey Dewey, *Relative Frequency of English Speech Sounds*, Harvard University Press, Cambridge, Mass., 1923.

[3] Harry M. Mason and B. K. Garrison, "Intelligibility of Spoken Messages; Liked and Disliked," *Journal of Abnormal and Social Psychology*, vol. 46, pp. 100–103, 1951.

economic, ethical, or aesthetic.[1] Words were also classified as economic, ethical, or aesthetic. The outcome? The economic students heard the *economic* words better than other words, etc. Moreover, each group of students *said* words of its own category more intelligibly than other words.

d. Application. The striking implication of these paragraphs is that we do not have a vocabulary of 1,000, 5,000, or any other number of equally serviceable words. Our vocabulary dwindles in terms of our familiarity with it from a few words that we say and hear easily, through borderline words that we know but do not know well, to words that we do not know. The difference between the well-known and scarcely known words is a matter of the amount of exercise we give ourselves with our words. We can get this exercise by attending lectures and hearing the words that we do not get in our daily social conversation, by reading widely, and by using in our speeches carefully chosen words that enhance our precision of statement.

3. THE AVOIDED WORDS OF YOUR VOCABULARY. The genesis of taboo words is treated in Chaps. 6 and 7. We observe here, however, that the effects of avoidance are the same as the effects of unfamiliarity. Obviously, the word appears low on word counts as it is avoided by society. The relative extent to which some words are avoided, and hence excluded from our experience and word counts, is indicated by one college population.[2] From the responses of 375 persons, including college freshmen, seniors, and faculty members, words were rated in "per cent of freedom." Ideally a word would have " 100 per cent freedom." Actually the following quantitative ratings were assigned from the "never-use," "seldom-use," etc., responses:

itch	62 per cent	bloat	48 per cent	puke	9 per cent
louse	59	guts	17	nasty	61
manure	41	harlot	19	slobber	26
naked	61	pus	41	stink	26
pregnant	28	sweat	63		

The taboo word is relatively unintelligible, as are other less frequently used words. The taboo word is more slowly detected on a pro-

---

[1] Robert L. Carlton, "An Experimental Investigation of the Relationship between Personal Value and Word Intelligibility," unpublished Ph.D. dissertation, The Ohio State University, Columbus, Ohio, 1953.

[2] E. R. Hunter and B. E. Gaines, "Verbal Taboos in a College Community," *American Speech*, vol. 13, pp. 97–107, 1938.

jection screen, as are other less frequently used words. The taboo word induces a delayed response to a statement like "An old piece of meat has an odor and is said to _____," or "A common synonym for perspiration is _____." This delay is also common when the response that is sought is any other less frequently used word. In fact, empirically, the taboo word only falls into place in quantitative studies in keeping with its frequency of usage, or the amount of oral-aural experience that we have with it.

PROBABILITY, PRONUNCIATION, (AND VALUES)

The foregoing paragraphs set the background for a discussion that was deferred from our earlier treatment of pronunciation. We have never heard a satisfactory explanation of why train callers are often hopelessly unintelligible. Other occupational cliques, for example paper boys and circus barkers, also seem to talk only to arouse curiosity or attract the attention of their listeners, not to impart information. This enigmatic behavior, we suggest, may relate to the *value* that the individuals place upon the words they are using. In turn, this low estimate of value may be an almost intuitive measure of the probability of the message, an awareness that all that is being said is 100 per cent probable anyway. "What else could I be barking except the features that are illustrated in the huge pictures before the tent, and what would I be saying except, 'Come in'?" Possibly the barking of the papers by the newsboy is only an announcement that he is around, like yodeling once was with chimney sweeps. The oft-said words are held in low esteem. Superior oral readers are known to slight the common words of our language like the nine words that make up one-fifth of the total. Again, the oft-said words are not valued highly.

The officials who are charged with maintaining satisfactory voice communication among pilots in their use of plane-to-ground radio frequently report the transmissions are substandard in spite of the adequate equipment. The pilots may view the words they utter, in requesting landing instructions, of relatively minor importance—in fact, nuisances—in comparison with their major job and special skill, flying. Moreover, the messages are routinized to the greatest possible extent. Hence, the messages seem to be almost 100 per cent delivered as soon as "contact" is achieved.

Teachers, lawyers, physicians, accountants, and a host of other specialists may follow the same procedure that is exemplified by the train caller and paper boy when the words of the occasion are highly probable, oft repeated, and almost taken for granted.

THE PROBABLE UTTERANCE

We treated in Chap. 4 the relative probability of words without regard to the context in which they occur, as "The color of snow is . . . ." However, the fruitfulness of the probability approach to words suggests that the concept might be applied to larger units of language. For example, what do you say when you are asked to describe your home town? On one occasion, about 2,000 people were asked successively, as a part of an interview by telephone, to describe the place from which they came. A surprisingly large number began their answer. "From a small town." This frequent response incited enough interest for the interrogator to follow with, "Where is this small town?" "How small is it?" Villages or settlements from 13 persons to cities of 200,000 were called small towns. The list included Albany (New York), Toledo, Dayton, and Youngstown (Ohio). A similar response to another question is "small college." The literal size of the institution is almost inconsequential. For example, a student said that he wanted to work in a speech clinic in a small college upon graduation. Some ill-conceived letters of recommendation might have resulted had his advisers not learned that he meant a school of 4,000 to 5,000 students, considerably above the median among American colleges and universities.

Another striking example of a highly probable response comes from experience with a mechanical unit that introduces a delay between the time a speaker utters a sound and the time he hears his utterance through a headset. Participants find this a frustrating though fascinating experience. A highly probable pair of words from a participant immediately after the experience is "beat it." His statement may be, "Let me try again; I want to 'beat it'" or the query, "Does anyone 'beat it'?"

YOUR VOCABULARY, A SUMMARY

These several paragraphs may seem to condone the limited vocabulary. The word counts enumerate the words of our language that are most familiar. By the same token, they reveal the words that are surprises as we hear them. There can be no justification for the limited vocabulary on the basis of "getting by" either as a speaker or a listener. The small vocabulary that was found in classroom speeches may indicate that one *could* do well in listening to his student colleagues even if he knew surprisingly few words. This can be really encouraging only to the person who is confronted with learning English in a hurry. The college student must look toward the rare end of his vocabulary if he is to understand lectures and literature and converse with the lecturers and writers.

1. REWARDS. With the larger vocabulary, you can understand the writings of another era; can more exactly identify the meaning of the writer or speaker; can employ synonyms rather than repetitions of the same word; can express opposites without excessive use of the prefix *un-*, *in-*, *non-*, or *not-*. You may be surprised to discover the number of rarely used words that come to you in featured radio newscasts—words you have been ignoring.

You have listened to the collegiate speaker who is bubbling over with enthusiasm but who lacks the vocabulary with which to give his ideas and excitement full expression. For example, "exquisite" may be the only word that he can use readily in expressing the superlative of his approval. This leads to "exquisite . . . exquisite . . . exquisite." The student leader who would make us go to the next football game finds himself shackled with the words "down," "down there," or "out there" as a synonym for the general locale of the playing field. Under the circumstances, he rests his case on a few highly probable words: "support," "team," "duty," "spirit," "fight," and the recurrent "out there," "down there," etc. You also know the student who has become facile with the campus jargon and who is unable to use spontaneously the appropriate language for his talk before his home-town church or school. "Red hot," "swell," "cool," and "gone" are near the top of his vocabulary.

2. ADMONITION: STUDY THE DICTIONARY. A large vocabulary is not defensible as a garment that one wears for display. An intimate familiarity with many more words than the minimum vocabulary for getting by is a necessity if one is to speak interestingly and exactly. This larger stock of words is a partial guarantee that you will understand what you hear, whether you ever want to say the new words or not. A *collegiate* dictionary will serve most of your purposes. There are several good ones. Some offer particular advantages. For example, although not of collegiate level, *Thorndike's Century Junior Dictionary* is different in that it indicates with each entry the frequency of usage of the word—if the word happens to fall within the 20,000 words frequently used in chil-

dren's literature. Study the dictionary for the many kinds of information that it offers about words: meaning, use (part of speech), derivation, spelling—including number and tense—and, in some instances, historical notes—these in addition to pronunciation.

3. AUDIENCE ADAPTATION. The audience is an aggregation of individuals each of whom has his own word count. Some speech is directed to mass nationwide audiences. The most frequent words of a generalized word count would apply to this broad audience. Other speech is directed to local audience, individuals of similar interests. The general word count would be modified appropriately by the word count of the particular language community. Much speech is directed to single individuals. Here a general word count modified by the word count of the language community is again modified by words of personal interest and value to the individuals.

Porjects for Practice

1. Explain the significance and application that would attend the discovery of the "relative probability of utterances." Could this study lead to an evaluation of the several "modes" of appeal that are commonly sought by speakers, advertising men, etc.? Reread the paragraph about "small town." Can we assume that the idea "small town" is appealing?

2. This is a cooperative class project. Transcribe the first 250 words of one of your recorded speakers. Make a word count of the passage. Treat singular and plural numbers as one word; treat-*ed*, -*ing*, etc., as instances of the root word; treat words that change form with tenses as different words, for example, "see-saw," "is-was," and the like. Alphabetize the words and keep the words that begin with the same letter on a single page. Put your name on all pages. Your instructor will distribute the pages, with one student taking all the *a*'s, another the *b*'s, another the *c*'s, etc. Collate the words from the several students' papers. Finally, a committee will determine (*a*) the total number of words, (*b*) the number of different words, (*c*) the probability of the 10 most frequent words, and (*d*) the words that were rarely used and who said them.

3. Discuss: Thorndike's word lists have put us in a linguistic strait jacket.

4. List 10 words that come from a specific geographical language community; 10 from a community of common interest. Call the attention of the class to 10 words that are typically overused in the speeches of your class.

5. Collect the *rare* meanings of 10 common words, for example, "disinterested."

6. Note the word for "mother" in at least six languages and frame from the words a notion of a "mother language." Now try two or three more words.

Does your plan fit? Who are some proponents of a mother language? What are their fields of study?

7. An early sentence in this chapter included the phrase "for controlling social behavior." This phrase relates to a popular theory of the origin of language. Discover these theories as the opportunities arise and discuss fully the relative merits of the theories with fellow students and teachers. One of your speeches might well be on some aspect of speech, for example, "Language," and you might use some of the ideas that you get about the origin and function of language in this speech.

8. Plot the rank order of words against their probability. Use Zipf's and Shannon's constant. Make the plot on log-log, four-cycle graph paper. Ausherman's words 1–9 (the . . . it) appear above. Others are word 10, "you"; 20, "on"; 30, "has"; 40, "very"; 50, "so"; 100, "say"; 150, "important"; 300, "front"; 600, "race"; 1,000, "apply"; 1,100, "depend"; 1,400, "crack"; 2,000, "quilt."

9. Answer the following questions with the aid of any good collegiate dictionary, for example, one published by Merriam, Harper, or Funk & Wagnalls. (The following entries have been taken from *Webster's New Collegiate Dictionary*.) Consult the table of contents, index, preface, list of abbreviations used, and read again the information about pronunciation. Read the explanation that precedes each section. The instructor may prefer to treat these 100 items as four 25's rather than two 50's. Compare the time you spend with the first 50 and the second 50 questions.

o   Note the time at the beginning of this exercise.

1   Indicate how the *au* in *raucous* should be pronounced by comparing it with common words.

2   Some words, such as *booze*, are marked *colloquial*. What does *colloquial* mean? See also the relevant early paragraph in the introduction of *Webster's New Collegiate Dictionary*.

3   What is the plural of *serum?*

4   Where is *Cannes?* How is it pronounced? Is it larger than Miami, Florida? What is the population of each?

5   Should *vice president* be hyphenated or written as two words?

6   When is *Mother's Day* observed?

7   What are *pince-nez* glasses? How is the phrase pronounced?

8   How did Wilhelm Richard *Wagner* pronounce his last name? When did he die?

9   What is the significance of the numbering of the three definitions of *villain?*

10   What is the difference between *in*sult and in*sult?*

11   Distinguish between *conscious* and *aware* as synonyms.

12   From what language and what words do we get *sophomore?* What is its literal meaning?

13   Is the *ocelot* hunted in Michigan?

14   From what people did we borrow *lariat?*

15   What is a *lame duck* in American politics?

16   What is wrong with the sentence: "The horse drug him"? Study the meaning of the verb and its principal parts.

17   May *stopped* be divided at the end of a line? If so, between what letters should it be divided?

18   In what three activities is the word *lineman* used?

19   When and from whom did we get *boycott?*

20   When *corn* is used to mean a grain, to what does it refer in England, Scotland, and the United States?

21   About how long is a *newt?*

22   Give three words that rhyme with *dawn.*

23   What does the name *Thomas* mean?

24   What color is mixed with red to form *purple?*

25   What is the feminine of *drake?*

26   Where is the *reichsmark* the unit of currency? How much is it worth in our money?

27   How tall is a horse that is *15 hands* high?

28   Give three antonyms of *morose.*

29   What does *au gratin* mean? How is it pronounced? In what trade is the term used?

30   When did the word *hello* come into use?

31   What is the abbreviation for the plural of *Mr.?*

32   Which spelling is preferred, *pedlar* or *peddler?*

33   What is the meaning of *Pecksniffian?* From what sources does the word come?

· 34   In chemistry, what is an *element?* What is the atomic weight of *osmium?*

35   What is the meaning of the prefix *ante-?*

36   What is the meaning of the suffix *-ling?*

37   What is the difference in meaning between *Atlas* and *atlas?*

38   What is the meaning of *skittles* in "not all beer and skittles"?

39   Is the use of *suspicion* acceptable in "I suspicioned him"?

40   What is a *spinner* in football?

41   What does the "AS" after *gospel* tell us about the origin of the word?

42   Is the *Red River* of Texas longer than the Red River of the North? How long is each?

43   What are synonyms for *&c.?*

44   Should we write "consumers' guide" or "consumer's guide" in forming the possessive plural of *consumer?*

45 Should *Spanish* be capitalized in "The tree is covered with Spanish moss"?

46 What is the rule for hyphenating words compounded with *self*, as when *self* is added to *love, self-love?*

47 Why are there two accent marks on *hesitation?*

48 How many cubic inches are there in a gallon?

49 What is Gresham's law?

50 What difference is there between the British and American pronunciation of *lieutenant?*

— (How long have you worked?)

51 Indicate the pronunciation of *tion* and *sion* in *nation* and *extension.*

52 Is *different than* acceptable?

53 Is the following acceptable: "Jackson had a larger supply of cannon"? What is the plural of *cannon?*

54 Which is higher, Longs or Pikes Peak? How much? Is the spelling *Long's* or *Longs?*

55 Who were the American *autochthons?*

56 Should *per cent* be written as one word or two? Is it an abbreviation? How can you tell?

57 With a few lines indicate the *Isthmus of Panama* and the direction you would travel in passing from the Atlantic Ocean to the Pacific through the Panama Canal.

58 What is the meaning of the vertical lines before *au lait?*

59 When was *John Tyler* president of the United States?

60 On what syllable is *abdomen* accented?

61 Distinguish between *expect* and *hope.*

62 From what language and what word do we get *salary?* What was its original meaning?

63 From what country did we get *pajamas?*

64 How many pipes does a *bagpipe* have?

65 What is the meaning of the expression *pony up?* Where is it used?

66 What is the past tense of *dive?*

67 Divide *iconography* and *iconoclast* into syllables.

68 In what professions is *trepan* used?

69 Who was the *Babbitt* of Sinclair Lewis? With what words has he supplied us?

70 What difference in meaning is given to the word *shoe* in England and the United States? What do the English call what we refer to as a *high shoe?*

71 Does a *carabao* have horns?

72 Give three words which rhyme with *bestirred.*

73 What does *Margaret* mean?

74 Is *cerise* a brighter red than maroon? What is the original meaning of the words, and from what language do they come?

75 If you crossed the border and changed a five-dollar bill into Mexican currency, how many *pesos* would you receive?

76 What is the difference between *blond* and *blonde?*

77 If a man weighs *13 stones*, how many pounds does he weigh?

78 Give two antonyms of *torso.*

79 In what profession is *corbel* used?

80 What was the original meaning of *wench?*

81 What does *Zool.* after *plantigrade* tell us?

82 Which spelling is preferred, *theatre* or *theater?*

83 In what play is *Jaques* a character? How is the name pronounced?

84 What is the chemical symbol for *hafnium?*

85 What is the meaning of the combining form *tele-?*

86 What is the meaning of the suffix *-art?*

87 What is the difference in meaning between *Creole* and *creole?*

88 What is the meaning of *spell* in the sentence: "She has him under a spell"?

89 Is the use of *like* as a conjunction sanctioned in careful usage, as in the sentence: "He runs like he was in a hurry"?

90 What is a *lob* in tennis?

91 What is the altitude of *Death Valley?*

92 What is the meaning of "L. fr. Gr." under *hydrophobia?* What is the original meaning of the word?

93 To what does *2* after *overmuch* refer?

94 Give two uses for the *colon.*

95 Should *Wednesday* be capitalized?

96 Should *baseball, football,* and *basketball* be written as one word, two, or hyphenated?

97 To what does *70* after *decorum* refer?

98 How should the plurals of *turkey* and *lily* be written? Give the rule.

99 How many square feet in an *acre?*

100 *Grimm's law* is in what field of knowledge?

101 Note the time at the end of this exercise.

Readings

Bodmer, Frederick, *The Loom of Language*, Lancelot Hogben (ed.), W. W. Norton & Company, Inc., New York, 1944.

Dale, Edgar, *Bibliography of Vocabulary Studies*, The Ohio State University Press, Columbus, Ohio, 1949.

Fairbanks, H., "Studies in Language Behavior, II: The Quantitative Differentiation of Samples of Spoken Language," *Psychological Monographs*, vol. 56, pp. 17–38, 1944.

Flesch, R., *The Art of Plain Talk*, Harper & Brothers, New York, 1946.

Hanley, M. L., *Word Index to James Joyce's Ulysses*, Madison, Wis., 1937.

Horn, E. H., *Basic Writing Vocabulary: 10,000 Words*, Department of Publications, State University of Iowa, Iowa City, Iowa, 1926.

Jespersen, Otto, *Language: Its Nature, Development and Origin*, The Macmillan Company, New York, 1922.

Lewis, M. M., *Infant Speech*, Routledge and Kegan Paul, Ltd., London, 1936, The Humanities Press, New York, 1951.

Mencken, H. L., *The American Language*, Alfred A. Knopf, Inc., New York, 1936; Supplement I, 1945, Supplement II, 1948.

Miller, George A., "Speech and Language," in *Handbook of Experimental Psychology*, S. S. Stevens (ed.), pp. 789–810, John Wiley & Sons, Inc., New York, 1951.

———, G. A. Heise, and W. Lichten, "The Intelligibility of Speech as a Function of the Context of the Test Materials." *Journal of Experimental Psychology*, vol. 41, pp. 329–335, 1951.

Morris, C. W., *Signs, Language and Behavior*, Prentice-Hall, Inc., New York, 1946.

Sanford, F. H., "Speech and Personality," *Psychological Bulletin*, vol. 39, pp. 811–845, 1942.

Seashore, R. H., and L. D. Eckerson, "The Measurement of Individual Differences in General English Vocabularies," *Journal of Educational Psychology*, vol. 31, pp. 14–38, 1940.

Steadman, J. M., "Affected and Effeminate Words," *American Speech*, vol. 13, pp. 13–18, 1938.

THE SPEAKER'S MEANINGS:
SPEECH AND EVALUATION

When one individual talks to another he seeks, of course, to communicate meanings. The meanings may vary from simple expressions about inner feelings to carefully and deliberately formulated ideas about the purpose of college, the nature of man, the structure of the universe, or the ideal life. Actually, as we have observed in Chaps. 2, 3, and 4, what passes between speaker and listener is a series of sound waves. Because they have a standardized pattern or form and a familiar order of occurrence, and because they have been associated with experiences more or less common to both speaker and listener, these waves awaken memories in the listener. Further, they stimulate him to make new associations and to create new meanings for himself. The words, then, serve only as stimuli for the listener. The meanings are created by the listener and come from within as well as from without. Knowing this fact, the careful speaker tries to select meanings whose effect upon the listener he can predict. The student who wishes to become a successful speaker seeks to acquire many meanings for different types of listeners. Furthermore, he endeavors to acquire meanings that can be tested and proved true. To the best of his ability, he discards meanings that are untrue and misleading.

How speakers and listeners accumulate their many systems, or constellations of meanings, and how these, in turn, affect the processes of communication and the further acquisition of valid meanings are prime considerations for any student of speech. We shall see that certain ways of thinking or "talking to ourselves" facilitate the acquisition of valid new meanings and that certain other ways act as barriers to communication. Realizing this, the student knows that listeners will not always use his words creatively, simply because he is the one talking.

126

How rigid barriers to new and more valid meanings are set up by old ways of thinking is vividly told by Leland Stowe in his book, *They Shall Not Sleep*. Near the outbreak of the war with Japan, when the Nipponese armies were invading Burma, the British governor and his attendants refused to believe the radio reports that the British troops had been cut to pieces and that their antiquated airplanes were useless. Belief in British supremacy over the Asiatics was such a rigid mental barrier that new raw *facts* could not break through. Even after the collapse, "they just couldn't believe it." The news reporters, on the other hand, were trying to get factual accounts of the collapse past the radio and telegraph censors.[1]

In free societies it is imperative that both speakers and listeners keep open the channels of communication. At the same time they must select and reject meanings on the basis of validity and social value. This process of selecting and rejecting meanings on the basis of their validity and social value Alfred Korzybski, in *Science and Sanity*, calls evaluation.[2] This double task of preventing fixed beliefs from acting as barriers to new and more valid meanings and of rejecting invalid systems of information after critical analysis, challenges the intellectual capacity and integrity of all free people and necessitates continuous refinement of skills in observing, classifying, reasoning, and communicating. In a word, learning, communicating, and evaluating are such closely interwoven activities that a blockage or distortion at any step affects our lives both personally and socially.

EVALUATING AND ABSTRACTING

Philosophers and scientists, too, once assumed that man was a rational being, capable of being trained to evaluate, to make choices on the basis of reason alone, and that emotion somehow interfered with logic. They thought man was made with a dual-control mechanism, one part for thinking and another for feeling, the two parts located in different areas of the body. As one took over, the other was shut off. If reason prevailed, emotions were suppressed. If emotions were stronger, reason was lost. As knowledge of the nervous system and the nature of

[1] Leland Stowe, *They Shall Not Sleep*, pp. 87–139, Alfred A. Knopf, Inc., New York, 1944.

[2] Alfred Korzybski, *Science and Sanity*, pp. 164, 194–203, The International Non-Aristotelian Library Publishing Company, 1933, 1941, 1948. Distributed by The Institute of General Semantics, Lakeville, Conn.

signals and symbols advanced, this concept gave way to one which recognizes the intricate interconnections between so-called feeling centers of the brain and so-called reasoning centers. They cannot be divided or separated. Hence, as we indicated in the previous section of this chapter, a new term *evaluation*, which includes both emotions and reasoning, is used to describe the choice-making processes. The important consideration in the modern world is not whether reason or emotion predominates in the process of deciding or choosing. The crucial test of the process of evaluating is the prediction of the results or sequences of the choice. If, for example, as you drive a car along a hilly highway, you are tense, fearful of an accident, and sense threat in every hill and every car, your evaluation is poor because so many predictions are untrue. If, on the other hand, as you drive over the hills, you are aware that there is the possibility of meeting a car on your side of the highway and that you must be prepared to turn off, your prediction is true and your evaluation is good. If a car does come over one of the hills on your side of the highway, and if, being mentally set for an emergency, you avoid the crash, your evaluation and your prediction may save lives.

From this illustration you probably have already inferred a significant point. That point is simply that in our complex world some predictions must be erroneous and the evaluations, therefore, not valid. In such cases the most accurate prediction is that your prediction is not very accurate and that you must be prepared for uncertainty.

This uncertainty affects a speaker in many ways. As a speaker you need to be alert for the unexpected, but not fearful of it. You need to rid yourself of any tendency to be too sure that listeners will criticize you severely, make fun of you, laugh at a particular joke, or applaud long and loud. You need to plan. But you need to catch facial expressions, body positions, and other signs of acceptance of, indifference to, or rejection of your meanings. Your ideas, voice, articulation, pronunciation, and phrasing have to be altered to suit the situation. Surprises and disappointments can be reduced and alertness and open-mindedness increased when such evaluative habits are formed. Even with the best of planning, unanticipated responses will occur. They need not surprise you, since you are set for uncertainty.

Basic to the personal development of alertness and adaptability is an awareness of how we acquire our meanings, our knowledge. It is difficult to say whether most of what we know, or believe we know, came to us by seeing or by accepting meanings handed down by authorities. Even the skilled scientist, who performs hundreds of experiments and makes refined observations, bases much of his knowledge upon the reports of reliable authorities in his field. Whatever the source of facts outside us, our nervous system reacts only to a small portion of the total external world. This reaction to a small part of the total quantity of stimuli gives us our meanings. The process is currently called *abstracting*, that is, a "drawing off," a summarizing. Perhaps the following illustration will clarify: At night you have undoubtedly driven toward a town or city, and from a distance you have seen the glow of light in the sky. You did not see the thousands of individual bulbs of street lamps, window lights, and door lights which contributed to the glow. But when you reached the edge of the city, you did see a few individual lamps. However, you no longer saw the glow above. If you could have taken one of the bulbs to a laboratory, you could have seen the filament glow, but you could not have seen the electric current which caused it to glow. You inferred that the individual brightness of all the lamps put together made the light you saw before reaching the city. You never did see both the lights and the glow.

You can never observe all the details of any object or event. You can observe only a few details of a part. In other words you abstract a part from the whole. Our meanings, then, are made up of observations of parts and of inferred relations between the parts. Our inferences are valid when we can predict relations after numerous observations. Many times, in fact most of the time, if we learn, our inferences have to be modified as observation is improved. For instance, astronomers believed through hundreds of years that Castor and Pollux, twin constellations which may be seen in the southwest during the summer, were actually two stars. Only a few years ago, when the gigantic telescopes were built, did they discover that each was a group of six stars and that across the great reaches of the heavens the human eye could not see the individual stars in each constellation.

What we can observe, then, is restricted by the limitations of our senses. Our ears miss high-frequency sounds that dogs can hear. Our eyes cannot see the ether waves which occur faster than 800,000 billion times a second, although waves below that frequency will give us the meaning of light and color. X rays which vibrate above 400,000,000 billion times per second can cause serious burns without our observing anything before the destruction is wrought.

Not only are our senses limited, but they are greatly affected by conditions before and during observations. Those conditions may exist either in the outside world or within our own bodies. Any one of us can report the increased intensity of stimuli when we have a headache or are excited. The warmth or coolness of water is governed, not only by its temperature, but by what one has experienced before feeling it. As a simple class demonstration, prepare three buckets of water of different temperatures, one cooled to about 60 degrees Fahrenheit, one warmed to about 98 degrees, and the third heated to 140 degrees. Place one hand in the 60-degree water, the other in the 140-degree water. After leaving both hands in the water for a minute or so, place them in the 98-degree water. Does it feel warm or cool? Does the quality of warmth or coolness inhere in the water? Or does the quality emerge from the changing relationships between parts of the body and different outside temperatures?

It should be apparent that the properties and qualities we assign to events and objects emerge from the interaction between the observer and the observed. The quality of a steak for dinner, the brightness of a light, the courage of a deed, the difficulty or ease of speaking to the class, the courage of an act, the truth of an idea, the worth of money are qualities which emerge as human nervous systems abstract the outside world. What they abstract is determined by their sensitivity and by factors which have influenced them. As we have already observed and shall observe further, symbol systems exert a predominant influence.

All knowledge, all meaning, it would seem, then, involves this process of abstracting. Abstracting involves the selecting, the drawing out of certain pertinent, relevant details from a collection or mass of stimuli. These abstracted details then serve as symbols for the collection. For example, from a box the details of the form are selected. Hence, a figure such as

although on a plane surface suggests a box. On the cruder levels of symbolic function, the following details may represent or symbolize a real flag, and these

may represent or symbolize a man. These selected or abstracted details are projected to the outer world by the motor nerves as gesture, model, or speech sign. That is, they are described by a gesture; they are made or drawn as in picture writing; or they are spoken or written.

When the highest brain centers are activated and more and more abstract symbols are produced, the process of abstracting can become infinitely continuous. From descriptions of the external world, inferences may be abstracted, and from inferences, still higher order inferences may be further abstracted. In this way we build the high-order abstractions of science and philosophy.

Since certain details of a situation are abstracted by a nervous system to become a symbol, it follows that a speech symbol may represent at least four entities. For example, the word *man* will represent: (1) the complex cellular structure (muscles, bones, nervous system, glands combined) which can be known by dissection, by use of the microscope, by biochemical studies, etc.; (2) the ordinary man you can see; (3) the individual psychological picture with your reactions to man; and (4) the symbolizing or talking we may do about man. Figure 24 illustrates these entities or levels.[1]

Since the same symbol actually refers to different events in the outside world, it is easy to confuse what we are thinking or talking about by losing sight of the level of abstracting or by identifying different levels. For instance, when we repeat the old bromide, "It is man's nature to wage war," are we speaking of biochemical man, of a man we know and can see, of our memory of a man, or of words spoken about man by ancient observers and repeated thousands of times since? To know what we are talking about, we must know what level of abstraction we are on.

IDENTIFICATION OF DIFFERENT LEVELS OF ABSTRACTION

Because one generation inherits from an earlier generation the cruder observations and the unconscious identifications of different levels of abstractions, meanings tend to become fixed and stereotyped. Thus for

[1] *Ibid.*, p. 384.

centuries even the learned people believed that flies had eight legs because Aristotle said so, that witches actually practiced witchcraft, that
ghosts haunted the churchyards, and that kings were divine. Thus each
generation accepted the identifications of levels of abstractions made
by preceding ones.

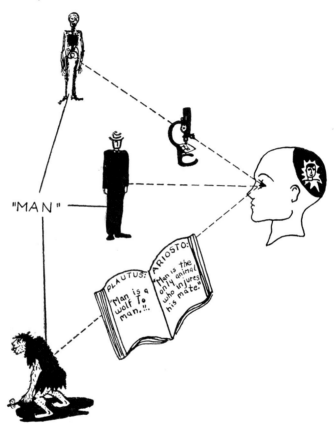

FIG. 24. A diagrammatic representation of four referents or entities which the term
man represents: (1) biochemical man, (2) the man we see, (3) the symbolized abstractions of man through the ages, and (4) the picture of man carried in our heads.

Perhaps you have done the same thing when, around a fireplace on a
rainy night, you have told tales of danger. You were unusual if you did
not feel uneasy as the stories became more and more gruesome. You
were perhaps identifying the story world with the real world to the point
that you became afraid.

Osa Johnson reports an amusing instance of identification of different levels of abstraction by the cannibals on the island of Malekula. She and her husband had returned to the island with films of the Johnsons and the natives taken the year before and were showing them to the natives. Seeing their first movies, the savages were literally struck dumb. There Osa, Martin, and the chief were watching the screen. They were on the screen. Who was who? The chattering began, and as other cannibals appeared in the movie the watchers shouted their names. Then suddenly, when the picture of a man who had been dead for a year was shown, the natives were awe-struck. The magic of the white man had brought him back to life.[1]

The natives, of course, identified the moving-picture level of abstraction with the level of actual events. Although the movie magic of Martin Johnson and its effect upon the behavior of the primitive peoples of Malekula may seem to represent an extreme example of identification, still the word magic practiced by our manipulators of symbols is no less ridiculous. If one accepts all advertising as true, one may be a man of distinction, have pleasant breath, make $25,000 a year, have the physique of Apollo, reduce taxes, have more services from state and local governments, and raise his children without fears or animosities. All one needs to do is drink the proper liquid, use the correct dentifrice, subscribe to a mail-order course in body building, take the right financial journal, vote the straight party ticket, and accept the latest theory of child raising. That educated persons identify the word level with the action level is clearly shown by mass responses to modern advertising and political propaganda.

Furthermore, that identification of the word level of abstraction with the event level of abstraction affects deep-seated physiological processes can be seen in the two following examples which are not uncommon. A college girl, nineteen years old, experienced abrupt changes in blood pressure and pulse rate and became nauseated whenever she heard the word "ammonia." Years before, when only six, she had swallowed ammonia and had been ill. All that was necessary to initiate physiological changes similar to those of the illness was the mere utterance of a word.

The social results of identification are tragic. Robert L. Duffus tells of a woman whose generalized hatred for Jews came from no real experience with a single one but only from abstractions made by others at

[1] Osa Johnson, *I Married Adventure*, pp. 135–137, J. B. Lippincott Company, Philadelphia, 1940.

high levels, beginning with her mother's reading of Dickens's *Oliver Twist*. The woman said:

> I remember quite plainly how angry I became when I learned the full extent of Fagin's operations as affecting Oliver. There was also a picture of the old Jew, showing him in all the horror imaginable—stooped, filthy, ragged, sly, sneaking, all the worst possible traits. Then I saw a few years ago Lon Chaney play the part on the screen. The performance capped the climax. Since then I have looked upon most Jews with somewhat of aversion.[1]

The sound and light waves from a piece of film made by actors in makeup were identified with human beings. This identification shut off new abstractions at an experience level and unconsciously blocked any attempt at realistic evaluation.

The threat to free people is great when social and political leaders identify their levels of abstraction. Rigidity, reluctance to change, or what has been called "cultural lag" is the natural accompaniment of identification of different levels of abstraction. Symbol systems become fixed and ultimately invite force or the threat of force. The radical revolutionaries, too, identify their meanings, their abstractions, with the truth and reject a consideration of any system that does not fit theirs. A speaker's unlimited belief in his belief leads to dogmatism, while the identification of personal meanings with truth leads to feelings of greatness, even grandeur, and to feelings of persecution when differences of opinion arise.[2]

If you will read the speeches of Adolph Hitler, especially those delivered during the very year German armies invaded Poland, you will sense the tragedy which befalls a country that accepts the identifications and projections of its leaders. Recurring again and again are such ideas as:

1. Germany has no territorial demand other than that of regaining our colonies.

2. The tension in Europe is caused by an unscrupulous press.

3. A gigantic Jewish capitalistic campaign is endeavoring to mobilize hatred against us peace-loving Germans.

4. National Socialism aims at the educational, economic, and social improvement of a national community.

[1] Robert L. Duffus, "Where Do We Get Our Prejudices?" *Harper's Magazine*, vol. 153, pp. 503–508, 1926.

[2] Richard M. Brickner, *Is Germany Incurable?* pp. 146–262, J. B. Lippincott Company, Philadelphia, 1943.

Although we hardly expect to hear in our American democratic society such unsane projections, still now and then we detect the faintly sour odor of projection of blame and self-glorification.

To bring the point home intimately, listen carefully to the talks at pep rallies. Some speakers identify fairness and all that is good with their cause, and all trickery with their opponents. Other speakers indicate that they look upon the game as a friendly rivalry, that they want to win but that basically the contest itself has values which outweigh defeat or victory. You should reflect carefully upon which evaluation represents sanity. You will observe, too, after the rally, that you did not do much reflecting while in the crowd, that in the crowd identification and projection came easily.

CONSCIOUSNESS OF ABSTRACTING KEEPS OPEN THE FLOW OF NEW MEANINGS

The socially responsible speaker has an obligation to know what he is talking about. Knowing, you recall, necessitates the acquisition of new meanings. Knowing, you also remember, is a process that takes place on different levels of abstraction. You can know some things about Korea without having been there. You can study maps, pictures, reports, statistics, yet you still cannot know the odors, the sounds, the fatigue, the frustrating routines, and the frightening engagements that gave meaning to the UN soldiers' everyday life. On the other hand, there are some veterans of the Korean campaign who know Korea on the sound, smell, and sight level so intensely that any other communication about Korea is met with the rebuff, "Don't talk to me about Korea. I know *all* about it. I've been there."

If you are to acquire rich new meanings, your lines of communication must be open. Karl Deutsch, in an essay "Higher Education and the Unity of Knowledge," considers from a social and historical point of view the answers to an important question: "What are the particular kinds of communication which must continue to function if knowledge is to grow?" Three of the four kinds of communication that he considers are of particular concern to the student of speech.[1]

The first is a set of channels which would involve the communication of novelty, of new experiences. These new experiences would include new

[1] Karl W. Deutsch, "Higher Education and the Unity of Knowledge," in *Goals for American Education*, Lyman Bryson, Louis Finkelstein, and Robert M. MacIver, (eds.), pp. 89–95, The Conference on Science, Philosophy, and Religion in Their Relation to the Democratic Way of Life, Inc., New York, 1950.

combinations between things, men, or *symbols*, even in the mind of a single individual. As a student you will wish to make discoveries through systematic observation. You will also wish to understand new combinations, new relations between symbolic representations of the world around you. If up to this point, you have kept open this set of communications, you have new ideas about speech. You have learned from your experiences in speaking and in observing the speech of others.

The second set involves the sharing of experiences between different human beings. It is cut off if other human beings are rejected as sources of information, if their testimony is treated as insignificant, or if their feelings are evaluated as not comparable to ours. The blockages in this second set of communications can be observed all around us. A college teacher may close the circuit by remarking to a sophomore, "That's a stupid question." A senior may dismiss the meanings of a professor with the retort, "What he knows isn't worth knowing." The labor agitator may refuse even to hear the representative of management. An industrialist may reject the efforts of a mediator to explain the other position. Obviously, learning ceases when this rejection of others occurs.

The third kind of communication of concern to us is that between man and nature. It breaks down if sense impressions, the first-order abstractions of the raw, natural world, are rejected as illusory or irrelevant. If few or no first-order observations are made or if they are not remembered, if nature is considered to be unknowable anyway or to be not worth knowing, then the descriptions basic to classifying and systematizing are not forthcoming. Consequently, too, the inferences necessary to our new and, we hope, more refined knowledge cannot be made. Under such a blockage, speech and language tend to function as ritualistic reiteration of the old superstitions, myths, falsehoods, and half-truths. Thus in China, as late as the early 1900's, education merely recapitulated old knowledge. In Tibet, new thoughts are outlawed. Even in this country, there are those who would return to the past.

Of especial significance will be your observation that the blockages in the three sets of channels described by Deutsch involve the identification of some level of abstraction with the abstraction of the truth. The abstraction is "I can learn nothing here." This shuts off any further effort to abstract, which, we have seen, is basic to learning. It is generally believed that this abstraction, "I can learn nothing here," is itself learned. Thus, by symbols, we can learn not to learn. By ignorance of ignorance, we intensify the ignorance. For instance, the UN soldiers, who had learned "only seeing is believing," could not free themselves to learn more from the higher abstractions of experts on Korea. In a way, then, they had learned a reaction which kept them from learning. They had learned *not to learn.*

A safeguard against this failure lies in the capacity of the human being to examine how he knows what he knows. By knowing about knowing, by critically examining all abstractions, and by continuously evaluating inferences, classifications, and descriptions in terms of low-level observations, one may reduce blockages to new meanings. Anyone who faces the responsibility of communicating to others needs to labor against the cultural forces which set up symbolic barriers to learning. If one cannot believe what another believes, he can at least learn why the other believes what he does. Dogmatic barriers to learning are broken and mutual understanding may be established.

Projects for Practice

1. Study Fig. 25 carefully. Let four or five students present in a narrative what Fig. 25 means to them. It is better for them not to hear one another. Are the meanings identical? In what does the "meaning" reside, in the picture or in the mind?

2. Secure from the library a copy of Murray's Thematic Apperception Test (TAT) cards, and explain how abstractions from them are further abstracted in the analysis of personality. Use one card to illustrate to the class how different interpretations are supposed to signify types of personality.

3. Give brief explanations of your decision on each of the following problems:

a. Assume that you have before you a light which will certainly flash if you press one and only one of the four switches labeled *ABCD.* How many chances out of 100 do you have of pressing the right one on the first trial? If, after you have pressed one switch, the light does not flash, how many chances in 100 do you have of pressing the proper switch on the second trial? Assuming two incorrect choices, how many chances do you have of making the correct decision on the third trial?

b. A student speaker became very nervous before every speech. A group of three speech teachers and three psychologists, after talking with the student, suggested that one of the following factors was probably the cause of the nervousness:

(1) The student had been previously criticized by his speech teacher.

(2) The student had a thyroid gland disturbance.

(3) The student had a deep-seated anxiety about groups of people.

FIG. 25. A picture such as those used in projective tests. Subjects are asked to make up a story which may be illustrated by the picture. What events have led up to the

situation pictured? What are the thoughts and feelings of the characters? What will be the outcome? The test is revealing to the degree that cooperation is given.

139

(4) The student was overconcerned about his grades. What are the chances in 100 that the first factor is the cause? Assume that further investigation shows that the first factor is not present, what are the chances in 100 that (2) above is a cause? Assuming now that medical examination has removed any possibility of the second being a cause, what are the chances that factor (3) is the cause?

c. Four students, Alec Smart, Tom Carlin, Chester Fall, and Truman Henry, were called before the Dean because one of them was suspected of having been the principal leader of a hazing incident that resulted in the serious injury of two freshmen boys. What were the chances in 100 that Smart was the guilty one? After Smart was found innocent, what were the chances in 100 that Carlin was guilty? After Carlin was cleared, what were the chances in 100 that Fall was guilty?

d. In which of the three instances is your abstraction likely to yield the most accurate prediction? Why?

4. Read "The Patriot: An Old Story."

THE PATRIOT

AN OLD STORY

It was roses, roses, all the way,
    With myrtle mixed in my path like mad:
The house-roofs seemed to heave and sway,
    The church-spires flamed, such flags they had,
A year ago on this very day.

The air broke into a mist with bells,
    The old walls rocked with the crowd and cries.
Had I said, "Good folk, mere noise repels—
    But give me your sun from yonder skies!"
They had answered, "And afterward, what else?"

Alack, it was I who leaped at the sun
    To give it my loving friends to keep!
Naught man could do, have I left undone:
    And you see my harvest, what I reap
This very day, now a year is run.

There's nobody on the house-tops now—
    Just a palsied few at the windows set;
For the best of the sight is, all allow,
    At the Shambles' Gate—or, better yet,
By the very scaffold's foot, I trow.

I go in the rain, and, more than needs,
    A rope cuts both my wrists behind;
And I think, by the feel, my forehead bleeds,
    For they fling, whoever has a mind,
Stones at me for my year's misdeeds.

Thus I entered, and thus I go!
    In triumphs, people have dropped down dead.
"Paid by the world, what dost thou owe
    Me?"—God might question; now instead,
'Tis God shall repay: I am safer so.

Robert Browning

Prepare a short speech in which you give your opinion of the patriot, the person speaking in the poem, and justify it. Is the patriot heroic, or is he filled with self-pity? Do you believe the speaker in this poem? Why?

  5. Read "Bredon Hill."

BREDON HILL[1]

In summertime on Bredon
    The bells they sound so clear;
Round both the shires they ring them
    In steeples far and near,
    A happy noise to hear.

Here of a Sunday morning
    My love and I would lie,
And see the colored counties,
    And hear the larks so high
    About us in the sky.

The bells would ring to call her
    In valleys miles away:
"Come all to church, good people;
    Good people, come and pray."
    But here my love would stay.

And I would turn and answer
    Among the springing thyme,
"Oh, peal upon our wedding,

[1] From *A Shropshire Lad*, by A. E. Housman, Henry Holt and Company, Inc., New York, 1924. Reprinted by permission of the publishers and by special permission of the Society of Authors as the Literary Representatives of the Trustees of the Estate of the late A. E. Housman, and Messrs. Jonathan Cape, Ltd., publishers of A. E. Housman's Collected Poems.

And we will hear the chime,
And come to church in time."

But when the snows at Christmas
On Bredon top were strown,
My love rose up so early
And stole out unbeknown
And went to church alone.

They tolled the one bell only,
Groom there was none to see,
The mourners followed after,
And so to church went she,
And would not wait for me.

The bells they sound on Bredon,
And still the steeples hum.
"Come all to church, good people—
Oh, noisy bells, be dumb;
I hear you, I will come.

A. E. Housman

Prepare a short speech explaining the poem and read portions of it to justify your interpretation. How do you justify or reject the reasoning of the speaker in the poem?

6. Read "Miniver Cheevy."

Miniver Cheevy[1]

Miniver Cheevy, child of scorn,
Grew lean while he assailed the seasons;
He wept that he was ever born,
And he had reasons.

Miniver loved the days of old
When swords were bright and steeds were prancing;
The vision of a warrior bold
Would set him dancing.

Miniver sighed for what was not,
And dreamed, and rested from his labors;
He dreamed of Thebes and Camelot,
And Priam's neighbors.

[1] Reprinted from *The Town down the River* by Edwin Arlington Robinson, copyright 1910 by Charles Scribner's Sons, New York, copyright 1938 by Ruth Nivison. Used by permission of the publishers.

Miniver mourned the ripe renown
That made so many a name so fragrant;
He mourned Romance, now on the town,
And Art, a vagrant.

Miniver loved the Medici,
Albeit he had never seen one;
He would have sinned incessantly
Could he have been one.

Miniver cursed the commonplace
And eyed a khaki suit with loathing;
He missed the mediaeval grace
Of iron clothing.

Miniver scorned the gold he sought,
But sore annoyed was he without it;
Miniver thought, and thought, and thought,
And thought about it.

Miniver Cheevy, born too late,
Scratched his head and kept on thinking;
Miniver coughed, and called it fate,
And kept on drinking.

Edwin Arlington Robinson

What kind of personality was Miniver Cheevy? Are there any similarities between him and anyone you know? What conventional suggestions are carried by the words "Thebes," "Camelot"? Who were "Priam's neighbors"? What is the significance of the lines

He mourned Romance, now on the town,
And Art, a vagrant.

Who were "the Medici"? What were their sins? What is the ironic contradiction in Miniver Cheevy's character?

7. Read "Elsa Wertman" and "Hamilton Greene" in Edgar Lee Masters' *Spoon River Anthology*. What lines indicate the different levels of abstraction on which Elsa and the sitters-by viewed her tears? How does the poem "Hamilton Greene" reveal that one's own verbal abstraction of himself and of his qualities may be a false inference? Would a lower-level abstraction, such as a close comparison of his own and his mother's features, be disturbing to Hamilton Greene? Why should it be? Do you know instances of people's being disturbed when they were told their "parents" were foster parents? Are the characters Elsa Wertman and Hamilton Greene of basic concern to

the poet, or is he using them as a way of making vivid a higher-level abstraction? If there is one intended, what is it?

8. Read "Which Died First?"

WHICH DIED FIRST?[1]

For some weeks following the tragic incident in which both Mr. and Mrs. Ferdinand Montoya lost their lives, it was taken for granted that a compromise division of the large estate of the deceased couple would be made between their respective families. The physician who pronounced them dead had filled in his report to the authorities with the hour of death as 3:10 for each victim, and the records were filed indicating simultaneous deaths.

The heirs of Ferdinand Montoya, therefore, were stunned when Mrs. Archibald Fawcett, mother of the deceased Evelyn Montoya, arrived at a private parley and insisted that the husband had expired *before* the wife—and that therefore, in view of the way his will had stood, his wife had fallen heir to all his property. By which she meant that the entire $700,000 or more now belonged rightfully to her as the legal heir of the deceased Evelyn Montoya.

To understand the situation it is necessary to know something of the ill-fated couple and of the strange manner in which death overtook them.

It would never have occurred to Ferdinand Montoya, Litt. D., or to his wife, Evelyn, to draw up a will. Each had enjoyed wealth from birth, and both, temperamentally inclined to literature and the arts, had extraordinarily little talent for handling practical affairs. However, at the suggestion of their attorney they had signed documents soon after their marriage bequeathing, in the event of the death of either, his or her entire possessions to the survivor. It need hardly be said that they failed to consider the eventuality of simultaneous death. The occasion of affixing their signatures to the wills had appealed to their sense of humor, and they had accordingly celebrated it with a theater party.

The tragedy occurred on an afternoon in March while the Montoyas were staying at their suburban home in Westchester County. The chauffeur had been released for the afternoon.

The Montoyas, it may be said, were surprisingly ignorant, even for persons of academic minds, of the care and operation of their automobiles. Although they possessed two, they drove very seldom. However, soon after lunch on that day Mr. Montoya and his wife decided to drive

[1] From *The Second Baffle Book*, by Lassiter Wren and Randle McKay. Copyright 1929 by Doubleday & Company, Inc., New York. Reprinted by permission of the publishers.

in the country. It was a cloudy March day, and the wind was blowing high, but the whim had seized them, and they made preparations for taking out one of the cars themselves. They were last seen by the house-keeper about two-thirty as they walked out of the house to the garage. She watched Mr. Montoya open the garage door for his wife and then turn back to the house as if he had forgotten something.

It was the housekeeper, some thirty minutes later, who sensed some-thing unusual in the fact that the *muffled* sound of a droning motor was coming from the garage. The housekeeper said later that for some time she had been working in the front of the house and that when she finally came to the rear (from the window of which the garage may be seen) she had no way of telling how long this condition had existed.

But after some minutes had elapsed the housekeeper became vaguely alarmed. Finally she decided to find out whether anything had gone wrong. At first hesitantly, and then more swiftly, as a dreadful thought entered her mind, she ran the distance separating the garage from the house and flung open the doors. Instantly she was engulfed in the pent-up fumes of deadly carbon-monoxide gas.

Within the garage both the Montoyas lay unconscious, and examina-tion revealed that they were dead. Both had been poisoned by inhaling carbon-monoxide gas. But which had died first?

When the matter finally came before a private referee, mutually selected to avoid publicity, the evidence was rather precise. Neighbors and servants supplied many details. The interior of the garage was examined minutely and photographs and notes taken at the time were observed.

The two cars were found jammed together. The engine of the right-hand one was running, hood up.

Mrs. Montoya was found in a sitting posture, her back supported by the rear wall of the garage. The upper front portion of her coat and dress was wet. Her right wrist was broken and her clothes badly soiled.

Mr. Montoya was found lying upon the floor of the garage, as indi-cated in the diagram.

On the switch which throws in the electric circuit (right-hand car) were found prints of the index finger and thumb of Mrs. Montoya. Upon the left rear mudguard of this car was an imprint of the right hand of Mr. Montoya. Both of the doors upon the right side of this automobile were found locked.

Upon the right rear mudguard of the left-hand automobile [see Fig. 26] was an imprint of the left hand of Mr. Montoya. (This car was out of repair and had not been in use for some time.) Its doors were all locked.

From the water faucet which projects from the lower center of the rear wall, a full stream of water was found running. The pool from it had washed away footprints which might have been useful in reconstructing the tragedy exactly.

The diagram in Fig. 26 may help you to determine who died first. Explain how the drawing is a lower level of abstraction than the language level. Explain how inferences are at a still higher level than description. Prepare a 3- to 5-minute speech you might make if you were an attorney for one of the heirs. Do the members of the class agree? Compare the majority opinion with that of another class.

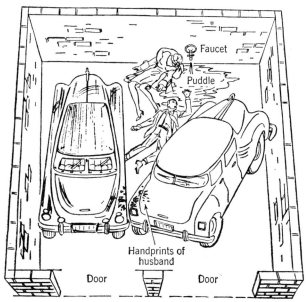

FIG. 26. Diagram showing the position in which the automobiles and the bodies of the Montoyas were found.

9. Korzybski, in *Science and Sanity*, points out that some higher-order abstractions free the individual while others inhibit him. Consider the following and determine their likely effects. Then try acting them out in class pantomimes.

Nervousness about nervousness
Shyness about shyness
Confusion about confusion
Knowing about knowing
Giggling about giggling

10. As a check upon the great disparity between high- and low-level abstractions, answer the following questions:

Have you ever told a lie?
Have you ever cheated?
Have you ever taken anything that did not belong to you?
Are you a liar?
Are you a cheat?
Are you a thief?
How many lies must a person tell before he is a liar?

Surely you will think of other questions which reveal a similar disparity between the low-level abstraction involved in specific action and the high-level abstraction involved in generalizations and qualitative statements. Here is a start: "He hit himself." What does the "he" refer to? The "himself"? Does all of "he" hit all of "himself"? Compare this statement with "I am scared to speak," "I make a fool of myself every time I try to talk." What part of "I" makes a fool of what part of "myself"?

11. Read the introductory portions of Claude W. Heaps' lecture, *Structure of the Universe*, given below. This is an example of meaningful high-order abstractions based on careful and systematic low-order abstractions. Full consciousness of the relative nature of inference is clearly revealed. Select the statements which reveal the speaker's awareness of the limitations of his high-order abstractions. Students interested in the clear communication of scientific facts would do well to read the entire speech and to select further remarks which reveal rigor of reasoning and consciousness of abstracting.

THE STRUCTURE OF THE UNIVERSE[1]

Claude William Heaps

It may seem, at first sight, presumptuous to attempt the discussion, in one hour or less, of such a comprehensive topic as the structure of the universe. Actually the subject is not as big as it sounds. There are, in one sense, as many universes as there are individuals; but the universe in this personal sense will be ruled out of the present discussion. A tremendous simplification is at once achieved when we limit our topic to the physical universe. We now inquire, what is the physical universe?

[1] Claude William Heaps, professor of physics at Rice Institute, delivered this speech at Rice Institute in the spring of 1943. One of a series of lectures which bore the general title "Science and Human Welfare," the talk vivified for a general audience an extremely difficult subject. This speech was included in the *Annual Report of The Smithsonian Institution for 1944*. Used by permission of Professor Heaps.

Eddington has defined it as the "theme of a specified body of knowledge, just as Mr. Pickwick might be defined as the hero of a specified novel." Such a definition emphasizes the epistemological point of view and therefore it suffers from lack of definiteness and simplicity. There is beautiful directness and decisiveness in the attitude of the mathematician who wrote an equation on one line in one of his published papers and said, "This equation contains everything we know about the physical universe." The conciseness of the language of mathematics is probably nowhere better exemplified than in this equation. On the other hand, the universe, if it can be described in terms of mathematical symbols and with one equation, may not seem like such a big subject after all.

To the physicist, matter, space, and time exist outside the human mind. The physical universe is an objective, dynamic arrangement of all matter, space, and time. In discussing the structure of the universe we merely attempt to describe some of the features of this arrangement. . . .

To begin this discussion of matter, space, and time we will try first to systematize our ideas of space, or size, in relation to matter. Imagine a long, horizontal line drawn so as to represent the "the x-axis." Let all objects in the universe be placed along this line in the order of their sizes. The smallest objects will be placed near the beginning of the line, at its left end. Larger and larger objects will be placed farther and farther to the right. We next divide the line into two parts by a vertical line. All objects to the left of this vertical line are too small to be seen with the naked eye, so this region is called the *microscopic* region. In it are placed different kinds of particles such as molecules, atoms, the proton, the neutron, the mesotron, the electron, positron, and neutrino. These particles are placed nearer and nearer to the origin of the line as they become smaller and smaller. It is worth noting that nature seems not to have given us anything smaller than the electron, in spite of the fact that there is plenty of room for particles between the electron and the origin of the line.

To the right of the vertical dividing line we place all objects large enough to be seen with the naked eye. This region is called the *macroscopic region*. We might put in here, stones, mountain, earth, solar system, spiral nebulae. The farther end of the macroscopic region may be given a special subtitle, the *astronomical* region.

We have arranged here various matter elements in a certain spatial relationship. The time concept is involved because this is an arrangement which may be correct only at one instant of time. It is possible that the position of some of these entities on the line is constantly changing. When an electron gets into rapid motion its mass is changed a little and it shortens one of its dimensions. It thus shifts its position on the line slightly to the left whenever it has a high velocity. The solar system may be slowly running down so that the planets gradually approach the sun. If this is the case the position of the solar system on the line is slowly shifting to the left.

Certain segments of this line have occupied the attention of various specialists. Astronomers deal with everything listed to the right of earth. Thousands of specialists work on the section from earth to atom. Physicists in recent years have concentrated intensively on the segment from atom to zero. The discovery of the positron, the neutron, and the mesotron within the last decade, has opened up a most fruitful field of research in physics. In this region, forever beyond the reach of the human eye, is probably contained most of the mystery of the entire universe. As K. K. Darrow has expressed it, "This field is unique in modern physics for the minuteness of the phenomena, the delicacy of the observations, the adventurous excursions of the observers, the subtlety of the analysis, and the grandeur of the inferences." . . .

Returning now to our linear lay-out for the universe we may note that everything to the right of proton is constructed out of the material included in the range from proton to zero. All matter in the universe exists in the form of bunches or aggregates of smaller parts. Protons, neutrons, electrons bunch to form atoms; atoms group into molecules; molecules group into stones and mountains; stones and mountains form the earth. In the astronomical field, planets group about the sun to form the solar system—a solar system which in the astronomical field is remarkably like the atom in the microscopic field.

The important unit of structure in the astronomical field is a sun. Practically all the stars which we can see on a clear night are distant suns, much like our own, although it is thought that only an extremely small fraction of these suns have planets around them like our own.

All these suns which can be recognized distinctly are grouped in a sort of flattened, disklike bunch which is whirling in empty space. Our own sun and planetary system is a member of this group, being located about 30,000 light-years distant from the center, or hub, of this gigantic disk. When we look into space along the plane of the disk the stars seem to be distributed very densely. We see the milky way. This bunch of suns is called a spiral nebula. It is sometimes called a galaxy, or an island universe. The word "universe" in this sense has a restricted meaning because our island universe is not the only one in existence. There are millions of others distributed throughout space as far as our most powerful telescopes have been able to penetrate.

The nebulae are by no means recent discoveries. Sir William Herschel, 150 years ago, suspected that they were distant groups of stars. The philosopher Kant believed that they were "systems of many stars, whose distance presents them in such a narrow space that the light which is individually imperceptible from each of them, reaches us, on account of their immense multitude, in a uniform pale glimmer." They have been described as looking like "candlelight seen through horn." . . .

We might now indicate . . . the approximate size of the largest bunch of matter, the spiral nebula, as 100,000 light-years. Also we might speculate as to the possibility of nebulae themselves forming still larger groups. Extensive surveys have been made by the astronomers at Harvard and Mount Wilson, of the distribution in space of the nebulae, and there is, indeed, evidence of grouping of nebulae. It is legitimate to add another bunch of matter to the line lay-out—the supernebula, or supergalaxy.

The supergalaxy is the largest known aggregation of matter in the universe. Its diameter may be of the order of a million light-years. At least that is the estimate made by Harlow Shapley of the diameter of the group of nebulae in which our own is located. Our local group contains perhaps 15 or 20 nebulae, but in some supergalaxies there are hundreds of members.

So far, then, our picture of the universe reveals a granular, or atomic structure. We start near the zero point of size, with a particle of definite size. A fundamental law of attraction operates to cause the small particles to group together to form larger particles, these larger particles again group to form still larger particles, and so on until we reach the limit of observation, the enormous supergalaxy. We are unable to put a stop at the right-hand end of our line, as we have done at the left end. Space may go on into infinity—possibly matter may go on bunching up into larger and larger aggregates with no limit as to the ultimate size of any final bunch, because there may never be any final bunch. Speculations of this kind may be interesting but they are not of much significance otherwise, because they take us outside the realm of possible human experience.

It seems probable that in detecting the supergalaxy man has reached the limits of observation in his probing of the depths of space. The new 200-inch telescope will be doing a fine job in helping to chart and analyze these enormous groups of matter.

The [imaginary] line diagram of the universe, limited at one end by the electron, at the other by the supergalaxy, has given a rather simple picture in terms of two variables, space and matter. The third variable, time, must now be considered. We have to consider the relationship between the various units of our structure as this relationship may change from time to time. Newton's Law of Universal Gravitation says that every particle of matter in the universe attracts every other particle. If forces of attraction cause matter to bunch up into aggregates of various sizes, why may not the various bunches themselves start coming together until eventually there results just one large, static bunch of matter floating quietly in an infinity of space? Such an end result seems logical, but it cannot happen until the kinetic energy of matter, the energy of motion, has been converted into radiation and transferred to infinity. Such a transfer of energy appears, in fact, to be going on.

A study of the motions of the various aggregates may be expected to throw some light on this question. We start with the smallest particles, electrons, for example. In addition to random motions caused by collisions with other particles, all electrons are supposed to spin. They may be thought of as being like tops which never run down. When an electron helps to form an atom, in addition to spinning it also revolves about the nucleus, just as the earth revolves about the sun. The aggregations of matter between atom and earth . . . may have various kinds of motion but when earth is reached we again have the spin about an axis and the revolution about the sun. Our sun, together with all the other suns in its group, forms a nebula which spins with high speed about a central axis. The spin velocity is very high, but the size of our nebula is so great that it takes about 2 million centuries for it to make one revolution. As Shapley puts it, this is the time required to "click off one cosmic year."

The motion of the supernebula is not known in accurate detail. It is possible that some sort of gigantic spin is present here also, but so far such a spin has not been detected. Instead, a very surprising sort of motion has been discovered, a motion which is just contrary to what we expect if matter is to agglomerate into one big bunch. The supernebulae appear to be receding from us. The supernebula to which our galaxy belongs maintains its fixed dimensions, and behaves more or less as a unit, but all the other supernebulae appear to be flying away from ours with high speeds. The farther away from us they are, the faster they seem to recede. There seems to be no good way of explaining such a phenomenon. One might assume that a primeval explosion started all matter out in all directions from an original concentration, but there are serious difficulties involved in such a theory. . . .

Readings

Deutsch, Karl W., "Higher Education and the Unity of Knowledge," in *Goals for American Education*, Lyman Bryson and others (eds.), Harper & Brothers, New York, 1950.

Johnson, Wendell, *People in Quandaries*, chap. 7, Harper & Brothers, New York, 1946.

Keyes, Kenneth S., *How to Develop Your Thinking Ability*, chaps. 1, 2, 4–9, McGraw-Hill Book Company, Inc., New York, 1950.

Lee, Irving, *Language Habits in Human Affairs*, chaps. 4, 5, 9, 11, Harper & Brothers, New York, 1941.

White, Leslie, *The Science of Culture*, chaps. 6, 7, Farrar, Straus & Young, Inc., New York, 1949.

7

THE SPEAKER'S MEANINGS: TESTING VALIDITY

In Chap. 6 we observed how the identification of words with the events and the objects they represented blocked lines of communication. We observed how tenacious acceptance of traditional meanings virtually blindfolded our eyes and deafened our ears. We learned that by talking to ourselves when we should be listening, we shut off signals or messages from the outside. The self-talk feeds back into the system and shuts off incoming circuits.

On the other hand, much that we hear and see should be shut off at some level. Undoubtedly, all of us listen to and read much nonsense, and although nonsense as play or comic relief has its place in a busy world, nonsense in the guise of sense is tragically misleading. As we listen to some political prophets, a few sports forecasters, and many radio hucksters, we wonder whether the world is not filled with Gratianos each speaking his infinite deal of nothing.

In a free society the individual must make his own choice between sense and nonsense. You had the chance to learn from the discussions and exercises of Chap. 6 that choosing sense is not easy. You also probably observed that some individuals who chose nonsense were no less forceful in the defense of their decisions than those who chose sense. What happened in your class was similar in many respects to what has happened in man's groping for more accurate observations and more valid interpretations of himself and of the world in which he lives.

As a speaker you will offer information, give advice, and urge action. The more thoughtful you become and the more careful you are in investigating the "facts," the more likely you are to become convinced of one thing: A speaker can hardly be certain of the "certainties" which with confidence and vigor he urges upon his listeners. On the other hand, excessive humility scarcely serves the need of democratic group action.

There are occasions when decisions, right or wrong, must be made, and to make them demands the best judgment of a group. As a speaker and as a listener in group action, you are socially obligated to arrive at the most valid meanings in your power.

You will discover as you continue a study of evaluating meanings that the problem of *relations* is the crucial one. In fact, thinking and speaking can be viewed from the vantage of discovering and symbolizing the relations which exist or are thought to exist between parts of the universe. As soon as you symbolize a relation between parts or events in the outside world, you of course introduce a new relationship—that between your symbols and the events the symbols represent. Let us consider the following example as a way of making this somewhat complex problem clear. An orchestra playing from a musical score records a symphony. A talented musician listening to the recording writes a new score as he listens. This score would be very similar, if not identical, to that from which the orchestra played. The tempo, pitch, loudness, and other relations were captured by means of the symbolic representation, the score. What would happen if the same notes were used but the relations between them were altered? The composition would no longer be the same. What would happen if the musician in transcribing the score did not hear certain notes that were on the record, or thought he heard notes that were not there? The music produced from his score then would be quite different from that of the recording.

In a sense, intelligent persons are writing their scores of the universe. They write them in the symbols of mathematics, the various sciences, literatures, and philosophies. Their adequacy is determined by validating the relations symbolized. In efforts to arrive at more valid relations educated men for centuries have been analyzing their methods of analysis. They have developed systems of mathematics and logic for testing the adequacy and validity of statements. They have elaborated quantitative measurements into systems of statistics.

In recent years scientists in numerous fields, particularly in mathematics, physics, medicine, psychiatry, biology, neurology, and psychology, have renewed their interest in a general methodology for improving human evaluations and human communications. One general methodology which has attracted the interest of many scholars is semantics.

How you develop your ability to analyze, to evaluate properly, depends, of course, upon many factors. Your studies in the social sciences, in literature, in mathematics, and in the physical and biological sciences should contribute to your capacity for analyzing meanings. Improvement in evaluation is a lifetime process. When improvement in evaluation stops, intellectual decay and death begin.[1] Much immediate help in testing the validity of your meanings can come from an application of even the elementary principles of semantics, logic, and statistics. General semantics is concerned with word-fact relations, logic tests word-word relations, and statistics is a method of testing quantitatively fact-fact relations.

SEMANTICS

The evaluation of word-fact relations of necessity involves a study of abstracting. You have already learned how all the meanings you carry around with you are abstractions, summaries of the multitude of objects, occurrences, and the abstractions of others to which your nervous system has responded. When you think about these, you are abstracting your abstractions. This is somewhat like the experience in a barber shop with mirrors on both sides of the room. You see a reflection of the reflection of the reflection, etc. To say that a memory of an event is identical to the event would be to say that a reflection of the man is the man. The mentally unhealthy identifications of the different levels of abstraction can be exposed by the application of six fairly simple rules.

1. KNOW WHOSE ABSTRACTIONS YOU ARE COMMUNICATING. When one speaks or listens, he is sending or receiving the abstractions made by a particular individual at a particular moment of time in a particular situation. For example a student may say to you, "Professor Smith told me we would have a test today." You may, in turn, say to another student, "Professor Smith said he would give us a test today." You may have thought you were communicating Professor Smith's abstraction. You never were, of course. You were communicating your abstraction of a student's abstraction of Professor Smith's abstraction. Your statement to be accurate would have had to be, "Student A said that Professor Smith said there would be a test." If this seems involved, think what happens when a statement passes through 10 intermediate steps. Think of the opportunities for misunderstanding and distortion. One who accepts rumor, gossip, or propaganda identifies the statement that reaches

[1] George Zipf, *Human Behavior and the Principle of Least Effort*, p. 202, Addison-Wesley Publishing Company, Cambridge, Mass., 1949.

him with an earlier abstraction of an event. He loses sight of the bias of the maker of the statement.

Many of a speaker's meanings come from books, magazines, or reports. The writers or compilers of these have their biases. To abstract a book properly one needs to know some of the biases of the author. Without knowing them one will be likely to attribute an objective, factual value to the author's meanings which they hardly merit. The American historian Allan Nevins remarked that in the very greatest of histories the element of partiality is strong.

The bias of speakers and audiences was observed by Aristotle, who was born in 385 B.C. If the audience esteems a given quality, said Aristotle, the speaker must say his hero has that quality, no matter whether he is "addressing Scythians or Spartans or philosophers." He also observed the ease with which words prejudice listeners. He wrote:[1]

We are also to assume, when we wish either to praise a man or blame him, that qualities closely allied to those which he actually has are identical with them; for instance, that the cautious man is cold-blooded and treacherous, and that the stupid man is an honest fellow or the thick-skinned man a good-tempered one. We can always idealize any given man by drawing on the virtues akin to his actual qualities; thus we may say that the passionate and excitable man is "outspoken"; or that the arrogant man is "superb" or "impressive." Those who run to extremes will be said to possess the corresponding good qualities; rashness will be called courage, and extravagance generosity.

In some of the books on argumentative speaking, the advice is to secure facts from an unbiased authority or source. Our view, however, is that no authority is without bias. Even governmental statistics and business reports reflect the biases of the compilers. Therefore, one must try to discover the bias that is assumed to be inherent in all human thought and communication. To be aware of it is to be less influenced by it. To become aware of the biases of the great reflective thinkers, the great historians, and the great scientists should make one more aware that he, too, has prejudices. The discovery of whose abstractions we are communicating and an awareness of the biased nature of the abstraction should cure us of credulity, train us to understand and tolerate a variety of abstractions, and finally teach us the certainty of uncertainty.

[1] Aristotle, *Rhetorica*, Rhys Roberts (trans.), 1367a, Oxford University Press, New York, 1924.

2. KNOW THE DATE OF THE ABSTRACTIONS. Not only do we need to know the source of the abstraction but we need to know its place in the time continuum. Words, being static, tend to give a timelessness to abstractions. "As fixed as the stars," once "true" to astronomers, is no longer "true." The stars of the Big Dipper are drifting in different directions, so that in time the Big Dipper will be an inverted frying pan. We have previously observed that Castor and Pollux, which according to Greek mythology were the bodies of twin brothers, are not twin stars at all but are each a constellation of six.

A speaker who uses abstractions of a historical nature must keep in mind that they were made in a given period, with social and cultural influences affecting the persons who made them.

The best proof of that fact is that an era like the so-called Middle Ages did not look the same to Walter Scott in the nineteenth century as it had to Voltaire in the eighteenth; it does not look the same to most of us in the twentieth century as it did to either Scott or Voltaire. And the differing perspectives are not primarily due to increases in the amount of information about the Middle Ages. They are ascribable principally to variations in the outlooks, and therefore in the back looks, of the lookers.[1]

Persons who falsely attribute timelessness to their abstractions find it difficult to adjust even to the slow changes in a culture.

3. KNOW THAT DETAILS ARE OMITTED FROM THE ABSTRACTION. The very process of abstracting prevents our knowing many of the details which are omitted. For instance, a scientist may look at a slide under his highest-powered microscope. He sees more than with the naked eye, of course, but there may be much unobserved. But the process of trying to fill in more and more of the details of our abstractions is the process of observing, learning, communicating. To know that some details are omitted, and to delay evaluations so that these details may be sought, are necessary if evaluations are to be appropriate. As a demonstration to illustrate the necessity of delaying evaluations, one of the authors performs the following experiment. Before class time he removes the whites and the yolks of several eggs from their shells by piercing each end with a needle and then blowing through one of the holes, but he leaves one untouched. After removing the insides, he fills the holes with melted

[1] Jerome Frank, *Fate and Freedom*, pp. 28–29, Simon and Schuster, Inc., New York, 1945.

tallow. In class, while talking about colloidal behavior, he breaks open the one egg containing yolk and white. Placing the contents in a glass, he pours alcohol over the egg to demonstrate how coagulation and flocculation result. At this point, by prearrangement, a student who has been skeptical starts an argument. The teacher becomes indignant. Taking two of the shells he squeezes them together over the student's head, who runs from the room, wiping his hair and face as if egg yolks and whites were covering him. For good measure, the instructor throws a shell or two at a white-faced student in the back row.

About half of the students in each class, even in graduate classes, report that they see the yolk in the student's hair, on his face, and running down the wall in the back of the room. A few students who are able to delay their reactions until more details are revealed are not taken in. They see the faked nature of the quarrel, the artificiality of the eggs. Instead of being disturbed, they are amused. Reactions not dissimilar to those of the disturbed students often occur when writers are unaware that many details are missing when they make their abstractions. You can find amusement by reviewing what some critics say that certain authors meant and then reading the vehement denials of a second set of critics. Verbal battles rage because even learned men lose sight of the lost details. "The Battle of the Books" is fought in every age, scientists versus mystics, ancients versus moderns, romanticists versus classicists.

A special type of abstraction, which particularly demands that the details be filled in, is the quantitative abstraction. A student who had received low ratings on an interclass speech project said, "All the other students received high ratings except me. Why did the judges have it in for me?" However, when he looked over the ratings, he found that out of 256 students, 45 had ratings as low as or lower than he. Speakers both in public and in private should guard against quantitative abstractions, unless they know the details making up the abstraction. The remarks "Everyone is going," "Most of the students cheated on the test," "Nobody knew the answers" usually tell more about the language habits of the speaker than they reveal about the topic being discussed.

4. KNOW THE POSSIBILITIES OF HIDDEN MOTIVES FOR THE ABSTRACTION. Many of the meanings held and expressed by individuals are prompted by consciously or unconsciously concealed motives. To know

the speaker, as we remarked earlier in this section, helps to reveal motives. That alone, however, is not enough. Obviously, your abstraction of the motives of others confronts you with one of the most difficult tasks in evaluating. It can keep you running in linguistic circles. The line between cynicism, skepticism, and habitual doubt on the one hand and gullibility on the other is a faint one and hard to trace through the intricate maze of human ignorance, cupidity, rationalization, pride, unselfish devotion, and moral and intellectual integrity. Since, however, most of our meanings are derived from speakers, books, monographs, or news stories which present the abstractions of interested persons, we must evaluate the possibility of hidden motives.

We live in an age when propagandists are using the pseudoscientific writings on race, economics, chemistry, biology under the slogan "Accurate Information" instead of under the more appropriate label "Accurate Misinformation." Two days before this was being written, a professor of philosophy who taught in a large Eastern university and who had labeled general semantics as a fascistic discipline was dismissed when he refused to answer whether he had belonged to the Communist Party. Whether he did and is hiding it or whether he did not and is defending what to him is a legal ideal that a man cannot be compelled to testify against himself remains to be seen. The point is that if he is guilty, then his motives for denouncing general semantics were probably not purely philosophical. If he is not guilty, our abstractions of his abstractions may be motivated by knowing that he was even accused of being a Communist. In an age of strong beliefs, persistent anxieties, and social conflict, the individual, of necessity, must penetrate the superficial significance of an abstraction and determine the motives behind it.

5. KNOW THE TRICKS OF "LINGUISTIC MAGIC." When we were young, we enjoyed the traveling magicians who came to our school about once a year. Gullible and mystified, we could not understand how the rabbit came out of the "empty" black hat, how the ring which had been hammered and bent could be shot from the pistol and become again circular. We did not understand that an empty hat could be switched for one containing a rabbit as we glanced quickly at something pointed out by the magician and that likewise good rings could be exchanged for cheap trick ones. Douglas Kelly has made a study of the psychologics of magic and self-deception and has suggested that the magicians employ

misdirection to deceive; misdirection includes misdirection of attention and misdirection by camouflage.[1]

When a speaker or writer utilizes misdirective language, he deceives and mystifies listeners in harmful ways instead of in entertaining ones. Students trained to detect the tricks of "linguistic magic" can reduce the self-deception their culture may have taught them as well as the deception by selfish but clever linguistic magicians. Let us look at some of the linguistic tricks that are used to misdirect the listener or reader.

First, there is the metaphor. Metaphors may make meaning vivid and speech and writing interesting. The danger in the comparisons lies in their being mistaken for the real object of which they are only a picture. As primitive peoples eat the heart of a deer to make them fleet, or the heart of a lion to make them brave, civilized man tends by metaphorical use of symbols to explain and to acquire abstract phenomena. He then loses sight of the metaphor and accepts the comparison as a fact.

The effect of the acceptance of the metaphor as a fact is that people see the world in the focus their pictures give. During different periods of man's history, certain metaphors have become dominant and have influenced the way man has looked at himself and the world. To the Greeks, a god was like a man; to the Jews and the Christians, man was like God, even though fallen. To the Puritans, man was corruption. To many moderns, man is a machine, to be kept in good running order by high octane fuels and frequent overhauls. Such comparisons may make our communication vivid but may also lead to rigidities and stereotyped pictures.

The anatomists were once restricted in their thinking because of the misdirective influence of metaphors like amygdaloid (almondlike), a structure within the basal ganglia of the brain; fasciculus (bundle of sticks); lenticular (like a lens), a structure within the basal ganglia. The metaphorical picture becomes so fixed that users of the metaphor cannot look for the objective variations from it. Scientists today are endeavoring to escape from the too rigid patterns of thought imposed by the comparison of the nervous system to a telephonic mechanism, and they are using a new metaphor drawn from the advances in electronics.[2]

[1] Douglas Kelly, "Mechanisms of Self-deception," in *Papers from the Second American Congress on General Semantics*, M. Kendig (ed.), pp. 53–60, The Institute of General Semantics, Lakeville, Conn.

[2] Norbert Wiener, *Cybernetics*, pp. 53–56, John Wiley & Sons, Inc., New York, 1948.

A second type of misdirection occurs in the use of honorifics (terms designed to honor or pay respect) and euphemisms (terms substituted for unpleasant ones). Many individuals are so accustomed to the identification of words with the things they represent that they act as if changing the term will transform the object. "A man who taught the fifth and sixth grades in Byers, Kansas, threatened to lick the children if they did not call him professor."[1]

The right to the honorific "professor" has been claimed by auctioneers, dancing masters, banjo players, and by an "immense range of virtuosi mainly frauds." So misused and abused, the term now often belittles instead of honors. A Nebraska editor who applied the term to a horse trainer, a barber, and the manager of a roller-skating rink wrote a vigorous protest when a colleague called him "professor." In general the term doctor is replacing professor on many campuses. The title "doctor" has been bestowed upon chiropractors, optometrists, chiropodists, and college professors, who for some reason prefer it to professor, whether they have earned it or been granted it *honoris causa*.

Euphemisms, to make work more distinctive, honorable, or profitable have been used by most of the professions. One can hardly read a professional or trade journal without encountering them. "Realtor" (real-estate agent), "insuror" (insurance agent), "weldor" (welder), "mortician" (after physician-embalmer), and "custodial engineer" (janitor) have appeared to change public attitudes toward the work, although the work remains unchanged. In like manner, people try to soften reality by using such words as "withdrew" for "failed," "resigned" for "dismissed," and "passed away" for "died."

Undoubtedly the need to soften unpleasant and painful experiences and to increase personal esteem is great. Undoubtedly too, honorifics and euphemisms contribute to a need that human beings have, a need for status. The danger in the use of honorifics and euphemisms lies in their deceptive misdirection and in their affinity to rationalization. In any case students of speech need to be aware of their insidious effects.

A third type of linguistic magic which misdirects and deceives is what might be called retrospective alteration. It occurs daily because there is a need for it; it is most deceptive because it omits many details; and it builds delusions because it silently assumes that nonverbal occurrences can be changed by verbal abstractions, that past events can be

[1] Quoted by H. L. Mencken in *The American Language: Supplement I*, p. 529, Alfred A. Knopf, Inc., New York, 1945.

altered by present talk. Retrospective alteration occurs when individuals try to change or alter past occurrences by speech. Have you noticed how the coaches and players of a team that has lost a contest will replay it with words? In the verbal replay, they will eliminate a fumble or bad pass or a foul by saying, "If that hadn't happened, the game would have been different." With words, they change certain events they want to change but keep the others identical. The rest of us too will retrospectively alter past events to suit present purposes. The retrospective alteration may change the attitudes of the uncritical, but to the analytical it sounds woefully like an alibi, an excuse, a rationalization.

Retrospective alteration appears often in historical interpretations. A historian who, *after* the Bolshevik revolution in Russia in 1917, traced its seeds to the French revolution of 1789 gave, *after* the complex events, a relationship which before they did not have, to him or to any other historian.[1] Past events, past interpretations were altered to account for unpredictable occurrences only *after* they had occurred. Scientific relationships are based upon predictions that are verified by subsequent occurrences. This is not intended to be unduly critical of historical writers, since they provide by their work the soundest link between past and present cultures. Yet, to be unaware that much of what is called history, according to historians like Charles A. Beard and Allan Nevins, better deserves the label of "twistory" is to be deceived by retrospective alteration.

6. KNOW THE COMMUNICATIVE PURPOSE OF THE ABSTRACTION. In addition to the many highly individual conscious and unconscious motives, human utterances have a general communicative purpose or end. A compliment may be sincere, or it may be prompted by a desire for a favor. In either case it serves to create good feeling. The motives would differ. The purpose served would be the same. Authorities have struggled with the task of classifying speech according to purpose, but no classification has met wide approval. For purposes of introducing the problem only, we shall accept the classification offered by Thomas C. Pollock.[2]

a. Phatic Communion. The term *phatic communion* Bronislaw Malinowski gave to speech which is used to establish the bonds of social

---

[1] Frank, *op. cit.*, p. 29.

[2] Thomas C. Pollock, *The Nature of Literature*, pp. 162–196, Princeton University Press, Princeton, N.J., 1942.

communion between individuals. Greetings, pretty compliments, pleasantries, jests, all serve to create a pleasant social atmosphere. A literal-minded person who abstracts "hypocrisy" from such communications needs also to be alert to the fact that the persons who use them create, in spite of the hidden motives, an air of well-being. Persons who are well adjusted socially find it difficult to understand the difficulty that the timid, shy, and hostile have in using speech for phatic communion. The socially maladjusted, on the other hand, and the ones with "world problems" on their minds simply cannot participate in the chit-chat, the small talk that often provides a common bond with others.

b. Referential Speech. Referential speech meets the purpose of pointing and explaining. If one directs a visitor to an office, there are objects and persons to which the words refer or figuratively point. (We could call referential speech *pointing* speech.) Referential speech may not only point to referents (objects, events, relations, abstractions) but may also seek to stimulate a certain attitude toward the referents or to act toward them in a specific way. Pure referential speech occurs when the speaker's primary concern is to communicate knowledge of the referents. Pragmatic-referential speech occurs when attitudes or actions are evoked in a predetermined way as knowledge of the referents is imparted. Referential speech is successful if the attention of the listener is directed to the referent. Pragmatic-referential speech is successful if the intended attitudes or actions are stimulated.

c. Evocative Speech. Evocative speech seeks to express or evoke (or both express and evoke) a human experience. It is the purpose of the oral reading of a poem or the speech of a character in a play. It is the purpose of a story teller. The speech may be fictional. It may be historically inaccurate. The important thing is that the psychological experience of someone is communicated through symbols to the listener. It may be trivial. The short rhyme

She

He

Me

can be read with inflections to suggest victorious courtship or forlorn retreat, or indifference to rejection. There is no referential person involved. How different this is from an actual Bill or Joe or Bob saying, "Mary rejected Jim and accepted me." The effectiveness of evocative speech is determined by the degree to which a listener experiences the intended psychological response. The verbal images in the short poem "A Memory" by William Allingham are successful if in addition to evoking mental pictures they revive in the reader or listener deeper feelings associated with the images themselves.

A MEMORY

Four ducks on a pond,
A grass-bank beyond,
A blue sky of spring,
White clouds on the wing:
What a little thing
To remember for years—
To remember with tears.

LOGIC

After an individual has thoughtfully and honestly examined the word-fact relationships involved in his meanings, he faces the necessity of seeing that the word-word relations clearly formulate and convey valid meanings. To make meaning clear, he must first of all conform to the conventions of English grammar. Although ungrammatical expressions like "I ain't got none" may communicate meaning to listeners, they too often cause confusion because of their ambiguity. Furthermore, their violation of accepted patterns of expression, like inappropriate dress or indecorous behavior, startles and distracts the hearer's attention from the meaning intended.

Beyond the requirements of grammar lie the requirements of logic. Each culture develops patterns of reasoning which are acceptable. Speakers within a particular culture cannot ignore those rules or conventions governing the relationships between statements. In our modern civilization "intuitive insights," "visions," or "divine revelations" are not sufficient reason for accepting meanings. Meanings, to be valid, must have logical connections with other meanings. The statement of the logical basis for the truth of a statement consists of giving reasons. Giving reasons comprises the explicit statement of connections between meanings. Rules governing this process have been formulated and called *logic*. Our purpose here will be to treat four basic principles of logic, principles which, if followed, should make speech more reasonable.

1. KNOW YOUR ASSUMPTIONS. Reasoning must always involve the taking of something for granted. Whatever is taken for granted is an assumption. Primitive man—and, for that matter, man not so primi-

tive—once assumed that what he could not see did not have physical existence. On the other hand, primitive man and many modern men assume that some things which cannot be demonstrated physically have a supernatural existence. Also, modern man, with his electronic microscopes and telescopes, his radar, and his Geiger counters, assumes that what he detects by extrasensory devices does exist whether he can see it or not and that it exists in the patterns he describes. We have seen in Chap. 3 how extrasensory devices have recorded the invisible sound waves and have made possible inference about the make-up of speech sounds. Furthermore, man has so humbled himself that he assumes that many things exist which he cannot yet detect but may detect eventually. He cannot prove they exist, but his assumption that they do leads to thinking which could not otherwise be possible. Korzybski expresses emphatically the idea that all reasoning rests upon assumptions. He writes:[1]

We see that no statement made by man, whether savage or civilized, is free from some kind of structural metaphysics involving s.r. [semantic reactions]. We see also that when we explicitly start with undefined words, these undefined words have to be taken on faith. They represent some kind of implicit creed, or metaphysics, or structural assumptions.

Assumptions, then, are often implied or hidden. Let us see on relatively simple levels of communication what the failure to examine an implicit assumption can lead to.

A student who reported to his instructor that another student was a sneering snob was asked why he thought so. He replied, "He sneers at me when I am talking." When asked why he thought the student was sneering, he said that the other student had pulled down the corners of his mouth. That was true. The student in question did pull down the corners of his mouth and had for years. He did it when he smiled, not to show contempt but to hide the braces on his teeth. What was the implied assumption? When a student pulled down the corners of his mouth, he was sneering. About all that needs to be done to expose the statement as one which cannot be taken for granted is to bring it out of the unconscious and to express it openly.

In general, each culture has deeply rooted and widely pervasive

[1] Alfred Korzybski, *Science and Sanity*, p. 153, The International Non-Aristotelian Library Publishing Company, 1933, 1941, 1948. Distributed by The Institute of General Semantics, Lakeville, Conn.

assumptions. Although a consideration of the history of ideas would be necessary to list very many of the assumptions underlying the culture of free people, we should call attention to several basic ones often used by speakers.

Civilized man assumes that truth is better than lies, that happiness is better than unhappiness, that each individual has inherent worth, that all events (physical, biological, psychological, and social) are related in some kind of system, even if they are not causally related, that we have a freedom of choice and can direct our own destiny. These and similar assumptions not proved underlie many of the reasons advanced to prove propositions.

A speaker has to be careful to select assumptions acceptable to his social group if he expects to persuade them to accept his meanings. For speakers and writers to do so always, however, would result in cultural stagnation. There must be free and independent spirits who will risk losing immediate popularity in order to destroy stratified cultural assumptions contradicted by new information. The urgency of this point of view is indicated by Charles A. Beard, the American historian.[1]

By discarding the inherited conceptions of theology respecting the nature of the earth, animals, and plants, by examining things with great care, by classifying them, by discovering their characteristics, and by experimentation, scientists accumulated an immense body of practical knowledge confirmed by consensus of the competent. They also disclosed sequences in natural phenomena which are correctly called laws.

The history of Christ and the Christian church, the story of Columbus, the accounts of Galileo, Bruno, Spinoza, Benjamin Franklin, and countless others show that to question old assumptions involves personal risk. Even today much of our education tends to be recapitulative. Students who question the teachers' assumptions are, we fear, too often considered troublesome. In all courses, such questioning, if it is followed by investigation and hard thinking and if it is expressed in the manner which shows that the student is aware of his own high order abstractions, is much to be desired.

2. AVOID CHANGING OR EXTENDING THE MEANING OF ANY TERM IN A GIVEN CONTEXT OF DISCOURSE. We have observed that nearly any term can be used to refer to different entities. The term *man*, you will

[1] Charles A. Beard, *The Discussion of Human Affairs*, p. 31, The Macmillan Company, New York, 1936.

recall, refers to at least four entities. In a given context, man should be limited to one entity, unless there is reason for shifting. In this case, attention should be called to the shift in the level of abstraction. In a drama class, a student took exception to the lines

> O, that this too too solid flesh would melt,
> Thaw, and resolve itself into a dew!

He reasoned, flesh is not solid. It is composed, he said, of many cells separated by air spaces; colloids bound by membranes are in motion, etc. Another student said flesh *was* solid. Anyone could see that it was. Both students were using the word "flesh" but they were using it to refer to different levels of abstraction. One was using it to refer to the microscopic and even submicroscopic characteristics. The other was using it to refer to the object he could see with the naked eye. The argument was resolved when the instructor called attention to the two different levels of abstraction the students were on. Furthermore, she pointed out that one student had ignored the Elizabethan culture in which the lines had been used and had overlooked the imaginative purpose of the metaphor.

The misuse of expressed and implied modifiers that state the quantity of terms often leads to an illogical extension of meaning. Study the following sample of political talk[1] to learn how a speaker extended the meaning of Professor Carstairs from "some men cannot be bribed" to "no men can be bribed."

It is well known that every man has his price, and when I said this, I was merely repeating the obvious. That's why I'm surprised to find even such an impractical idealist as Professor Carstairs denying that all men can be bought. He certainly has a blind faith in human nature to think that people are capable of resisting the lure of money. And he doesn't know any history, which is full of examples to refute him. It is absurd to hold that no one can be bribed.

In the second place we are likely to extend meaning because we do not know or we forget that terms like *not, no, none* before a noun give the same significance as *all* or *every one of*. For example, if a dean reports, "Jones is not a student at State," he has in a sense said, "All the students at State have been checked. Jones is not one of them." Now let us suppose that we learn that all students at State are to receive an educational subsidy. Can we infer that Jones will not receive such a

[1] Monroe Beardsley, *Practical Logic*, p. 285, Prentice-Hall, Inc., New York, 1950.

subsidy? Definitely not. Such an inference would have been possible only if all students at State were to receive all the educational subsidies. This meaning would be implied in such a conclusion but would not have been in the premise.

3. EXPOSE QUESTION-BEGGING ABSTRACTIONS (*Petitio Principii*). Sometimes, when confronted with the urgency to show how we know what we know or how we arrived at our meanings, we face great difficulty. Too often we commit the fallacy of begging the question by merely repeating the abstraction in different words (iteration), by reasoning in a circle (using the statement to prove a reason which is then used to prove the statement), or by assuming a higher-order abstraction which includes the original abstraction.

During political campaigns persons influenced greatly by partisan feelings often make statements about party candidates of whom they know little. When asked how they know, they frequently clutter up the talk with such answers as "He just is," or "Everybody knows he's the best candidate." They clutter it even more when they use intermediate premises. The persons pressed may say, "Our candidate has the best training because he has had important committee assignments, and he has had those because of his training." Usually, of course, both iteration and reasoning in a circle are camouflaged by many irrelevant and redundant words. Be alert for them in your own speech and in the speech of others.

Actually the fallacy of *petitio principii*, through assuming a larger general principle (higher abstraction), contributes much to students' difficulties in giving a speech. A student ready to walk to the front of the class feels a little tension in the stomach and notices his mouth is somewhat dry. He assumes the larger principle that this is stage fright or nervousness and behaves as if the tension were the result of stage fright. In many instances this reaction can be checked by recognizing that the slight tension is merely a living organism's way of providing alertness. Many students unfortunately perpetuate the uneasiness by assuming still a larger principle and saying to themselves or aloud, "I never could speak anyway." Each specific performance is assumed to be a failing effort because all such efforts are destined to fail (the more general assumption). A careful study of the symbolic mechanisms underlying *petitio principii* will reveal that many habitually poor evaluative responses, such as anxiety, timidity, self-pity, etc., involve this fallacy.[1]

[1] Alfred Korzybski, *op. cit.*, pp. 443–451.

Culturally, too, many of the prolonged, irreconcilable arguments that divide and antagonize stem from recurrent fallacies of begging the question. These arise from the attempts to answer unanswerable questions. Whenever talk becomes concerned with attempts to answer unanswerable questions, then the fallacy of assuming what needs to be proved is likely to occur with greater and greater frequency. With some amusement, we read and reread about the disputations of the Middle Ages. How many angels can dance on the head of a pin? Is there space between Heaven and Hell? If there is, can angels go from Heaven to Hell without passing through the intervening space? Today we hold our disputations on such questions as the following: What is the mind? What is the id? The unconscious? The subconscious? What is art? What is love? What is the greatest literary work? The answers to such questions involve abstractions at a very high level. When a disputant on such a question is pressed for answer, he can find no low-level abstraction to point to. He, therefore, changes labels or words for the original assertion and submits them as reasons.

To know that unanswerable questions are meaningless represents an advance in thinking. To expose the meaningless nature of many of the questions discussed as educational topics, however, would be to make oneself exceedingly unpopular. Yet one still should suspect a failure to ask meaningful questions whenever talk becomes clogged with *petitio principii*.[1]

4. REDUCE CONFUSION ABOUT CAUSE. As we have indicated frequently, the understanding of relationships between objects, events, and symbols provides the basic *logic* to our thinking. Most of that basic logic we have learned from our particular language culture. Especially is this true in the case of our persistent assumption of and quest for causes. The frequency in daily speech of such statements as the following suggests how entrenched is belief in *cause:*

His success was *due to* hard work.
His fifth foul *lost* the basketball game.
The rough green *caused* me to miss that putt.
Increased output *resulted in* an oversupply of goods.
The industrialist *used his influence to secure* rebates.
The attractive jacket *sold* the book.

[1] Percy Bridgman, *The Logic of Modern Physics*, pp. 28–32, The Macmillan Company, New York, 1938.

At a more scholarly level of communication the assumption of cause is no less important. In a widely used American history textbook,[1] we read on a single half page, selected at random, the following sentences: "These events (business stagnation, labor conflict, agrarian unrest) *roused* all the President's fighting qualities . . . . Time . . . *has softened* judgments . . . . Cleveland *made* W. Q. Gresham of Illinois Secretary of State. He *appeased* the hunger for spoils . . . . He more than *doubled* the number of positions under the merit system . . . ." It would seem that the idea of cause is "involved in the meaning of all transitive verbs."[2]

Much daily confusion obtains in any discussion of cause. We hear that better school spirit will result from more pep rallies and from fewer rallies, from more dances and from fewer dances. We hear that students will work harder if we do away with grades and if teachers grade more severely. Obviously, it is easy to state a cause. To show that the causal system exists requires labor and rigorous thinking.

The first step in improving evaluation by reducing confusion about cause is to determine the significance of the word expressing cause, whether it is a verb, noun, or conjunction. Read the following three statements expressing beliefs about the Montoyas' deaths.

1. Mrs. Montoya died first *because* a woman is weaker.
2. Mrs. Montoya died first *because* the position of the fingerprints indicated Mr. Montoya had entered the garage last.
3. Mrs. Montoya died first *because* the judge decided she did.

The three *because*'s have quite different meanings. The first is an explanation of physiological causation that would explain her dying first. The second is a statement of reasons why we should believe she died first. And the third is a kind of legal definition based on a judge's ruling.

One of the truly great writers on rhetoric, Richard Whately, wrote over a hundred years ago:[3]

The Premise by which any thing is proved, is not necessarily the Cause of the fact's *being* such as it is; but it is the cause of our *knowing*, or being con-

---

[1] Arthur Schlesinger, *Political and Social Growth of the United States, 1852–1933*, p. 189, The Macmillan Company, New York, 1925.

[2] Monroe Beardsley, *op. cit.*, p. 441.

[3] Richard Whately, *Elements of Rhetoric*, pp. 76–77, James Munroe and Company, Boston, 1856.

vinced, that it is so; *e.g.* the wetness of the earth is not the Cause of rain, but it is the Cause of our knowing that it has rained. These two things,—the Premise which produces *our conviction*, and the Cause which produces that *of which* we are convinced,—are the more likely to be confounded together, in the looseness of colloquial language, from the circumstance that (as has been above remarked) they frequently coincide; as *e.g.* when we *infer* that the ground will be wet, from the fall of rain which *produces* the wetness. And hence it is that the same words have come to be applied, in common, to each kind of Sequence; *e.g.* an Effect is said to "follow" from a Cause, and a Conclusion to "follow" from the Premises; the words "Cause" and "Reason," are each applied indifferently, both to a Cause properly so called, and to the Premise of an Argument; though "Reason," in strictness of speaking, should be confined to the latter. "Therefore," "hence," "consequently," &c., and also, "since," "because," and "why," have likewise a corresponding ambiguity.

Whately further explained that the multitude of words which bear this ambiguous meaning contributes to our confusion, especially since they are the very ones we depend upon to discover and to explain relationships. If confusion is to be avoided, the significance of because must first be determined.

The second consideration which must be given great weight, if evaluation of causal relations is to be sane, is that causation is seldom simple. Most events are so interrelated and stem from so many causes that singling out one circumstance is misleading. Even in the rigorous logic of physics the assumption of definite causation has been modified, and in its place we find the theory of probability. This may be somewhat crudely illustrated by the following example: If you have loaded dice that make it probable you will roll 7 or 11, you cannot be sure that any one roll will be 7 or 11. You are confident, however, that with the loaded dice the probability of rolling 7 or 11 is greater than if you use honest dice. In other words, there is no definite causal relation between the loaded dice and the number rolled. The force of the roll, the surface on which the dice are rolled, etc., are factors which also influence what dots turn up. All we can say is that after thousands of rolls with the loaded and the honest dice, the chances of 7 or 11 turning up are greater with the loaded dice than with the honest ones.

That the assumption of a probability theory presents grave problems to all of us interested in the science of human behavior and human relations goes without saying. To oversimplify, however, is to stupefy.

We can take hope in the words with which Hans Reichenbach closes a chapter on predictive knowledge.[1]

The picture of scientific method drafted by modern philosophy is very different from traditional conceptions. Gone is the ideal of a universe whose course follows strict rules, a predetermined cosmos that unwinds itself like an unwinding clock. Gone is the ideal of the scientist who knows the absolute truth. The happenings of nature are like rolling dice rather than like revolving stars; they are controlled by probability laws, not by causality, and the scientist resembles a gambler more than a prophet. He can tell you only his best posits—he never knows beforehand whether they will come true. He is a better gambler, though, than the man at the green table, because his statistical methods are superior. And his goal is staked higher—the goal of foretelling the rolling dice of the cosmos. If he is asked why he follows his methods, with what title he makes his predictions, he cannot answer that he has an irrefutable knowledge of the future; he can only lay his best bets. But he can prove that they *are* best bets, that making them is the best he can do—and if a man does his best, what else can you ask of him?

The full significance of this statement may be felt socially when educated speakers refrain from perpetuating the oversimplified causal systems and accept the responsibility of no longer implying they possess unlimited prophetic powers. Descriptions of possible factors affecting the events of the future will take the place of promises that too often are not kept and prophecies that too often do not come true. In all fairness, the student should keep in mind that both a theory of causation which, centuries old, is as we have seen a part of our language structure and the newer theory of probability are assumptions. He must decide which he will try to use.

STATISTICS

That we live in a world where quantitative measurements are becoming more and more important is apparent to a casual reader of the newspaper, the weekly news magazines, or the professional journals. The popularity of census figures, election polls, and sales and welfare quotas indicates that a large share of educated people acquire many of their meanings from enumerations and measurements.

The complex nature of quantitative measurements and the difficulty of understanding them contribute to the many invalid meanings speak-

[1] Hans Reichenbach, *The Rise of Scientific Philosophy*, pp. 248–249, University of California Press, Berkeley, Calif,. 1951.

ers acquire and perpetuate. We shall consider only six of the most common statistical errors that distort meanings. Speakers may reach more valid conclusions if they avoid these statistical blunders.

1. MAKING QUANTITATIVE COMPARISONS OF NONCOMPARABLE DATA. In recent years certain critics of public schools have claimed that the reading level of high school students is much lower than it was 20 years ago. To prove this claim, they have cited average reading scores taken on corresponding classes at 5-year intervals. But we may question whether the large high school population of today is comparable to the more select high school population of 20 years ago.

One of the grave injustices done to immigrants in the United States was the charge once made in a census report that the tendency toward criminality among the foreign-born was twice as great as among the native-born. Figures showed that in our prisons 1,768 prisoners per million population were foreign-born, while only 898 per million of the native population were in prison.

The foreign-born and native populations were not comparable. The foreign-born population included a small proportion of children, while the native population included a very large proportion. A fairer comparison between populations of voting age revealed that there were 3,270 foreign-born white prisoners and 3,395 native prisoners per million males.

2. MAKING ERRORS IN SAMPLING. We are often confronted with the necessity of measuring certain characteristics which are representative of a large group or population. Furthermore, to be of any value, the characteristics must be determined not by a few but by many sets of measurements. A track coach is not interested in a single jump of a high jumper. A student planning to enter a profession is not influenced by the income of one person in that profession. A baseball scout is not influenced by a single home run. A store planning to locate in a new area cannot decide on the basis one day's observation of pedestrian traffic.

Obviously, it is impossible in any case to make measurements on 100 per cent of the instances. What the store does is to record the number of pedestrians on a number of days at different times of the year and at different times of the month. The student secures a professional report of the average income, based usually upon the survey of only a part of the members of a profession. This partial enumeration, or measuring, is called sampling. A sample which is not representative of all of a given population is called biased.

It is at once apparent that the method of sampling is crucial. The validity of the generalizations made about a population will frequently be determined by the method of sampling. The pollsters have learned that lists of people made up from telephone directories are economically biased because they omit representation of those who cannot afford a telephone. College debaters have made the error of considering salaries only in tool- and dye-making and in the welding and electrical trades as a basis for the generalization that wages were rising as fast as living costs. A glaring instance of biased sampling occurred when a New York newspaper, in an optimistic editorial, cited statistics that indicated economic conditions were improving. The figures showed that retail sales in April of a given year were better than in April of the preceding year. The report neglected the fact that Easter had occurred in March of the preceding year and in the third week of April of the given year and that Easter sales not included in the first were included in the second.

3. USING A MISLEADING MEAN (AVERAGE). As you well know, a mean is made up of the total scores divided by the number of measurements. If there are a small number of scores at either end of the scale which deviate widely from the rest, the mean is likely misleading. An example of how misleading a mean can be is illustrated by the following instance: A promotional agency, proclaiming the desirability of a residential area, gave figures to show that the average annual income of the 40 families living there was $12,000. What they neglected was that three persons who lived on the fringe of the district had incomes of $100,000 a year and that the average for the other 37 was $4,865 a year.

4. USING MISLEADING PERCENTAGES. Years ago, after a well-known university had opened certain courses to women, a news report carried the information that 33⅓ per cent of the women enrolled had married into the faculty. Of course, the important item was the number enrolled. There were three. One had married a faculty member.

A study of stuttering spasms published in a professional journal claimed that under certain conditions one subject had a 700 per cent increase in stuttering. This subject had one spasm under one condition and seven under another. Other subjects who had twenty spasms under one condition and thirty under the other had only a 50 per cent increase. Although only 19 stutterers were examined and although 8 of them showed no increase, the average increase, largely accounted for by the 1 case, was 600 per cent. This misuse of statistics leads to egregiously faulty meanings. Percentages based on fewer than 100 measurements of observations are likely to lead to wrong impressions.

5. ACCEPTING AN INSIGNIFICANT DIFFERENCE AS A REAL DIFFERENCE. Let us suppose that it was very important to know the average weight of the men at both X and Y colleges and to determine which school had the heavier men. Since we cannot measure all the men, we take a sample of 10. (That is too small, but we wish to keep this easy.) Those weights run as follows:

X 225 190 180 175 175 160 160 150 140 115   Average 167.5
Y 200 195 185 170 165 165 170 155 150 150   Average 170.5

We might conclude that the men at Y were, on an average, heavier than the men at X. However, the difference may be only accidental and determined by our *chance picking* of the men in our sample. A second sample might include the following weights:

X 200 195 180 175 170 165 160 160 155 145   Average 170.5
Y 220 195 175 180 170 165 155 155 135 120   Average 167.5

The limits of this book prohibit consideration of the ways of testing differences between averages. Our concern is to warn speech students against using differences in averages as indicating real differences when in reality they may be chance differences. Students who debate, who are planning to enter business, law, teaching, will wish to read further in statistics.[1]

6. DO NOT BE DELUDED BY DECEPTIVE GRAPHS. As a speaker wishing to present specific material vividly, you may wish to use a graph. Or you may discover graphs you will want to adapt for use before an audience. When you either use the meanings from graphs or communicate by means of graphs, you must be sure they are fair ones. Compare the two graphs in Fig. 27 on the political affiliations of college graduates. Both are based on the same facts. One is deceptive, since it magnifies the facts by introducing the second dimension of width to the dimension of height.

Projects for Practice

1. Below are a series of arguments recently observed in reading and in

[1] An excellent and not too difficult introduction to the field of statistics can be found in J. P. Guilford, *Fundamental Statistics in Psychology and Education*, McGraw-Hill Book Company, Inc., New York, 1950.

discussion. Determine whether each is logical. If not logical, which error of logic is involved?

    a. It is generally recognized by all the newspaper editors and most of the radio commentators in this country that the conservative businessmen are interested in the welfare of their country. On the other hand, the so-called liberal professors of social science and philosophy cannot be classified as the strong businessmen of our country. Therefore, it logically follows that the professors are not much interested in the welfare of the country.

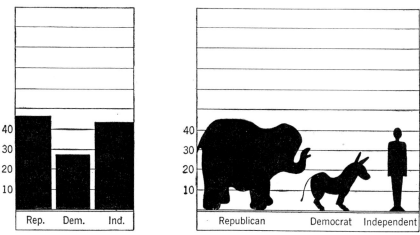

Fɪɢ. 27. Two graphs presenting the same facts. One graph is grossly deceptive.

    b. Children naturally like circuses, parades, and pageantry. Adults, however, are not children. Therefore, it is ridiculous for adults to be entertained by parades and circuses.

    c. The church is an institution which has done much to alleviate the anguish and suffering of mankind. Scientific experimentation is after all not a part of the church. Therefore, scientific experimentation has not alleviated the suffering of man.

    d. The methods of science are exact and rigorous, and have made it possible for new knowledge and new techniques to be used for the welfare of man. Religion and philosophy, on the other hand, do not possess the rigorous methods of science. Therefore, religion and philosophy cannot contribute to the welfare of man.

    e. The human mind is not identical with matter. It is intangible. It does not occupy space. The body, on the other hand, is tangible and does occupy space. Therefore, the mind is not a part of the body but separate from the body. The human body is the expression of the human mind. The mind is spiritual, and spirituality is greater than material substance. Therefore, it is unlikely that the mind could be an expression of the body. Instead, the body is the expression of the transcendental human mind.

f. The world has order because the thought that knows the world is itself an ordering. Hence, the thought is a part of the world, and since it has order, the world must have a natural order. The generalized principles of science are necessary because they are ultimately laws of thought that are involved and presupposed in every experience in past, present, and future. Science, therefore, is absolute and truth is everlasting, since science is the order of thought, and thought is a part of the natural law.

g. The logical positivists say that all truth is relative to the individuals who are interpreting it. The individuals do not agree. Therefore, there can be no agreement on what is truth. If there is no agreement on what is truth, then the statement made by the logical positivists cannot be true, since they themselves cannot agree upon what is true. If there is no truth to the statement of the logical positivist, then we need to pay no attention to it.

2. Arrange the following groups of statements in an ascending order of abstraction, placing the lowest order first and the highest order last.

The quarterback fumbled on his own 2-yard line during the final game.
The poor ball handling in the final game lost the conference championship.
The quarterback threw away the final game.
The ball was seen to roll away from the quarterback on the 2-yard line.

3. Study the following passages from "An Essay on Man," to determine whether the metaphor is taken as a fact. Explain how proper evaluation may be prevented because of the metaphorical distortion. Determine whether there may be unanswerable questions. Why do you think so? Do you detect the error of begging the question?

II

Presumptuous Man! the reason wouldst thou find,
Why formed so weak, so little, and so blind?
First, if thou canst, the harder reason guess,
Why formed no weaker, blinder, and no less?
Ask of thy mother earth, why oaks are made
Taller or stronger than the weeds they
     shade?
Or ask of yonder argent fields above,
Why Jove's satellites are less than Jove?

X

Cease then, nor Order Imperfection name:
Our proper bliss depends on what we blame.
Know thy own point: This kind, this due de-
  gree
Of blindness, weakness, Heav'n bestows on
  thee.
Submit.—In this, or any other sphere,
Secure to be as blest as thou canst bear:

Safe in the hand of one disposing Pow'r,
Or in the natal, or the mortal hour.
All Nature is but Art, unknown to thee;
All Chance, Direction, which thou canst not
  see;
All Discord, Harmony not understood;
All partial Evil, universal Good:
And, spite of Pride, in erring Reason's spite,
One truth is clear, *Whatever is, is right.*

Alexander Pope

If Pope's apparent logic had prevailed, what would be the state of the world?
4. What semantic, logical, or statistical trick is played in each of the following?

  a. In remote areas of the Ozarks, any reference to *leg* is a grave social blunder. A leg of mutton, table legs, etc., become a limb of mutton, table limbs, etc.

  b. A doctor reported that he had administered penicillin in 18 advanced cases of scarlet fever and that in none was there noticeable benefit. Penicillin, therefore, was not indicated in cases of scarlet fever. Is the sampling a fair one?

  c. A student reasoned that students generally become more intelligent as they progress through college. He showed that the mean-point average of college seniors was higher than that for college freshmen. Is this use of averages sound?

  d. A speech teacher secured ratings on four performances by each of 350 students. Three evaluators contributed 660 ratings, while 40 contributed the other 740. What criticism may be made?

  e. In a survey of college graduates for the purpose of investigating their incomes, political and religious beliefs, marital status, and other facts which would provide data for generalizations about a college educa-tion, questionnaires were sent to a sample of 17,053 persons. This sample was selected in a manner to satisfy the requirements of proportional representation of geographic areas, types of college or university, etc. Of the number receiving the questionnaire, 36.2 per cent replied to the first request, 16.9 per cent replied to the second request, and 31.8 per cent did not reply, while 2.5 per cent *refused* to reply or to be interviewed. For some reason, replies were not received from 7,570 or 44.4 per cent of the persons on the list to be surveyed. Is the sampling adequate? What facts should be known about the replies before the sample can be accepted as sound?

5. The data from a study by Havemann and West[1] show that, of the businessmen who had been A students in college, 29 per cent made over $7,500 a year, 27 per cent made from $5,000 to $7,500, 36 per cent made from $3,000 to $5,000, and only 8 per cent made less than $3,000. Of the businessmen who had been C and D students, the respective percentages were as follows: 24, 22, 42, 12. Prepare a chart which will make these figures vivid without distorting them.

6. Search for other data on average incomes in professions you are considering. Prepare graphs based on these facts.

7. Prepare a 5-minute speech based on all the data you can obtain about the profession you are planning to enter, and, using graphs, present it to the class.

8. Correlations between intelligence test scores and reading comprehension scores were calculated for a random sample of 600 college freshmen. The correlation was .62. A correlation between the same tests was calculated for a sample of 150 students in a reading clinic. The correlation was .10. What explanations of the difference in correlations can you make?

9. Forty freshmen who had made poor comprehension scores on a reading test were asked to read two 400-word passages aloud five times. The average number of miscalled words on each of the five readings is shown.

Reading	Words miscalled
1	34
2	25
3	23
4	19
5	17

The students were given a comprehension test after each reading. Their average score on each test was 60, 71, 74, 77, 76.

  a. Draw a chart which will vivify the above data.

  b. What conclusions can you draw? If it is shown that the differences between each pair of average scores except 77 and 76 were "significant," what conclusions would you draw?

[1] Ernest Havemann and Patricia Salter West, *They Went to College*, pp. 25–37, Harcourt, Brace and Company, Inc., New York, 1952.

10. In a study of culture in the United States, Charles Angoff and H. L. Mencken used the following statistics among many others to show that culture in one state was very low.[1]

STUDENTS IN COLLEGES (PER 100,000 OF POPULATION)

Rank	Number
1. District of Columbia	2598.18
2. Nevada	1294.45
3. Utah	1294.16
4. California	1241.54
5. Oregon	1184.58
. . . .	
40. Mississippi	444.14
41. New Mexico	419.44
42. West Virginia	408.54
43. Maine	407.92
44. Florida	389.01
45. Alabama	383.09
46. Arkansas	327.88
47. Delaware	289.75
48. New Jersey	270.42
49. Connecticut	221.17
United States	730.25

What would you like to know about the population before you would accept the figures as a fair index?

11. In another part of the same study, Angoff and Mencken argued that the same state was not a desirable place in which to live.[2] They used the following average temperatures to prove it:

Rank	Annual	Summer	Winter
1. Vermont	38	65	18
2. North Dakota	39	65	8
3. Minnesota	41	66	11
14. Iowa	48	72	21
35. California	57	70	45
43. Mississippi	64	80	47
46. Texas	66	82	49
48. Florida	71	81	60

a. Using the data given, show how averages are a very misleading method of estimating desirability of a climate.

[1] Charles Angoff and H. L. Mencken, "The Worst American State," *The American Mercury*, vol. 24, p. 12, 1931.
[2] *Ibid.*, p. 370.

b. What is the fallacy involved in evaluating the climate of a whole state by a state average?

Readings

Guilford, J. P., *Fundamental Statistics in Psychology and Education*, 2d ed., chaps. 2, 4, McGraw-Hill Book Company, Inc., New York, 1950.

Huff, Darrell, *How to Lie with Statistics*, W. W. Norton & Company, Inc., New York, 1954.

Lee, Irving, *Language Habits in Human Affairs*, chaps. 7–9, Harper & Brothers, New York, 1941.

Thoules, Robert, *How to Think Straight*, Simon and Schuster, Inc., New York, 1939.

THE ORGANIZATION OF SPEECH

At all levels of life, the structuring or organization of parts into wholes follows relatively well-established designs. The colloids of the human body, the molecules of steel, the human beings within a stable society, although constantly in changing relationships, still move in highly predictable patterns. In abnormal conditions, such as cancerous diseases, structural flaws, and revolutions, the breakup of established designs may be followed by chaotic and unpredictable changes and end in the destruction of a particular structure. On the other hand, dynamic alterations of pattern often are followed by new alignments of parts and by a revitalized and stronger organization.

Although social structures are no longer thought to be as rigid as Alexander Pope's "An Essay on Man" suggested, still society, to be at all cohesive, must impose forms of organization upon its members. But either to persuade and coerce its members into desirable behavior on the one hand or to dissuade and restrain them from undesirable activity on the other, a society must first of all group and classify individual human responses.[1] The principal tool by which society classifies is, as we have seen, articulate speech. If you will reflect but a moment upon organizing groups like the home, the church, the school, the state, and upon regulative terms like *good* and *bad*, *clean* and *unclean*, *smart* and *dumb*, *brave* and *cowardly*, *lawful* and *unlawful*, *successful* and *unsuccessful*, *religious* and *irreligious*, you will sense the tremendous organizing effects speech has upon your own personality and upon your relations with other members of any social group. Edward Sapir, who was a distinguished anthropologist, wrote that even such highly per-

---

[1] George Zipf, *Human Behavior and the Principle of Least Effort*, pp. 275–276, Addison-Wesley Publishing Company, Cambridge, Mass., 1949.

sonal activities as ways of breathing fell into categories of polite and impolite and, therefore, became organized physiological responses partly as a result of social forces.[1]

The very act of learning involves perception of patterns, *Gestalten* (shapes), configurations. More and more, the authorities on the psychology of learning emphasize the importance of this organizing function of the mind and of speech. In fact, much research indicates that learning is painfully slow and inferior in quality if organization is not also present. In learning which involves symbols, the organizing function is even more important. If this theory is true, as it now seems to be, it means that if you have learned to talk, you have also learned to organize. The simplest human act, the simplest kind of speech involves organization to some degree.

It is urgent that beginning students of speech understand the full significance of this view. If they do, they will lighten their labor in organizing not only their speeches but all their work. If they understand that the real question, then, is not whether they should organize ideas, but which one of a number of correct patterns of organization they wish to apply to a given problem, much of their uncertainty can be eliminated.

ORGANIZATION AND MEANING

So that you may more fully understand the relationship between organization and meaning, let us look at the following sentence, which is made up of words quite familiar to you.

s	t	o	d	e	y
y	u	t	a	c	a
a	o	s	e	n	w
s	e	i	r	e	e
t	s	e	e	t	h
i	n	n	b	n	t
t	e	o	d	e	s
a	s	y	l	s	i
h	e	n	u	s	s
w	k	a	o	i	i
f	a	f	h	h	h
o	m	i	s	t	t

[1] Edward Sapir, "The Unconscious Patterning of Behavior In Society," *Selected Writings of Edward Sapir in Language, Culture and Personality*, p. 545, University of California Press, Berkeley, Calif., 1951.

Before reading further, look at the sentence again. Have you understood its meaning? How have you tried to organize the letters? Have you persistently tried to organize them from left to right and from top to bottom? We suggest now that you forget the left-to-right pattern imposed by your culture and look at the lower right-hand corner first. Read up four letters and draw a light horizontal line. Proceed by reading up each column of letters. Do the letters now fall into recognizable patterns?

As one further simple illustration of the fact that organization yields meaning, look at the three ways of arranging the simple words "he," "only," "her," "watched." Those words may be arranged in one of the three following sequences: (1) "Only he watched her," (2) "He watched her only," (3) "He only watched her." The same words have quite different meanings according to their order.

Language is inevitably an orderly arrangement of symbols, so much so that some aspects are predictable. The order of letters is relatively fixed and may call to our minds spelling. The order of sounds is one aspect of pronunciation. The order of words is less rigid and a matter that allows the speaker considerable latitude. Again, though, some arrangements of the words are more natural than others. In contrast to the sentences suggested above, the sentence "Mary held a rose" has no alternative arrangements of words which would make sense to us; however, we could add or insert "between her index finger and thumb" after "rose," after "held," or before "Mary," and we seem to have complete freedom to interchange the words "index finger" and "thumb." This somewhat oversimplified introduction to the problem of organizing our knowledge has, we hope, served to clarify the principle that "knowing," or "having meanings," depends upon perceiving the structure, the relatedness of the parts, in a whole. In brief, we may summarize by stating that having meanings implies some organization of details.

Much of the structure, or organization, of the universe is still unknown. Much is only hypothesized or guessed at. A great deal, however, is "known." As human meanings have evolved, they have fallen into organized patterns in biology, chemistry, physics, geology, psychology, history, religion, ethics, etc. The very development of man's complex patterns of symbols has given man the power to perceive and to express many types of relations between objects and events. In addition to relations of space and time, he has formulated symbols for expressing relations of cause and effect, linear and nonlinear relationships between events, and the dynamic relations of objects in motion expressed by modern calculus. These make possible new observations and open up new sources of meanings and stimulate still newer patterns of organization. Similarly, the very fact that there exist terms for various racial, religious, psychological, social, economic groupings of people, and terms for expressing interactions between groupings, leads scientists to develop ways of measuring quantitatively such relations.

As college students, you will find it necessary to remember much that has been reported by experts. If you will remember that remembering depends largely upon perceiving the organization as well as the details of any subject area, your efficiency will increase. Your training in this course should help you understand the chronological, economic, and psychological structure of history, the imaginative and ideational relations in literature, and the operational, functional, and quantitative designs of science. As your powers of observing and thinking develop, and as you study for classes in science, in the humanities, and in the arts, you will develop abilities in perceiving and formulating more and more intricate symbolic patterns. You will, thereby, increase your understanding of the intricate structure of the universe in which you live. Your development of your own speech will contribute much to your general education.

At times, your thinking may seem to be without a pattern or organization of any kind. Your daydreaming, your reflections upon tasks at hand, your conversation with close friends may seem to lack the organization which we have said is inherent in speech. This type of association has been called "free association" by psychologists and psychiatrists, who have studied it both in individuals and in groups. The lack of structure, however, is more apparent than real. For in free association there is an unconscious pattern. Ideas have submerged, or unconscious, interrelations. For example, a college student who was very fearful of speaking, particularly to older men, responded in a series of words to stimulus words. The first word was "blue." Each response word, in turn, was used as a stimulus to evoke another oral response. The sequence of responses was as follows: "Lake Michigan," "holiday," "beach," "swimming," "accident," "spit-it-out," "embarrassment," "father." The student insisted that for 12 years, at least, an incident involving the need to speak quickly while on a holiday with several friends had remained buried in his memory. His oral responses, at first apparently without organization, developed a chronological pattern which brought to consciousness his bitter childhood experience.

The discovery of the structural pattern of our own ideas may be as informative about *us* as the discovery of the structure of the outside world is informative about *it*.

ORGANIZATION AND COMMUNICATION

The fact that the free association of words or images has an unconscious organization and that the discovery of that structure is beneficial to the speaker makes possible the therapeutic use of speech for students who suffer stage fright or any other mild anxieties. However, except in groups whose individual members are working together on mental hygiene, the free-association type of talk, with its hidden structure, becomes a barrier to communication. Listeners generally expect to understand quickly and easily. They cannot grasp the hidden structure of free association and become confused and irritated. It is for this reason that many of the very loosely organized public speeches, which resemble free association, create tensions and send the listeners away talking both inwardly and overtly about their frustrations instead of about the speaker's speech. The public speaker, therefore, is compelled to discover the more clear-cut patterns that audiences prefer.

The speaker has many types of patterns to choose from when he talks. Whatever one he selects, however, he should choose on the ground that it is the best to attain his purpose in speaking. If the purpose is to while away the time, little organization is required. If, however, busy people are meeting for a serious purpose, a quickly perceived design is essential. In any case, the organization of a talk emerges from the speaker's perception of his goal in relation to the audience, topic, and occasion. That organization which leads listeners to have images and ideas similar to those of the speaker will most likely achieve the speaker's purpose, while that pattern which has hidden or ambiguous relations between parts confuses and annoys listeners. If a person hopes to communicate well, he must choose his plan of organization carefully.

PATTERNS OF ARRANGEMENT

If you will review for a few moments the books you have read, the movies you have seen, or the lectures you have heard, you will be aware of the widely different patterns the communicators used to present their ideas. Even when the topics or ideas are very similar, their shapes, their arrangements, are quite different. As a student you will have the opportunity to observe that many different patterns may be, so far as we can judge, equally satisfactory. You will also observe that within a speech you may vary the patterns somewhat, but that the over-all plan must be logically and emotionally consistent. To help you with your early planning, we suggest that you study the following plans carefully, modifying and combining them to suit your own purposes and materials. The important consideration is to think about each one in relation to your subject, your audience, and the occasion.

1. IMAGINATIVE PATTERNS. Centuries before printing was invented, when speech was the principal means of communication, philosophers speculated about the types of discourse. They observed that poetry and drama had a different form, a different pattern, from history and public speeches. To the former two types of discourse they applied the general term *poetic*, while the latter two, they said, belonged to *rhetoric*. The arrangement of materials in poetic was from image to image and was determined emotionally. The progress in rhetoric was from idea to idea and was based on logic. A modern speaker does not need to be bound by these arbitrary distinctions. Story tellers, travel lecturers, book reviewers, and even some public speakers have developed their discourses largely by images rather than by ideas. Robert Greene Ingersoll's vision of war and vision of peace, both parts of his "Decoration Day Oration of 1888," draw heavily upon the imaginative structure of Percy Bysshe Shelley's "Queen Mab." Compare the imaginative progression of a part of Shelley's poetry with one short passage of Ingersoll's oratory, and you will see how a skillful orator piled image upon image much as the poet did.

FROM "QUEEN MAB"

"The Present and the Past thou
    hast beheld:
It was a desolate sight. Now,
    Spirit, learn
The secrets of the Future.—"

. . . .

"Here now the human being stands
    adorning
This loveliest earth with taintless
    body and mind;"

. . . .

The term
means tha
results, un
In all hon
written—
seems to i
the other
remember
in explain
he has the
motive, it
saying he
such exist
lower leve
person has
environme
avoid it. V
endless lis
of respons
have been
complex p
single fact
We bec
tendency
even curso
inner sour
pain and p
those of r

unhampered in our actions and in our thinking. The responses we make during infancy, childhood, adolescence, and early adulthood tend to become more or less fixed, and the symbols which are associated with our satisfactory responses become clustered around habitual responses. These give us our typical ways of thinking and reacting, in other words, our temperaments.

As we indicated in Chap. 8, the organizing of responses or the patterns of behavior, even in such personal behavior as breathing habits, are in a large degree learned from the culture. Motives, too, are learned by the symbols of acceptance or nonacceptance which are applied to unpatterned childish behavior. Would you remove your shoes and sit on the floor when invited to a friend's house? Would you throw refuse upon a stranger passing your door? Would you give away anything a new acquaintance admired? Would you place tight bandages upon your baby's head and leave them there for a year? In some societies these are patterns of response so deeply inculcated that to fail to behave in a similar manner would lead to ostracism.

In this long process the role of authority is, of course, great. Authority, however, is not always present. The parent, the teacher, and the minister, the most common sources of authority, are seldom with the child on the way to school, on the playground, and in the "shack" or at the "hangout." Dominant childhood associates begin to assert their values through reward and punishment. Thus, early in the lives of individuals arise conflicting sources of authority and of symbolic values. To be on the side of the law or against it, to be for tradition or opposed to it becomes an issue. Literature is filled with the accounts of the gap between age (authority-tradition) and youth. Shakespeare's *King Lear*, Balzac's *Père Goriot*, D. H. Lawrence's *Sons and Lovers*, Stevenson's *Crabbed Age and Youth* attest to the conflicting motives between conformance and revolt. History, too, is replete with accounts of young revolutionaries in politics, in science, in literature. The term *Young Turks* has even characterized a group of young reformers in the National Speech Association. The satisfactions derived from early responses lay down patterns of response which are likely to persist. Here again we must emphasize the importance of recognizing the difference between symbolic behavior and nonsymbolic behavior. For example, the one who is against traditional values on the action level becomes a problem child, a disciplinary case, a juvenile delinquent, a criminal, a revolutionary. The one who somehow checks his revolt against authority and tradition

arrangements, are quite different. As a student you will have the opportunity to observe that many different patterns may be, so far as we can judge, equally satisfactory. You will also observe that within a speech you may vary the patterns somewhat, but that the over-all plan must be logically and emotionally consistent. To help you with your early planning, we suggest that you study the following plans carefully, modifying and combining them to suit your own purposes and materials. The important consideration is to think about each one in relation to your subject, your audience, and the occasion.

1. IMAGINATIVE PATTERNS. Centuries before printing was invented, when speech was the principal means of communication, philosophers speculated about the types of discourse. They observed that poetry and drama had a different form, a different pattern, from history and public speeches. To the former two types of discourse they applied the general term *poetic*, while the latter two, they said, belonged to *rhetoric*. The arrangement of materials in poetic was from image to image and was determined emotionally. The progress in rhetoric was from idea to idea and was based on logic. A modern speaker does not need to be bound by these arbitrary distinctions. Story tellers, travel lecturers, book reviewers, and even some public speakers have developed their discourses largely by images rather than by ideas. Robert Greene Ingersoll's vision of war and vision of peace, both parts of his "Decoration Day Oration of 1888," draw heavily upon the imaginative structure of Percy Bysshe Shelley's "Queen Mab." Compare the imaginative progression of a part of Shelley's poetry with one short passage of Ingersoll's oratory, and you will see how a skillful orator piled image upon image much as the poet did.

FROM "QUEEN MAB"

"The Present and the Past thou
    hast beheld:
It was a desolate sight. Now,
    Spirit, learn
The secrets of the Future.—"

. . . .

"Here now the human being stands
    adorning
This loveliest earth with taintless
    body and mind;"

. . . .

No longer now the wingèd habi-
    tants,
That in the woods their sweet lives
    sing away,
Flee from the form of man; but
    gather round,
And prune their sunny feathers on
    the hands
Which little children stretch in
    friendly sport
Towards these dreadless partners
    of their play.
All things are void of terror: Man
    has lost
His terrible prerogative, and stands
An equal amidst equals: happiness
And science dawn though late upon
    the earth;
Peace cheers the mind, health reno-
    vates the frame;
Disease and pleasure cease to
    mingle here,
Reason and passion cease to com-
    bat there;
Whilst each unfettered o'er the
    earth extend
Their all-subduing energies, and
    wield
The sceptre of a vast dominion
    there;
Whilst every shape and mode of
    matter lends
Its force to the omnipotence of
    mind,
Which from its dark mine drags the
    gem of truth
To decorate its Paradise of peace.

Percy Bysshe Shelley

From "Decoration Day Oration of 1888"

A vision of the future rises:

I see our country filled with happy homes, with firesides of content—the foremost land of all the earth.

I see a world where thrones have crumbled and where kings are dust. The aristocracy of idleness has perished from the earth.

I see a world without a slave. Man at last is free. Nature's forces have by Science been enslaved. Lightning and light, wind and wave, frost and flame, and all the secret, subtle powers of earth and air are the tireless toilers for the human race.

I see a world at peace, adorned with every form of art, with music's myriad voices thrilled, while lips are rich with words of love and truth; a world in which no exile sighs, no prisoner mourns; a world on which the gibbet's shadow does not fall; a world where labor reaps its full reward, where work and worth go hand in hand, where the poor girl trying to win bread with the needle—the needle that has been called "the asp for the breast of the poor"—is not driven to the desperate choice of crime or death, of suicide or shame.

I see a world without the beggar's outstretched palm, the miser's heartless, stony stare, the piteous wail of want, the livid lips of lies, the cruel eyes of scorn.

I see a race without disease of flesh or brain,—shapely and fair,—the married harmony of form and function,—and, as I look, life lengthens, joy deepens, love canopies the earth; and over all, in the great dome, shines the eternal star of human hope.

Robert Greene Ingersoll

Young speakers will find it difficult to sustain throughout a whole speech the image-by-image arrangement. However, they can do much to break the regularity of speeches otherwise organized if, in parts that permit it, they will weave in descriptive patterns. They need not strive for the "purple patches" of an Ingersoll or a Henry W. Grady. They may merely use simple images to give life and warmth to abstract ideas.

Observe Woodrow Wilson's vivid description of the frontiersman's westward march and how it gave warmth and life to the subject, "The Course of American History."

. . . But, until they [the American people] had turned their backs once for all upon the sea; until they saw their western borders cleared of the French; until the mountain passes had grown familiar, and the lands beyond the central and constant theme of their hope, the goal and dream of their young men, they did not become an American people.

When they did, the great determining movement of our history began. The very visages of the people changed. That alert movement of the eye, that openness to every thought of enterprise or adventure, that nomadic habit which knows no fixed home and has plans ready to be carried any whither,— all the marks of the authentic type of the "American" as we know him came into our life. The crack of the whip and the song of the teamster, the heaving chorus of boatmen poling their heavy rafts upon the rivers, the laughter of the camp, the sound of bodies of men in the still forests, became the characteristic notes in our air. A roughened race, embrowned in the sun, hardened in manner by a coarse life of change and danger, loving the rude woods and the crack of the rifle, living to begin something new every day, striking with the broad and open hand, delicate in nothing but the touch of the trigger, leaving cities in its track as if by accident rather than design, settling again to the steady ways of a fixed life only when it must: such was the American people whose achievement it was to be to take possession of their continent from end to end ere their national government was a single century old. The picture is a very singular one! Settled life and wild side by side: civilization frayed at the edges,—taken forward in rough and ready fashion, with a song and a swagger,—not by statesmen, but by woodsmen and drovers, with axes and whips and rifles in their hands, clad in buckskin, like huntsmen.

2. SPATIAL PATTERNS. Talks on astronomy, geography, military tactics, football strategy, and weather often necessitate some use of spatial patterns. If care is taken to group the spatial details which are contiguous, instead of merely enumerating a long list of items, and if they are connected by transitional phrases, then the audience will visualize, understand, and remember more easily. Walter Orr Roberts's lecture "Stormy Weather on the Sun," given under the auspices of the Smithsonian Institution on March 22, 1951, contains many such phrases as the following:[1]

> The sun is a gaseous sphere. As you go down toward the center . . . . There near the nucleus . . . . It is here in the depths . . . . Lying directly on the surface . . . . The transition layer between the spotted surface . . . . At the edge of the sun . . . . The intercession of the moon between the earth and the sun . . . . The corona . . . surrounds the eclipsed sun . . . .

3. TEMPORAL PATTERNS. One important determiner of arrangement is time, the sequence in which events occurred. The first-grade child, in recounting the events of a birthday party, is likely to say "and then"

[1] Walter Orr Roberts, "Stormy Weather on the Sun," *Annual Report of the Smithsonian Institution*, pp. 163–174, 1952.

often. The party is a sequence of events, and the sequence is the order in which they occurred. The influence of time pervades all human experience. It is continuous and nonrecurrent, facts that are exploited currently by funeral directors as they place clocks on the fronts of their establishments. The effect of time sequence on our composition is marked. The student's weekly letter home may narrate the events from Monday through "today." The account of a trip may progress from "when we left" to "when we returned." The recipe book explains the ingredients of the cake in the order in which they are added. The directions on the can of polish go from "first" to "finally." The argument for the city income tax may run chronologically. The award of a distinctive prize may begin with "This girl has always been outstanding" and include references to successive accomplishments. In short, time is a great common denominator among speakers and listeners and provides a natural genesis for ordering ideas. Time influences the verbal accounts of children who have never given a passing thought to "organization," of persons who have no formal education, as well as eminent scholars who write series of volumes on world civilization.

In recounting the past, a speaker wishing to use a time arrangement need not always arrange the events in the order in which they occurred, from first to last. Successful dramatists like Kaufman and Hart have begun with a significant late event and have retraced scene by scene the occurrences leading up to it. Short-story writers often use the "flashback." Eulogies and character sketches, too, may begin with an individual's latest and most significant contributions and retrace the two or three main streams of influence upon the character.

4. TOPICAL PATTERNS. Another grouping of ideas is a view of the parts that comprise the whole. This may include the notion of sequence that we discussed in the preceding paragraph, but having treated time order, we shall not include it here. We look at a shelf of books and may see red covers, blue covers, etc. We take another view and may see history books, English books, etc. In either instance, with possibly no conscious deliberation on our part, the books fall into categories that when summated account for all the books. Such *classes* of events, ideas, objects, or attributes give us the basis for many of our groupings of ideas or orderings of sequential portions of our composition, oral or written. Books are principally classified by topics in libraries. Botany and zoology include systems of elaborate classifications. The yellow pages of the telephone directory classify business houses by topics (although

we also need the *sequential* alphabet in order to locate a particular firm). In discussions of such topics as "We Need Sidewalks," "Public Parks Are Beneficial," "The Student Body Should Support Our Activity," groupings of ideas come to mind, possibly with a single word as the common denominator, for example, "safety," "property values," "health"; with parks, "juvenile delinquency"; with sidewalks, "adult recreation"; with our activity, "attract students," "meet the competition," "improve morale," "put classwork into operation," "get more for our tuition." These three, two, or five groups (there is no fixed number) when summated should equal the *point, topic, central idea,* or *thesis* that we are interested in developing.

The topical method is useful because many of our meanings are extremely general. Even when we attempt to bring those meanings down to specific instances they are still somewhat elusive. About the best we can do is to relate them to other somewhat less general ideas. Let us suppose, for instance, you were trying to explain an American college to someone who was not familiar in any way with one. Would you begin with the buildings and campus? The curricula? The students? The faculty? The athletic program? How would you proceed? You would probably do the best you could by talking about major aspects of college, knowing full well that some topics would have to be omitted. The order in which you took up the topics might not matter.

This method is easy, perhaps too easy, since it does not always require rigorous thinking and complete classification. It has been used by popular speakers and writers under various disguises. Thomas Dewitt Talmadge, under the topic "Big Blunders," amplified five actions which he called blunders. Logically there could have been ten or twenty. The only limits would be the audience's staying powers. On the other hand, the method permits even rigorous thinkers to treat an obviously limited number of aspects of complicated problems. The statement of the topics gives the listeners the mental pegs from which Macaulay, the historian, thought a speech should be suspended. Many examples of the excellent use of this type of organization appear in the scientific speeches printed in the *Annual Report of the Smithsonian Institution.*

5. GRAPHICAL PATTERNS. Walter Lippmann, columnist and author of books on politics and social philosophy, when speaking before a medical association, chose the subject "The Living Organism of Our Society." His patterns of thought were drawn from a living human, which the medical men could quickly visualize. A geologist talking on oil in Michi-

gan used the familiar pattern of a mitten with a free little finger and a free thumb suggestive of the map of Michigan. The oil fields were "placed" in relation to the thumb, the palm, and the base of the imaginary mitten. Scientific, philosophical, theological, and other types of highly abstract talks may be more easily followed if a graphic pattern to relate the parts can be used. At the same time, as we pointed out in Chap. 7, the graphic or metaphorical pattern should not be permitted to induce false or inaccurate relations. A state may roughly resemble a hand, but there are differences which cannot be forgotten. A society may seem roughly to resemble a body, but there would be confusion about what part was the "head" and what part the "tail." If care is taken to avoid metaphorical fallacies, however, and if the graphic analogy is selected judiciously, a graphic organization of parts greatly facilitates the communication of meaning. In reality, the graphic method makes use of the fact that visual experience involving spatial relations makes up our most common thought patterns and that visualization, although oversimplified, is quick and easy.

6. LOGICAL PATTERNS. The arranging of ideas according to some logical pattern is a common one when the speaker's purpose is to prove his main idea. The subordinate thoughts stand as proof for the primary or main idea. The logical pattern may be a deductive one in which a general truth is brought to bear upon a particular case in question. If, for instance, in Chap. 6 you believed Mrs. Montoya died first, your general knowledge of fingerprints, of the manner of springing between jammed cars, etc., would be used to prove the particular statement: "Mrs. Montoya died first." Each subheading might be proved by the specific facts observed. Obviously, this is the method used most frequently in debate, both legal and legislative.

The pattern may be an inductive one in which a number of particular occurrences are adduced to prove a general rule or theory. For instance, proof that yellow fever was carried by the mosquito was accumulated by observing the specific instances in which individuals who were exposed to mosquitoes which had fed on yellow fever victims caught the disease, while other individuals not exposed did not catch it. This method may be developed along relatively simple designs which lead to a general rule, true only part of the time. Or it may be extended into intricate experimental designs involving refined statistical procedures and yielding rather close measurements of probability. This method is well suited to talks before scientific groups who demand rigorous logical procedures. It is poorly suited to general audiences, since they find the procedures somewhat difficult to follow.

7. PSYCHOLOGICAL PATTERNS. Although all the patterns thus far suggested should be used only in terms of their suitability to a particular audience, and should, therefore, be evaluated for their psychological effectiveness, still their characteristic forms do not depend upon psychological considerations alone. There are, however, other patterns of organization, which are primarily formed around points of interaction among the speaker, the subject, the audience, the time. These patterns evolve primarily from psychological considerations. Speeches before hostile audiences, speeches on topics foreign to listeners' interests, speeches on intricate and complex subjects before uninitiated audiences need an organization that proceeds from the known to the unknown, from the accepted to the unaccepted, from the interesting to the less interesting. Of course, in some situations, the speaker must recognize that the entire speech may be only a preparation for later, more advanced developments.

PREPARING THE DETAILED PATTERN

After the speaker has selected his speech topic, he needs to plan the development of his speech. What he includes, of course, is determined by what he knows and by what is suitable to the audience. Methods of analyzing the audience will be explained in Chap. 9. For the present, let us say that if the speaker expects to hold the attention of the audience, he must be sure to have a variety of ideas, illustrations, examples, comparisons, instances, etc., to develop each division of his speech. Beginning students have found the following outline of procedure helpful.

1. Write out concisely what you expect to achieve by your speech. How do you hope the audience will react?

2. Whether you express it at the beginning of the delivered speech, at the end, or whether you only imply it, phrase carefully the statement that you think will motivate the audience to do what you wish.

3. Select your pattern of organization.

4. Divide your ideas into two, three, or four principal parts, according to the patterns you have selected.

   a. If imaginative, what are the three or four large pictures you wish to paint?

   b. If spatial, sketch the broad outlines of each division.

c. If temporal, what are the main units of time or stages of development?

d. If topical, what is the basis of division? Have all important topics been covered? Do any of the topics duplicate one another? Is any one topic as comprehensive as the whole subject? The main partitions of your speech should follow only one principle of division. If they do not, they will be likely to overlap.

e. If graphical, are the comparisons consistent throughout? Are they more familiar and vivid than the ideas themselves?

f. If logical, does each of the main arguments support the statement of purpose, theme, or thesis?

g. If psychological, are the motives carefully analyzed? Are they strong and important enough to justify their use?

5. Without too much concern at first for order, write down all your ideas and facts, using a plan similar to that suggested below.

Materials Chart

Main idea:

I. Specific instances
  1.
  2.
  3.
II. General illustrations
  1.
  2.
  3.
III. Comparisons or analogies
  1.
  2.
  3.
IV. Anecdotes or incidents
  1.
  2.
  3.
V. Quotations
  1.
  2.
  3.
VI. Statistics
  1.
  2.
  3.

6. Organize the ideas and facts given under Project 5 into the pattern you have selected. The following outline form is suggestive:

Organization Chart

   1. Statement of specific response wanted from the audience:
   2. Statement of theme or central idea:

Introduction

  I. Type   Purpose
  II. Materials

Body

Main idea I.
   Division *A*.
      Materials 1.
            2.
            3.
   Division *B*.
      Materials 1.
            2.
            3.
Main idea II.
   Division *A*.
      Materials 1.
            2.
            3.
   Division *B*.
      Materials 1.
            2.
            3.

Conclusion

  I. Type   Purpose
  II. Materials

7. Prepare an appropriate introduction and conclusion. Introductions should arouse interest in the subject and establish friendly relations between the speaker and the audience. A conclusion should show that the speaker knows he has completed his treatment of the subject. It should clinch matters or ask for future consideration.

Projects for Practice

   1. Organize the following list of categories into a system of main and subordinate parts:

    a. Words
       Phrases
       Sentences
       Paragraphs
       Books
       Clauses
       Chapters
       Works
       Volumes
    b. Nervous system
       Spinal column
       Brain
       Cerebrum
       Cerebellum
       Medulla and pons
       Central nervous system
       Autonomic nervous system
       Sympathetic division
       Parasympathetic division
2. Organize the following items according to a correct time sequence:
    Valley Forge
    Fighting in the South
    Military campaigns
    Operations around New York
    The contest over taxation
    Movement toward independence
    Colonies of the coastal plain
    New England
    The indentured servants
    The Puritans
    The Cavaliers
    The Colonies

3. Picture your chief interest today. Trace it back through the four most significant events which contributed to it.

4. Describe your greatest skill. Trace its development through the three or four most significant stages.

5. Picture the complex automotive industry today. Trace it backward through the three or four most important stages of its development.

6. Arrange the following sets of ideas in a chronological order, and be prepared to give your reasons for the arrangement.
    a. Distribution
       Organization

       Invention
       Production
   b. Application
       Exploration
       Discovery
       Speculation
       Scientific calculation
   c. Recovery
       Disease
       Prognosis
       Observation
       Diagnosis
       Treatment

7. Organize the following facts to fit each of the situations suggested:
Two young men have pleaded guilty to killing a customer in a drugstore they were holding up. Both have come from slum homes which bred criminality. Both have participated in 20 armed robberies. Both have wounded men in previous holdups. Both have been paroled after each of three convictions. The state in which they were found guilty permits capital punishment.

   Situation: Put yourself in the place of the judge giving the verdict.
   Assignment: Organize a speech explaining that verdict to the class.

   Situation: You want the class to feel sympathy for the men. You are pleading for leniency.
   Assignment: Organize a speech to persuade the class that leniency should be shown.

   Situation: You believe severe punishment is necessary to defend society against further attacks.
   Assignment: Organize a speech to get the class to believe as you do.

8. Organize the following facts to fit each situation suggested:
A teen-age girl in the second year of high school was missing from school for 4 days. She was arrested for shoplifting in a department store, but released when the manager refused to prosecute. Her home, 2 months previously, had been broken by a divorce. Her scholastic record and her conduct until that time had been good. She refuses to promise good conduct in the future. Her intelligence and aptitude scores are high.

   Situation: You are her counselor presenting her case to the school's personnel and guidance committee.
   Assignment: *a.* Organize an explanatory speech presenting her case without any recommendation.
   Assignment: *b.* Organize a speech recommending a course of action.

9. Organize the facts given below to fit each situation suggested. Try the effectiveness of organization plans by delivering your speeches to the class.

Fifty per cent of A students from professional schools earned over $7,500 at the time of a survey. Only 37 per cent of the D students earned as much. Eleven per cent of the A students who were teachers or clergymen earned $7,500. Only 4 per cent who had been C and D students earned as much. Of graduates in government service, 24 per cent of the A students were making $7,500. Only 9 per cent of the C and D students were making $7,500. Twenty-nine per cent of the A students who went into business earned $7,500. Only 24 per cent of the C and D students who went into business made $7,500.

Reports from alumni of colleges are as follows:

"A college education does not pay off in money. If money is your goal, go to a vocational school." (An engineer)

"If I were going to college again, I should take more cultural courses and study professional ones less." (A successful businessman)

"College is the best place one has to learn. If I were doing it over, I should drop most activities except my fraternity and spend my days in the library." (A prominent lawyer)

"I consider extracurricular activities, especially the social type, a waste of time and money." (A career woman and housewife)

"Maintain average grades and get into every activity possible. That is my advice to a young man in college." (An eastern businessman)

Younger graduates are more active in extracurricular activities than older ones.

a. Of graduates who were fifty years of age or older, 26 per cent had participated in three or more activities.
b. Of those forty to forty-nine years of age, 30 per cent had participated in three or more activities.
c. Of those under thirty, 42 per cent had been in three or more activities.
d. Colleges are providing more extracurricular activities.

Situation 1: Explain to a group of freshmen the problems of choosing activities.
Situation 2: Make an appeal for more participation in more activities.
Situation 3: Make an appeal for limited participation.

Readings

Baird, A. Craig, and Franklin H. Knower, *General Speech*, chaps. 6 to 8, McGraw-Hill Book Company, Inc., New York, 1949.

Brigance, William Norwood, *Speech: Its Techniques and Disciplines in a Free Society*, chap. 11, Appleton-Century-Crofts, Inc., New York, 1952.

9

THE MOTIVATION OF SPEECH

The term *motivation* implies the idea of cause. To be motivated simply means that if one has a certain motive, a particular kind of behavior results, unless, of course, a counter motive checks or alters the response. In all honesty, however, we must recognize that much that has been written—and much that we may say—about motivation and motives seems to involve two fallacies. One is the fallacy of *petitio principii* and the other is the oversimplification of cause. Motivation, it must be remembered, cannot be observed directly. It is inferred. It is easy, then, in explaining why one person seeks high office, to infer that within him he has the motive for power or prestige. Once we have inferred such a motive, it is easy to explain another person's seeking high office by saying he is motivated by the prestige or power motive, as if we knew such existed. In reality, of course, we have not explained much at the lower levels of abstraction. We have not explained *why* a particular person has a desire for power and another, living in relatively the same environment, does not, when it is within his grasp, or why he may even avoid it. We have covered up our ignorance at times by postulating an endless list of motives and counter motives. We then explain variations of response by simply asserting that one of the counter motives must have been operating. Furthermore, we have often oversimplified the complex process of motivation by attributing a given response to a single factor.

We become especially impressed with these two difficulties, the tendency to oversimplify and the reasoning in a circle, when we have even cursorily examined the most scholarly attempts to discover the inner sources of behavior. Plato thought that plants had desires and felt pain and pleasure, that although their feelings were more limited than those of man, such processes as growth and turning toward the sun indicated desire. Human behavior was driven by three sets of energy: desire, emotions, and knowledge. Desire was derived from the loins, emotion from the heart, and knowledge from the head. Aristotle believed that the whole vitality of any organism lay in its *soul*, that the plant soul had vegetative powers, the animal soul sensitive powers, and the human soul rational powers. The motive force of behavior lay in the soul. On the other hand, when Aristotle considered the practical problem of man's action, he stated that the common *end* (motive) of all men was happiness and its constituents, which were good birth, friends, wealth, children, beauty, health, strength, honor, virtue, etc.

Happiness, he said, was what all men sought in some of its constituents. Locke, too, thought that nature "had put into man a desire for happiness and an aversion to misery," and that these principles "continuously operate and influence all our actions without ceasing." Freud thought that desire or pleasure, often disguised in the symbolism of dreams, verbal slips, and even accidents, was the deepest motive of human behavior. William James thought that "the pleasures and pains which action brought modify and regulate it," and that the "thoughts of pleasures and the pains acquire themselves impulsive and inhibitive power."

In spite of the incompleteness of all theories of human motivation and in face of the many contradictions and the recurrent oversimplification, we can proceed by accepting the principle that desire, wish, need are among the chief mainsprings of human behavior.

Much, of course, remains unexplained. The task of discovering what men desire is tremendous and constantly recurring, because culture determines needs and culture changes. However, with the caution that, of all human beliefs, the formulations about motive are among the most tentative, we may proceed. If we are to talk at all, and certainly if we are to talk about talking, we must consider the best guides we have at the present.

MOTIVATION RESTS UPON NEED

Like all behavior, the act of talking, as well as the content of talk, rests upon basic needs. The idea of need carries with it the connotation of want or lack. For example, when you have plenty of air to maintain a balance between oxygen and carbon dioxide you have no motivation to seek more air. Let there be a scarcity of air and you will seek it at once. Similarly, at a more complex level, persons who feel the lack of social recognition are motivated to secure it.

Obviously, the needs we feel vary greatly from individual to individual and from time to time within a single individual. One student places social recognition by his friends above everything else, above learning, above grades. Another becomes indifferent to their praise or blame and sacrifices good will for academic superiority. But even the first student's desire for socializing and fraternizing will be risked on occasion if academic probation threatens his stay at college, while the second student, in spite of his satisfaction in academic superiority, does not "rub it in" too much for fear he will lose all social acceptance and become isolated.

The individual at any moment will determine consciously or unconsciously what his needs are. He will do this in accordance with his capacities and his previous experiences.[1] The determinants of an individual's needs, or motives, then, will encompass physiological processes, cultural influences, and patterns of response (temperament).

1. PHYSIOLOGIC NEEDS. Even though a speaker can do little to change the physiologic determinants of a listener's motives, he cannot afford to be unaware of or indifferent to them. Generally, people who are hungry care little for patriotism. People who are cold are not moved by promises of salvation. In Germany and in Russia promises of a greater and grander nation moved the masses but little. Force and threats of force made more converts than appeals to national pride. Even freedom could be sold for the promise of regular meals, clothing, and a warm house. In labor disputes appeals to patriotism and a sense of duty carry less weight than promises of more take-home pay to provide cars, refrigerators, television sets, and groceries. That physiologic needs operate with great strength to determine behavior is shown by the facts that infants in need of vitamin D choose cod-liver oil over foods without vitamin D[2] and that "civilized" persons have resorted to cannibalism when starvation threatened.[3]

A physiologic determinant of behavior, which may be laid down in the

[1] Jules Massermann, *Principles of Dynamic Psychiatry*, pp. 107–112, W. B. Saunders Company, Philadelphia, 1946.

[2] C. Davis, "Results of Self-selection of Diets by Young Children," *Canadian Medical Association Journal*, vol. 41, p. 257, 1939.

[3] Norman Munn, *Psychology*, 2d. ed., p. 265, Houghton Mifflin Company, Boston, 1951.

genes, is thought to be the type of physique. Although the investigations are still far from conclusive, enough observations and sufficient generalizations have been made to indicate the possibility of a relation between physique and temperament.[1] At least, a student analyzing human responses to symbols cannot afford to be unaware of this influence. In general, individuals who are large of stomach, flabby in muscle, and overrelaxed are thought to be fond of socialized eating and ceremonial occasions. Similarly, they are supposed to be tolerant of others, almost indiscriminate in their affections, and, in turn, eager for approval and affection from others.

The athletically built, on the other hand, prefer action to talk or reflection. The Admiral Halseys, the General George Pattons, the driving football coaches, the "hard-boiled" top sergeants are representative of this class. They are courageous, adventurous, and often callous to the feelings of others as well as to the fine arts. They respond to the motive of power and relish taking risks.

The delicately chiseled individuals, on the other hand, tend to be less moved by either social or physical factors. Generally apprehensive and somewhat unpredictable, they resist social pressure, prefer their privacy, and find it difficult to share ideas or feelings.

Naturally, most individuals have mixtures of these three classes of physique and temperament. At times in many individuals, the various physical characteristics, as well as the variations in temperament, are so inextricably blended that a complete analysis is impossible. On the other hand, after one has had experiences speaking at football banquets, English and art clubs, and honorary scholastic fraternities, he is well aware that not only must he change the ideational content but also the manner of speaking, the appeals to interest, and the refinement or coarseness of language. Furthermore, he develops more and more appreciation of the contributions made by the highly varied but still classifiable types of physique and temperament.

2. CULTURAL NEEDS. Upon basic physiologic needs our human *culture* builds patterns of response. The particular human society into which we are born teaches us how to satisfy our hunger, how to win society's approval and avoid its punishment, when and how to satisfy sexual needs, in what ways to express ourselves, and to what extent we can be

---

[1] See William Sheldon and S. S. Stevens, *The Varieties of Human Temperament,* Harper & Brothers, New York, 1942.

unhampered in our actions and in our thinking. The responses we make during infancy, childhood, adolescence, and early adulthood tend to become more or less fixed, and the symbols which are associated with our satisfactory responses become clustered around habitual responses. These give us our typical ways of thinking and reacting, in other words, our temperaments.

As we indicated in Chap. 8, the organizing of responses or the patterns of behavior, even in such personal behavior as breathing habits, are in a large degree learned from the culture. Motives, too, are learned by the symbols of acceptance or nonacceptance which are applied to unpatterned childish behavior. Would you remove your shoes and sit on the floor when invited to a friend's house? Would you throw refuse upon a stranger passing your door? Would you give away anything a new acquaintance admired? Would you place tight bandages upon your baby's head and leave them there for a year? In some societies these are patterns of response so deeply inculcated that to fail to behave in a similar manner would lead to ostracism.

In this long process the role of authority is, of course, great. Authority, however, is not always present. The parent, the teacher, and the minister, the most common sources of authority, are seldom with the child on the way to school, on the playground, and in the "shack" or at the "hangout." Dominant childhood associates begin to assert their values through reward and punishment. Thus, early in the lives of individuals arise conflicting sources of authority and of symbolic values. To be on the side of the law or against it, to be for tradition or opposed to it becomes an issue. Literature is filled with the accounts of the gap between age (authority-tradition) and youth. Shakespeare's *King Lear*, Balzac's *Père Goriot*, D. H. Lawrence's *Sons and Lovers*, Stevenson's *Crabbed Age and Youth* attest to the conflicting motives between conformance and revolt. History, too, is replete with accounts of young revolutionaries in politics, in science, in literature. The term *Young Turks* has even characterized a group of young reformers in the National Speech Association. The satisfactions derived from early responses lay down patterns of response which are likely to persist. Here again we must emphasize the importance of recognizing the difference between symbolic behavior and nonsymbolic behavior. For example, the one who is against traditional values on the action level becomes a problem child, a disciplinary case, a juvenile delinquent, a criminal, a revolutionary. The one who somehow checks his revolt against authority and tradition at the verbal level is negativistic, troublesome, a crackpot, a reformer, a critic, a complainer.

In mobile and highly labile societies in which authorities change and differ, the people's ideas of what is "tradition," "good form," or "honest" and the ideas of what is "new," "revolutionary," or "poor taste" become hopelessly involved. The sources of authority and freedom, of satisfaction and dissatisfaction, and of motivation are, therefore, wavering and uncertain. The variability of human behavior and the confusion of authority lead to some strange contradictions. Many can be devout followers of traditional systems of ethics and yet not flinch at a questionable but quick profit. They can be devout defenders of Americanism, yet feel free to cheat on a war contract. To become more and more perplexed at the contradictions of human motivation, one only need read the daily newspapers for 2 weeks. Today's metropolitan paper carried the stories of a school superintendent who in 2 years had embezzled $150,000, a university professor who had killed his family, a young and successful doctor who had taken the life of his wife and daughter, a convict who had risked his life for scientific research, a millionaire who had given away his fortune to churches and charities, a factory worker who had been badly burned saving a mother and child from a burning building, and a truck driver who wrecked his automobile carrier and permanently crippled himself to avoid a boy on a bicycle.

These are, of course, the dramatic, the exceptional cases which made the headlines. Yet in every group there will be a large portion of individuals whose daily problem is one of reconciling conflicting motives. To slight study or to strive a little harder, to speak one's mind or to keep silent, to ignore injustice or to strike against it, are commonly experienced motivational conflicts.

CONFLICTING NEEDS CHECK AND ALTER MOTIVATION

Listeners who are receiving advice from a speaker often are hearing admonitions contrary to what they heard the day before. In the modern world, with millions of books, magazines, newspapers, and propaganda sheets pouring from the presses each week and an unceasing supply of talk spilling from the television sets, radios, and talkies, the average listener in his short lifetime is literally bombarded with words by the "old guard," the "Young Turks," the promoters of security, the advocates of "let's-take-a-chance," the proponents of progressive activities in education, the defenders of good, solid substance in our schools. The areas of living are so many that naturally all of us accept upon the word of some authority our course of action. When subjected to advice from contradictory authorities, we find our decisions more difficult. Numerous conflicts between motives arise. In fact, one philosophical writer believes the conflicts are so deep-seated that they reach the very roots of our ways of thinking and that the conflict between systems of thinking leads to general confusion in education, religion, politics, ethics, etc.[1] The speaker needs to be aware that individuals who do have conflicting motives are likely to be vascillating, erratic, tense, and anxious.[2] In these conditions their responses are impulsive, poorly reasoned, and nonadaptive. In controversial speech situations, which according to some writers include over half of all our talking,[3] sensitivity to the motivational conflict is essential, as we shall see in Chap. 15. Without sensitivity to the underlying but often unexpressed conflicts, a speaker or a group leader can not help the individuals find a stronger and more common symbolic bond.

SATISFACTION REINFORCES MOTIVES

Although from the preceding section a student might get the impression that people generally are confused and disorganized, obviously such is not the case. People do live unified and satisfying lives. They do become doctors and scientists. They do build automobiles and airplanes. They do have homes and families. They do support schools, charities, and churches. Thus, in spite of varying degrees of uncertainty and perplexity, main patterns of response and characteristic traits and temperaments are established. These, as we hinted earlier, grow out of previous satisfactions. Nothing succeeds like success. A child keeps clean and pleases his mother. It is easier to be clean the next time. A boy hears the cheers of his playmates as he knocks down another "toughy." Later, when he is grown, he will fight harder and take more blows if the nation goes to war. A little girl recites a poem well, the class applauds, and the teacher beams. Watch her. In a few years she

---

[1] Oliver Reiser, *The Promise of Scientific Humanism*, pp. 6–10, Oskar Priest, New York, 1940.

[2] Bertrand Frohman, *Brief Psychotherapy*, pp. 73–124, Lea & Febiger, Philadelphia, 1948.

[3] A. Craig Baird and Franklin H. Knower, *General Speech*, p. 351, McGraw-Hill Book Company, Inc., New York, 1949.

will likely be acting in high school plays. Later, if she does not continue acting, she will remain interested and feel akin to actresses. These obviously oversimplified and probably overstated interpretations at least make the point that all of us do develop certain main currents of thinking and lay down main courses of action. Words which can touch off those main lines of activity are more likely to evoke a response than are symbols which are irrelevant to them, while words that are counter to them run the danger of evoking resentment, dislike, and even active opposition to the speaker of the words.

MOTIVATIONAL PLANS

If talk, any talk, is to be effective in sharing experiences, in securing accurate information, in giving information or advice, in getting something done, it must take into account the main patterns of response in the persons toward whom it is directed. One does not stop a harassed doctor to ask about a minor scratch. Catch him off guard at the golf club—if you can—and you might dare to. Neither do you ask a mechanic to adjust your carburetor when he is engaged in reassembling a timer. A talker must time and aim his talk carefully if he is to have any chance of evoking the desired responses. To do this he must make some good guesses about what his auditors are like, what they do, when they do it, what their satisfactions are. Although planning the motivation involves guessing, information improves that guessing. With it a speaker can plan how to connect his motives with those of his listeners, so that both he and they may find satisfaction in the talk or in the action proposed by the talk.

Traditionally many systems or plans for analyzing listeners' motives have been devised. Nearly all are helpful, and all, of course, are incomplete, since even while one is analyzing, auditors are changing. The following outline has been as helpful to the beginning student as any we have tried.

MOTIVATIONAL PLAN

I. Purpose of speech situation
II. Listener's probable response patterns
    A. Predominant types of listeners
        1. Physical characteristics
            a. Massive viscera (large abdomen), round chest, flabby
            b. Hard muscles, sturdy, upright
            c. Fragile, slender, delicate, poorly muscled

2. Temperament types
  a. Ceremonious, gregarious, sociable
  b. Assertive, bold, direct, competitive, adventurous
  c. Introvertive, socially inhibited, unpredictable
3. Intellectual interests
  a. Fine arts
  b. Literature
  c. Science
  d. Social science
  e. Athletics and recreation
B. Common social and symbolic bonds which unite the individuals in the audience
  1. Family
  2. Community
  3. Religion
  4. Political
  5. Economic
  6. Social
    a. Fraternal
    b. Recreational
    c. Educational

As we have indicated, the patterns of our social groups reflect the organizational words of our speech. Those organizational words also provide a cultural pattern of motives. To analyze and to know the speech of social groups is to discover the main lines of motivation.

The ethical speaker will attempt to discover his own and his listeners' common purpose, their common symbolic bond. To do this involves the discovery of their principal response patterns, whether they are determined by cultural or physiological factors; and to make this discovery the speaker must inquire about them: Who are they? What is their work? What church do they go to? What is their recreation? What is their general economic status? Their fraternity or lodge? Their home life?

Then the speaker must determine how his thoughts, his set of values, his advice will bring satisfaction to these people he has learned to know. The beginning student often asks how he can do all this. In fact, some beginning students are so much appalled by the seeming immensity that they unconsciously resist all attempts to make a motivational plan. After students recognize the task for what it is—a kind of lifelong systematic study of people, they find it stimulating. Some facts may be learned in the library, others in the psychology laboratory. Most must come from talk with all kinds of people. Samuel Johnson, the English lexicographer, wit, conversationist, critic, essayist, and poet, emphasized this fact 200 years ago. In *The Rambler*[1] he wrote:

Among the numerous requisites that must concur to complete an author, [or orator] few are of more importance than an early entrance into the living world. The seeds of knowledge may be planted in solitude but must be cultivated in public. Argumentation may be taught in colleges and theories formed in retirement; but the artifices of embellishment, and the powers of attraction, can be gained only by general converse. The orator who wears out his days and nights in perpetual research is too apt to lose in his elocution what he adds to his wisdom.

The writer or the speaker who does not invent his topics to suit the beliefs and experiences of his audience will have no "facility of inculcating his speculations, of adapting himself to the various degrees of intellect." He will talk to most unintelligibly and to all unpleasantly.

VALUES IN STUDYING MOTIVES

Although in all truth we must approach the study of motivation with reservation, particularly when we read lists of sure-fire appeals and a simple set of rules on how to influence people, still some effort to understand response patterns of humans must underlie our generalization in sociology, economics, psychology, history, anthropology, and so on. As we study speech further, we shall need to inquire into the motives for substituting symbolic action for direct physical activity, the hidden motives for inhibiting all speech (hysterical mutism), the motives for persistent lying (pseudologia fantastica), the motive for lisping (psychogenic sigmatism), and other speech forms with concealed motivation. Although in the present state of knowledge a satisfactory systematization of motives is impossible, study and observation will awaken us to possible forces we would otherwise fail to observe. In Chap. 14, "Public Address," and in Chap. 15, "Group Discussion," further attention will be given to the direct application of what knowledge we have to specific situations.

Projects for Practice

1. Keep a notebook for 3 days of the times you hear "I want," "I wish," "Give me," etc. Can you classify these expressions of need?

[1] Samuel Johnson, *The Works of Samuel Johnson*, Arthur Murray (ed.), vol. VI, p. 167, London, 1753-1755.

2. Keep a record for 3 days of the instances when acquaintances or friends inhibited wishes because of social taboos or pressures.

3. Keep a record of your observations of minor social conflicts: arguments, quarrels, disagreements, traffic jams. Can you determine motives?

4. For 1 week try to symbolize your main wishes. Write down your desires. At the end of the week, how many were fulfilled? How much thwarting of desires was there?

5. Prepare a 4-minute speech on one of the commonly listed basic drives.

Readings

Barnett, H. G., *Innovation*, chaps. 2-4, McGraw-Hill Book Company, Inc., New York, 1953.

Brembeck, Winston, and William Howell, *Persuasion*, chaps. 4-6, Prentice-Hall, Inc., New York, 1952.

Dewey, Richard, and W. J. Humber, *The Development of Human Behavior*, chap. 7, The Macmillan Company, New York 1951.

Monroe, Alan H., *Principles and Types of Speech*, 3d ed., chap. 10, Scott, Foresman & Company, Chicago, 1949.

STYLE IN SPEECH

Let us suppose that 10 of us are given the same exercise as an assignment in speaking. The gist of our mutual task is a topic sentence and 10 pieces of evidence, and with these in common we are to make speeches independently to sections of our class. Each of us frames the best possible speech that he can prepare, all having the same thesis. We do not confer; we make our speeches. Unknown to us, recordings are made, and the 10 records are brought back to us for comparison. We find much similarity among the recordings. We hear the same subject over and over, and the 10 pieces of evidence are in each recording. But we are struck with the dissimilarities from one recording to another. There are differences in voice, of course; we take these for granted and ignore them with little effort. The differences that arouse our curiosity in these particular replayings of the records are matters neither of voice nor of logic. One of us used questions again and again. Another seemed especially to take his audience into his confidence with "you," "we," "I," and "let us"; his sentence: "I took a little poll among our fellow students last night, and—you may find this hard to swallow—I found. . . ." was both effective and singular among the speeches. In fact, the 10 of us were as different in the ways we phrased our speeches as we are in facial features. This difference was one of *style*, the phrases and sets of phrases, the sentences and sets of sentences in which we said our principal idea, subordinate ideas, and 10 pieces of evidence.

STYLE SPANS LANGUAGE

Obviously, style is closely related to language, a topic that we treated in Chap. 5 principally as a set of code symbols. Our interest in the earlier treatment was with single words as they might be tallied in a word count; *style* has broader compass. It includes the phrase, sentence, paragraph, and passage, and is intimately entwined with the concepts of the speaker. It includes the tendency that a person may have to say "for example" or "remindful of the time . . . ," to cite *particulars* and *facts* in support of assertions, and to say "like winding a watch," or "poor, penniless, pitiful. . . . " If counting were to be done with respect to style, the tally marks would summate separate categories of sentences of particular lengths, of questions and statements, anecdotes, figures of speech, and the like. Indeed a potent difference between *word counts* and *stylistic counts* would lie in the decisions that would be left to the enumerator.

In the counting of words, the clerk would follow a few rules like those of Project 2 in Chap. 5. An enumerator of stylistic events, however, would first decide what kinds of occurrences were to be counted. He would then have to decide, line by line, whether the event occurred. These decisions would be difficult. We have an interesting illustration of a discrepancy that arises from this kind of judgment in this book. We cited in Chap. 4 a study in which the most frequent length of a sentence in classroom speeches by college students was 12 words. Also in Chap. 3 we presented in tabular form some results that related to another extensive study of classroom speeches.[1] In this study the 6,688 words were attributed to 325 sentences, nearly 21 words per sentence. It is almost unthinkable that the two sets of college students differed this much in the average length of their sentences. Rather, the investigators probably differed in their rules about what constitutes a sentence in transcribed material.

THE SPEAKER AND HIS STYLE

A style in speech is unique to a speaker; it is personal. The distinguished French naturalist, Buffon, addressed the French Academy in the middle of the eighteenth century on a subject that has been translated, "Style is the man himself."[2] This thesis has remained popular, and to accept it precludes an atomistic enumeration of the characteristics of good style. Buffon's principle suggests an inherent unity among *idea, language,* and *speaker.* We take no exception from this. The speaker is a bundle of experiences, and his ideas and the sentences in which he

[1] J. C. Kelly and M. D. Steer, "Revised Concept of Rate," *Journal of Speech and Hearing Disorders,* vol. 14, p. 223, 1949.

[2] G. L. L. de Buffon, "Discours sur le style" (1753), in *Pages Choisies,* pp. 66–74, Librairie Larousse, Paris, 1934.

states them will naturally emanate from the same fountainhead of experience. Figuratively, allowing for some intermediate reflecting, the experience does the talking. We may be sure that rural living gave rise to the language of "You can't make a silk purse out of a sow's ear," "Don't look a gift horse in the mouth," and "sowing wild oats." The experience of an older culture than ours gave rise to the question, "Is the game worth the candle?" One speaker—not an entire community— put the final touch to each of these sayings, and his language, we may be sure, arose from his experiences—his patchwork of neural pathways. The preservation of these old sayings is quite another matter. We may suppose that "we, the people," through successive generations, found in each phrase an equivalent of a single word and learned the phrase and its use in the same manner that we learned the remainder of our vocabulary. We have judged the words and the idea that is aptly expressed by the language to be ideally blended. The style of the phrase was given it by a singular person. The continual employment of such phrases may be equally singular to your style. You may be saying, in effect, "My experience also leads me to that phrase." The language of any exchange of ideas is personal, drawn from a reservoir of experiences as we have abstracted them.

We shall first examine aspects of the informal, untutored style.

1. REPETITIVE PATTERNS. Style is learned, of course, and comes to be the framework for the habitual utterances of the speaker. This is notably obvious with a person's expletives and slang. A listener notes these expressions quickly as they recur, and if the listener is given to mimicry, he exploits the habitual phrases of his subject. The recurrent aspect of informal style is remindful of *probability*, which was treated with respect to language in Chap. 5 as interpretation of the different frequencies with which words occur. Indeed, the expletives in an individual's speech are not only amenable to a frequency tabulation and a *probability* interpretation but, more than likely, can be predicted to occur in a particular place in the sentence, and the course of the remainder of the sentence is notably subject to probability. Once a particular speaker embarks upon an oral sentence, how many words will he utter before he finishes the sentence? What are the chances that the subject of the sentence will precede the predicate? How many sentences will be spoken before an example is introduced? Before a story is told? These questions relate to aspects of an individual's habitual oral style. Unless a deliberate plan to change the style is introduced, the habits of

one year in these regards are the habits of another year. This consistency in style leads to observations like, "Yes, Bill *would* say that," "You know who I mean, the lad who always says, 'thunderation,'" "Birdie got involved in one of his long sentences and I couldn't get away," or "Ray only gave a three-joke speech tonight."

a. Type-token Ratio. It is not obvious why some speakers should repeat their words more frequently than other speakers do; yet we are measurably different in this regard as we are different in our build, features, gait, or fingerprints. A measure of this feature of our language is the type-token ratio.[1] This ratio is only an arithmetical determination. The number of different words, or *types*, in a passage is divided by the total number of words, or *tokens*, that are used. With passages of about 500 words, this ratio tends to be a reliable index for an individual and to vary systematically from one person to another. This is as though a neural pattern were established by the saying of a word and as though the pattern called for the re-use of the symbol at the first opportunity.

b. Parallel Sequences. With appropriate measures, other repetitive patterns may be disclosed that are differentiating among individuals. For example, a series of similar phrases, like the ones in the passage from Samuel (Sunset) Cox in Chap. 11, is frequently recommended as an attribute of style in speaking. The construction is sometimes called *parallel.* Except as a speaker encourages himself to employ this structure and thereby alters his untutored style, the supposition is reasonable that the form recurs for much the same reason that a word reappears in a style that has a low type-token ratio.

One repetitive pattern occurs in alliterations, that is, a series of successive words that begin with the same sound; another is exemplified by a series of modifiers either preceding or following a noun or verb; and some speakers tend to repeat words or phrases immediately upon saying them the first time. Interestingly, the series is often a pattern of three: three alliterative words, three adjectives, or three phrases—like the series that you read only now. These patterns of language have received general approval from rhetorical critics and have been observed to narrow a gap between prose and poetry.

The question is interesting whether the employment or avoidance of the repetitive patterns is the more difficult. Herrick, in his speech "A

[1] H. Fairbanks, "Studies in Language Behavior. II. The Quantitative Differentiation of Samples of Spoken Language," *Psychological Monographs*, vol. 56, pp. 17–38, 1944.

Neurologist Makes Up His Mind" (Appendix A), refers to individuals who suffer from aphasia. Frequently, when these brain-damaged patients are relearning speech, they cannot do other than repeat a word or phrase that they have succeeded in saying. "Good morning," when said once, is continued until it "wears out" or until the patient is given some help in stopping the pattern, for example, until a finger is put to his lips. A therapist who requests "count from one to four" may hear "1, 2, 3, 4, 1, 2, 3, 4, 1, 2, 3, 4 . . . " This "press to continue" may be related to some normal patterns of casual speech, as "good morning, good morning," "no, no, no," "I think so; yes, I think so." One of the properties of the cortex apparently is a capacity to inhibit the continuation of a verbal pattern that has been released into action.

The following question is sometimes asked: Is the person who stutters unable to make the next sound—this is the usual view—or unable to stop making the sound he is "stuttering"? These are challenging queries. Should the pressure toward the repetitive pattern in normal language yield to measurement, the resulting data might put some of our traditional merits of language in an odd category. Many of our figures of speech and much that goes with poetry and repetitive phenomena —supposedly difficult to achieve—might be found to exemplify our weaknesses and not our strengths in producing language. One is reminded of George Bernard Shaw's statement in the preface of one of his plays.[1]

It may be asked why I have written *The Admirable Bashville* in blank verse. My answer is that I had but a week to write it in. Blank verse is childishly easy and expeditious (hence, by the way, Shakespear's copious output), that by adopting it I was enabled to do within the week what would have cost me a month in prose.

c. Repeating Ourselves. The reminiscing storyteller who repeats his list of anecdotes in the manner of a practiced monologuist is usually excused on the basis of defective memory. Has he really forgotten that he told the story earlier? Perhaps so, and in this event one wonders whether the story was told the first time to impart information or to satisfy an urge to talk. Either urge to talk or fondness for the story—the kind of fondness that attends favorite songs—would be as plausible an explanation of the repeating behavior as is faulty memory.

[1] George Bernard Shaw, *The Admirable Bashville*, p. 7, Dodd, Mead & Company, Inc., New York, 1917. Used by permission.

2. SPILLING OVER. In somewhat the same vein that the repetitive pattern in style may be a tribute to man's frailty instead of his ingenuity, we suggest the further possibility that the mere utterance of language patterns may frequently fulfill some need of the individual. Talking aloud to oneself is a popular pastime, more so than it is credited with being. When talking aloud to oneself is the topic of a discussion, no one ever asks, "What is it?" In fact, an awareness that people talk to themselves seems to be universal. The practice is commonly termed childish, which may account for our apparent desire to explain it away. The popular rationalization is that this behavior is really social, for there is always an imagined audience.

Talking to oneself—the mere uttering of language, alone—may serve as self-entertainment like whistling, whittling, and some fishing and hunting. Another example of language for personal satisfaction has roots in a study of the oral language of schizophrenia.[1] Structured interviews were conducted among hospitalized patients and their responses were recorded. The language of the responses was analyzed for (1) core materials, or the essential words of the patients' ideas, (2) contributing modifiers, or helpful but nonessential words, and (3) meaningless material, or spilling-over words. As much as one-third of the verbal flow of the patients was comprised of irrelevant words. The professional staff had surmised that the patients seem to need to talk and had noted that, after a gush or oral sense mingled with spilling over, the patients were composed. Many aspects of normal behavior have been understood better as extreme deviations have been found in abnormal patterns. Most of us have felt some shock upon hearing recordings of what we say. Students and teachers alike may study those surprising recordings that have been made and try to find how much spilling-over language is there.

Indeed, personal satisfaction is a fairly common accompaniment of speaking. The parties at which "I had a swell time" are often the ones at which we were very spontaneous with talk. Our examples have their roots in conversation. Does the satisfaction that attends verbal flow in "little speech," in conversation, carry over to the platform? The biographies of orators often attest to the statement, "He was a lively conversationalist" or imply, "He dominated the small talk of the dining room."

[1] James J. Calvert, "Verbal Behavior as a Predictor of Personality Syndromes," unpublished Ph.D. dissertation, The Ohio State University, Columbus, Ohio, 1950.

3. SUMMARY. In concluding this discussion of the private view of speech, its repetitive patterns and excess verbalization, let us reflect about whether the similarities among the manifold occasions on which we talk outweigh the dissimilarities. Will our motivations that lead to conversation propel us toward other kinds of speaking? The speaker, with his attitudes toward important issues, with his experiences and reservoir of language, his propensity for wit or gravity, and his pride or modesty—he is surely about the same individual for any one season of life. His listeners may be his cronies in a conversation or strangers in an audience; there may be many or few of these listeners. They include employees and employers; but irrespective of the differences, these listening people have grown up in the same culture, speak the same language, heard the same broadcasts, know the same brands. In short they are people who have topics and ideas in common with each other and with the speaker. The bond between this speaker and his listeners is strengthened by his private patterns of language. These are likely to be similar in gravity and wit, economy and waste of words, in sketchiness or completeness from one circumstance of talking to another. The elements that encompass conversation are likely to extend beyond.

The style of oral utterance is highly personal. We have focused our attention on the speaker's natural style, speakers who drive school buses, teach in programs of civil defense, have coke dates at the student union, and give advice to freshmen on how to study. Their style of speech is purely personal, and only a little more practiced version of their style of speech of a year ago. Our purpose in this section has been to understand this aspect of speech and to appreciate how deeply imbedded it is in speaking behavior, and to consider further the possibility that style reveals some of the motivations that impel an individual to speak.

THE LISTENER AND THE SPEAKER'S STYLE

We noted earlier that style in speech is determined somewhat by the listener. Let us take another view of the social nature of speech and pursue the listener's contribution to a speaker's style.

1. THE SOCIAL INFLUENCE. In effect, the speaker announces his views to listeners in his successive statements. Thus, the language, the fabric of style, arises from his set of *personal* abstractions and is directed to people who represent other *personal* sets of abstractions, neural

pathways, or meanings as treated in Chaps. 6 and 7. This inherently social character of speech is revealed in our most frequently used words: the, of, and, to, a, in, that, it, is, *I*, for, be, was, as, *you*, with, *he*, on, have, by, not, at, this, are, *we*, *his*, but, *they*—28 words that account for more than one-third of the words that we use.[1] Six of these most popular words—those that are italicized—refer to people. No word specifies any other life or object. The *personal* words are the most specific of the lot. Speech is social, always!

2. THE PROJECTIVE INFLUENCE. At least one principal objective of speech is to gain acceptance or approval by our listeners. Our endeavors in speaking lead inevitably to listeners; thus it would seem to follow, "Know your listeners." But this dictum cannot be achieved. Herrick assures us, in Section IV of "A Neurologist Makes Up His Mind" (Appendix A), that he does not understand his wife's mind. We cannot *know* precisely what a listener, other than oneself, experiences when he hears the word "purple," when he bites a cherry seed, when he misses a train, or gets a diploma. Our best guess is that his inner experiences are much like ours. "Purple means to me the shade of grandmother's dress. I have that shade in mind." "When I bite on a cherry seed by accident I experience a feeling like the world has let me down, one of the most surprising and disappointing feelings that I know." From our experience with the projects of Chap. 6 particularly, we know that these deeply imbedded personal feelings cannot be said and heard with exact correspondence in meaning. Listeners are neither like each other nor like us. "Purple" is not the hue of grandmother's dress, except for one person. Some listeners do not go to football games, do not read comic books, do not like history, do not know parental love, do not belong to your church or any church, do not fear cherry seeds, automobile accidents, horses, atomic bombs. We are in a baffling predicament.

3. THE INFLUENCE OF UNDERSTANDING. Our style is personal; our listener's style is personal. Your awareness of this circumstance is in itself an achievement. It is a leavening influence upon a phraseology that might otherwise be didactic. The humility that is engendered by this awareness often occasions a language pattern of "it-seems-to-me." Rigid definitions are thus avoided, and with them the style of the positive statement is lost. Rigid style is quite as likely to impede understanding or meaning as to foster it. Consider these examples: "Did you call

[1] Godfrey Dewey, *Relative Frequency of English Speech Sounds,* **p. 19,** Harvard University Press, Cambridge, Mass., 1923.

Jim a *scholar?* I'd say he is a *pupil."* "This is not *reorganization* but a new mode of *functioning."* "Ours is not a *democratic* government but a *Republic."* These lecturelike pronouncements are not in keeping with an awareness of the listeners' part in communication; no awareness of the listeners' diversity of styles has modified the positive statement. In effect, our ongoing language becomes a series of puzzles to be solved by listeners immediately—if at all. It is small wonder that humor comes into speaking, indeed that it makes up a considerable portion of the discourse of the stage, dining room, and platform. The humor, of course, is funny in varying degrees among the listeners, and this again is humorous. At the same time we suspect that the overt act of laughing is one of very few on which the speaker can rely as a sign that his style is in some degree comprehensible and effective.

4. SOLUTION I: PERSPICUITY. Style must be as clear as possible. This would surely mean that the language should be ordinary words. But common language is only a beginning. Repetition of the idea with other words is helpful, indeed simply repeating the same word two or three times may serve to tell the listener, "The essence of my view lies in this word; please carry it away with you." The idea can also be repeated and thereby clarified with an *illustration.* The words "for example" imply that the speaker is not going to carry his ideas any further for the moment. He is backing up to say the last idea again more clearly, for he is about to use specificity. The *comparison* serves a similar purpose. The idea is retold, this time in a different context and presumably one that is already familiar to the listener.

Frequently, the effect of the comparison can be caught on the fly with no backward reach in time. The comparison is built into the first saying of the idea through a *figure of speech,* for example, a *simile* or the *metaphor.* There are numerous figures of speech. You use many of them, probably. Some classifications continue with *figures of language,* but the two sets of *figures* become confusing if extended through several categories. Broadly speaking, all of them serve the end of clarity. Enough segments of your idea and sufficient associations between your idea and your listener's experience will make your idea clear. The unknown and unfamiliar object or the unfamiliar concept becomes comprehensible through the swift analogy to a familiar object or concept. Fragments of the whole idea and facts about the fragments kindle an understanding among your listeners, and when they have sufficient facts, evidence, illustrations, and the like, your ideas approach clarity.

Objects are more vivid, as a rule, than words about the objects; hence the inestimable value of "Here is the book end that . . . ," or "This is a shin guard that . . . ," or "These wounds I got . . . "

5. SOLUTION II: INTEREST. The second attribute that the listener requires from language is that it be interesting. We approached humor above from the viewpoint of the frustrated speaker who acknowledged that didactic prose was a little silly in a situation where the complete transfer of thought was impossible anyway. We come to humor now as a way of gaining attention. However, humor is only one way of holding attention. Indeed, as the cook in the restaurant is reputed to have said, "Even chicken can get tiresome." The speaker himself is the most interesting "event" in a conversation, discussion, or speech. He is thousands of miles of telephone wire encompassed in a few cubic feet, and every segment of the wire stores experiences that are singular to one person. The *anecdote* is one way this experience is converted to fact again and one device by which style is enlivened.

We have treated probability with respect to the word that is coming next and again with relation to the personal traits of style. We suggest that it also relates to interest values in style. By way of illustration, a study that was cited in Chap. 4 showed that readers may be able to detect both where a word had been omitted from 12-word sentences and what the original word had been. Thus the progress of the sentence followed a familiar pattern and could be guessed to a surprising degree. Possibly when a story is described with the words, "It took an odd twist," the speaker is saying something important about style. The interest value of a story may well be related to the probability-improbability of the outcome. Is not that conversationalist interesting who "outsmarts" you, who tells a story where you least expect it, who reverses the usual order of a pair of common words? The classroom lecturer who seems dull—is he the one whose style is entirely probable? We should guess so, and while making this guess, we should suggest the inherent interest value of the *concrete* or *specific* over the *abstract* or *general*, of the *hyperbole*, of the *anecdote* and *illustration*. They are events in speech that can hardly be guessed before they happen.

STYLE IS APPROPRIATE

The final topic of the preceding section suggested the possibility that interest values are associated with stylistic events of low probability. In the present section we must add the cautious note: *within limits.*

Style in speech is somewhat stereotyped by the form of the speech and the occasion, and *stereotyped* implies a condition in which events are more predictable or probable, not less so. Original speech occurs in innumerable circumstances, but the same style of speech is not appropriate for all of these. Each of the 14 instances listed below exemplifies a *form* of speech: conversation, discussion, debate, eulogy, or the like. An occasion is also implied. The following quotations are small segments of the meanings.

1. A conversation: "Where does the line fence belong?"
2. A scout meeting: "This is the way to bandage a broken finger."
3. A telephone: "Should the budget committee make provision for a paid assistant secretary?"
4. A conversation: "Welcome to our neighborhood; I hope you will attend the Tenfield Heights Church."
5. A conference: "How can we reduce the stock of luggage?"
6. A conference: "Should the powers of the executive branch be curtailed?"
7. A radio speech: "If you are registered, vote tomorrow."
8. An assembly address: "Use your summer vacation to further your academic objectives."
9. A demonstration: "This is the way we reduce the tension in the muscles of the arm."
10. Along the side line: "That tackle cuts left when he lines up with his feet like this."
11. A testimonial dinner: "Jim Lawson not only directed a successful campaign for our united appeals, but . . . "
12. A memorial service: "The four students who . . . "
13. A class reunion: "Who put the ducks in the swimming pool?"
14. A strike meeting: "Are we getting anywhere with present negotiations?"

Any suggestion that the improbable is so linked with interest that these statements might be shifted randomly among the speaking situations is preposterous. Convention has established decorum, propriety, or good taste in speaking, and violations are egregious blunders.

STYLE, CONCEPT, AND UTTERANCE

The phrases and sentences of speech turn thought into language, and the voice converts the language into sound waves. In the main, we have proceeded atomistically to treat concept formation, voice, and language as individual components of the process of speaking. The present exception to the principle is deliberate and is both (1) an example of concurrent treatment of related aspects of speech and (2) an attempt to suggest one relationship between style and the central nervous system.

The phrases and sentences of style are spoken as units of several words. These units exist acoustically as periods of sound between pauses and physiologically as breath pulses between inhalations.[1] A suggestion that concept formation and the unit of language that lies between pauses may be intimately related is offered by Marcel Verzeano.[2] He reports that Stanley Cobb ascertained the length of patients' phrases before and after lobotomies were performed, an operation in which fibers of the brain which connect the frontal cortex with subcortical structures are severed. The operation reduced the length of the patients' phrases and increased their number. Verzeano continues:

One possible explanation of this phenomenon might be that severing a certain number of association fibers in the frontal lobes limits the complexity of the concepts which the subject may form and thus the length of the phrases by which those concepts are expressed is also limited. On the other hand, in order to transmit the same amount of information with shortened units, the patient has to increase his number per unit time.

The alteration of phrase length in this manner seems to us to have tremendous significance. *Phrase* and *sentence* have been used in this chapter in their traditional meanings: groups of words and a complete idea. No dimension of a concept has been implied heretofore. Possibly the 12-word sentence that typified student speaking indicates an extent of an idea, and the pause-language-pause sequence in speech follows a time pattern that accommodates the central nervous system and is related to concept formation specifically. Verzeano has also investigated the flow of speech through quantifying the phrases that lie between pauses. But what is a pause? How much time must lapse in the flow of speech to constitute a pause? Verzeano delimits the pause arbitrarily and assigns it a singular value from one analysis to another.[3] He made successive analyses of the same sample of unrehearsed speech from

[1] R. H. Stetson, *Motor Phonetics: A Study of Speech Movement in Action*, pp. 1–9, North-Holland Publishing Company, Amsterdam, Netherlands, for Oberlin College, 1951.

[2] Marcel Verzeano, "Time Patterns in Speech for Normal Subjects," *Journal of Speech and Hearing Disorders*, vol. 15, pp. 197–201, 1950.

[3] Marcel Verzeano, "Time Patterns of Speech for Normal Subjects. II," *Journal of Speech and Hearing Disorders*, vol. 16, pp. 346–350, 1951.

eight speakers and used varying times from o.1 to o.8 second of silence
to indicate a pause. He found approximately 60 "phrases" per minute
when he considered a pause as any silence exceeding o.1 second. His
electronic tally was really of pauses, not phrases. Since each pause might
be viewed as terminating a phrase, we shall refer to the *phrases per
minute*. There were 30 phrases per minute when the pause was considered to be o.2 second, 20 phrases per minute with an o.5 second pause,
and 12 phrases per minute with an o.8 second pause as the minimum
separation time. Obviously, with short separation times between phrases
or units of speech there would be relatively many phrases, and each
would be short. Verzeano found the average length of the phrase to
be o.77 second when the phrase was the interval of speech between
pauses of at least o.1 second. However, when lapses of o.8 second were
the minimum breaks to count as pauses, the phrases were, on the average, 4.3 seconds long.

The segments, units, or phrases of our discontinuous flow of speech
are obviously relative. Their parameters depend on the definition that
we assign to the boundaries. When the minimum boundaries of a phrase
are taken to be any interruption that is about one-half the time that
we consume in saying one syllable, the average length of a continuous
pattern of speech is about three-fourths of a second, the time required
for us to say three or four syllables. Is this the time span of a concept?
On the other hand, when we say that a break, in order to count as a
break, is at least as long as the time we would spend in saying "seventy-
seven" or "runway five right," the continuous pattern of speech is
about the length in number of syllables of the following lines:

> The time has come, the Walrus said,
> To talk of many things:
> Of shoes—and ships—and sealing wax—
> Of cabbages—and kings—

Is this the length of a concept in talking? The phrase in this instance is
about 50 per cent longer than the 12-word sentences that were found to
be common in classroom speeches.

The impact of this discussion lies in the possibility that the scope, or
magnitude, of the mental sweep that accompanies, or *is*, concept formulation, and at the same time encompasses the process of coding the
concept into language, may be amenable to measurement. In this event,
all of us will want to reassess the importance of fluency in speaking.

SUMMARY

Our ideas are expressed in a time sequence, a succession of words. We can hardly imagine that our nervous system is generating words one by one with the orderliness of a conveyor belt. Rather, concepts are presumably generated, usually fully worded. These groupings of words are unique to the person who is originating the speech. They comprise his style. When this style is untutored, a notable repetition of words and phrase structures is characteristically present.

We strive to improve the untutored style and, in part, we add more repetitive patterns. Our most effective improvements in style may result from our efforts to extend our natural clarity and the traits of our style that evoke interest among our listeners.

The occasion on which the speech occurs imposes restrictions upon our language. These constitute appropriateness and call for suiting the language to the idea and both to the occasion. Appropriateness in style is learned behavior, is somewhat unique to each culture, and serves to maintain the status of the probable word, sentence, and idea over the improbable.

Projects for Practice

1. Identify speakers whom you would expect to say something like the following and formulate another list from whom these phrases would seem incongruous.

   a. I am reminded of Abraham Lincoln's remark. . . .

   b. That view looks like one that I once saw through binoculars. In our assault on Sicily. . . .

   c. There are 47 colors in that window.

   d. The quarterback was supposed to stand still with the ball for one second. Our watches show that he moved at 0.7 second.

   e. Load your eyeballs with the maroon job.

   f. For Wednesday, read Chapter 7.

   g. If you feel thwarted and frustrated by somewhat jaundiced glances from your colleagues. . . .

   h. The kid took the count all right.

   i. That would depend on whether you have relative or absolute loss in mind.

   j. Just to remind you, as though it made any difference whatsoever, whichever road you take from the Old Oak Corner you are apt to find army worms if you will take the time to stop your fancy automobile and look over the fence into a stubble field all right.

2. Prepare a series of quotations that seem to you to typify persons whom your classmates know well. What is the percentage of correct identifications? If you read the phrases aloud, try to avoid mimicry, at least until you discover that the words alone do not carry the meaning.

3. Note the personal references in the speeches of Appendix A, particularly (a) the first section of Herrick's speech and the reference he makes later to his experimentation, (b) the references Lowell makes to his relationship with his school, and (c) the personal pronouns in Yeager's speech.

4. Compare the number of personal pronouns per 100 words in two speeches in Appendix A. Compare these numbers with ones you obtain from two newspaper editorials.

5. Determine your type-token ratio from the transcription of your record in Chap. 5. The sample is too small to be reliable but will suffice for a comparison within your class.

6. The lines of a play are written as dialogue and simulate conversation. Compare the style of a few scenes from modern plays with the style of observed conversation.

7. Study the following examples of public address. The *notes* relative to style are incomplete. Add to them.

Words	*Notes*
HENRY CLAY: "He my master! He my master! He my master! Sir, I would not own him for my slave."	Repeated phrase. Exclamations. Personal language. Low type-token ratio. Figurative language. Terse. Contempt.
JOHN C. CALHOUN: "I have now, Senators, done my duty in expressing my opinions fully, freely and candidly, on this solemn occasion. In doing so, I have been governed by the motives which have governed me in the stages of the slavery question since its commencement. I have exerted myself, during the whole period, to arrest it, with the intention of saving the union if it could be done; and if it could not, to save the section where it has pleased Providence to cast my lot, and which I sincerely believe has justice and the Constitution on its side."	Personal language. Varied sentence length. Three modifiers following verb. Clear. Value concepts: duty, justice, constitutionality. Figurative language.

HENRY GRADY: " . . . that somehow or other we have caught the sunshine in the bricks and mortar of our homes, and have builded therein not one ignoble prejudice or memory."

Personal language. Figurative language, including details in the abstracting (bricks and mortar).

RUFUS CHOATE: "I say that there is not an occupation of civilized life, from the making of laws and poems and histories, down to the opening of New Jersey oysters with a broken jackknife, that is not better done by a bright than a dull man, by a quick than a slow mind, by an instructed man than a gross and simple man, by a prudent, thoughtful, and careful man than by a light and foolish one."

Long sentence. Repetition. Modifiers (one critic observed that Choate typically "drove a substantive and eight"). Incongruity or "lack of probability."

8. Find four examples of style that seem interesting to you and try to account for the interest value.

9. Find illustrations in contemporary speeches of sentences that are (a) loose, periodic; (b) single, compound; (c) long, short; (d) declarative, interrogative; and (e) ones that contain parallel constructions within them. The textbook from which you studied composition may suggest other categories of sentences that you can illustrate.

10. In the third paragraph of the following passage Wendell Johnson offers an interesting basis for the criticism of public address.[1] Do you know cases that support the suggested view? Can you prepare a paragraph that illustrates more than one level of abstraction? Review Chap. 8 for ideas about this.

How does a speaker manage to sound "dull"? If you try to recall the dullest speakers you have heard it is quite likely that you will find that they tended strongly to pitch everything they said at about the same level of abstraction. In general, speakers are dull because either they seldom rise above the level of *detailed* description, and so leave one with an undirected feeling of "So what?" or they seldom descend to the level of description, and consequently leave one with the disappointment that comes from having got nothing when presumably something had been promised. In either case one feels frustrated. . . .

[1] Wendell Johnson, *People in Quandaries*, pp. 276–278, Harper & Brothers, New York, 1946. Used by permission.

When we experience such reactions, we refer to them obliquely by saying that the speaker was dull.

And how does a speaker manage to sound "interesting"? It is a common notion that a speaker is interesting if he talks about something in which the listener is already interested. Teachers of public speaking tend to put a great stress on the importance of "choosing the subject," so that it will be well-suited to the audience. Now, a moment's reflection will serve readily to remind you of the many dull speeches you have heard on subjects in which you were definitely interested. . . .

If you will observe carefully the speakers you find to be interesting, you are very likely to find that they play, as it were, up and down the levels of abstraction quite as a harpist plays up and down the strings of her harp. There is a fairly systematic order about it, but there is variability as well. A harpist who lingers too long on one string offends our ear; just so, the speaker who remains too long on the same general level of abstraction offends our evaluative processes—no matter what his subject may be.

11. Explain and exemplify: vividness, the concrete, direct discourse, the fable, the parable, nuance words, and at least four other elements of style. Suggestion: You may start with Herrick's phrase "three-pint capacity of a human brain" (Appendix A) and proceed to find several more elements of style in the speeches of Yeager and Lowell.

12. Laughing was described as an *overt* sign that a speaker is effective. What are others? What ones have you experienced as a speaker? What kind of evidence from other people gives Herrick some confidence that he is understanding them? (Appendix A, Section IV of "A Neurologist Makes Up His Mind.")

13. The mixed metaphor has been frowned upon by literary critics. Under what circumstances might the mixed metaphor hold advantages over the sustained metaphor? Notice Herrick's use of "marriage and divorce" in successive sentences (Appendix A).

14. Note and evaluate the use of questions in Yeager's speech (Appendix A). Questions that are answered by the speaker are called *direct;* the ones he asks but does not answer are called *rhetorical.* Does Yeager employ either kind exclusively?

15. The following game has been used for measuring a basic characteristic in language, the amount of information per symbol.[1] You may find the game revealing as you work with the idea of probability in connection with language. Select a phrase or sentence, for example, "The glass is colored." Ask

---

[1] C. E. Shannon, "Prediction and Entropy of Printed English," *Bell System Technical Journal*, vol. 30, pp. 50–64, 1951.

another student, not a member of your class, to guess the successive letters. Count "space"—the space between words—as a 27th letter. With each guess of a letter tell your partner "right" or "wrong; the letter is ___." The more wrong guesses you get, the more improbable the actual events would seem to be. You would want many "guessers" before you generalized much. How probable are the words "oysters" and "broken jack-knives" in the Choate passage of Project 7? We would guess that no one would expect those particular words to be in the sentence.

16. Cite instances of inappropriate style that have come to your attention. Which error is the worse, levity where solemnity is the order of the day or the reverse?

17. Humorous speeches are rare on the floor of the Congress of the United States. Notable exceptions include Private John Allen's "Fish Hatchery for Tupelo" and "The Expense of Burying a Congressman," James Proctor Knott's "The Glories of Duluth," and Thomas Corwin's "In Reply to General Crary." Members of the class will report on these speeches. Discuss the place of humor in legislative speeches. Earlier we suggested that a speaker's style tends to be consistent. An interesting exception to this was exemplified by Thomas Corwin. He did not speak much as a member of Congress, but of the speeches he gave there, only the "Reply to General Crary" was humorous.

18. We suspect that the elaboration of the section "Style Is Appropriate" contained no surprises for you; in other words, the content was almost entirely predictable. You could have passed an examination on the topic without reading the section. The balance between the improbable—highly informative—and the appropriate is difficult to maintain. Turn back through this book and note passages that were surprises.

19. You may have learned laws in connection with your high school or college courses, Ohm's law, Boyle's law, Archimedes' principle, etc. What is unique in the style of a law? Here are some "laws" that grew in a university circle. Do they meet your criteria for the style of a law?

    a. Stroud's first law: The reason people eat what they do for breakfast is that they're not wide enough awake yet to think.

    b. Johnson's law: One thing leads to another.

    c. Harlow's law: Practice consumes time even though improvement in performance fails to occur.

    d. Lewis's law: If you talk about any theory often enough, you will somehow come to believe it yourself.

    e. Brown's law: Buttered toast always falls so as to do the greatest amount of damage.

    f. Davis's law: The way to live a long time is to get an incurable disease and treat it.

g. Adam's law: **There's more to vision than meets the eye.**

h. Dahlstrom's law: There is small comfort in large differences beyond the third decimal place.

20. Discuss the validity of the following paragraph:[1]

It has long since been observed that emotion introduces rhythmicity in speech:

If his emotions rise during the course of his words, his rhythm, by repetition of words and phrases and by other methods, begins to approach the regularity of poetic rhythm. All great orations indicate this, as the orator warms to his work. He never reaches, except in flashes, the actual regularity of metric pattern, but he is aimed in that direction. If the emotions reach a white heat it will be difficult for him to avoid a regularity in essence metric.

21. The excerpt from Lewis Carroll's *Through the Looking-glass* attributes—in our estimation—short concepts and slow concept formation to the Walrus. Read the lines aloud in a manner to suggest that your ability to form concepts and to say them in language is taxed by the long phrases between the dashes. What is your guess of the length of phrase that you "think" at one time?

Readings

Brewster, William T. (ed.), *Representative Essays on the Theory of Style*, The Macmillan Company, New York, 1928.

Brigance, William Norwood, *Speech Composition*, Appleton-Century-Crofts, Inc., New York, 1937.

——— (ed.), *A History and Criticism of American Public Address*, McGraw-Hill Book Company, Inc., New York, 1943.

Goodrich, C. A., *Select British Eloquence*, Harper & Brothers, New York, 1852.

Hudson, Hoyt H., "De Quincey on Rhetoric and Public Speaking," *Studies in Rhetoric and Public Speaking in Honor of James Albert Winans*, Appleton-Century-Crofts, Inc., New York, 1925.

———, *The Epigram in the English Renaissance*, Princeton University Press, Princeton, N.J., 1947.

Pyles, Thomas, *Words and Ways of American English*, Random House, Inc., New York, 1952.

Reid, Loren D., "'Private John' Allen: A Humorist in Politics," *Quarterly Journal of Speech*, vol. 28, pp. 414–421, 1942.

Sanford, W. Paul, *English Theories of Public Address*, 1530–1828, H. L. Hedrick, Columbus, Ohio, 1938.

[1] C. Wood, *The Craft of Poetry*, E. P. Dutton & Co., Inc., New York, 1929, quoted in Verzeano, "Time Patterns of Speech for Normal Subjects," *Journal of Speech and Hearing Disorders*, vol. 15, p. 199, 1950.

Spencer, Herbert, "The Philosophy of Style," *Essays Scientific, Political, and Speculative*, vol. 2, pr. 333–369, D. Appleton & Company, Inc., New York, 1891.

Wallace, Karl, "On Analogy: Redefinition and Some Implications," in *Studies in Speech and Drama in Honor of Alexander M. Drummond*, H. A. Wichelns and others, Cornell University Press, Ithaca, N.Y., 1944.

11

THE SPEAKER'S GESTURES AND BEARING

A feature of speech is its acoustic-auditory character, that which we get from the telephone and radio. Speech also has visual components, the basis for a silent motion-picture industry. This chapter will develop the idea that the visual aspects are important adjuncts to much speech but that the visual components alone do not offer a very satisfactory set of symbols for communication. The silent movies could not convey the lines through action. They were spelled out in the English alphabet and English words for American viewers.

Most visible action is labeled *gesture*. However, we shall note that even much of the auditory aspect of speech may be considered to be gesture. Thus, through semantic juggling, what we see and what we hear in speech become dual sets of simultaneous gestures.

The foregoing view assumes plausibility as we toy with our television sets. We may first watch speech as the sound section is turned low. We watch hands and read lips, and speech seems to be revealed by the gestures. As we slowly turn up the audio section of the television set, we may be struck with the idea that sound and sight are doing the same thing. Both are revealing meaning. Both are gestures. This brief exercise with the television set has traced in a few minutes the outcome of years of thoughtful observation on the part of nineteenth-century scholars.

The uniqueness of the implied similarity between the sound and sight of speech suggests that we review some of the inherent characteristics of speech

SMALL TALK VS. PURPOSIVE SPEECH

Someone is around when we talk, and we talk because there is someone around. Not to talk—unless talking is taboo, as in a study hall or theater audience—simply does not imply sensible behavior. We may or may not sit silently by a stranger in a city bus, but if the ride lasts for some time as from one city to another, the silence becomes noticeable and the urge to talk overcomes us, as it does with students in a hallway as they await a class. Such circumstances account for some of our least purposive talking: "Surely rained last night," "Who will take the American League this year?" "Cold, isn't it?"—simply, in colloquial idiom, "passing the time of day." Purposive speaking is quite another matter. Statements, one by one, are vital and the responses are important, for each response may affect the statement that follows. In the following account, every quotation (acoustic) and description (visual) from the original series of events is of first-order importance; both the original saying of the *words* and the bodily movements that went along with the words were pertinent to life and death.

THE DEATH OF THE SHERIFF

WEST BLUFF, Jan. 13. James White, a farmer living near here, was the sole eye witness to the gun battle in which Sheriff Ben Lucus, 65, was slain by two men late yesterday.

White was driving his pickup truck from his home near Harborville to West Bluff about 4:30 P.M. yesterday when he saw the sheriff with two men.

"I know Ben well and thought I'd better stop and see if he needed any help," White related.

"Ben's car was headed toward West Bluff, the same as mine. Apparently he had passed the two men, then stopped his car and walked back to them.

"As I drove past, the sheriff was standing with the two men in front of him. He was searching one man for weapons. The men had their hands up.

"I stopped my truck at the roadside between where the sheriff was standing with the men and where he had parked his car.

"'Keep your hands up, keep your hands up,' I heard the sheriff warning the men as I got out of my truck cab.

"One of the men was black-haired, about 5 feet 7 inches tall. The other was blond, and taller, about 6 feet, I'd say. Ben was searching the blond who was standing directly in front of the sheriff. The black-haired fellow was to the side and a little to the rear.

"Just as I stepped to the road, I saw the right hand of the black-haired fellow dart into his jacket and he stepped back quickly.

"'Look out, Ben, he's drawing a gun,' I called in warning.

"Ben grabbed the blond fellow close to him as a shield as he shouted at the other fellow to drop the gun.

"Suddenly the blond one jerked away from the sheriff, whirled to the side and moved toward my truck.

"Then the shooting started.

"The black-haired one was firing at the sheriff and Ben was firing at him. Then Ben moved back to the side of my truck and fired one shot at the blond one.

"As the sheriff fired, the blond one tossed his revolver over the truck into the road shouting 'I give up.' I saw a piece of the gun handle fly off as the revolver struck the paving.

"Ben had been wounded all that time and was dying on his feet, but I didn't know it. I glanced quickly at the black-haired gunman. He was standing at the roadside with the revolver held in both hands in front of him. It looked like he was trying to reload it.

"'Don't worry about this one' (the blond), I yelled, 'watch the other one, Ben. He's reloading,' I called.

"Ben just stood there by the truck, revolver leveled at the gunman and motioned him to come to him. The gunman started to walk toward the sheriff. The sheriff started to walk alongside the truck toward the gunman. As Ben reached the front end of the truck he suddenly collapsed.

"'He's down,' one of the gunmen shouted.

"That's when I decided it was time for me to leave. I figured the gunmen had heard my shouts to the sheriff and I'd be the next one to get shot.

"I started running toward the sheriff's parked car, figuring on fleeing in it. I thought they'd take my truck and as far as I was concerned they could have it.

"But before I reached Ben's car, one of them shouted at me.

"'Stop.'

"I kept running but yelled back over my shoulder: 'I haven't done anything.'

"'You never will do anything again if you don't stop right now,' one warned me in a grim voice.

"That stopped me. I froze in my tracks.

"As I stood there, the two men rushed past me. Neither made any move toward me. They just ran past and leaped into the sheriff's car.

"The black-haired one got under the wheel. They drove away fast.

"Then I turned and saw the sheriff. He was lying two or three feet in from the road side. As I knelt beside him he sort of opened his mouth and moved his head a trifle.

"I saw a car coming. I stopped it. It contained two women. I wanted them to get help from West Bluff but they seemed to be hysterical at the sight of the sheriff lying there on the road.

"I yelled at them to go on but to tell someone in West Bluff to send help.

"Then I saw another car approach. I stopped it. Rev. Johnny Spahr, 18, associated with the Church of Christ here, was the driver. He helped me make the sheriff comfortable and then drove to West Bluff for help."

THE "FIST LANGUAGE" AND ABSTRACTIONS

"The Death of the Sheriff" could be retold with the participants of any linguistic background, or it could be translated into any language. It could be rewritten with animals replacing human antagonists. The behavior patterns would not differ much in any instance, for a principal characteristic of the story is the physical movement of attack and defense, a "fist language." Words and voice replace some of the violence of a completely elemental version. Interestingly, the fourth character of the drama was a messenger, a narrator of the action to the three chief participants. His messages to the sheriff were heard by the assailants, as well, and thus became common knowledge and part of the fiber of events.

Verbal fights may parallel the animalistic duel of "The Death of the Sheriff." With more at stake, for example more lives, or less at stake, the sides substitute discourse for fists and guns and rely on ballots to decide the outcome. Vestiges of the "fist language," "sign language," "body language," etc., that antedated words—as physical struggle preceded discourse—may be observed in our culture as accompaniments of the "word language" of either the prosecution or the defense, the affirmative or the negative. We call the physical accompaniment of word language *gesture*. However, in "The Death of the Sheriff" you possibly observed that "fist language" was the entire event, both idea and action, not merely an accompaniment of a word. A gesture, indeed, is or may be an abstract of a feature of the thought, topic, or argument that is under development. The gesture symbolizes a segment, usually a vital segment of the whole idea. In somewhat the same manner that a military force may be referred to figuratively as "caisson," an election as "ballot box" or "November 2," a ship called a "sail," or a library called a "magazine rack"—in somewhat the same manner, the Empire State Building is abstracted as height, "a raised hand pointing upward," or a water wheel as a continuous rotation, "a hand in circular movement." A precursor to this routine behavior of the talking adult lies in the genetic development of the language of the child who is learning to talk. The behavior of the child has been aptly described by Latif.[1]

[1] I. Latif, "Physiological Basis of Linguistic Development and of the Ontogeny of Meaning," *Psychological Review*, vol. 41, pp. 76–77, 1934. Used by permission.

It is through the intervention of its elders that the general movements and postures of an infant gradually pass into symbolic gestures. A hungry infant, for instance, soon comes to react to the sight of the nursing-bottle by writhing, wriggling and directing its head and eyes towards it—general indications of food-adience. At the creeping stage an infant will creep towards its bottle. This is its direct response to the sight of the nursing-bottle. This response, however, has a "significance" for the interested mother, inasmuch as she understands it to mean that the infant wants food. The general behaviour of the child may thus be termed a *whole-body* language, since the attitude and activity of its whole body convey meaning to an onlooker.

But this whole-body language of the infant soon comes to be abbreviated, through the solicitous participation of the mother. As soon as the infant shows a nascent attitude of food-adience, the mother brings the bottle and thus cuts short the adient efforts of the infant. Whenever it stretches out its hand towards an object, the attentive mother is there to put the object in its hand. Such coöperation on the part of the mother, soon reduces the whole-body language of the infant to mere "conventional" gesture, in which *only a part* and that the earliest part of an action is substituted for the entire action. The responses of the infant thus become merely symptomatic, i.e. symbolic.

OUR UNIQUE GESTURES

Experience among us bears out Latif's explanation, but we may reserve the privilege to fill in the details for a particular child ourselves. Each infant follows the general pattern and exhibits additional individual differences. Accordingly, there are manifold individual differences in both the child's and the adult's *abstractions of the features* of an object or idea by gesture. Why should there not be? The pattern that is to be abstracted is unique in each instance. There would be as many ways of handling each moment in the "Death of the Sheriff" as there would be sheriffs or hoodlums who might participate and terrains where the fight might occur; there would be various gaits in the infant's crawling to his food source and differing amounts of frustration and tension among infants when the food, once gained, turned out to be sour, hot, or cold. "Missing the nail and hitting the finger" elicits widely differing reactions among us, and thus our abstractions of the event would differ, our abstractions either by language or by gesture. The feature to one human organism of a geyser, for example Old Faithful of Yellowstone Park, is its height, to another its sound, another its color, and to still another its regularity. The abstraction by signs—and signs are the essence of gesture—is thus different from one observer to another.

In special cases gestures or physical abstractions are formalized, practiced, and presented as a component of an art as in a dance and sometimes are given the sanction of an entire culture, as the sign language of the hula of the Hawaiians. Some nonverbal abstractions may stand alone in a communication within a cultural pattern, as the shaking or nodding of the head in our culture, the wiggle-waggle of a finger that is pointed generally downward to mean "no" in Mexico, or the raising of the eyebrows at the dinner table to mean "yes" or "please" in Greece. The conventional sign language of the Hawaiian hula, given below,[1] also extends gestures to include a set of symbols with specific meanings.

Word	*Action*
Moon	Arms above and in front of head; palms front
Idea	Finger (one, usually index) pointed to forehead
Tears	Rubbing eyes with a downward stroke as though brushing tears away
Wind	One arm out; three hand circles in a horizontal plane above the head
Rain	Two hands, downward, like playing a harp
Valley	Two hands, far to sides, making downward swing
Ukulele	Like holding and strumming a guitar
Fish	Two hands, palms together, wiggling forward
Poi (a particular food)	One circle of one index finger as though cleaning a cooking bowl; then to mouth
Sleep and Dream	Two hands, palms together, head resting at side on back of hand
Kiss	Brushing hand downward over lips, terminating with palm facing audience
Smile	Touching two index fingers at sides of mouth

DESCRIBING GESTURES

The view that gestures are partial representations of ideas or of selected features of ideas, concepts, attitudes, materials, topics, reasoning processes, pleadings, announcements, etc., that we are uttering does not lead easily to subdivisions or classifications of gestures. Obviously, we have largely deprived ourselves of the convenience of classifying gestures according either to purpose or to type, unless we might so classify our thoughts; for we have linked the gesture to the essence,

[1] Contributed by Maizie Kobayashi, international graduate student, The Ohio State University, Columbus, Ohio.

the substance, the content of talking. In turn, the development of an idea may follow patterns that can be named but hardly categorized under names that differentiate gestures. Descriptive words, imperfect at best, may be more relevant than classifications: "clear," "cogent," "important," "closely reasoned," "ambiguous," "illogical," "abstruse," "trivial," "factual," "figurative," "complete," "emotional," etc. The gesture is simply present; it exists. It is inherent in the speaker's ideas. The line that the thought takes is the line that phrases and images take, and gestures are therein. Neural sets, predispositions, biases interact with the present circumstance and produce a stream of verbal consciousness. Grammar, the order of words, the length of the sentence—these are dimensions in which the oral abstract is revealed. The speaker believes that his concept has greater or less urgency, and this attribute affects the manner of his utterance.

I. SCALING GESTURES. Gestures might be classified or scaled in keeping with the "magnitude of the urgency" that they depict. They might also be classified according to the extent to which they seem to have a specific meaning. Such scaling is generally not feasible. You may wish to try to make such evaluations, however. Gestures that are uniquely descriptive and ones that seem to convey a lot of emphasis can be assigned *plus* values fairly easily. Furthermore, in our attempts to classify gestures, we should keep in mind that a gesture is more a sample of one person's "gesture traits" and not so much a sample of a universally used gesture language. Thus the gesture would be evaluated or described largely in reference to the general run of gestures of the *same speaker*.

2. EXEMPLIFICATION. An oral argument is underway about a tax levy which would support a civic auditorium of unprecedented size for the community. Two speakers allude to the height of the tower that would cap the edifice. They also speak of the tremendous floor space of the building. Both speakers are vehement, one favoring the levy and one opposing it. Both might happen to use similar gestures when conceptualizing height; a set of similar gestures with reference to area; a set with reference to the site; and other sets to denote the "amount of happiness that attends operatic or symphonic performances," "the pride of citizens in public improvements and civic centers," "the size of the current municipal debt," "the vision [or lack of vision] of the city fathers," "the recent increase in juvenile delinquency in the city," "the comfort of the upholstered seat," etc. In execution, the gestures

might be similar or not from speaker to speaker or from topic to topic. Onlookers without the advantage of sound effects might witness small movements and large movements, sweeping and slashing movements, pointings upward and downward, and up, down, and level movements of either or both hands. The feature of these words is that they *describe;* they describe each movement. Describe what? Describe either a *topic* that is conceptualized by the speaker or the speaker's notion of relative *urgency* of his idea about the topic. *Describe* here is akin to specifying an amount: much or little. The amount that an idea weighs with us may range on one scale from neutral, indifference, or zero to an extreme positive deviation. Thus, as you view gestures you might devise *for the speaker you are watching* a scale that would range from minimum movement to extreme movement *for him* and enter tally marks along a three-, five-, or seven-point scale.

THE MONOTONY OF GESTURES

Gestures we now take for granted as part of the speaker's revelation of his notions and his attitudes about his ideas. Occasionally we may observe gestures about gestures in the same manner that we have words about words. These gestures occur most frequently on the stage and probably always as part of a humorous circumstance. For example, one person in a play may be describing a second character and ridiculing one of his typical patterns of gesturing. The speaker catches himself in the act of employing the disdained gesture. *He freezes, grimaces at his upswung arm, reaches with his other hand, and seems to pull the offending member to his side.* Similarly, impersonations may include gestures about gestures—someone's else, usually. These gestures are interesting and specific. They represent an absence of monotony.

1. THE RECURRENT GESTURE. The recurrent pointing of the index finger toward the listeners is not a specific nor interesting gesture. Any explanation of this monotonous pattern involves guesses and "reading ourselves into another person's behavior"—a hazardous practice that we hope to avoid now and then. Let us look down this index finger for a moment from the speaker's vantage point. The "thinker" conceptualizes silently or orally, and when orally, he, by definition, says his concepts. He has a purpose, and—it lies in the audience. Words are his first line of offense as he endeavors to make himself understood and to achieve his purpose. Words seem not to be enough. He would italicize or use capital letters if he were writing. He has two messages, and they are

concurrent: (1) thought and (2) importance of the thought. He resorts to the recurrent gesture and jeopardizes all by monotony.

2. DEGREES OF DIFFERENTIATION. The language was one of signs instead of words with the American Indians, and the burden for intelligibility fell upon the "gesturer" and the "listener" and their ability to differentiate the visible symbols. This language required the specific gesture. There would be no monotony. (We can wonder, in jest, whether an audible stamp of the foot served in the visual language for a visible index finger in an aural language.)

Between the extremes of sign language and the recurrent gesture lie the countless instances of our appropriate gestures that do not convey total meaning in themselves. Our public speakers who were debating about the civic auditorium used these. Differentiations are not required between "house," "bungalow," "cabin," "mansion," etc., for the gestures only abstract successively selected features of a building.

The recurrent pecking index finger can be no more than a repetitious abstract of "Get this."

3. MEASURING MONOTONY. We are familiar with type-token ratio from the preceding chapter: the number of different words in a passage divided by the total number of words in a passage. We venture an analogy; if it is figurative, it is only because we are uncertain that we can count gestures with the same reliability that we can tally words. At least we can imagine the results that we might get if we were to divide the several "shapes" of gestures by the total number of gestures used by a speaker. Back to our index-finger pointer. He is a monogesturer. We count his jabbings. He jabs 10 times in one minute. His gesture ratio is 1/10. He might earn a ratio of 1/50, 1/100, or 1/1,000, depending only on the length of the time sample we chose to study. Our query remains whether this person is abstracting his concepts with gestures or is abstracting his egocentric attitude toward his mission.

A LARGER DEFINITION OF GESTURE

We have treated *gesture* as almost synonymous with movements of the hand. We need not hold such a limiting definition, although one conventional use of the word does restrict it to "hand play." The following paragraph may be taken to refer to gesture in a somewhat broader view.[1]

[1] G. Mallery, "Sign Language among North American Indians," *First Annual Report of the Bureau of Ethnology, Smithsonian Institution*, vol. 1, pp. 279–280, 1881.

Even among the gesture-hating English, when they are aroused from torpidity of manner, the hands are involuntarily clapped in approbation, rubbed with delight, wrung in distress, raised in astonishment, and waved in triumph. The fingers are snapped for contempt, the forefinger is vibrated to reprove or threaten, and the fist shaken in defiance. The brow is contracted with displeasure, and the eyes winked to show connivance. The shoulders are shrugged to express disbelief or repugnance, the eyebrows elevated with surprise, the lips bitten in vexation and thrust out in sullenness or displeasure, while a higher degree of anger is shown by a stamp of the foot.

This larger definition of gesture to include any movement on the part of a speaker or listener is interesting and perfectly valid.

1. VOICE AS GESTURE. A further extension of gesture allows it to include much of the sound of speech, or what Herbert Spencer termed *signs of feeling*.[1] In Spencer's view, Fairbanks was investigating gesture when he successfully associated the emotional accompaniment of voice with the pitch and rate of utterance, a topic of our Chap. 3.

All speech is compounded of two elements, the words and the tones in which they are uttered—the signs of ideas and the signs of feelings. While certain articulations express the thought, certain modulations express the more or less of pain or pleasure which the thought gives. Using the word *cadence* in an unusually extended sense, as comprehending all variations of voice, we may say that *cadence is the commentary of the emotions upon the propositions of the intellect.* This duality of spoken language, though not formally recognized, is recognized in practice by everyone; and everyone knows that very often more weight attaches to the tone than to the words. Daily experience supplies cases in which the same sentence of disapproval will be understood as meaning little or meaning much, according to the vocal inflections which accompany it; and daily experience supplies still more striking cases in which words and tones are in direct contradiction—the first expressing consent, while the last express reluctance; and the last being believed rather than the first.

Spencer, in an essay published in 1857, is treating concisely some of the import of our chapter "The Sound of Speech." We are not restating the importance of vocal behavior. Rather, we want you to appreciate that the auditory and visual components of speech are so closely allied that some scholars hardly distinguish between them. This is particularly true among anthropologists.

[1] Herbert Spencer, "The Origin and Function of Music," *Essays Scientific, Political, and Speculative*, vol. 2, p. 421, D. Appleton-Century Company, Inc., New York, 1891.

2. LANGUAGE AS GESTURE. There is one further extension of gesture. The most extreme scope that is accorded the word *gesture* is the view that calls words or language gestures. Although we are not propounding this idea, or even Spencer's, we hope that you recognize the reasonableness that it represents if one is willing to differentiate between concepts, ideas, or subject matter and the utterance of these ideas, and to label the one *thinking* and the other the *saying* or *gesturing* the thought. We would prefer to think of unrehearsed or off-the-cuff speech as the manifestation of concepts, and view language, ideas, voice, and gesture as aspects of the talking man or of man, talking. Importantly, each of us must make clear the sense in which he uses *gesture*. In the discussions of this book the word means "bodily activity in speaking—and listening." All of us should respect the privilege of specialists in anthropology, philosophy, linguistics, etc., to employ the word as they wish, now that we sense the scope of the idea that they may have in mind.

CONCRETE GESTURES

Earlier we observed that the abstractions represented by our gestures are not often differentiating among the concepts that they accompany. A few, of course, are, as the shaking or nodding of the head *in our culture.*

1. EXPERIMENTAL EVIDENCE. In an experimental situation an actor practiced 35 manual gestures. These were photographed and shown to students, men and women, for identification both as slides and as motion pictures. There was greatest agreement among the viewers when they saw gestures that implied *worship* and *entreaty*. But generally, and even in these instances, there was little evidence of agreement about the concepts that were abstracted or represented by the gestures.[1] Several other studies have failed to establish any easy recognition of the emotional states that are portrayed by facial expressions in still pictures. On the positive side, laughter is recognized fairly well; amazement about as well; and happy states are often distinguishable from sad ones. Largely though, in our culture gesture must be considered as playing a supporting role in the identification of meaning in talking and listening.

There is one series of studies that provides an interesting exception

[1] L. Carmichael, S. O. Roberts, and N. Y. Wessell, "A Study of the Judgment of Manual Expression as Presented in Still and Motion Pictures," *Journal of Social Psychology*, vol. 8, pp. 115–142, 1937.

to the dismal prospect for the visual transfer of meaning of the preceding generalization. Two researchers in speech determined experimentally that when they worked within a family of 11 emotional states, students could match pictures of simulated portrayals of emotions and the names of the emotions quite well. The correct identifications ranged upward from 80 per cent when the viewers saw motion pictures of the portrayals and were well above chance when the identifications were from still pictures.[1]

2. CLARIFYING MEANING. The foregoing studies and the results are remindful of information theory and measurements that are based on the reduction of uncertainty. How much is the listener's uncertainty reduced by the facial states of the speaker? The results of Dusenberry and Knower indicate that if the uncertainty involved a pair of *yes-no* responses, as "These two pictures are *sad* or *happy*," the uncertainty could be almost completely reduced by the portrayals of the emotions. In fact, a third, fourth, and so on, up to an eleventh member, were added to the "vocabulary," and still the "right" picture reduced uncertainty significantly within the stated vocabulary. Never mind how far this might be extended. It is already important insofar as communication is concerned. Instances, by no means exceptional, arise in which the words alone in a sentence cannot be clearly meaningful. For example, "I wouldn't take anything for that picture" may mean either that the picture is worth everything or nothing to me. Gestures—manual, facial, vocal (if this time you will let us treat voice as gesture)—might resolve completely our one-in-two chance of guessing the right or intended meaning. Similarly, the ongoing panorama of "visible abstractions of concepts"—in other words, gestures—may be studied and taught in this context: reducing the uncertainty of the listener.

INEVITABILITY OF GESTURES

We have reiterated the view that gestures are revelations of concepts. Between the concept and the visible trace of the gesture lie muscles. These, in turn, are activated by the nervous system, and the manifestation of this activity within the muscle is a series of action currents. These action currents are small electrical discharges and attend every movement of a muscle. They are present only during muscular activity

---

[1] D. Dusenberry and Franklin H. Knower, "Experimental Studies of the Symbolism of Action and Voice—I: A Study of the Specificity of Meaning in Facial Expression," *Quarterly Journal of Speech*, vol. 24, pp. 424–436, 1938.

and are detectable with instruments that measure small electrical currents. One investigator applied needle electrodes to selected muscles at the surface of the body of several men.[1] The attachments ranged from the region of the vocal mechanism to the thigh. The students then pronounced a series of monosyllables as *top, top, . . . top*, at each of several rates. Action currents were recorded from every electrode with each syllable, and—at ordinary rates of repetition—only with the syllable. In other words, even a single syllable is "said" by the whole body, not merely by the mouth and larynx.

The important exception to syllable-to-syllable differentiation occurred with fast repetition rates. In these instances, the muscles of the abdomen seemed to "freeze" and to exhibit action currents continuously instead of only during the syllable. The visual recordings from these muscles resembled visual records of acoustic noise. The muscles of the mouth and larynx and of the walls of the lung cage continued to differentiate between successive syllables.

The close relation between the syllable of speech and muscular movement throughout the body is consistent with the view that the concept is revealed through the gesture as well as through language. E. Jacobson added further experimental verification of this. He found that we also get the muscular reactions in the speech mechanism if we only think the words.[2]

When the electrodes are connected in the speech musculature of the trained subject, the string shadow is practically quiet during relaxation. But promptly after the signal is sounded to engage in mental activity involving words or numbers, marked vibrations appear, indicating action-potentials. Soon after the subject hears the signal to relax any muscular tensions present, the vibrations cease and the string returns to rest.

THE SPEAKER'S BEARING

We might dispense with the topic of the speaker's body with an impertinency, "Posture is inevitable and that's that!" Therein lies a truism: posture, some posture, is always with us from the high chair to the wheel chair. In much and possibly most of our talking, posture is an unconscious and habitual adjustment to an activity of the moment that

---

[1] R. H. Stetson, "Speech Movements in Action," *Transactions of the American Laryngological Association*, vol. 55, pp. 29–41, 1933.

[2] E. Jacobson, "Electrical Measurements of Neuromuscular States during Mental Activities," *American Journal of Physiology*, vol. 1, p. 205, 1931.

is more demanding than talking: sitting at a dining table, driving an automobile, walking, riding in a train, etc. In the bustle of living, a conference of utmost personal importance is often arranged to occur while we engage in one of these activities, and more aspects of our posture are determined by the other activity than by talking. Occasionally, posture is entirely set by the activity of speaking, as in public address.

We cannot apply to posture the full force of the argument that seems to suit gesture, namely, that gesture is an active representation of a concept. Even in public address, posture cannot be very differentiating among concepts nor reveal much of the thought. Yet it may contribute somewhat, and the *somewhat* is important. The speaker who seeks to affect the ideas of his audience may well assume a bearing that manifests his attitude of high interest: (1) He could scarcely do other than face his listeners and have them in the best possible view. He looks at them directly. Possibly it is incidental that the forces that bring this about achieve a highly salutary reciprocal effect—that he is also in the best view of the listeners. (2) The speaker is as close to his listeners as possible. Were he sitting instead of standing and in a living room instead of an auditorium, he would be leaning a bit forward in his chair and in position to shift his attention from right to left to center easily. (3) On the platform, this same interest attitude makes him erect and, as Henry Moser says, "Puts him in position such that were he to faint he would fall forward."

We suggest not only that the speaker's foursquare-to-the-listener position is of importance but that the relevant advice predominates in importance among the bits of advice that are frequently given about posture. Necessarily, the distractions that may attend posture are to be eliminated: pacing and rocking, either to and fro or left and right. Principally, though, face the listeners squarely and in a manner that is in keeping with alertness, vigor, confidence, and the attitude, "Let's make the most of this short time."

Projects for Practice

1. Prepare to reenact in class "The Death of the Sheriff."
2. Prepare to reenact the interview between the newspaper reporter and the witness that resulted in the story "The Death of the Sheriff."
3. There is a story about several blind men who felt an elephant and then described the animal. Each man, of course, experienced a different feature of

the elephant. Extend this story to make further illustrations of our limited abstractions that are possible through signs.

4. John Crowe Ransom, poet and critic, has written about Antony's speech over the body of Caesar, beginning with the words, "If you have tears . . . ": "Considering its brevity, his [Antony's] speech has had perhaps the most astonishing success recorded for us anywhere in the annals of oratory, whether history or imaginative speaking."[1]

The lines of the speech dictate some of the speaker's movements. The speech as a whole exemplifies the oneness of action and words. Few speeches in oratory have language that bespeaks the posture, movement, and gesture more completely than this one. Indicate the gestures that you would use in reading the speech. Practice the gestures. Discover through renditions of parts of the speech in class the likenesses and differences among the several sets of gestures that have been prepared.

FROM "JULIUS CAESAR" (Act III, Scene 2)

If you have tears, prepare to shed them now.
You all do know this mantle: I remember
The first time ever Caesar put it on;
'Twas on a summer's evening, in his tent,
That day he overcame the Nervii:
Look, in this place ran Cassius' dagger through:
See what a rent the envious Casca made:
Through this the well-beloved Brutus stabb'd;
And as he pluck'd his cursed steel away,
Mark how the blood of Caesar follow'd it,
As rushing out of doors, to be resolved
If Brutus so unkindly knock'd, or no;
For Brutus, as you know, was Caesar's angel:
Judge, O you gods, how dearly Caesar lov'd him!
This was the most unkindest cut of all;
For when the noble Caesar saw him stab,
Ingratitude, more strong than traitors' arms,
Quite vanquish'd him: then burst his mighty heart;
And, in his mantle muffling up his face,
Even at the base of Pompey's statuë,
Which all the while ran blood, great Caesar fell.
O what a fall was there, my countrymen!
Then I, and you, and all of us fell down,
Whilst bloody treason flourish'd over us.

[1] John Crowe Ransom, "Poetry: I. The Formal Analysis," *The Kenyon Review*, vol. 9, pp. 449–450, 1947.

O, now you weep; and I perceive you feel
The dint of pity: these are gracious drops.
Kind souls, what, weep you when you but behold
Our Caesar's vesture wounded? Look you here,
Here is himself, marr'd, as you see, with traitors.

William Shakespeare

5. Study the following paragraph from M. M. Lewis's *Infant Speech*[1] and prepare further illustrations of the development of words from gestures preparatory to discussing the topic in class.

A child, [Stern] tells us, is trained to link a word with its accompanying situation, so that he comes at length to respond to the word alone. The chief aid to this linkage is furnished by movements or gestures; either those of the adult, or those of the child. In the former case, the child responds first to the adult's gestures—for instance, his mother's outstretched arms—and then he is trained to respond to the accompanying words, so that ultimately these alone acquire the power of evoking the appropriate movement. In the second case, the process of training begins from one of the child's own gestures. These may be of three kinds: (*a*) spontaneous—for instance, dancing a doll or looking at a clock; (*b*) imitative; or (*c*) induced—for instance, the child is induced to touch his nose. The adult constantly introduces a word when the child is making a gesture, and ultimately the word acquires the power of evoking the gesture.

6. Discuss a question that is not answered in this chapter: When should I gesture? Is the viewpoint of the chapter consistent with your answer?

7. Discuss the application of conditioned reflex to the learning of words and gestures.

8. Contrast the description of gestures in this chapter with the following one from a standard textbook in social psychology.[2]

F. H. Allport has classified gestures into three kinds: *emotional, demonstrative,* and *graphic.* An *emotional* gesture is a natural bodily movement in pleasant or unpleasant states of excitement. It is not made for purposes of communication but expresses or comprises the emotion experienced. A *demonstrative* gesture consists in pointing. It calls attention to objects or persons and sometimes signifies the source or goal of an activity. Hence it is greatly limited in its purpose of communica-

[1] M. M. Lewis, *Infant Speech*, p. 110, Routledge and Kegan Paul, Ltd., London, 1936, The Humanities Press, New York, 1951. Used by permission.

[2] D. Katz and R. L. Schanck, *Social Psychology*, pp. 348–350, John Wiley & Sons, Inc., New York, 1938. Used by permission.

tion. *Graphic* gestures mimic the objects or situations they represent. For example, in sign language, walking is indicated by a slow movement of the fingers, running by a rapid movement.

To this threefold classification may be added at least three more types of gestures: the *symbolic*, the *habitual*, and the *autistic*. Language gestures not only point or portray; they also symbolize. Apart from the artificial development of a sign language based upon the written alphabet, many of the gestures in the vernacular of the deaf-mutes are *symbolic*. Doubt is expressed by moving the fists up and down in alternation. This gesture does contain a graphic element in that it portrays the rival pull of opposed forces. Nevertheless it is sufficiently formalized to be unrecognizable through its graphic features alone. Among normal people many gestures have also become conventionalized for language purposes—instance our use of the thumbs-down signal, which the Romans employed before us. In many cultures movements of the hand symbolize religious meanings in sacred rituals. Among the Egyptians the uplifted arms and hands designated life or the vital principle. Art has stylized gestures into a language of emotional expression. In India the dancing girls learn thousands of formalized gestures, no less than twenty meanings being represented by the extended fingers of the closed hand alone.

Habitual gestures are not used for communication, nor do they necessarily express emotion. They are the movements which characterize a personality and which become fixed in the course of the individual's development. Examples are: the folding of the arms, the bobbing of the head, the placing of the tips of the fingers of one hand against the tips of the other, the placing of the hands upon the hips, running the hand through the hair—to mention only a few. These habitual gestures may have little stimulating value save when the person who exhibits them is well known. In such instances they may be telltale signs of the maker's intentions. One man may pull his ear when in doubt; in another person this gesture indicates an adverse decision; in still another it may have no characteristic expressive significance. Many professional and occupational habits have a gestural component. The diplomat carries over his bowing into personal situations, and the politician his hand-clasping and back slapping. The doctor, the lawyer, the machinist reveal their callings through the characteristic gestures of their trade.

Habitual gestures are concomitants of behavior which have been more or less accidentally conditioned to situations. They have little meaning in the individual's own life, though they can be used to interpret his intentions and to indicate his cultural background. *Autistic* gestures are also characteristic responses of an individual, but they do have a definite relation to his personality. Just as autistic thinking is self-directed thinking, so autistic gestures are the individual's reactions to his own conflicts. Moreover, they are not externally directed toward the solution of a conflict. Many so-called nervous habits are included in this category. Biting the fingernails, stretching the arms as a result of embarrassment, and pinching the lips with the fingers are in many cases autistic gestures.

9. Discover other classifications of gestures. What are the principles of classification? Explain one of these classifications to your class and relate it to the material of this chapter.

10. Examine the hand positions of a comic strip character over a period of several days. Is sameness or variety the rule?

11. Explain the statement, attributed to R. D. T. Hollister of the University of Michigan, "Too many students spend too much time on the platform gathering raindrops." Demonstrate the fault while you read a passage that you have practiced.

12. Discuss the statement in this chapter, "Any explanation of this . . . pattern involves . . . 'reading ourselves into another person's behavior'— a hazardous practice that we hope to avoid now and then." Point out instances in which the practice has not been avoided by the authors.

13. Try the type-token game with gestures. Do not practice it consistently. The listener has more important functions than to serve as a tally clerk for gestures.

14. Discuss the possibility of being specific in the sign language of the American Indian as described by one writer.[1]

> The signs are made almost entirely with the hands, either one or both. . . . Thus the sign for man is made by throwing out the hand, back outward, with index finger extended upward. . . . Woman is indicated by sweeping downward movement of the hand at the side of the head, with fingers extended toward the hair to denote long flowing hair or the combing of flowing locks. . . . *Fatigue* is shown by downward and outward sweep of the two hands in front of the body, index finger extended, giving a gesture-picture of utter collapse. *Bad* is indicated by a motion of throwing away.

15. Practice reading the following minor selections about war and peace, amplifying the words with appropriate gestures. Do you find that you are using a few "shapes of gestures" repeatedly? As you try to substitute or add other shapes, do you find yourself conceptualizing differently? This chapter stresses gesture. However, comparisons are frequently made between the

[1] J. Mooney, "Sign Language," *Bulletin of the Bureau of American Ethnology,* vol. 30, pp. 567–568, 1910.

relative specificity of language and that of action, with the implication that words are much more specific than action in conveying meaning. Is this implication justified in these two passages?

a. [At Camp Charlotte, Cornstalk eloquently asked for peace and promised to stay off the warpath. There were many chiefs there, but one great figure was missing—one who refused to ask for peace. This was Chief Logan the Mingo. His influence was so great that it was important for Dunmore (Lord Dunmore, Governor of Virginia) to get his name on a treaty of peace, so the Governor sent John Gibson to invite him. The result was one of the greatest orations ever uttered by a savage (1774). Logan spoke English, but could not write. Gibson, however, understood the Mingo language. As Logan's spirit welled up, he burst forth in a strong expression of his indignation at the wrongs he had suffered. It was written down by Gibson and delivered to Dunmore beneath the famous Logan Elm. "Perhaps the finest outburst of savage eloquence of which we have any authentic record," said Theodore Roosevelt; and Thomas Jefferson wrote of Logan's oration in terms so glowing that some of his enemies accused him of writing the speech himself.]

I appeal to any white man to say if he ever entered Logan's cabin hungry and he gave him not meat; if ever he came cold and naked and he clothed him not? During the course of the last long and bloody war, Logan remained idle in his camp, an advocate for peace. Such was my love for the whites that my countrymen pointed as I passed and said, "Logan is a friend of the white man." I had even thought to have lived with you but for the injuries of one man. Colonel Cresap, the last spring, in cold blood and unprovoked, murdered all the relations of Logan, not even sparing my women and children. There runs not a drop of my blood in the veins of any living creature. This called on me for revenge. I have sought it. I have killed many. I have fully glutted my vengeance. For my country I rejoice at the beams of peace; but do not harbor a thought that mine is the joy of fear. Logan never felt fear. He will not turn on his heel to save his life. Who is there to mourn for Logan? Not one.[1]

b. [A northern Congressman speaks against the imminent war between the States.][2] Mr. Chairman: I speak from and for the capital of the greatest of the States of the great West. Before we enter upon a career of force, let us exhaust every effort at peace. Let us seek to

[1] David W. Bowman, *Pathway of Progress: A Short History of Ohio*, p. 71, American Book Company, New York, 1943. Used by permission.

[2] Samuel Sullivan (Sunset) Cox, "On Secession," *The Congressional Globe*, 36th Cong., 2d Sess., pt. 1, p. 372, 1861.

excite love in others by the signs of love in ourselves. Let there be no needless provocation and strife. Let every reasonable attempt at compromise be considered. Otherwise we have a terrible alternative. War, in this age and in this country, sir, should be the *ultima ratio*. Indeed, it may well be questioned whether there is any reason in it for war. What a war! Endless in its hate, without truce and without mercy. If it ended ever, it would only be after a fearful struggle; and then with a heritage of hate which would forever forbid harmony. Small States and great States; new States and old States; slave States and free States; Atlantic States and Pacific States; gold and silver States; iron and copper States; grain States and lumber States; river States and lake States;—all having varied interests and advantages, would seek superiority in armed strength. Pride, animosity, and glory would inspire every movement. God shield our country from such a fulfillment of the prophecy of the revered founders of the Union! Our struggle would be no short sharp struggle. Law, and even religion herself, would become false to their divine purpose. Their voice would no longer be the voice of God, but of his enemy. Poverty, ignorance, oppression, and its handmaid, cowardice, breaking out into merciless cruelty; slaves false; freemen slaves, and society itself poisoned at the cradle and dishonored at the grave;—its life, now so full of blessing, would be gone with the life of a fraternal and united Statehood. What sacrifice is too great to prevent such a calamity?

16. It is alleged that gestures are more likely to accompany the onset of a conceptualization than the completion of the idea. Assume that a sentence represents a concept. Practice reading a passage and discover where in the sentences you and a partner are prone to gesture.

17. Tie an object to a cord and whirl the object in the manner of a sling shot. Before you make a test run describe the sound that you expect to hear. After the whirling, describe the sound you have made. You have imitated an imagined and a real sound. Discuss these imitations as gestures. What other gestures have you made in this exercise?

18. Explain to a group of fellow students
    a. Your favorite hair style
    b. Your favorite ride at the fair
    c. How to play soccer, lacrosse, quoits, or curling
    d. Common mistakes in swimming

19. The word *gesture* appears often in a standard encyclopedia. Find some references to the term and decide what meaning the writer had in mind.

20. The gestures of what culture are shown in the painting "The Last Supper"? Study the gestures that you find in murals and friezes.

21. Discuss the statement, "Speech is total bodily activity." Treat the topic with experimental evidence, genetic evidence, starting with the infant, and a philogenetic analogy, for example a cat's response to an enemy. A student of biology may helpfully explain to the class the contributory role of endocrine glands in rapidly making the body a more capable source of speaking.

22. Compare the point of view of this chapter with one of a century ago as represented by a standard book in elocution materials.[1]

> Motions towards the body indicate self-esteem, egotism, or invitation; from the body, command or repulsion; expanding gestures express liberality, distribution, acquiescence or candor; contracting gestures, frugality, reserve, or collection; rising motions express suspension, climax, or appeal; falling motions, completion, declaration, or response; a sudden stop expresses doubt, meditation, or listening; a sudden movement, decision or discovery; a broad and sweeping range of gesture illustrates a general statement, or expresses boldness, freedom, and self-possession; a limited range denotes diffidence or constraint, or illustrates a subordinate point; rigidity of the muscles indicates firmness, strength, or effort; laxity denotes languor or weakness; slow motions are expressive of gentleness, caution, deliberation, etc.; and quick motions, of harshness, temerity, etc.

23. Study and discuss Herbert Spencer's essay "The Origin and Function of Music" in the light of your present views of speech.

24. Discuss the following statements from T. Hewitt Key's lectures in University College, London, 1841–1873.[2] What name would you give this theory of the origin of language?

> Now it is all but universally admitted that some portion of language owes its origin to an imitation of the sounds of nature. The *moo-cow* and the *baa-lamb* of the child, the *cuckoo*, the *peewit*, the *whip-poor-Will* of N. America, and the *tuco-tuco* of S. America, are simple but irresistible examples of this law. . . .
>
> Now when a stone tied to a string is whirled violently around, the ear catches very distinctly a sound which we may represent by the utterance of the noise *whirr*, and the more so, if we roll out the final liquid. Such a sound, especially if accompanied by a circular movement of the hand, would serve as a natural symbol of the idea of revolution:

[1] Charles David Bell and Alexander Melville Bell, *Bell's Standard Elocutionist*, new ed., pp. 25–27, William Mullan and Son, London, 1879. Alexander Melville Bell was the father of Alexander Graham Bell.

[2] T. H. Key, *Language: Its Origin and Development*, pp. 2–8, George Bell & Sons, Ltd., London, 1874.

but more than this; the sound is one which actually plays a part in existing languages, and that to an extent which to my mind is irresistibly convincing. For example, the German has *wirr-en*, to twist, the French *virer*, the English *veer*, as the weathercock, and to *wear* (a ship). The same sound forms an important part of *whirl*, *whorl*, *world* (the round globe), *warp*, *worm* in the double sense of the wriggling creature so-called, and the helix of a screw, *wort* in the sense of root, as spiderwort. It is also heard in the initial letters of *wr*ithe, *wr*eath, *wr*ench, *wr*est, *wr*ist, *wr*ing (a towel or a bird's neck), *wr*iggle, *wr*ap, *wr*y. The Latin exhibits the same in *uer*tere, in *uer*mis a worm, in *uer*minari, which unites the two meanings "to breed worms" and "to writhe with pain"; both uses, however different in their application, involving the idea of turning. The adj. *uarus* "with crooked legs," and *uarices* "varicose veins" have the same origin.

25. Compare with the foregoing A. H. Sayce's account of the origin of language, given below.[1]

Gestures, in the proper sense of the term, are only partly the same for all races of men; no doubt the instinctive element preponderates in them, but we have to allow also for a certain element of conventionality. There is not the same physiological reason why a shake of the head should denote a negative as there is why a particular expression of the face should indicate pleasure, or pain, or surprise, or why a feeling of shame should bring a blush to the cheek. . . . Gestures are rather a sign for the intellect than for the emotion, and since the same feeling must express itself similarly in the case of every one while the same thought need not, it is evident that that which expresses thought admits the element of conventionality more than that which expresses feeling. Pain must always be pain, and affect the nerves and muscles in the same way; what is thought of, on the contrary, may be conceived very differently, and represented in an equally varying manner. Hence it is that we share the play of feature with the brutes, whereas gestures —embodying as they do a rational rather than an emotional element— are for the most part peculiar to man. Man is man in virtue of language, and it was gestures that first made language possible.

But gestures alone are often but a poor resource for either the child or the traveller. They fail to express the meaning intended. Let us suppose a child, for example, to have been scratched by a cat, or frightened by a herd of cows. . . . If it be unacquainted with the names of cat and cow, it can only point out those animals by imitating

[1] A. H. Sayce, *Introduction to the Science of Language*, 4th ed., vol. 1, pp. 106–111, Kegan Paul, Trench, Trubner & Co., London, 1900. Used by permission.

the sounds they utter; and *miow* and *moo-moo* become the nursery names for "cat" and "cow." And what still goes on in the nursery was a general procedure in the childhood of mankind. . . . Now if we are to infer anything from the habits of the nursery, and of those savage tribes which best represent the infancy of mankind, onomatopoeia must have played a large part in the formation of language. Its advocates have done much harm to what Professor Max Müller has happily termed "The Bow-Wow Theory," by endeavoring to trace back words as we now find them to an onomatopoeic origin; but this does not prove that the theory when scientifically applied is false. . . . Besides gestures and onomatopoeia, there is a third way in which we can make ourselves intelligible without knowing the articulate language of those to whom we are speaking. This is by making use of interjectional cries. Like the play of feature, interjectional cries are the same for all men; we all make much the same kind of exclamation when hurt, or angry, or surprised. . . . The origin of language, then, is to be sought in *gestures, onomatopoeia,* and to a limited extent *interjectional cries*. Like the rope-bridges of the Himalayas or the Andes, they formed the first rude means of communication between man and man.

26. Discuss (*a*) a standard for evaluating gestures; (*b*) a program for improving my gestures and bearing.

27. *Role playing* is a current term for impromptu acting. Usually, the outline of a speaking situation for a group is given to a class, and then part of the class improvises as the scene is depicted. The performances are typically overdone in the circumstance in which the participants "act" as though they were "acting." Try this one, and then make up other sets of roles. Notice the importance of gestures in the portrayals.

> The Executive Committee of Joaquin College has decreed that students will not be permitted to have automobiles at college. Protests have been raised, and a round-table discussion is in process at the front of the auditorium before a student-faculty assembly. The discussants are President Sapir, who wants to hurt no feelings; Professor Knobit, who has said openly for 15 years, "No student with a car ever gets more than C in my class"; Miss Inez Marquis, who is a bit too popular with the students for a first-year teacher; Stanley Moon, with high grades, no money, and a tendency to be brash; Sue Hardy, who received a convertible for becoming 21 unmarried.

28. There are McGuffey clubs in some communities. The members studied the McGuffey readers. The annual meeting of these clubs is frequently a reading contest with poems read in the manner of exercises in elocution.

Prepare a short poem for the next meeting of your class. Part of the period will be devoted to a McGuffey Day contest.

29. In the speeches of Appendix A, the ones by Herrick, Yeager, and Baird contain the word *gesture*. Do you believe the three speakers give the same meaning to the word?

Readings

Alport, F. H., *Social Psychology*, Houghton Mifflin Company, Boston, 1924.

Crocker, Lionel, *Public Speaking for College Students*, American Book Company, New York, 1941.

Ehrensberger, Ray, "An Experimental Study of the Relative Effectiveness of Certain Forms of Emphasis in Public Speaking," *Speech Monographs*, vol. 12, pp. 94–111, 1945.

Gray, Giles Wilkeson, "Problems in the Teaching of Gesture," *Quarterly Journal of Speech Education*, vol. 10, pp. 238–252, 1924.

Stanislavski, Constantin, *An Actor Prepares*, Theatre Arts, Inc., New York, 1936.

Stetson, R. H., *Motor Phonetics*, 2d ed., Oberlin College, Oberlin, Ohio, 1951.

Woolbert, Charles Henry, *Fundamentals of Speech*, rev. ed., Harper & Brothers, New York, 1927.

12

INTERPRETATIVE SPEECH

From the very first of this book, we have emphasized the fact that speech is a distinctively human activity. Because man has a hearing mechanism responsive to a wide range of sound waves and a neuro-muscular mechanism that functions to associate and reproduce sounds, he creates a whole new world, the world of symbols. He has extended this world by his skill in writing and printing. Man lives, therefore, in an environment of spoken and printed symbols as much as in an environment of objects, events, and other human beings. The more educated man becomes the more he extends the limits of both his physical and his symbolic environments. Discoveries in all the sciences, advances in medicine, research in the humanities and the arts require observation of the nonverbal world and new formulations in the symbolic one.

Any college student can early decide whether his symbolic environment is to be restricted and narrowed to his immediate activities on low levels of abstraction: feeding, gossiping, dating, exercising, or watching the movies or television. Or he can decide that there is a brave new world of human symbolizing, a world, difficult at times to be sure, but one worthy of exploration.

To explore the symbolic world requires that the student himself must symbolize, that he must read and talk about what he reads. He will talk about the talking of sensitive human beings before him: scientists, philosophers, poets, dramatists, painters, musicians, theologians. He will remember from Chaps. 6 and 7 that he is abstracting their abstractions and that he is, in a sense, creating new meanings of his own. He is not parroting. His meanings will not be identical to the ones he abstracts, but they will be sufficiently similar in structure and pattern, let us hope, to be accurate. He will be aware, of course, of the ambiguity of many meanings that he encounters. Further, since his view of knowing may be somewhat different, especially if he accepts the principle of abstraction, he will be alert to the confusion that results when authors identify different levels of abstracting.

In the earlier chapters we were primarily concerned with the meanings you, as a potential speaker or writer, acquired. Now we become more and more interested in the meanings you communicate. Naturally, the two processes of "getting" and "giving" meanings are not separate distinct processes. What you try to communicate will be determined chiefly by what meanings you have.

Much of the speaking you do, especially while in college, may be called interpretative speaking. The oral reports in history, the reviews of books in English, the critiques in philosophy and social theory, the survey of theories of learning in psychology and education, and the talks in art or music classes involve a rather direct communication of the communication of others.

We shall consider this interpretative speech under the two headings "Referential Interpretation" and "Evocative Interpretation."

REFERENTIAL INTERPRETATION

Organization plays the key role in referential interpretation. Since structural relations provide the hard central core of meaning, it is obvious that if you are to report the meanings of others you must report the structure, the pattern, the organization of those meanings. In general, referential interpretation may follow one of the two broad patterns, depending upon whether the report is based upon a single work (or group of works) or whether it centers upon a general broad concept and draws upon a number of different creative works.

If the report is concerned with a single unified work, you may (1) make clear its main divisions, (2) present its details, (3) summarize the whole around its most significant contribution to human expression, (4) show its relations with other works in the same field of communication, or (5) report upon the distinct stages in the production of the work. Although, of course, your chief task will be to communicate the intended meaning, you should seek at the same time to give your listeners an understanding and appreciation they could not get by themselves. To achieve this goal you need to do sufficient collateral reading to place both the work and its creator in the proper setting of *their* symbolic world.

The second broad pattern of referential interpretation focuses attention upon an idea, a style, or a pattern of creativity which runs through the productions of a number of different individuals. The development may (1) trace the main abstraction through different contributors, (2) analyze its effect upon human thought and action, (3) consider the validity or humanizing value of the abstraction, and (4) array the views of its proponents and opponents side by side without choosing between them. The varieties and types of abstractions which lend themselves to these patterns of referential interpretation are merely suggested by the following topics: transcendentalism in philosophy and literature, the Gothic style in architecture, impressionism in art, romanticism in literature, antibiotics in medicine, the split-T offense in football, progressive education.

The tracing of abstractions is, of course, basic to the other methods, whether in your presentation you limit yourself to it alone or not. Hence, let us see how you would proceed if you applied that method to your report.

Let us suppose that you become interested in the value or danger of metaphorical language, a topic considered in Chap. 7. You want to discover what great thinkers have said about the validity of metaphors. By referring to card indexes in the library, reader's guides to literature, special bibliographies, handbooks on philosophy, language, or culture, encyclopedias, etc., you discover that Plato, Aristotle, St. Thomas Aquinas, Thomas Hobbes, William Harvey, John Locke, Emanuel Kant, Charles Darwin, and William James wrote on the use or misuse of metaphorical language. In the course of your pursuit, you may contrast the following statements by William Harvey, discoverer of the circulation of the blood, and by Charles Darwin, whose research led to the theory of natural selection and a new outlook in the biological sciences.

Nature endeavours to find the truth by means of anatomical dissections and experiments, is met by such a multitude of facts, and these of so unusual an aspect, that he [who enters on a new path] may find it more difficult to explain and describe to others the things he has seen, than he reckoned it labour to make his observations; so many things are encountered that require naming; such is the abundance of matter and the dearth of words. But if he would have recourse to metaphors, and by means of old and familiar terms would make known his ideas concerning the things he has newly discovered, the reader would have little chance of understanding him better than if they were riddles that were propounded; and of the thing itself, which he had never seen, he could have no conception. But then, to have recourse to new and unusual terms were less to bring a torch to lighten, than to darken things still more with a cloud: it were to attempt an explanation of a matter unknown by one still more unknown, and to impose a greater toil on the reader to understand the meaning of words than to comprehend the things themselves. And so it happens that Aristotle is believed by the inexperienced to be obscure in many places; and on this account, perhaps, Fabricius of Aquapendente rather intended to exhibit the chick in ovo in his figures than to explain its formation in words.

Wherefore, courteous reader, be not displeased with me, if, in illustrating the history of the egg, and in my account of the generation of the chick, I follow a new plan, and occasionally have recourse to unusual language. Think me not eager for vainglorious fame rather than anxious to lay before you observations that are true, and that are derived immediately from the nature of things.[1]

Several writers have misapprehended or objected to the term Natural Selection. Some have even imagined that natural selection induces variability, whereas it implies only the preservation of such variations as arise and are beneficial to the being under its conditions of life. No one objects to agriculturists speaking of the potent effects of man's selection; and in this case the individual differences given by nature, which man for some object selects, must of necessity first occur. Others have objected that the term selection implies conscious choice in the animals which become modified; and it has even been urged that, as plants have no volition, natural selection is not applicable to them! In the literal sense of the word, no doubt, natural selection is a false term; but who ever objected to chemists speaking of the elective affinities of the various elements?—and yet an acid cannot strictly be said to elect the base with which it in preference combines. It has been said that I speak of natural selection as an active power or Deity; but who objects to an author speaking of the attraction of gravity as ruling the movements of the planets? Every one knows what is meant and is implied by such metaphorical expressions; and they are almost necessary for brevity. So again it is difficult to avoid personifying the word Nature; but I mean by Nature, only the aggregate action and product of many natural laws, and by laws the sequence of events as ascertained by us. With a little familiarity such superficial objections will be forgotten.[2]

[1] William Harvey, *On Animal Generation*, from *Great Books of the Western World*, vol. 28, pp. 336–337, Robert Maynard Hutchins (ed.), Encyclopaedia Britannica, Inc., Chicago, 1952.

[2] Charles Darwin, *The Origin of Species*, from *Great Books of the Western World*, vol. 49, p. 40, Robert Maynard Hutchins (ed.), Encyclopaedia Britannica, Inc., Chicago, 1952.

As you continue your pursuit, you will learn that Sigmund Freud sided with Darwin rather than with Harvey, and that many modern scientific writers do use metaphorical language to make their ideas clear.

After what will probably seem like endless research in the library and after talking with students and professors who can give helpful hints, you will discover less well-known but no less significant writers like Ludwig Wittgenstein, Morris Cohen, Irving Lee, I. A. Richards, Ernst Cassirer, Sir James Frazer, and many others. You will become convinced that the search is as endless as the quest for the lost Atlantis. And so it is. But the quest will have led you to organize, to abstract, and to be willing, as time and interest and energy permit, to look further.

Much of your interpretation of referential writing will of necessity be more limited in scope. The plan you follow need not be essentially different, however, whether you are writing a research theme for English, a report for history, or preparing a major speech project. You will inquire, question, read, search, but you will relate your abstractions of abstractions to some system of knowledge. You will use these abstractions in conversation and in recitation, inadequate though they may be at times, but as you read and remember and write, and as you listen and speak, they will become more and more vivid and clearly organized.

EVOCATIVE INTERPRETATION

Do you like to listen to tall tales? Or read novels? Or poetry? Or go to the movies? Why? To be entertained? Or to gain information? Or to be convinced of a great truth? Rather than any of these, is it not that you thereby share more human experiences than you could ever share if you had to abstract them from the action, nonword level? We have observed that symbolizing is a distinctly human activity. It becomes important, not alone because we can make maps that fit territories (not that making accurate maps is not important), but because by symbols we can share the experiences of the lonely and the gay, the grief-stricken and the jubilant. Although as we read the myths, the yarns, the confessions, the poems of the men of literature, we know that they have omitted much, falsified some, and at times expressed the biased and rationalized opinions of frustrated men, still there is that great and valuable residue—human beings sharing their humanity.

The use of language (and speech) as literature, according to Thomas

Clark Pollock, is to express and evoke a human experience.[1] The validity of logical propositions, the consciousness of abstracting, the structure of language, and even the accuracy of predictions, from the literary or evocative viewpoint do not alone determine the value of language (speech). For example, stories have other values than truth. Although it is true that a news story or an on-the-scene broadcast depends upon honest reporting, fictionalized or poetic interpretations are likely to lose value if they are reportorial. The poetic use of speech and language, which for our purposes includes that in novels and plays as well as that in poetry, consists of symbols used not to indicate external objects and events but to evoke in the reader an experience.

The following passage by Sir James Jeans illustrates the use of symbols to convey accurate, referential facts.[2]

And now Galileo catches Jupiter in the field of his telescope and sees four small bodies circling around the great mass of the planet—like moths round a candle-flame. What he sees is an exact replica of the solar system as imagined by Copernicus, and it provides direct visual proof that such systems are at least not alien to the architectural plan of the universe. And yet, strangely enough, he hardly sees the full implications of his discovery at once; he merely avers that he has discovered four new planets which chase one another round and round the known planet Jupiter.

Contrasted to the passage above, the following words by Alfred Noyes illustrate the use of language to evoke an experience, the tremendous experience of discovery.[3]

> He showed me,
> Looking along his outstretched hand, a
>   star,
> A point of light above our olive-trees.
> It was the star called Jupiter. And then
> He bade me look again, but through his
>   glass.
> I feared to look at first, lest I should see
> Some wonder never meant for mortal eyes.
> He too, had felt the same, not fear, but
>   awe,

[1] Thomas C. Pollock, *The Nature of Literature*, p. 176, Princeton University Press, Princeton, N.J., 1942.

[2] James Jeans, *The Universe around Us*, p. 4, The Macmillan Company, New York, 1944.

[3] Alfred Noyes, *Watchers of the Sky*, pp. 142–144, Frederick A. Stokes Company, Philadelphia, 1922. Reprinted by permission of J. B. Lippincott Company.

As if his hand were laid upon the veil
Between this world and heaven.
Then . . . I, too, saw,
Small as the smallest bead of mist that
clings
To a spider's thread at dawn, the floating
disk
Of what had been a star, a planet now,
And near it, with no disk that eyes could
see,
Four needle-points of light, unseen before.
"The moons of Jupiter," he whispered
low,
"I have watched them as they moved, from
night to night;
A system like our own, although the world
Their fourfold lights and shadows make so
strange
Must—as I think—be mightier than we
dreamed,
A Titan planet. Earth begins to fade
And dwindle; yes, the heavens are open-
ing now.
Perhaps up there, this night, some lonely
soul
Gazes at earth, watches our dawning moon,
And wonders, as we wonder."

Alfred Noyes

Too often the limitations of experience, both actual and symbolic are
barriers to the communication of experience. One who has never felt
awe as he gazed at a sky full of brilliant stars will be little moved as he
reads the poetic account of Galileo. To learn to share symbolic experiences requires that one learn to see and feel first of all.

In addition, limited symbolic experience of course prevents the sharing
of experiences. For instance, most students will have some responsiveness to the poem "Leisure."

LEISURE[1]

What is this life if, full of care,
We have no time to stand and stare.

[1] From W. H. Davies, *The Collected Poems of W. H. Davies*, p. 120. Copyright
1929 by Jonathan Cape & Harrison Smith, New York. Reprinted by permission of
the publishers and author's widow.

No time to stand beneath the boughs
And stare as long as sheep or cows.

No time to see, when woods we pass,
Where squirrels hide their nuts in grass.

No time to see, in broad daylight,
Streams full of stars, like skies at night.

No time to turn at Beauty's glance,
And watch her feet, how they can dance.

No time to wait till her mouth can
Enrich that smile her eyes began.

A poor life this if, full of care,
We have no time to stand and stare.

William Davies

During Indian summer and the first warm days of spring, who has
not just stood and stared? Who cannot recall those feelings pleasantly
as he reads the lines? On the other hand De la Mare's "The Listeners"
presents an experience that can probably be felt only by those who
have acquired, through reading, sensitivity to such symbols as phantom
listeners and the "sound of iron on stone."

THE LISTENERS[1]

"Is there anybody there?" said the Traveler,
    Knocking on the moonlit door;
And his horse in the silence champed the grasses
    Of the forest's ferny floor:
And a bird flew up out of the turret,
    Above the Traveler's head:
And he smote upon the door again a second time;
    "Is there anybody there?" he said.
But no one descended to the Traveler;
    No head from the leaf-fringed sill
Leaned over and looked into his gray eyes,
    Where he stood perplexed and still.

[1] From *Collected Poems* by Walter de la Mare. Copyright, 1920, by Henry Holt
and Company, Inc. Copyright, 1948, by Walter de la Mare. Reprinted by permission
of the publishers.

But only a host of phantom listeners
   That dwelt in the lone house then
Stood listening in the quiet of the moonlight
   To that voice from the world of men:
Stood thronging the faint moonbeams on the dark stair
   That goes down to the empty hall,
Hearkening in an air stirred and shaken
   By the lonely Traveler's call.
And he felt in his heart their strangeness,
   Their stillness answering his cry,
While his horse moved, cropping the dark turf,
   'Neath the starred and leafy sky;
For he suddenly smote on the door, even
   Louder, and lifted his head:—
"Tell them I came, and no one answered,
   That I kept my word," he said.
Never the least stir made the listeners,
   Though every word he spake
Fell echoing through the shadowiness of the still house
   From the one man left awake:
Aye, they heard his foot upon the stirrup,
   And the sound of iron on stone,
And how the silence surged softly backward,
   When the plunging hoofs were gone.

Walter de la Mare

However, given *this symbolic experience*, a student should be able to share Louis Untermeyer's fun in writing the nursery rhyme "Jack and Jill" as a parody of "The Listeners," whereas without it he could hardly participate in the amusement.

WALTER DE LA MARE

TELLS THE LISTENER ABOUT JACK AND JILL[1]

Up to the top of the haunted turf
   They climbed on the moonlit hill.
Not a leaf rustled in the underbrush;
   The listening air was still,

[1] From *Selected Poems And Parodies* by Louis Untermeyer. Copyright by Harcourt, Brace and Company, Inc., New York, 1935. Reprinted by permission of the publishers.

And only the noise of the water pail
  As it struck on a jutting stone,
Clattered and jarred against the silence
  As the two trod on alone.

Up to the moonlit peak they went;
  And, though not a word would they say,
Their thoughts outnumbered a poet's love-songs
  In the first green weeks of May.

The stealthy shadows crept closer;
  They clutched at the hem of Jill's gown;
And there at the very top she stumbled,
  And Jack came shuddering down.

Their cries rang out against the stillness,
  Pitiful and high and thin.
And the echoes edged back still further
  As the silence gathered them in.

Louis Untermeyer

Students who, through good reading and listening habits, acquire wide symbolic experiences can share more and more the thoughts and . feelings of all men. Without such wide verbal experience one would remain as narrow and provincial as the illiterate of Hilltown.

Those students whose major interest and special ability lie in the areas of literature, language, music, and art will frequently feel the need of evocative speaking. Because they have enjoyed the sharing of experience, they will wish others to do so. They will not be content merely with giving information about a work of art. They will wish their hearers somehow to feel it. Often this desire demands that they supply their listeners with enough symbolic background for appreciating it. The background material, although informative in nature, must be selected because of its special pertinency to the artistic work. Material irrelevant to the end of evoking appreciative feeling not only is useless but often irritates the listener.

Of the many available means for providing an adequate symbolic experience for the appreciation of a painting, a musical composition, or a piece of literature, a beginning speaker will find helpful any one or any combination of the three methods which are given here.

1. An Account of Relevant Historical Events. Any work of art is produced by a creative, sensitive human being who lives in some place at some time. Byron and Shelley lived shortly after the French Revolution and during the economic and political reformation in England; Tennyson lived while the exciting discoveries in science were being reported; Sherwood Anderson lived in Midwestern American villages and towns when factories were being built and the lives of people were becoming mechanized. F. Scott Fitzgerald wrote during the jazz age of the early twenties. Grant Wood and Thomas Hart Benton painted into their pictures their interpretations of a period when lechery and greed were countered by prudery and comstockery.

The significance of painting or a piece of literature is lost to subsequent generations unless by collateral reading they discover the concrete details or events which were symbolized in the work of art. Only a literate minority will be curious enough to keep the meanings alive through a study of the history of the period. Even they, because of the passage of time, lose much of the original significance. On the other hand, they may discover meanings that the people of the period, including the artist or composer or writer, did not discover. Speakers who are talking because they want to associate with the literate minority in perpetuating the meanings of works of art must of necessity familiarize themselves with historical details relating to those works. Let us suppose, for example, that you like the poetry of John Greenleaf Whittier. You are probably already familiar with "Snowbound" and "Telling the Bees." Suppose you now read "Ichabod," like it, want to tell someone about it, and even read it aloud. First of all, you must find out who Ichabod was; what the name means—whether Whittier was referring to the Ichabod of the Bible; and if not, to whom he was referring. As a hint, you will discover the intensity of dislike that New England abolitionists had for any one who even spoke tolerantly of slavery. You will learn how the great Daniel Webster, often spoken of as "Jovelike," on a certain March day in 1850 did an about-face and betrayed New England abolitionists like Whittier. The meaning of the name Ichabod (the glory has departed) becomes highly significant. The poem now has a meaning quite different from what it had before you gleaned the associated historical facts.

What has been said of the necessity for collateral historical meanings in this instance could be repeated in the case of nearly every piece of literature, of nearly every painting, and of many musical compositions.

Each artistic production becomes more meaningful to the degree that we extend our historical knowledge about it. Yet we must caution again that this history is partly personal. By our own symbolizing we are recreating the past.

2. A SELECTION OF PERTINENT BIOGRAPHICAL DATA WHICH GIVE SIGNIFICANCE TO THE WORK. Of even more worth than the pertinent historical facts are the personal, biographical data which contribute meanings to literature, music, and art. Da Vinci's long quest for the face of the Christ in "The Last Supper," Breughel's peasant backgrounds, Byron's unhappy childhood and tempestuous love affairs, Shakespeare's childhood horror of charnel houses, Chopin's love of Poland all throw intense light upon their works. In greater or lesser detail, speakers wishing to evoke appreciation must ferret out significant biographical data before they present a particular work. The presentation of biographical as well as historical facts may follow the principles set down for narrative speaking.

3. AN INTERPRETATION OF HIDDEN SYMBOLISM. Early in this book we observed that we can get meanings from meanings of meanings. Another way to put it would be: A symbol may stand for another symbol, which may stand for an object which, itself, is symbolic of an idea. Let us take the symbol *hand*, for example. It stands for a

But the

may itself be symbolic of something else, such as *friendship* or *power* or *death*. It should be apparent, then, that although the sentence: "Raise your hands in praise" may mean a literal raising of the hands, the sentence: "If thy right hand offend thee, cut it off" does not necessarily mean a literal cutting off of the right hand. It more probably means severing relations with a servant or a follower. The flexibility of symbolizing permits each artist, whether he be a writer, a musician, or a painter, great freedom in his use of symbols to express his experience. At the same time, many conventional forms of literary symbolism are so well established that knowledge of the symbolism is necessary for a more intimate sharing of human experience. For example, the bridge in Thornton Wilder's *The Bridge of San Luis Rey* is more than a bridge that falls. "Bridge" is a traditional literary symbol. Traditionally, it refers to a mythical "sword bridge" over a river which must be crossed if Psyche (the Soul) is to be liberated from the magician who has imprisoned her. You will see the relation of this idea to the commonly held belief that the soul is imprisoned in the body till death. Then it is liberated. In Tennyson's *Idylls of the King*, as in the legendary accounts of King Arthur and his Round Table, Guinevere is symbolic of psyche or soul; the Holy Grail refers to the dish used by Jesus at His Last Supper and is, therefore, symbolic of purification.

Many of the modern short stories and plays have a new significance to students who will take the time to look up the titles in a good dictionary of folklore, mythology, and legend. One cannot possibly get the full import of that finest of short stories, "The Apple Tree" by John Galsworthy, without also reading the myth of Hippolytus, preferably as told by Euripides. One should also know the symbolic tradition of *apple*. The play *The Green Bay Tree* more sharply states its theme when one knows the traditional symbolism of the bay tree.

Obviously, this is not the place to attempt more than a brief admonition to be alert to hidden symbolic meanings and to become acquainted with the sources of meanings. Student speakers who accept this responsibility become a part of that literate minority who help to perpetuate our symbolic heritage. That heritage, through the ages, has accumulated meanings and values which humanize and enrich the lives of those who can share it. The number who can share it must be increased, if modern education is worthy of the name.

Projects for Practice

Projects designed to develop skill in referential interpretation:

1. What does the term *liberty* mean to you? Who said, "Give me liberty or give me death"? What did he mean? In what documents of democratic government is liberty mentioned? Do our liberties today express the evolution of human thought? For a start, look at *The American Spirit* by Charles A. Beard, or Merle Curti's *The Growth of American Thought*. Then read and report on one of the following:

The Constitution of the United States: first 10 amendments
John Milton, *Aeropagitica*
Charles Louis de Secondat, Baron de Montesquieu, *The Spirit of Laws*

Alexander Hamilton, John Jay, and James Madison, *The Federalist*
Francis Bacon, "The Advancement of Learning"
Thomas Hobbes, *Leviathan*

2. Let the class divide its labor and organize material on liberty.

3. Is the freedom of expression you enjoy in your classes related to the writings listed above? How?

4. What are the laws governing freedom of speech on radio and television?

5. Are there restrictions upon free speech today? If there are, what are they?

6. What responsibilities does free speech entail?

7. Report on Jean Jacques Rousseau's treatment of speech in Part I of *The Origins of Inequality*.

8. Read the following quotation from Francis Bacon's *The Advancement of Learning* and compare or contrast with the point of view expressed in Chap. 7.

And lastly, let us consider the false appearances that are imposed upon us by words, which are framed and applied according to the conceit and capacities of the vulgar sort: and although we think we govern our words, and prescribe it well "*loquendum ut vulgus sentiendum ut sapientes*"; yet certain it is that words, as a Tartar's bow, do shoot back upon the understanding of the wisest, and mightily entangle and pervert the judgement. So as it is almost necessary, in all controversies and disputations, to imitate the wisdom of the mathematicians, in setting down in the very beginning the definitions of our words and terms, that others may know how we accept and understand them, and whether they concur with us or no. For it cometh to pass, for want of this, that we are sure to end there where we ought to have begun, which is, in questions and differences about words.

Projects designed to develop skill in presenting historical background, biographical data, and explaining hidden symbolism:

1. Read "Ichabod."

ICHABOD

So fallen! so lost! the light withdrawn
　　Which once he wore!
The glory from his gray hairs gone
　　Forevermore!

Revile him not, the Tempter hath
　　A snare for all;
And pitying tears, not scorn and wrath,
　　Befit his fall!

Oh, dumb be passion's stormy rage,
    When he who might
Have lighted up and led his age,
    Falls back in night.

Scorn! would the angels laugh, to mark
    A bright soul driven,
Fiend-goaded, down the endless dark,
    From hope and heaven!

Let not the land once proud of him
    Insult him now,
Nor brand with deeper shame his dim,
    Dishonored brow.

But let its humbled sons, instead,
    From sea to lake,
A long lament, as for the dead,
    In sadness make.

Of all we loved and honored, naught
    Save power remains;
A fallen angel's pride of thought,
    Still strong in chains.

All else is gone; from those great eyes
    The soul has fled:
When faith is lost, when honor dies,
    The man is dead!

Then, pay the reverence of old days
    To his dead fame;
Walk backward, with averted gaze,
    And hide the shame!

        John Greenleaf Whittier

What is its significance? Why does Whittier feel so intensely about Ichabod? Why was the name Ichabod chosen for the title? Read an explanation of Daniel Webster's speech on March 7, 1850. Reread "Ichabod." Can you call up the intense feelings you have had toward someone who has been disloyal to you or your group? Tell about the experience. Prepare a 5-minute speech in which you present background material, and also read the poem in a way to increase a listener's appreciation.

2. Read Shakespeare's Sonnet 107, "The Mortal Moon."

THE MORTAL MOON

Not mine own fears, nor the prophetic soul
Of the wide world, dreaming on things to come,
Can yet the lease of my true love control,
Suppos'd as forfeit to a confin'd doom.
The mortal moon hath her eclipse endur'd,
And the sad augurs mock their own presage;
Incertainties now crown themselves assur'd,
And peace proclaims olives of endless age.
Now with the drops of this most balmy time
My love looks fresh, and Death to me subscribes,
Since, spite of him, I'll live in this poor rhyme,
While he insults o'er dull and speechless tribes:
And thou in this shalt find thy monument,
When tyrants' crests and tombs of brass are spent.

William Shakespeare

What is the meaning you abstract from it? Read Leslie Hotson's *Shakespeare's Sonnets Dated*, pages 4 to 21. Prepare a 3-minute speech explaining the poem in terms of Hotson's interpretation.

If Hotson's work is not available, consider the following facts: The Spanish Armada which sailed against England in 1588 was placed in battle array in the manner of a crescent moon. It was defeated, and England was saved from invasion. Shakespeare refers to the defeat of Mark Antony's ships in the words, "Alacke our Terrene (Mediterranean) Moone is now Eclipst, and it portends the fall of Antony." The year of 1588 figures in strange prophecies of the day of doom. The people of Shakespeare's time felt that after the defeat of the Armada there was no longer need for apprehension but that a new period of peace was ushered in.

3. Bring a good recording of Chopin's "Polonaise" (Op. 40, No. 1) to class. Give the historical background and play a passage of the record. Interpret the passage in terms of the background.

4. Bring a good recording of jazz or "boogie woogie" to class. Before playing part of it, prepare the listeners to appreciate it by relating those historical events which are most pertinent to the particular composition. You must select carefully.

5. By talking with music teachers and students and by research, determine what Liszt was trying to express in "Les Funerailles." Present a talk to the class which gives them an adequate symbolic experience for a deeper appreciation of the composition.

6. Select any worthwhile composer, painter, or writer to introduce to the class in the ways outlined.

7. Read parts of *The Ballad of Reading Gaol* by Oscar Wilde. Do biographical facts help us to understand his intense loneliness?

Tell about times when you have felt resentful over insensitivity to suffering. Is this poem symbolic of anything besides Wilde's suffering?

8. Read "Kubla Khan" by Samuel Coleridge.

KUBLA KHAN

In Xanadu did Kubla Khan
A stately pleasure-dome decree:
Where Alph, the sacred river, ran
Through caverns measureless to man
Down to a sunless sea.

So twice five miles of fertile ground
With walls and towers were girdled round:
And there were gardens bright with sinuous
    rills,
Where blossomed many an incense-bearing
    tree;
And here were forests ancient as the hills,
Enfolding sunny spots of greenery.
But oh! that deep romantic chasm which
    slanted
Down the green hill athwart a cedarn cover!
A savage place! as holy and enchanted
As e'er beneath a waning moon was haunted
By woman wailing for her demon-lover!
And from this chasm, with ceaseless turmoil
    seething,
As if this earth in fast thick pants were
    breathing,
A mighty fountain momently was forced:
Amid whose swift half-intermitted burst
Huge fragments vaulted like rebounding hail,
Or chaffy grain beneath the thresher's flail:
And 'mid these dancing rocks at once and
    ever
It flung up momently the sacred river.
Five miles meandering with a mazy mo-
    tion

Through wood and dale the sacred river ran,
Then reached the caverns measureless to man,
And sank in tumult to a lifeless ocean:
And 'mid this tumult Kubla heard from far
Ancestral voices prophesying war!

The shadow of the dome of pleasure
Floated midway on the waves;
Where was heard the mingled measure
From the fountain and the caves.
It was a miracle of rare device,
A sunny pleasure-dome with caves of ice!

A damsel with a dulcimer
In a vision once I saw:
It was an Abyssinian maid,
And on her dulcimer she played,
Singing of Mount Abora.
Could I revive within me
Her symphony and song,
To such a deep delight 'twould win me,
That with music loud and long,
I would build that dome in air,
That sunny dome! those caves of ice!
And all who heard should see them there,—
And all should cry, Beware! Beware!—
His flashing eyes, his floating hair!
Weave a circle round him thrice,
And close your eyes with holy dread,
For he on honey-dew hath fed,
And drunk the milk of Paradise.

Samuel Taylor Coleridge

Tell what it means to you. Read Chap. 19 of *The Road to Xanadu* by John Livingston Lowes. Prepare a 4-minute speech intended to increase our appreciation of "Kubla Khan." You may read the poem aloud after the talk.

9. Read the play *R. U. R.* by Carel Kapek. What idea is the author trying to convey? Is the outcome particularly significant so far as the individual characters are concerned? What is the symbolic significance of the words "Go Adam, Go Eve"?

10. Read "The Killers" by Ernest Hemingway. Is this story limited to only a few individual characters, or is it somehow a representation of the calculated intellectual and emotional murder which we commit and experi-

ence on the word level? Have you observed the "assassination of character" by gossip, by political attack, and by insinuation? Prepare a speech in which you use "The Killers" (or a similar story) to convey your experience in witnessing verbal murder in a quarrel or cheap gossip.

11. Read *Salome* by Oscar Wilde. Is the head of John the Baptist a symbol of Wilde's head? Is the slaying of John the Baptist a symbol of the "moral" murder of Wilde by a society which, like Salome, demands a victim? Can you show that although Wilde himself may like his symbolism, others reject it? Does this rejection of his symbolic meaning intensify his loneness?

12. Select a print of an expressionistic painting by Van Gogh to show to the class. Are the twisted cypresses, rooms, flower gardens symbols of twisted inner thoughts? Read an account of Van Gogh's life.

Present a talk on a print of a painting which illustrates the use of a pictorial symbol for ideas and values. The following are suggested:

> Botticelli, *The Madonna Crowned*
> Filippo Lippi, *The Virgin and Child*
> (What especially is the significance of the apple in the infant Jesus' hand)
> Hieronymus Bosch, *The Ship of Fools*
> Pieter Breughel, *Dutch Proverbs*
> Giorgio Chirico, *Horses*
> Francesco Cossa, *Allegory of Autumn*

13. Prepare and tell a condensed version of John Galsworthy's "The Apple Tree," showing how a knowledge of the symbolism enriches its meaning.

14. Prepare and tell a condensed version of Mordaunt Shairp's *The Green Bay Tree.*

15. Select any other appropriate story or play for an interpretative review for the class.

16. Read Edwin Arlington Robinson's "The House on the Hill." Is this poem merely a description of a house? Or does it have a symbolic significance? Why is *House* capitalized in the poem?

The House on the Hill[1]

> They are all gone away,
> The House is shut and still,
> There is nothing more to say.

> Through broken walls and gray
> The winds blow bleak and shrill:
> They are all gone away.

[1] Edwin Arlington Robinson, "The House on the Hill," from *The Children of the Night*, Charles Scribner's Sons, New York.

Nor is there one to-day
To speak them good or ill:
There is nothing more to say.

Why is it then we stray
Around that sunken sill?
They are all gone away,

And our poor fancy-play
For them is wasted skill:
There is nothing more to say.

There is ruin and decay
In the House on the Hill:
They are all gone away,
There is nothing more to say.

Edwin Arlington Robinson

17. In light of this chapter, read "Sweeney Among the Nightingales," and then read T. H. Thompson, "The Bloody Wood," in *T. S. Eliot: A Selected Critique*, edited by Leonard Unger. Do you agree that T. S. Eliot is only seeking to trouble and delight readers with Sweeney's antics?

SWEENEY AMONG THE NIGHTINGALES[1]
ὤμοι, πέπληγμαι καιρίαν πληγὴν ἔσω

Apeneck Sweeney spreads his knees
Letting his arms hang down to laugh,
The zebra stripes along his jaw
Swelling to maculate giraffe.

The circles of the stormy moon
Slide westward toward the River Plate,
Death and the Raven drift above
And Sweeney guards the hornèd gate.

Gloomy Orion and the Dog
Are veiled; and hushed the shrunken seas;
The person in the Spanish cape
Tries to sit on Sweeney's knees

Slips and pulls the table cloth
Overturns a coffee-cup,

[1] From *Collected Poems of T. S. Eliot*, copyright, 1936, by Harcourt, Brace and Company, Inc., New York, and used by permission of Faber & Faber, Ltd., London.

Reorganised upon the floor
She yawns and draws a stocking up;

The silent man in mocha brown
Sprawls at the window-sill and gapes;
The waiter brings in oranges
Bananas figs and hothouse grapes;

The silent vertebrate in brown
Contracts and concentrates, withdraws;
Rachel *née* Rabinovitch
Tears at the grapes with murderous paws;

She and the lady in the cape
Are suspect, thought to be in league;
Therefore the man with heavy eyes
Declines the gambit, shows fatigue,

Leaves the room and reappears
Outside the window, leaning in,
Branches of wistaria
Circumscribe a golden grin;

The host with someone indistinct
Converses at the door apart,
The nightingales are singing near
The Convent of the Sacred Heart,

And sang within the bloody wood
When Agamemnon cried aloud,
And let their liquid siftings fall
To stain the stiff dishonoured shroud.

T. S. Eliot

18. Prepare a supporting or a rejecting talk of 3 minutes on the following theory that the many modern short stories, plays, and novels of violence are symbolic of our inner conflicts:

A question frequently asked by viewers of the contemporary scene is: Why do brutality, violence, and futility play the leading roles in the movies, on the stage, radio, and television, and in short stories and novels. Although the literature of every age has had its share of assault, murder, and suicide, still the current portrayal of human degradation appears particularly vengeful. "Death of a Salesman," "A Streetcar Named Desire," and "Come Back Little Sheba," all closing on a note of despair and futility, play to crowded houses in the villages as well as in the cities. "True Detective," "Dragnet," "Badge 714," "The Shadow," and "The Falcon" spill out over national networks their sounds of violence. The pocket editions of Mickey Spillane sell in the millions.

One answer to the question is that the fictional assault expresses our inner frustrations and anxieties. The verbal violence is a symbolic projection of revolt by people who have no serenity of soul.

Readings

Adler, Mortimer, *How to Read a Book*, chaps. 9, 11, 12, Simon and Schuster, Inc., New York, 1940.

Benét, William Rose, *The Reader's Encyclopedia*, pp. 537–538, 1091–1092, Thomas Y. Crowell Company, New York, 1948.

Brooks, Cleanth, and Robert Penn Warren, *Understanding Poetry*, chaps. 4–6, Henry Holt and Company, Inc., New York, 1950.

Cooper, Charles W., *Preface to Poetry*, chaps. 7, 8, Harcourt, Brace and Company, Inc., New York, 1943.

Cross, Milton, *Encyclopedia of the Great Composers and Their Music*, vol. 1, pp. 164–178, 433–447, Doubleday & Company, Inc., New York, 1953.

Dictionary of Folklore, Mythology, and Legend, Maria Leach (ed.), vol. 2, pp. 1094–1097.

Dictionary of World Literature, Joseph T. Shipley (ed.), pp. 564–569, Philosophical Library, Inc., New York, 1943.

Hartnoll, Phyllis, *The Oxford Companion to the Theatre*, pp. 759–762, 780, Oxford University Press, New York, 1951.

Muther, Richard, *The History of Modern Painting*, vol. 4, pp. 105–150, E. P. Dutton & Co., Inc., New York, 1907.

The Nineteenth Century (*The Great Centuries of Painting*, planned and directed by Albert Skira), pp. 106–134, Skira, Inc., Publishers, New York, 1951.

13

INTERPRETATIVE READING

In the preceding chapter you observed some of the problems of interpreting and communicating meanings when you use your own patterns
of expression. You may well wonder what problem of interpreting is
involved when you read aloud the exact words of the author. Without
experience or reflection, you may say no abstractions of abstractions
are involved. In reality, however, even though you read the exact words
of an author, you are still abstracting meanings in subtle ways. Your
tone of voice, your rate of speech, your inflections, your loudness, as
well as facial expression and physical bearing, lift out the meanings of
the writer. In addition to the principles of interpretative speech which
we have discussed, principles which apply equally well to interpretative
reading, we must consider additional basic principles that should help
you when you communicate the exact words of another.

ORAL READING AND THE DISCOVERY OF MEANING

Some students may wonder why reading, particularly reading aloud,
should be taught in college. They may think that since formal reading
instruction was discontinued in the grades and since reading aloud was
not generally taught in high school, they have advanced beyond the
stage when such an elementary training will be fruitful. Experiments,
however, show:

The development of a high degree of efficiency in the various types of reading
required in contemporary life does not occur at any one age or grade level.
Neither is it completed, as some erroneously assume, in the elementary
school. It is a type of growth that begins in the kindergarten and primary
grades and continues throughout high school and college and not infrequently
long after formal education is complete.[1]

[1] William S. Gray (ed.), "Reading and Factors Influencing Reading Efficiency,"
Reading in General Education, p. 31, American Council on Education, Washington,
1940.

The records of the achievements of college students also reveal that the early college years represent a period in which the more complex skills in reading, including the analysis and interpretation of meaning, can be developed more rapidly.

That oral reading contributes to this development is argued by Eduard C. Lindeman, professor emeritus of social philosophy at the New York School of Social Work, Columbia University. After commenting upon the contributions made to family living by oral reading at the fireside, he adds:[1]

I was also encouraged to move toward experimentation by the fact which I had only then learned: namely that there is a functional correlation between the ability to read aloud and effectiveness of silent reading. In other words, I had learned that *persons who do not read well aloud, in most instances do not read well at all.* Reading, in short, is something more than seeing words in sentences. Reading is a way of acting our ideas. To read aloud is to add a new dimension to the acting. Thus, when I say that reading is one of the dramatic arts, I am implying that it is a device for bringing ideas to life. Good readers and good listeners become actors in a living play.

Much of literature is not vital until it is read aloud. Miniver Cheevy's frustration and the Patriot's disillusionment could hardly be fully felt with silent reading alone. An oral reading of much of literature is essential to understanding because it was written to be read aloud. The oral reader, then, must have such freedom from self-concern, such concentration, and such control of his speech mechanism that he can communicate the nuances of meaning and emotion the author intended.

BASIC TECHNIQUES IN INTERPRETATIVE READING

Although the use of technical devices cannot of itself make readers with insight, sensitivity, and a sure responsiveness to the meanings of literature, still the close observation and patient application of basic techniques can open the mind to new meanings and vivify their oral expression.

1. OBSERVING THE WRITER'S UNITS OF THOUGHTS. Generally thoughts are expressed by groups of words, not in a word-by-word manner. As language develops in the individual, single words expressing a whole idea give way to groups of words. The infant's "Mama" may mean "I want mama," or "That is mama." Later, as his responses to the world

[1] Eduard C. Lindeman, "Reading Among Friends," in *The Wonderful World of Books*, Alfred Stefferud (ed.), p. 61, The New American Library, New York, 1953.

become individualized and specific, he uses thought units made up of groups of words focusing upon a central idea. These thought units help further to differentiate and refine his responses.

In spontaneous speech, the thought units are indicated chiefly by pauses, some extremely brief, some long. In writing, the thought units are, in part, set off by punctuation marks, although punctuation is in fact chiefly a convention designed to assist the eye. Furthermore, as a convention, it undergoes changes. Consequently, in reading any passage the interpreter must determine thought units without relying too much on punctuation. In many instances the oral reader will supply punctuation marks of his own. In others, he will ignore the punctuation marks that are printed.

Observe what distortion to the thought occurs when you read the following selection aloud and group thought units only on the basis of punctuation.

ATALANTA IN CALYDON[1]

Before the beginning of years
   There came to the making of man
Time, with a gift of tears;
   Grief, with a glass that ran;
Pleasure, with pain for leaven;
   Summer, with flowers that fell;
Remembrance fallen from heaven,
   And madness risen from hell;
Strength without hands to smite;
   Love that endures for a breath;
Night, the shadow of light,
   And life, the shadow of death.
And the high gods took in hand
   Fire, and the falling of tears,
And a measure of sliding sand
   From under the feet of the years;
And froth and drift of the sea;
   And dust of the labouring earth;
And bodies of things to be
   In the houses of death and of birth;
And wrought with weeping and laughter,
   And fashioned with loathing and love

[1] Algernon Swinburne, *Collected Poetical Works*, vol. 2, pp. 258–259, Harper & Brothers, New York.

With life before and after
And death beneath and above,
For a day and a night and a morrow,
That his strength might endure for a span
With travail and heavy sorrow,
The holy spirit of man.

Algernon Swinburne

Now observe faithfully as you read the first two stanzas of Browning's "Soliloquy of the Spanish Cloister" what is lost by observing all marks of punctuation.

Gr-r-r—there go, my heart's abhorrence!
Water your damned flower-pots, do!
If hate killed men, Brother Lawrence,
God's blood, would not mine kill you!
What? your myrtle-bush wants trimming?
Oh, that rose has prior claims—
Needs its leaden vase filled brimming?
Hell dry you up with its flames!

At the meal we sit together:
Salve tibi! I must hear
Wise talk of the kind of weather,
Sort of season, time of year:
Not a plenteous cork-crop: scarcely
Dare we hope oak-galls, I doubt:
What's the Latin name for "parsley"?
What's the Greek name for Swine's Snout?

Robert Browning

The student who is just beginning his study of oral reading must make sure to avoid the common error of using each line of the passage as a thought unit. Notice the distortion of thought and the singsong rhythm when "Paul Revere's Ride" is read as if each line represented a thought unit.

Listen, my children, and you shall hear
Of the midnight ride of Paul Revere,
On the eighteenth of April, in Seventy-five;
Hardly a man is now alive
Who remembers that famous day and year.

Henry Wadsworth Longfellow

Now mark the thought units and reread.

The student will discover that the more adept he becomes in expressing the thought units of the author the more distinctive and individual variability he will show. Poor readers tend to be uniform, while trained readers show variability.

Lynch conducted an investigation in which groups of trained readers and untrained readers read the same paragraphs that represented factual prose, expressions of anger, and expressions of grief respectively. The readings were recorded and, by means of special photographic apparatus, were subjected to extensive analysis.[1] The analysis was summarized by Lynch in the following paragraph that includes references to patterns of word groupings as well as to other closely related patterns:

For the majority of measures experienced readers tended to vary more among themselves in reading the selections than did the inexperienced subjects. This shows that there are many individual differences in the effective reading of a given passage, particularly if the material is of an emotional nature, and that no one way may be set down as the right way to interpret a given selection. In spite of this variability, however, certain consistent tendencies among the trained readers differentiated them from the members of the untrained group. The trained readers used longer pauses between phrases for each passage, a much slower rate of speech within phrases for the third passage, a wider pitch range and greater pitch variation for all passages, a more marked tendency to set off significant words by using large inflections, and a significantly greater tendency to use more complex and fewer simple pitch inflections than did the subjects in the inexperienced group. The trained group in reading the emotional passages shortened the polysyllabic words and prolonged the pauses between phrases. Both groups raised the pitch level in the expression of emotion, the passage expressing anger exhibiting the greatest rise. In no case was the impersonation of a male or female character obtained by lowering or raising the pitch.

As we have hinted earlier, the expression of thought units in the oral interpretation of poetry poses critical problems. The regularity of length of lines and the use of rhyming words tend to lead the inexperienced reader to fall into a singsong chant. Even experienced interpreters read rhyming words at the same or very nearly the same pitch.[2] To make

[1] Gladys E. Lynch, "A Phonophotographic Study of Trained and Untrained Voices Reading Factual and Dramatic Material," *Archives of Speech*, vol. 1, pp. 24–25, 1934.

[2] Wilbur Schramm, *Approaches to a Science of English Verse*, p. 58, University of Iowa Studies, no. 46, 1935.

this tendency all the worse, high school pupils in many literature classes have been taught the traditional practice of scanning and dividing lines into metrical feet. Thus, a line of iambic pentameter will be read:

the PLOWman HOMEward WENDS his WEARy WAY

Obviously, this grouping is sheer nonsense. The line might be read:

The plowman/homeward wends/his weary way

That the metrical foot is not a unit of a line of poetry, and that it does not express the rhythm of the line, is clearly shown by Schramm's careful, scientific study already referred to. Schramm secured recordings of a number of distinguished poets reading their own poetry. Among these were Stephen Vincent Benét, Robert Hillyer, T. S. Eliot, Vachel Lindsay, and Hamlin Garland. By means of (1) an oscillograph which recorded the sound wave so that it could be studied for pitch and quality, (2) a high-speed output-level recorder which registers the intensity of the sound, and (3) a strobophotographic camera which graphs the pitch (all three registered the duration of sounds and pauses in detail), such characteristics as rate, stress, inflection, and phrasing (grouping of words in units) could be determined with accuracy. In no case did a poet read as if he were scanning. Furthermore, the poets do not think of metrical feet when they are composing. One of Schramm's conclusions was that lines of poetry should be thought of "not as a group of little segments which we call syllables and metrical feet, but rather as a continuous flow of melody broken only by unvoiced consonants and phrasal pauses." The interpreter will do well to forget rules of scansion in preparing to read. Instead of scanning, he should seek to discover the subtleties of meaning and to express them by flexibility of voice. The melody will emerge as the meaning flows in appropriate thought units.

2. EXPRESSING THE RELATIONS BETWEEN THE UNITS OF THOUGHT. As we have observed in Chap. 8, comprehending the meaning of anything depends upon a perception of the relations between the parts of a whole as well as upon a perception of the individual parts. We have observed how individuals with intellectual disturbances may be able to perceive the component parts of a picture, map, or paragraph but are unable to get meaning from the whole. To know, to understand, to

comprehend involves the mental grasping of complex relations. Even in the reading of short passages, the relations between parts give the cues to the meaning of the whole. As an experiment, read the following telegraphic message:

Gladstone   prime minister   England   described   Constitution   United States   "most wonderful work   struck
off   by   brain   purpose   man."   statement
sometimes   taken   mean   framers   Constitution waved
aside   past experience and   create   original   fundamental law.   Nothing   further from   truth.   no reflection on
founders   Constitution but   tribute   to   considered judgment   that   Constitution   product of   accumulated   experience   centuries.   Constitution has   roots
soil   past.   life   continuous unfolding   experiences
laws have   debt   pay   heritage   past   reflection   conditions   of   they have grown.   those who
seek   understand   American Constitution cannot start with
Constitution   but   go back   years   include   background

Before reading further, write a paragraph on what the words mean to you. Now read the complete passage and compare its meaning with what you abstracted.

It was Gladstone, the great prime minister of England, who once described the Constitution of the United States as the "most wonderful work ever struck off at a given time by the brain and purpose of man." This statement has sometimes been taken to mean that the framers of the Constitution waved aside all past experience and proceeded to create an entirely original and novel fundamental law. Nothing could be further from the truth. It is no reflection on the founders of the Constitution, but rather a tribute to their considered judgment, to say that the Constitution of the United States is a product of the accumulated political experience of centuries. The Constitution has its roots deep down in the soil of the past. Just as life is a continuous unfolding of new experiences which grow out of past experiences, so too laws have their debt to pay to the heritage of the past and are a reflection of the conditions out of which they have grown. That is why those who seek to understand the American Constitution cannot start with the Constitution itself, but must go back many years to include the background from which it emerged.

Look at any picture, read history or literature, listen to any musical composition, and you will be convinced that it is not the individual elements, words, or notes which alone give meaning. It is the relation between them.

Relations between the parts of a sentence, a paragraph, a poem, an essay, a story give it meaning. The oral reader must perceive the relations as the writer perceived them. The order of words, the connectives of speech, and vocal inflection show the relations.

In extended passages connective and relational words provide many of the cues to the thought relations intended. Various writers on rhetoric have classified the grammatical, logical, and rhetorical relations between the different parts of a sentence, between sentences within a paragraph, between paragraphs, between chapters, and between books. Any classification, no matter how extended, seems incomplete.

However, students may find the following classification of thought relations and relational words helpful, since experience shows that a study of the relational and connective words in writing sharpens perception.

    1. Coordinate relationships

RELATIONS BETWEEN THOUGHTS OF NEARLY EQUAL VALUE	RELATIONAL WORDS
Addition, harmony, agreement	Again, and, furthermore, moreover, likewise
Contrast or opposition	But, however, yet, on the other hand
Alternation or choice	Or, either . . . or, neither . . . nor
Consequence or reason	For, consequently, hence, therefore
Repetition	(Frequently none) to re-peat, again
Parenthetical	(Usually dashes or parentheses show the thought more or less added to or inserted between other thoughts)

    2. Subordinate relationships

RELATIONSHIPS IN WHICH ONE THOUGHT MODIFIES ANOTHER (By qualifying, limiting, describing, comparing, showing the reason for, or result of, conceding, stating a condition of, etc.)	RELATIONAL WORDS
Reason	Because, as, since
Cause	Because, as, since
Condition	If, unless, provided that
Concession	Though, although, even though
Degree	As much as, less than, more than
Purpose	That, so that, in order that, lest
Place	Where, wherever
Manner	As if, as, as though
Result	So that, such that
Time	When, whenever
Descriptive (thought units which list characterizing details) Restrictive (thought units which figuratively point at and identify)	Who, which, that, where, when, what

In conversational speech even an untrained voice is somewhat responsive to the relations between thought units. In interpretative reading, however, the voice is likely to be unresponsive to the many fine shades of expressed or implied relations between units of meaning. To increase insight into the meaning and develop responsiveness in the voice, the student should make full analyses of the thought relations and practice expressing them aloud. It is good in practice reading to drop relational words and to try to let the voice alone carry the implied relationship. An illustrative analysis is made of a poem with which you are already familiar. Keep in mind as you read this that another analysis might be equally appropriate.

Main question:	What is this life
Descriptive detail:	If full of care
Condition:	We have no time
Purpose:	To stand and stare
Repetition:	No time to stand
Additive detail (place):	Beneath the boughs

Repetition:	And stare
Manner:	As long as sheep or cows
Repetition:	No time to see
Additive detail (time):	When woods we pass
Additive detail (place):	Where squirrels hide their nuts in grass
Main idea:	
Answer to question:	A poor life
Repetition:	This
Repetition of condition:	If full of care
Repetition of main idea:	We have no time
Repetition of purpose:	To stand and stare

The elaboration of an idea and a mood by additional thought units is well illustrated in the following selection:[1]

Main idea:	I continued in a happy somnambulistic state,
Amplified by description:	Blousy, dishevelled,
Additive details:	Dropping hairpins, tennis balls, and notebooks wherever I went,
	Drinking tea with Dr. Lily Campbell and the professors, lapping up talk of books and history,
	Drinking tea with classmates and Elizabeth Boynton, the librarian,
	Having dates or nearly dates with the two M's on either side of me, Macon and Morgan,
Repetition and addition:	Having dates with Leonard Keeler,
	Who was working out campus thefts and misdemeanors with the first lie detector,
	Falling asleep in all afternoon lectures,
	Late for every appointment
Parenthetical detail:	(Once when I entered English history on time the whole class burst out laughing.)

At times even though the wording would seem to indicate a heaping up of images or details, the meaning may call for a telescoping or a blending of the details to reduce their number and significance. For example, in reading the first speaker's words in the selection below, the reader should seek to reduce "trees, meadows, mountains, groves, and streams" to a single blurred detail, and in reading the second speaker's words he should amplify the number and augment the importance of

[1] Agnes de Mille, *Dance to the Piper*, p. 75, Little, Brown & Company, Boston, 1952. By permission of the publishers and the Atlantic Monthly Press.

each image. Two young women, when asked what they saw on a rural holiday, replied in sequence:

Repetitive: "—Not much have I!
Condensation: Trees, meadows, mountains, groves, and streams,
                   Blue sky and clouds, and sunny gleams."
Contrast: The other, smiling, said the same,
                   But with face transfigured and eye of flame:
Additive: "Trees, meadows, mountains, groves, and streams!
                   Blue sky and clouds, and sunny gleams."

In view of the discussion and the illustrations of relations between thought units, analyze "Atalanta in Calydon" again. In view of this analysis, read the selection aloud. Do you have new meanings? Pay particular attention to the significance of additive details.

3. RESPONDING TO THE MOOD OF THE AUTHOR. At the pep rally or at the game you unashamedly use the language of others to express your own feelings. The words may signify desperation, as "Hold that line," or intense hope, as "We want a touchdown." The feelings are sincere and are a part of your system of social values. Literature, too, although more elegant in style, is made up of deep and universal emotions. It is a written record of the hopes, aspirations, fears, faith, despondency, and anger of men. To read any significant passage of literature without the appropriate emotional response is to fail to share in great human experiences.

Perceiving the author's mood, as well as his meaning, demands creative activity by the interpreter. The cold print must be brought to life. For example, the two words "good night" are without meaning until read aloud. Then they may mean resignation, repressed anger, unleashed disgust, a final farewell, plaintive longing, or loving gentleness. The ambiguity of the words is dispelled when the reader gives them his evaluation.

The attitudes or feelings shown by the reader are not the writer's but his own. The feelings, as well as the words, must be remembered and revived from past experiences suggested by the reading. Their nature and their intensity are the result of at least three highly interrelated factors. First, there is the reader himself: his personal capacities for perceiving the feeling of a writer and for reviving his own; his background of experience, both actual and symbolic; his pattern of physiologic response, phlegmatic or sensitive, impulsive or restrained. Second, there is the written composition: the choice and arrangement of words; the denotations and connotations; the melody or cacophony of sounds; the internal relations of the parts; and the external relations of the whole to the time, place, and persons who read it and hear it read. Third, there are the external cues a reader may have received from biographical and historical accounts of the author and the events to which the selection is related. A positive aesthetic response results from a synthesis of all three factors.

Most students have little difficulty in expressing their feelings before friends. There is abandonment in language, facial expression, and movement. On the other hand, many students perform in a colorless, inhibited manner when reading before a class. The formality of the social setting, the unfamiliarity of the language, and the unreality of the author's mood, as well as the lack of systematic training in oral interpretation, combine to check the student's oral responses. In learning to overcome these factors the following procedures are helpful: context copying, tone copying, group response.

a. Context Copying. Nearly all literature is written in or about a particular social context. Poets have often written their poems for their cronies at the inn or in the coffee house as well as for the larger audience. They have even written down for themselves what was visioned in a dream or what was a sudden outburst of symbolizing. Storytellers have created their yarns for companions at the campfire or on the trail. Essayists have enclosed their reflections in letters to be read aloud to relatives and neighbors. Recreating in make-believe the social context in which the literature was first received is one way of transforming the inhibiting formality of the classroom into a warm and receptive atmosphere. The young reader can lose much of his self-concern when he reenacts the situation before a small group. In fact, many stutterers do not stutter in playing a role or speaking dialect. Many of the inhibiting and conflictive forces are released when one becomes for a while another personality. Role playing has this beneficial effect in interpretative reading as well as in discussion and in mental hygiene. It is not difficult to recreate a scene in which the young George Gordon Byron, wounded by the criticism of early poetic attempts, rebellious at the requirements of Trinity College, and riotous in his living, reads aloud to the idolizing friends gathered in his room. What he reads is the newly finished poem, "Thoughts Suggested by a College Examination." With a few bravos for encouragement, a somewhat Byronic rebel in a modern college can bring to life the satiric lines:

THOUGHTS SUGGESTED BY A COLLEGE EXAMINATION

HIGH in the midst, surrounded by his
    peers,
MAGNUS his ample front sublime uprears:
Placed on his chair of state, he seems a
    god,
While Sophs and Freshmen tremble at his
    nod.
As all around sit wrapt in speechless
    gloom,
His voice in thunder shakes the sounding
    dome;
Denouncing dire reproach to luckless fools,
Unskill'd to plod in mathematic rules.

Happy the youth in Euclid's axioms
    tried,
Though little versed in any art beside;
Who, scarcely skill'd an English line to
    pen,
Scans Attic metres with a critic's ken.
What though he knows not how his fathers
    bled,
When civil discord piled the fields with
    dead,
When Edward bade his conquering bands
    advance,
Or Henry trampled on the crest of France;
Though marvelling at the name of Magna
    Charta,
Yet well he recollects the laws of Sparta;
Can tell what edicts sage Lycurgus made,
While Blackstone's on the shelf neglected
    laid;
Of Grecian dramas vaunts the deathless
    fame,
Of Avon's bard remembering scarce the
    name.

Such is the youth whose scientific pate
Class-honours, medals, fellowships, await;

Or even, perhaps, the declamation prize,
If to such glorious height he lifts his eyes.
But lo! no common orator can hope
The envied silver cup within his scope.
Not that our heads much eloquence require,
Th' ATHENIAN'S glowing style, or Tully's
    fire.
A manner clear or warm is useless, since
We do not try by speaking to convince.
Be other orators of pleasing proud:
We speak to please ourselves, not move the
    crowd:
Our gravity prefers the muttering tone,
A proper mixture of the squeak and groan:
No borrow'd grace of action must be seen;
The slightest motion would displease the
    Dean,
Whilst every staring graduate would prate
Against what he could never imitate.

The man who hopes t' obtain the prom-
    ised cup
Must in one posture stand, and ne'er look
    up;
Nor stop, but rattle over every word—
No matter what, so it can *not* be heard.
Thus let him hurry on, nor think to rest:
Who speaks the fastest 's sure to speak the
    best;
Who utters most within the shortest space
May safely hope to win the wordy race.

The sons of science these, who, thus re-
    paid,
Linger in ease in Granta's sluggish shade;
Where on Cam's sedgy banks supine they lie,
Unknown, unhonour'd live, unwept for die:
Dull as the pictures which adorn their
    halls,
They think all learning fix'd within their
    walls:

In manners rude, in foolish forms precise,
All modern arts affecting to despise;
Yet prizing Bentley's, Brunck's, or Porson's
    note,
More than the verse on which the critic
    wrote:
Vain as their honours, heavy as their ale,
Sad as their wit, and tedious as their tale;
To friendship dead, though not untaught to
    feel
When Self and Church demand a bigot
    zeal.
With eager haste they court the lord of
    power,
Whether 't is Pitt or Petty rules the hour;
To him, with suppliant smiles, they bend
    the head,
While distant mitres to their eyes are
    spread.
But should a storm o'erwhelm him with
    disgrace,
They 'd fly to seek the next who fill'd his
    place.
Such are the men who learning's treasures
    guard!
Such is their practice, such is their reward!
This much, at least, we may presume to
    say—
The premium can't exceed the price they
    pay.

                                        Lord Byron

In the biographies and collections of letters of numerous English and American writers, the curious student will find vivid descriptions of social contexts which may be copied as particular passages are read aloud. Edna St. Vincent Millay receives a copy of a poem which she reads, or she sends one to her mother. John Keats, ill, and lonely, but deeply in love, writes a letter and a sonnet to Fanny Brawne. Robert Louis Stevenson reads a letter aloud before sending it from Samoa. Mark Twain on a lecture tour tells a yarn about life on the Mississippi.

By copying context, students may abstract moments of the past at lower and more meaningful levels.

b. Tone Copying. The language of literature, being formal, may itself inhibit the reader's emotional response. By first expressing the mood of the selection in his own colloquial language, the student may break the inhibitions imposed. This method, first proposed by A. E. Phillips and used by numerous subsequent authorities on interpretative reading, includes a long classification of attitudes and moods and suggests both familiar, colloquial language and literary language for expressing them. Listed were attitudes of admission, advice, affection, aggrievance, agony, amazement, anger, and so on, through the alphabet. The list, although repetitious, stimulates the perception of nuances of feeling. As a test of your own perception of mood, classify the accompanying colloquial expressions of mood according to the brief list of attitudes included.

1. Advice
2. Aggrievance
3. Amazement
4. Aversion
5. Boldness
6. Mockery
7. Obstinacy
8. Warning
9. Affection
10. Complaint

I won't leave. They can't put me out of my room.
Don't let on, the authorities won't find out who broke it.
After all I have done for the school, they have denied me the award.
If I were you, I should go right to the President with the complaint.
We lost. Our team lost to that school. Oh, no!
The big baby. He whined like a hurt child.
Well, well if it isn't old Bill. How are you, pal?
I can't stand that sort of thing. It goes against the grain.
I walked right into his office and told him he couldn't do that to me.
He avoids me completely. He won't even talk to me.

Now try matching the colloquial expressions with the quotations from Shakespeare, below.

I'll tell you what you shall do. Our general's wife is now the general; confess yourself freely to her; importune her help to put you in your place again.

The dearest friend to me, the kindest man,
The best condition'd and unwearied spirit
In doing courtesies.

Brutus hath riv'd my heart:
A friend should bear his friend's infirmities,
But Brutus makes mine greater than they are.

What! fifty of my followers at a clap!
Within a fortnight?

O, he's as tedious
As is a tired horse, a railing wife;
Worse than a smoky house: I had rather live
With cheese and garlick, in a windmill, far,
Than feed on cates, and have him talk to me,
In any summer-house in Christendom.

Let it fall . . . though the fork invade
The region of my heart.

My lord of Gloster, I have long borne
Your blunt upbraidings and your bitter scoffs:
By heaven, I will acquaint his majesty
Of those gross taunts that oft I have endured.

Aye, and that tongue of his that bade the Romans
Mark him, and write his speeches in their books,
Alas! it cried, *give me some drink, Titinius,*
As a sick girl.

In the way of bargain, mark ye me,
I'll cavil on the ninth part of a hair.

Hark! Who lies i' the second chamber?

Although few or none of us have had the horrible experience of a scene
like that described in Robert Frost's "'Out, Out—'" we can call up
sensations of somewhat similar scenes—a serious automobile accident
that resulted from carelessness, a bad cut with a knife. The sudden
shock followed by the horrible consequences of witnessing death can be
experienced only through such experience as we have had and by recall-
ing with abandonment the voice and physical responses evoked then.

Read Robert Frost's poem "'Out, Out—'" aloud at the first reading.
Recall and express aloud past experiences of shock. Reread the poem.

"Out, Out—"[1]

The buzz-saw snarled and rattled in the yard
And made dust and dropped stove-length sticks of wood,
Sweet-scented stuff when the breeze drew across it.
And from there those that lifted eyes could count
Five mountain ranges one behind the other
Under the sunset far into Vermont.
And the saw snarled and rattled, snarled and rattled,
As it ran light, or had to bear a load.
And nothing happened: day was all but done.
Call it a day, I wish they might have said
To please the boy by giving him the half hour
That a boy counts so much when saved from work.
His sister stood beside them in her apron
To tell them "Supper." At the word, the saw,
As if to prove saws knew what supper meant,
Leaped out at the boy's hand, or seemed to leap—
He must have given the hand. However it was,
Neither refused the meeting. But the hand!
The boy's first outcry was a rueful laugh,
As he swung toward them holding up the hand
Half in appeal, but half as if to keep
The life from spilling. Then the boy saw all—
Since he was old enough to know, big boy
Doing a man's work, though a child at heart—
He saw all spoiled. "Don't let him cut my hand off—
The doctor, when he comes. Don't let him, sister!"
So. But the hand was gone already.
The doctor put him in the dark of ether.
He lay and puffed his lips out with his breath.
And then—the watcher at his pulse took fright.
No one believed. They listened at his heart.
Little—less—nothing!—and that ended it.
No more to build on there. And they, since they
Were not the one dead, turned to their affairs.

Robert Frost

---

[1] From *Mountain Interval* by Robert Frost. Copyright, 1916, 1921, by Henry Holt and Company, Inc., New York. Copyright, 1944, by Robert Frost. Reprinted by permission of the publishers.

c. Group Interaction. Just as group discussion facilitates speech activities for students in public speaking, so, too, does group interaction in oral reading contribute to feelings of security and a we-are-all-in-this-together attitude. Such response breaks the inhibition of the formalized classroom. Certain selections lend themselves particularly well for this type of reading. In fact, more of the author's mood may be revealed by such reading than by a single reader. The success of group reading will depend largely upon the absence of a blasé, this-is-childish attitude and the discovery of what earlier generations knew so well, that group participation in reading can be as pleasurable as group participation in athletics, music, square dancing, or any other creative recreation. In group reading students should imaginatively create an appropriate scene so that the group response will seem as natural as conversation or discussion.

Projects for Practice

1. Let four students form a conversational group, two who know the way and two who are seeking. Before class they should have formulated their meanings from the poem "Up-Hill" by Christina Rossetti. The intensity of an important guest should, of course, be revealed by voice, and manner. The symbolic significance should be thoroughly understood.

Up-Hill

READER 1:	Does the road wind up-hill all the way?
READER 2:	*Yes, to the very end.*
READER 3:	Will the day's journey take the whole long day?
READER 4:	*From morn to night, my friend.*
READER 1:	But is there for the night a resting-place?
READER 2:	*A roof for when the slow, dark hours begin.*
READER 3:	May not the darkness hide it from my face?
READER 4:	*You cannot miss that inn.*
READER 1:	Shall I meet other wayfarers at night?
READER 2:	*Those who have gone before.*
READER 3:	Then must I knock, or call when just in sight?
READER 4:	*They will not keep you standing at that door.*
READER 1:	Shall I find comfort, travel-sore and weak?
READER 2:	*Of labor you shall find the sum.*
READER 3:	Will there be beds for me and all who seek?
READERS 2 and 4:	*Yea, beds for all who come.*

Christina Rossetti

2. If some students who like to gossip can catch the chatty, gossipy tone of the following stanzas from Byron's *Don Juan*, they can give a demonstration of a nineteenth-century gathering of a rather fast group. The tempo should be lively. Read enough about Byron to know whether Donna Inez may not be a caricature of Annabella Milbanke.

DON JUAN

MAN 1: In Seville was he born, a pleasant city,
    Famous for oranges and women—he
  Who has not seen it will be much to pity,
    So says the proverb—and I quite agree;
  Of all the Spanish towns is none more pretty,
    Cadiz, perhaps—but that you soon may see:—
  Don Juan's parents lived beside the river,
  A noble stream, and call'd the Guadalquivir.

MAN 2: His father's name was Jóse—*Don*, of course,
    A true Hidalgo, free from every stain
  Of Moor or Hebrew blood, he traced his source
    Through the most Gothic gentlemen of Spain,
  A better cavalier ne'er mounted horse,
    Or, being mounted, e'er got down again,
  Than Jóse, who begot our hero, who
  Begot—but that's to come—Well, to renew:

WOMAN 1: His mother was a learned lady, famed
    For every branch of every science known—
  In every Christian language ever named,
    With virtues equall'd by her wit alone.
  She made the cleverest people quite ashamed,
    And even the good with inward envy groan,
  Finding themselves so very much exceeded
  In their own way by all the things that she did.

WOMAN 2: Her memory was a mine: she knew by heart
    All Calderon and greater part of Lopé,
  So that if any actor miss'd his part
    She could have served him for the prompter's copy,
  For her Feinagle's were an useless art,
    And he himself obliged to shut up shop—he
  Could never make a memory so fine as
  That which adorn'd the brain of Donna Inez.

WOMAN 3: Her favourite science was the mathematical,
    Her noblest virtue was her magnanimity;

Her wit (she sometimes tried at wit) was Attic all,
   Her serious sayings darken'd to sublimity;
In short, in all things she was fairly what I call
   A prodigy—her morning dress was dimity,
Her evening silk, or, in the summer, muslin,
And other stuffs, with which I won't stay puzzling.

. . . .

WOMAN 1:   In short, she was a walking calculation,
      Miss Edgeworth's novels stepping from their covers,
   Or Mrs. Trimmer's books on education,
      Or "Coelebs' Wife" set out in quest of lovers,
   Morality's prim personification,
      In which not Envy's self a flaw discovers;
   To others' share let "female errors fall,"
   For she had not even one—the worst of all.

. . . .

MAN 1:   'T is pity learned virgins ever wed
      With persons of no sort of education,
   Or gentlemen, who, though well born and bred,
      Grow tired of scientific conversation;
   I do n't choose to say much upon this head,
      I 'm a plain man, and in a single station,
   But—Oh! ye lords of ladies intellectual,
   Inform us truly, have they not hen-peck'd you all?

Lord Byron

3. The poem "The Song of the Shirt" requires a larger group and a more formal setting. It could be done as a sort of television dramatization. The narrator at one side begins the story. The working women carry it on from there. One adaptation concludes these projects.

4. The group reading of ballads can serve to heighten the emotional responsiveness of those who are inhibited and can offer a vivid contrast to the traditional method of interpreting a ballad.

A ballad is a realistic story in verse, a story in which the plot is paramount. The action occurs rapidly. There is little time for description or characterization. The ballad, more than any verse form except dramatic verse, was intended to be spoken.

Traditionally the interpretation of a ballad called for an impersonal, objective tone. Although the story might concern murder, hanging, or illicit love, the reporter is apparently little moved. He is a kind of callous news reporter who is no longer shocked by ugly realism.

To begin with, Sir Walter Scott's ballad "Lord Randal" might be read by a man and woman. Then a student who aspires to be a journalist could read the ballad as if he were reporting what had been said by the characters.

LORD RANDAL

"O where hae ye been, Lord Randal, my
    son?
O where hae ye been, my handsome young
    man?"
"I hae been to the wild wood; mother,
    make my bed soon,
For I'm weary wi hunting, and fain wald
    lie down."

"Where gat ye your dinner, Lord Randal,
    my son?
Where gat ye your dinner, my handsome
    young man?"
"I din'd wi my true-love; mother, make
    my bed soon,
For I'm weary wi hunting, and fain wald
    lie down."

"What gat ye to your dinner, Lord Ran-
    dal, my son?
What gat ye to your dinner, my handsome
    young man?"
"I gat eels boiled in broo; mother, make
    my bed soon,
For I'm weary wi hunting, and fain wald
    lie down."

"What became of your bloodhounds, Lord
    Randal, my son?
What became of your bloodhounds, my
    handsome young man?"
"O they swelld and they died; mother,
    make my bed soon,
For I'm weary wi hunting, and fain wald
    lie down."

"O I fear ye are poisond, Lord Randal,
    my son!
O I fear ye are poisond, my handsome
    young man!"

"O yes! I am poisond; mother, make my
   bed soon,
For I'm sick at the heart and I fain wald
   lie down."

                   Sir Walter Scott

5. Other poems which lend themselves delightfully to group reading are E. B. White's "The ABC of Security," which may be found in *The New Yorker*, May 9, 1953, and Archibald MacLeish's "Colloquy for the States, 1943," which may be found in his *Collected Poems 1917–1952*, published by Houghton Mifflin Company in 1952.

6. Read the following adaptation of "The Song of the Shirt":

THE SONG OF THE SHIRT

NARRATOR:

With fingers weary and worn,
   With eyelids heavy and red,
A woman sat, in unwomanly rags,
   Plying her needle and thread—
      Stitch! stitch! stitch!
   In poverty, hunger, and dirt,
And still with a voice of dolorous pitch
   She sang the "Song of the Shirt!"

WORKING WOMAN 1:

"Work! work! work!
   While the cock is crowing aloof!
And work—work—work,
   Till the stars shine through the roof!
It's O! to be a slave
   Along with the barbarous Turk,
Where woman has never a soul to save,
   If this is Christian work!

WORKING WOMAN 2:

"Work—work—work
   Till the brain begins to swim;
Work—work—work
   Till the eyes are heavy and dim!
Seam, and gusset, and band,
   Band, and gusset, and seam,
Till over the buttons I fall asleep,
   And sew them on in a dream!

WORKING WOMAN 3:

"O! men with sisters dear!
   O! men with mothers and wives,
It is not linen you're wearing out,

But human creatures' lives!
   Stitch—stitch—stitch,
  In poverty, hunger, and dirt,
Sewing at once, with a double thread,
  A shroud as well as a shirt.

"But why do I talk of Death?
  That phantom of grisly bone,
Ihardly fear his terrible shape,
  It seems so like my own—
  It seems so like my own,
  Because of the fasts I keep,
Oh! God! that bread should be so dear,
  And flesh and blood so cheap!

WORKING WOMAN 4:   "Work—work—work!
  From weary chime to chime,
Work—work—work—
  As prisoners work for crime!
Band, and gusset, and seam,
  Seam, and gusset, and band,
Till the heart is sick, and the brain benumb'd,
  As well as the weary hand.

WORKING WOMAN 5:   "Oh! but to breathe the breath
  Of the cowslip and primrose sweet—
With the sky above my head,
  And the grass beneath my feet,
For only one short hour
  To feel as I used to feel,
Before I knew the woes of want
  And the walk that costs a meal!

ALL WORKING WOMEN: "Seam, and gusset, and band,
  Band, and gusset, and seam,
Work, work, work,
  Like the engine that works by steam!
A mere machine of iron and wood
  That toils for Mammon's sake—
Without a brain to ponder and craze,
  Or a heart to feel—and break!"

NARRATOR: With fingers weary and worn,
  With eyelids heavy and red,
A woman sat, in unwomanly rags,

Plying her needle and thread—
Stitch! stitch! stitch!
In poverty, hunger, and dirt,
And still with a voice of dolorous pitch,—
Would that its tone could reach the rich!—
She sang this "Song of the Shirt!"

Thomas Hood

Readings

Clark, S. H., and Maud May Babcock, *Interpretation of the Printed Page*, chaps. 1–3, Prentice-Hall, Inc., New York, 1940.

Lowery, Sara, and Gertrude Johnson, *Interpretative Reading*, chaps. 1, 2, Appleton-Century-Crofts, Inc., New York, 1942.

Schramm, Wilbur, *Approaches to a Science of English Verse*, University of Iowa Studies, no. 46, Iowa City, Iowa, 1935.

Tresidder, Argus, *Reading to Others*, chaps. 6–8, Scott, Foresman & Company, Chicago, 1940.

14

PUBLIC ADDRESS

One person talks; several listen—that is public speaking, public address, or public talking. To many of us this is the principal application that comes to mind with the word *speech;* and at its best, public address represents a skill on the part of the central figure, the speaker, that both students and their elders frequently covet. Public speaking has held a place of esteem in our civilization throughout recorded history—at least since Aristotle formulated a lasting set of rules for speakers, and even earlier with the formal suggestions by the Sicilian Corax for pleaders in cases of equity. Indeed, public speaking either antedates or goes to the very roots of Western history. Only experience as a listener and an awareness of the responsibility of the public speaker could have led to Moses' protest against becoming a leader: "I am not eloquent. . . . I am slow of speech, and of slow tongue," and the Lord's tacit acceptance of the importance of these skills for the leader: "Is not Aaron the Levite thy brother? I know that he can speak well. . . . Thou shalt put words in his mouth."

WHY DO I MAKE SPEECHES?

Turn through the pages of the collected speeches of an American orator and ask the question: Why did he make this speech? Now, enumerate a few speeches that *you* have made and ask the same question. The most obvious first answer may not lie in a single reason, and the ultimate all-engrossing answer may not lie on a conscious level. The following possible answers may apply to your next speech; however, the listing is not complete. You can add others.

1. *I am invited to speak.* This enters into many speaking situations. Through a letter, telephone call, or face-to-face question one is invited to speak. A topic for the speech may be suggested as a part of the invitation or not. The invitation, indeed, may come as a surprise at the banquet table

302

or upon our return to the "old school," or may come formally months ahead of the event.

2. *To make speeches is part of my job.* Speeches made in the classroom might be considered either here or with the preceding reason. Apart from the college classroom, many positions carry with them the obligation for making speeches. Clergymen, school principals, and college presidents certainly accepted the role of speech makers when they accepted their work. The same is hardly less true for industrialists, managers, publishers, professors, and businessmen. Moreover, at least the clergymen and schoolmen assumed the responsibility for filling in occasionally when the invited, outside speakers fail at the last minute to appear for scheduled speeches. Some school assemblies might be dismissed under these circumstances, but not all of them. The person who is in charge is often obligated to carry on.

3. *I have something to say.* With this attitude either our *ideas* or our vested interests may be taking over. We attend the hearing about the proposed new school law, civic auditorium, or budget with the intention of supporting a point of view. No personal invitation need pave the way for this appearance; neither does an obligation to our job or position prod us into either attending or speaking.

There are other motivations that bear upon the output of speech at public gatherings. Some of these reasons are highly personal, perhaps not admitted, and sometimes not even recognized by the speaker.

1. *I must become known.* The aspirant to public office may utilize several means to call the attention of a political party and prospective backers and voters to himself. One method is public address. However, the urge to become known need not relate to a specific purpose.

2. *I am in a competitive circumstance.* Possibly a student is 2 or 3 years behind a brother who excelled. Pressures, either from outside—the family, neighbors, fraternity—or from within—"I must do as well as Jim," cause the student to use public address as a means of winning. The unwitting "other person" may even have been named by someone else as opponent, and the whole contest may be played unannounced for the benefit of a home-town neighbor or an unofficial selection committee of neighbors, former schoolmates, or one or the other set of parents.

3. *I "need" to talk.* Here is the unnamed, unrecognized, and unadmitted cause for many prolonged sessions and stolen shows at public meetings. The content of the utterances may be an "exposition of the obvious," a resaying of what already has been offered, or, fortunately, an appropriate contribution to the meeting. The motivation, though, is a compulsion to talk, and the important personal consequence is a catharsis, a feeling of well-being and "all's right with the world."

Obviously a single speech may be accounted for by more than one of the foregoing six explanations, not to mention others that are not enumerated. Also, you may be questioning whether you can assign a specific reason to why you make a speech, much less why someone else makes speeches. The length of the sustained speech should not be taken as an indication of the motivation that produced it. Some people do not find sufficient occasions for making the speeches that they need to make. On the highly conscious level, a candidate for a state legislature, himself a college teacher of political science, observed seriously: "A problem nowadays is to find a *stump*, and I am curious whether or not this has always been the case with candidates for lesser offices." Nor could his backers find public stumps for him.

A final observation about these relevancies to speaking is that the speaker is always responsible for the fact that he is speaking. In every circumstance he selects "yes" from a "yes-no" choice. True, it may be difficult to turn down certain invitations, but they can be declined. It may be difficult not to talk when called upon by surprise at a dinner table, but in the final analysis the one-who-is-given-an-opportunity-to-speak *can* decline. The person who accepts a position that calls for public address does so of his own volition.

HOW DO I MAKE SPEECHES?

Ingrained motivations for speaking are no more subtle than the deeply rooted formulas for the speeches that emerge. Speakers of a lifetime often reveal in their reminiscences that their speeches have followed few rules consciously applied. Critics view the body of speeches that have come from such a one, however, and find that a single plan is common to the lot. Our purpose is not to recommend an outline of your completed speech, rather, to help you make consciously the inevitable decisions that accompany speechmaking.

I. YOUTHFUL PUBLIC ADDRESS. Public address is interestingly illustrated in a popular procedure in elementary education, *sharing*. This is a practice in which a child lets the rest of his group know about a rich experience that he has had. The effectiveness of the device is so great that a child of the kindergarten or first grade may clap his hands with glee at the circus, the zoo, or on discovering a snake, turtle, or frog and exclaim, "I am going to share this!" The youngster merely stands before, or more often among, his group and recounts an event. No time limits are imposed. The youthful listeners and the speech can continue until the speaker runs down, and the rules of the game seem to allow a speaker to mount the rostrum as often as he wishes, any time that he feels, "I should share this." Now, we are not condoning this entire behavior pattern with the grown-up child—at least until the child reaches the United States Senate. Time in the college classroom, and on the public platform must be regulated and allotted. However, there are some features of sharing that might be carried upstairs to the college.

The sharing speech is an abstract of the speaker's current state of knowledge on one subject. An idea has not been blown up or inflated with materials that have been searched out and tested. Rather, a state of the neural pathways has been revealed through abstracting and unconsciously selecting details, incidents, observations, etc., from the stockpile of information. In the process, enthusiasms, prideful attitudes, and disappointments make the account an admittedly personal and public revelation of one stock of neural patterns, a private evaluation.

2. THE PUBLIC ADDRESS OF MATURITY. Let us move to another and somewhat contrasting group of speakers, senators; possibly we should say "world senators" to emphasize that the discussion is generalized. These particular senators have been in their posts a dozen years, have served on important committees, listened to testimony relevant to the work of the committee assignments, and sponsored laws to correct abuses in the areas of their specialization; they are the persons whose opinions are sought by news reporters, party leaders, colleagues, and collegiate public speakers. These senators are busy: reading and answering mail, seeing callers, attending committee meetings, holding news conferences, participating in legislative sessions, writing reports, reading reports, etc. For one or more of several possible reasons, the senators also make speeches to outside groups: to earn money, to repay a personal obligation, to educate the public, to feel the pulse of the electorate, to do the expected thing, to receive an honor, to help a cause, to oblige the urge to speak, etc. The public addresses that result are likely to be sharings of the senators' experiences. The outlines that are prepared for the speeches are abstracts of ideas, one person's idea in each case, and the speeches that are delivered are abstracts of complete views of topics as the topics exist in the neural patterns of these extra-special senators. In the first projected versions of the speeches—and there may not be time for a rethinking or another version—experience is the sole guide to the sustained development of the ideas, all familiar ones. Were the resources of the senators on these ideas to be exhausted, the

speakers continuing until each was to say, "I know nothing more that pertains to this topic," a long, long session would occur. From this finite but enormous total, the complete case, the speakers abstract or take out their public addresses.

We, you and we, are neither elementary school children nor world senators. How does this notion of public address fit us? More than we might suppose and from the viewpoint of "How do I relate to my speech," it fits all of us perfectly. For example, one of us is booked to speak at a neighboring college in connection with career day, and the subject is to be "Job Opportunities in an Aspect of Speech"—a singular aspect. The speech was in some measure prepared as we put down the telephone, accepting the assignment. The abstract that occurred as a flash might be described as (1) your college has a long tradition in speech; (2) you students have an acknowledged interest that overlaps this singular specialty; (3) there are more openings in this specialty than there are people trained for it; (4) this specialty offers a reward of personal satisfaction; and (5) here are the requirements. A speech, an abstract drawn from a backlog of experience, would have followed this pattern if an impromptu presentation had been required. With time for specific preparation, an abstract was shaped that included more details than the instantaneous one provided.

a. Inventing. Two aspects of public address may at first thought seem to be inconsistent: *invention* and *abstraction*. They need not be inconsistent. Invention implies an emphasis upon building the speech. From this view a speaker starts with an idea that he intends to dwell upon for the available time. His task is to array reasoning and evidence, or analogies and inference, in such a manner that he makes the most plausible accounting that he can envisage for his cause. This emphasis on the development of the idea seems to imply: Sustain your idea before listeners for as many minutes as possible. In this context, questions arise in the mind of the speaker-to-be. Where do I get material? What are the divisions of this topic? Can I insert an appeal to, let us say, patriotism? Have I had an experience that bears out my contention? Did Aesop write a fable that is relevant to this topic? The emphasis in this approach to sustained speaking is on building the case: analogies, arguments, illustrations, fables, quotations, facts, anecdotes, and the like.

The process of inventing a complete speech may be largely in keeping with our practices in court procedures. A lawyer accepts an obligation for framing and presenting for his client the best case of which he is capable, a circumstance with few exact parallels in real life. He builds this case eve nthough the client is assigned him by the court. He takes professional pride in a job well done, and he faces an obligation to do his utmost. A counterpart that is less binding in its outcome lies in intergroup debate, as intercollegiate debate.

b. Abstracting. Apart from the concept of inventing or building the sustained speech is a view that the utterance is an abstract of the ultimate, or complete development of an idea. This idealized development may be admitted to be unattainable, to be beyond the limitations of a single person, even a generation. At this level we run into the frayed question, What is truth? We back away, take another view, and decide that the idealized development lies in the neural patterns of any one of us, complete as of the present moment. At a later time we may have other or different neural patterns, and the complete view of a topic may differ from the one we possess now or, in other words, the one that we *are* now. The possibility of the age-seventy view does not alter the fact that at this moment the stock of our attitudes and information may be measured as a complete entity for *now*. The sustained oral utterance in this sense becomes a summary, précis, or abstracting of the current state of affairs. The abstraction may conform to a 10-minute time limit or a 3-minute one; it is necessarily personal, for it springs from sets of neural patterns that are as individual as, again, fingerprints.

The view that a public address is an abstracting of a set of neural patterns need not be in opposition to the notion of invention, only supplementary. If we assume that invention with respect to public address implies adding something to our stock of knowledge on a particular topic for a specific purpose, we can then suppose that the added information has either altered or accommodated a previous arrangement of neural patterns and that our actual abstracting in process occurs in the light of the current state of the neurograms at the moment of utterance.

In the process of abstracting our present complete ideas, we reject innumerable possible views—the ones that we do not hold. Of the remaining ones we may select topics that appear to be the most rewarding. The ultimate selection is, of course, completely unique.

This process reminds us of information theory, treated briefly in Chap. 4. Why can some books be skimmed while others must be read carefully? Do we find that some portions of chapters of textbooks are often more important than others in reviewing for an examination? Freshness and significance in a speech may arise from presenting those portions of the abstract that are seldom treated, with only passing reference to the frequently employed approaches. The oft-used "(1) A change is necessary; (2) this substitute is practical," leaves an opposing debate team as well as an audience little to do but await the end of the speech. Nothing new is likely to occur unless it be a little fresh evidence.

WHICH SUBJECT SHALL I USE?

The kindergarten child shared with his classmates an event in which he participated, something that happened to him. The world senator in our earlier illustration spoke from a background of committee work. If we accept even in general terms the idea that a public speech is an abstract of the case-as-known-by-one-person, we largely accept a notion that speech is autobiographical. Often, very often, the speaker is assigned a subject. The assignment, if not made directly, is implicit, as, "The topic of the ton-mile tax will be under discussion in our group." Herein lies the implication, "Among the members of our group you are viewed as an authority on this topic" or "If you have not made your views known on this subject, please do so and before our group." Your subject has been chosen. At other times, as when we attended the round-table discussion that was conducted before a student-faculty assembly on the banning of student-owned automobiles, the subject of anything we might say was selected for us by the topic for the meeting. One way or another, the topic is assigned us for most of our public speeches. As to the remaining ones, the query: "Which subject shall I use?" applies.

1. SUITING YOUR AUDIENCE. Let us treat our question about subjects with special reference to the classroom, your class—now. Your speeches emanate from your experience—past events, but as uttered your speech is neither a past fact nor an imaginary flight into the future. This *present-indicative* aspect of public address is very important and affects both our choice of subject and our treatment of the topic. There is no present interest among your listeners in becoming girl or boy scouts or members of high school fraternities; however, your listeners are potential members of honorary societies. Your audience is not now concerned with operating a bomb sight, problems of celestial navigation, or the techniques of discharging a torpedo, but everyone of your listeners has a stake in national defense, both civil and military. College students,

having made their choice of a college, are not especially interested in the advantages of this one over ones that you almost chose or the one you attended last year; but they are interested in knowing of the college courses that offer unusual advantages and in graduate and professional schools. Thus, of utmost importance, you speak in the present.

2. SUITING YOURSELF. Some topics, events, or situations arise and become dated quickly: Thanksgiving and Christmas seasons, San Jacinto Day, Memorial Day, Columbus Day, a play, dance, concert, lecture, an editorial, Sadie Hawkins Day, Founders Day, examination week, equinox, Twelfth-night, or Tag Day. Sports and the personalities of each sport are seasonal. Some other topics are continuing in timeliness: conservation of natural resources, liberal education, Great Lakes commerce, world government, etc. We could enumerate the topics of speeches by the score and still not answer your question: "Which topic shall I use?" You are the one who faces up to listeners on a particular occasion, a class session—you, a complex outgrowth of a singular environment and heredity. Can you take a measure of the factors that have contributed to your present self? Are you held in special esteem for such reasons as more age, more size, or especially recommended physical make-up? Do you enjoy prestige because of your scholastic standing, wide travel, student offices? Have you enjoyed success in earlier speeches? In the process of assigning yourself a topic for a speech, you may profitably examine these advantages that you enjoy, as well as all your attitudes and interests. The abstract that you will present, both in its topic and its point of view, will derive from this background. What have you done? If you have had experiences with sailing, you doubtless find yourself conversing about boats. The same neural patterns that guide your conversations are in operation in your public speeches: the same points of view about labor unions, management, ranching, racial problems, public medicine, military academies, public schools, small families as opposed to large families, and the like. Perhaps you have met a distinguished creator of wood prints, stained glass windows, pipe organs, or hand-blown glass. Your interest, then, or at least your information, is unique with respect to these arts. Perhaps you have known a painter, a jockey, a railroad engineer, and this person has aroused in you predispositions toward art, horses, or transportation. The crux of the discussion is that your attitudes are not universal ones but are singularly personal. Where you have lived has conditioned your view toward peoples of different colors. Experience has affected your

neural patterns about sports: cricket, hockey, water skiing, archery, skeet, etc.

Earlier we have seen that in conversation you talk about occurrences, events, and ideas—all of interest to the listener—that evolve from experiences, such as you have now probed, perhaps of another year or of the last few minutes. These topics arise naturally and easily and give rise to brief abstractions. An analogy from conversation to public address is implicit, and our failure to make the transfer arises, in part, from our practice and familiarity with conversation and our inexperience with public address or possibly an unfortunate experience or two with it. The fact remains that the essence of the subject for a speech lies in the experiences and the beliefs that arose and are arising from the living speaker. Where you have been, what you have done, what you believe— these make your topics. This relationship is so close that all of us have learned to conjecture—fairly satisfactorily—what some speakers will talk about. For example, a reporter who has returned from the Orient is almost obligated to discuss political matters of the East and West. A person whose reputation is entirely with art chooses his subject from art. And you? Examine minutely a list of the books you have read, the places you have visited, the jobs you have held, your present objectives, the ideals that you hold most highly.

The range of speech subjects is as broad as human affairs, sports, hobbies, literature, morals, mores, history, biography, science, etc.— in short, all human experiences and thinking. For you, however, the range is bounded by your experience and thinking. Therein lie many topics of interest to your listeners. Some speeches entail giving a wider scope to some little experience of yours—generalizing, moralizing, "figurative application," an abstract of part of your personal philosophy with an incident as a point of departure. Thus a touchdown may lead to high-order abstracting: abstracting about abstractions. Bruce Barton gave through the Biblical phrase "They knew not Joseph" a compelling reason for continuous advertising on the part of our manufacturers. This kind of development is interesting to study as an onlooker. There is really no logical tie-up between the Biblical story of Joseph's successors and advertising. Yet the notion of continuous advertising seems easy to accept when presented in the figurative connection. Simply, a generation grew up who did not know Joseph. Another generation might grow up without knowing about script. Therefore advertise all the time. This game can be played in reverse. Some speakers narrow down or simplify large, mass human endeavors to a single feature or moral. International affairs become "a game of chess." Western migration symbolizes "courage."

We still have not selected a topic for you. "We must select the subject for our speech as early as possible." The preparation of the abstract is far less wearisome than the frustrating periods spent in, "What shall I talk about?" An experienced clergyman admonished his student listeners: "It is not the study of Virgil that is difficult; it is the worry about the study of Virgil that is tiring." So it is with "my next speech." Right there in "my" lies the nub of the matter. Who is making the speech? You are. If we were making it, the subjects might derive from one of these attitudes, circumstances, or events—all personal: "Out with the Boy Scouts, or a Night of Bedlam," "Refinishing Furniture for Fun," "The Noise about Us," "The Subjects Students Choose for Speeches," "An American Orator of 1850," "Life in a Small Community," "Job Opportunities in Speech," "Military Applications of Speech," "The Uniqueness of a College of 400 Students"—and a host of others. We would not speak on "The Western Reserve," for we have only read a book about it; "The Canal System in America," for we have only read interesting articles about it; "The Circuits of Electronic Computers," for we have only listened to experts describe them; "Scandals in Sports," for we only know what we read in the newspapers.

But you, you the surgeon-in-training, the baby sitter, the reader of poetry, the musician, the student of genetics, the subway rider, the secretary, the connoisseur of painting, the circuit maker, the waitress at a summer resort, the editor, the catcher of abalone, the watch repairman, the student of philosophy—you are the one to abstract your views for your listeners. We shall be interested in *which of your many subjects you choose.*

MESHING GEARS WITH LISTENERS

We have learned that our success with listeners is relative. Our words are neurograms, their words are neurograms, and the patterns do not quite match. Our plight could be worse, as when we try to match neural patterns with another age. We have seen in Chap. 7 that abstractions of events of a different age are affected by the metaphors of that age. Sir Toby's (*Twelfth Night*) line, "Nay, if you be an undertaker, I am for you," does not read very hard. Out of context it seems to say, "I am about to die; you, being a funeral director, may have me." In context it must be a little senseless to many readers and go somewhat like this: "If you are a funeral director, I shall kill you," for the stage direction *"Draws"* accompanies the line. The word "undertaker" is the troublemaker. Shakespeare and his fellows knew the word as meaning "meddler." With this in mind the line makes sense: "You meddler, I'll fight you."

Our problems of adequately meshing gears—we assume that gears never get in quite the same relationship with each other twice—with listeners in public address is not quite as difficult as is Shakespeare's in this century. There are some similarities, however. Shakespeare cannot say to an actor, a director, or to listeners, "No, I didn't mean that at all." The interpretation of his lines in a public reading of them must stand. Even another authority—who may be as wrong as the one who set the manner of the first reading—can only affect subsequent readings of the lines, not the erroneous neural patterns that were established by the first and erroneous reading. Similarly, in public address, the typical one-way flow of language, from the speaker to the listener, forbids the correcting of erroneous impressions when they are made—and frequently forever. Small wonder that lecturing teachers are surprised by what they find on examination papers! Also small wonder that arguments develop in the wake of speeches over what the speaker really said. Gears that have meshed or rather have had the opportunity to mesh with the same gear do not mesh with each other.

1. AVOIDING MISUNDERSTANDINGS. Dangers inherent in the one-way communication system include the following: (1) the listeners may overinterpret the statements and views of the speaker, for example, "Shakespeare disliked all meddlers," (2) they may misinterpret or put the wrong meaning into the words, for example, "Sir Toby disliked funeral directors," or (3) they may fail to get any meanings, for example, "What was Sir Toby yelling about?"

Precautions against these pitfalls are more easily taken after the speaker becomes aware of the enormity of the task that he assumes when he attempts to share his thoughts with listeners. Such awareness is kindled by a period for questions after a speech. These sessions can be supplemented in the classroom by a test that the speaker prepares before his speaking assignment and administers after his speech. Either procedure is likely to elicit signs of the particular inefficiency that befell the speaker: the listeners' overinterpretation, misinterpretation, or failure to grasp the ideas.

a. Phrases that Orient the Listener. Special precautions are in order, as these phrases illustrate: "Mind you, I only said that we . . . not that we . . . ." "Let me repeat that last statement." "Let's take another look at this . . . ." "Now I come to the second reason for my favoring . . . ." "Possibly an example will make the predicament in which we find ourselves more clear." "This term is a tricky one; I think we had better explain it." This kind of cautious statement might be termed *spelling out*, and viewed as similar to asking a telegrapher to read back your message to you before he sends it. The phrases seem natural; we hear them so often that we scarcely notice them. They are only illustrative of a cardinal fact: public address makes special demands upon the speaker to be clear, as clear as he possibly can be.

b. Accept the Responsibility for Explanation. As curricula become more and more specialized, students, of course, become specialists. Institutions of higher learning that were not so long ago single, integrated units are now a diversity of departments, perhaps colleges. The educative process which, again, was recently fairly uniform, one that involved rhetoric, literature, language, philosophy, and mathematics, is being enlarged by the diversity of technical curricula, at least for more and more students. These students find barriers as they try to explain their specialties to one another. The temporary frustration that ensues is shrugged off with a laugh and "Oh, well," or it is met head on and overcome. There is no shrugging off technical materials that must be explained to the public, if financial support for the technical program is to be forthcoming. Certain new processes must be explained to the directors of organizations, if the materials are to be exploited fully in the production schedule of the firm. Some technical materials must be explained to fellow students, if they are to pass examinations. In short, explanation through public address is an inherent part of our culture that is characterized by specialization, and the task of making the explanation falls sooner or later on the technician who understands how the gadget or the instruments of the laboratory work, as well as the accompanying theory.

Explanation is in no sense the sole responsibility of the engineer. It is a normal component of much public address. For example, the argument for an increase in student activity fees is not well made unless the student taxpayers know how the present fees are being spent. This takes some explaining. Possibly an indication of the importance of explanation lies in the attention that is given to *expository aids.*

c. Aids to Explanation. The blackboard seems to us to be an inevitable part of a classroom. Why the blackboard in a speech classroom? For examination questions? Only rarely. For lists of new words? Occasionally. For students to "say back the book"? Now and then. Mostly the blackboard with one, three, five colors of chalk is a visual aid to explanation. The explanation or derivation of a formula or equation is spelled out for all of us to see. The wiring diagram, with its attendant code of symbols, is put on the board for all to see. The instructor, who holds a tuning fork that is vibrating 256 times a second, turns to the blackboard to draw pictures of typical positions of the prongs, in effect, to make still drawings of the moving object. Much else has come to the aid of expository speaking; *teaching aids,* these developments are called. Possibly they began with maps and globes. Slides—multicolored ones, moving pictures—with sound, filmstrips, pointers with illuminated tips—these along with a family of *audio aids* remind us how far we have extended the principle embodied in blackboard and maps. Without electric current, a projector, or an extension cord, we can get along with the *chart,* a many-colored illustration that tells us at once where our student-activity fee is going. We see a dollar sliced in the manner of a pie, unevenly; the pieces of various sizes represent the different allotments from the fund. A graph such as you made when you studied Chap. 7 shows us vividly the incomes of a representative sample of professions contemplated by members of the class. Another graph might indicate growth, for example, of our Army in 1910, 1930, and 1950. There are three arrays of soldiers in three rows, with one drawing of a soldier representing a stated number of troops. Sometimes numbers are not rounded off, and one drawing is meticulously divided at the shoulder or midline to indicate a fraction of a unit and incidentally to emphasize the exactness of the chart. Charts may combine drawings and language with varying emphasis. The typical organizational chart of an administrative unit requires both drawing and words as exemplified in Fig. 28. Debaters frequently employ a chart to reinforce their oral explanation of a proposed plan.

The striking feature of visual aids as employed by the speaker is that they are almost entirely self-explanatory. They may reinforce the narration of an event or make more vivid the reasons that contribute to an argument, but in themselves visual aids are clarifying, expository. Some indication of the value of these materials to speakers is indicated by these examples: many universities have visual aids laboratories; a state organization of colleges has a teaching aids committee; a medical college has a medical drawing department; and military services have visual aids coordinators to prepare for reports to committees of Congress, etc.

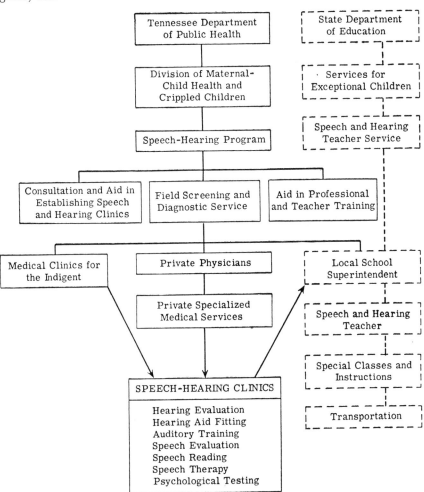

FIG. 28. The organization chart indicates the scope of an activity and suggests the responsibilities of the members of each unit.

d. *Application.* We assume, of course, that you are now preparing your aids for your next speech. A few suggestions may be in order. (1) A chart may be more helpful in an explanation than an object that the aid represents, for you can make the chart any size you wish and eliminate distracting details. However, the object—if it happens to be an object that you are reducing to a chart—can be a visual aid in itself. (2) An aid should help the speaker, and any intimation that the speaker is really helping the aid is calamitous. Sometimes it happens, too, that the speaker seems to have nothing to say beyond the chart, and he spends his time unnecessarily reading it or explaining the obvious. Never give a speech a second time without reviewing the speech with the aids that accompany it. (3) In many speeches the chart, blackboard, or projection screen appears to take the role of the speaker's listeners. Rather, the aid should bolster what you have to say to the audience out front. (4) Slides break, equipment fails to function, and charts tear, get mislaid, or cannot be appropriately used in the assigned room. Always be prepared to give the speech without the aid, for sometime you may have to. When you face this you can ponder the question, "Am I man or mouse?" and then proceed to give your speech, we hope, with no allusion to your misfortune.

2. SUMMARY. Insofar as language is concerned, if one word or set of words seems to be more certain to convey our ideas than other words, then we employ the more effective ones. This may mean ultimately that 86 per cent of our audience grasps 74 per cent of what we say, rather than 84 per cent of the people getting 71 per cent of the content. If illustrations, analogies, restatement, transitional sentences will raise the percentages further, we have no choice but to use them.

Insofar as visual aids are concerned, if a graph will raise the comprehension of our ideas even slightly, we have no alternative, in view of our objectives and the responsibility that is ours to be as clear as possible, but to say it with pictures. Indeed the responsibility of a speaker toward communicating his ideas to the best of his ability is somewhat akin to that of the lawyer who is obligated to make the best case possible for his client.

SHAPING THE ABSTRACT

Often a speaker has little opportunity to plan his public address. Speaker Jones hurriedly, possibly in a few minutes, prepares to substitute for a scheduled speaker who has been unable to fill an engagement. Speaker Bolar, while attending a dinner, is asked to give his views on a topic that has been presented. Speaker Chance finds that a public hearing is about to be concluded without an adequate presentation of his point of view. In situations like these the speeches that are delivered

are planned and uttered almost simultaneously. The abstract is shaped
to the self-chosen time limit. The abstract may have come to mind in an
habitual organization, with topics 1, 2, etc., only needing to be arranged,
or ordered, before being said. The language is the habitual phraseology
of the speaker, and the humor—if humor occurs—arises from neural
associations with "occasions like this one," "the phrases that I am
again saying," "other discussions that I have heard or in which I have
participated on this topic." Every speaking experience is a preparation
in some degree for the inevitable occasional impromptu speech.

1. EXEMPLIFICATION. Another pattern in public speaking provides
the speaker ample time to shape his speech before delivering it. In the
interests of the listeners' getting the most for their time invested, we
hope that this pattern predominates. This procedure allows for preparation. The life story of a prepared speech would be hard to write. It would
include the biography of the speaker, with a special chapter pertaining
to "The Speech."

TELEPHONE: Speak to the Elephants Club of Highbury on the Ton-mile
tax? Hm, April 17. Yes, that's free on my calendar. All right, I'll do it.

SELF: I've done a lot of talking for this tax but I've made no speeches.
Bill Smith and I were talking about it last week, and Bill is from Highbury.
That's why they have asked me: Bill told them I was for the tax. I suppose
in that trucking center of Highbury no one is for the tax. Well, I told Bill all
I know about it. Guess I'd better find out some more facts and dot the *i*'s
and cross the *t*'s on some of the things I was saying to Bill. Anyway I'll want
to tell them how the roads are (1) for personal travel, (2) for motor transport,
and (3) for national defense; how many we have in this state and the kinds
we have; how much they cost and how long they last. They boil down to a
charge against the federal government (everyone in the land has a stake in
the roads in this state), state and local government, and the people who use
the roads. This last charge is not equitable, for it's on an arithmetic progression, the more gas you burn, the more tax you pay, and on a slight progression
in license plates, the heavier the vehicle, the more the plates cost. But there's
the rub, the wearing out of a road is disproportionately greater with heavy
vehicles (trucks with lots of wheels, weight, and speed). I'll put in some calls
and then go around to the library.

TELEPHONE: Bureau of motor vehicles, will you send me a summary of
vehicle licenses in this state: automobiles, trucks, individual owners and fleet
owners, motorcycles—everything you put licenses on. Weights, too . . . .
Yes, good suggestion, send me your last report to the Governor. Why didn't
I think of that?

Telephone: State Highway Department, will you send me a copy of your last annual report to the Governor? By the way, does that include comparisons of the costs of building and maintaining roads over the last several years? Those tests that were run down East, Delaware or Maryland, on damage to roads by different vehicles? Do you have a check on the approximate weight per vehicle and the miles traveled by each weight in the state? Say, who checks up on whether there is a way of comparing the freight that moves through our state and the freight that moves within and out from our state? . . . You say a committee of the legislature made a study of this? I'll look into it. Thanks for that annual report of yours.

Telephone: Hi-go Trucking Company, you folks contribute to a little newspaper, I believe, that attacks the ton-mile tax. Would you send me over a few recent ones? I'd appreciate a copy of the issue that took up the report of the committee of the legislature last session.

Self: Now I'll go over to the library and get a book or two on principles of taxation and see what I can find on the ton-mile tax. It'll be a joke on me if I turn out to be wrong on this thing. Right off I'd have to tell that story of Grover Cleveland's that Jim Smart was telling the other day.

We shall never know how the speech to the Elephants came off. We are confident, though, that the information that was carried to Highbury was much more complete than the earlier abstract that Bill Smith received. Prejudices were tested, facts were tested, and a more complete view of the ton-mile tax evolved. Our speaker may have produced from his experience a few bad-luck stories from days when automobiles and highways were ill-adapted to each other, some accounts of his recent cross-country travel, a joke about men typically saving license plates; possibly he described the sound of rubber sanding cement, the odor of sliding tires, the feel of the bumps at the edge of a narrow pavement, the view from a high precipice of traffic below; possibly he was able to add an entirely new idea to his knowledge of roads, that 60 per cent of traffic fatalities occur on 276 curves in the state, while only 40 per cent occur on 8,000 miles of straight roads, and that the straightening of the curves only awaits additional revenue.

2. Selecting Details. Preparation of the speech alters the abstract with which we begin. With preparation we have a more complete view of our topic and are ready to shape the abstract into our most representative effort. A time limit becomes important, whether the limit is assigned, set by convention, or determined by the good sense of the speaker. The abstract is shaped to the time limit, possibly by the selection of the *aspects of the topic* that will be handled or by the *selection of*

details that will be given with each topic. The speaker may not face this choice as an absolute or arbitrary one, but he does have to reduce his total knowledge of the subject to fit a time limit, and this is absolute.

3. IMPROVING LANGUAGE. The language of the speech may become a chief concern during the period of shaping the abstract. Many manuscripts of speeches must be prepared for publication. Many more are written simply as a step in preparing the speech. Some are written as safeguards against inexactness. Most manuscripts are edited several times before they are considered final. At this stage the speaker seems to be able to raise himself by his own bootstraps, for he substitutes words, rearranges sentences, inserts a vivid expression, changes statements to questions, inserts qualifying words, checks grammatical usages —all to the advantage of clarity, interest values, exactness, and with the aim of the best possible speech within the time available.

4. DOCUMENTING MATERIALS. "This is clover honey," reads the label, and the housewife buys a jar for her clover-honey-eating family. The bees left no tag "clover" but the apiarist read the signs—color, texture, smell, and taste—and attributed the honey to its source.

The public speaker borrows materials as prolifically as do the bees. Indeed, except for materials that may develop from imagination and reasoning, all the speaker knows has come from outside, either by way of another's thinking and observation or through his own observation. All this material has filtered through the speaker's network of neural patterns and has been subjected to his interpretation. Thus, there is an it-seems-to-me aspect to all that he utters. This inherent subjectivity in speaking is reason enough for the public speaker to give his listeners the sources of his materials. An analogy, however, arises from the scientist's report of an experiment. The speaker, similarly, is saying, in effect, "If you will examine these sources and if you will approach them with a predisposition like this, you will arrive at the same view that I am supporting: Our city needs more industry" or "A winning team is desirable" or "Private enterprise must be retained."

Failure to credit the source of material in writing is a violation of ethics and, in some instances, of law, and is called *plagiarism*. Although the rules governing the use of materials in speaking are not so strict, important materials *should* be attributed to their sources. Typical phrases that may be used to document material are these. "According to H. L. Mencken in his book *The American Language* . . . ." "I found in Louis Mumford's book *The Condition of Man*, published in

1944, this statement . . . ." "Perhaps you remember the line in William Saroyan's play *The Beautiful People,* . . . ." "I am sure that you remember the speech by Mercutio in *Romeo and Juliet,* . . . ." "I was talking with Professor Baker, last week, and asked him this question . . . . Professor Baker replied . . . ." "Last week's *New Yorker* had an interesting cartoon by Peter Arno that depicted . . . ." "According to an editorial in the *New York Times* of January 12, 1955 . . . ." "Did you hear with me the statement made in Assembly last Tuesday by Professor Barnes?" "Further facts in line with these data are presented in the *Encyclopedia of Social Sciences* in the article on 'Mercantilism,' written by Professor Keates of Yale University."

Poor documentation is afforded in such statements as "The bulk of the material for this speech comes from a book on capitalism." "Forty per cent of college students in 1947 were G.I.'s." "Television will be popular in Mexico in 1960." The missing documentation does not tell the listeners where they can confirm the materials that you are presenting. Many students do not realize the potential value of documentation, and some view it as a confession of weakness or a sure contribution to dull speaking. On the contrary, it affords added respect for the speaker by the audience; it contributes to the authenticity of the speech. Without documentation, the audience is at a loss with respect to sources of material, reliability of the material, the prejudices of the authors of statements that are used as evidence, or the amount of misinterpretation that is introduced by the speaker. And, as Walter Dill Scott observed, facts suggested to the mind are held as true.[1] Unfortunately, however unreliable the source, listeners may believe that every home in Mexico will have a television set in 1960.

THE FRAILTY OF LISTENERS

Possibly you have supported some cause, and in the course of your effort you have appeared before a committee for a hearing. Reasonable, personable individuals, possible friends of yours, seemed as committeemen to have become obstinate, penny pinching, illogical, and quarrelsome. Multiply the oddity of a committee by some huge number, and you may approximate the strange unpredictable body of listeners, known as an audience. You are in an audience often—your student

[1] Walter Dill Scott, *Influencing Men in Business,* p. 49, The Ronald Press Company, New York, 1921.

assembly perhaps. You know how it behaves. Students shuffle to their seats, remindful of Jaques' line of A.D. 1598 to 1600, "A whining school-boy creeping like snail unwillingly to school." The chatter and clatter subside slowly as the speaker is announced. He is given a minute or two to prove himself . . . and thereon hangs the balance! Can he make us listen? We are willing to give him a few seconds free, but from then on he has to command our listening. Otherwise, we shall pass remarks among us, study a lesson for the next class hour, doze, or—if permissible —leave. If we do listen, what do we remember? The least we get is a point of view. Upward from there we carry away (1) a well-turned phrase, (2) an interesting fact or two, (3) a one-sentence summary of the speech (the theme, central idea, or thesis), (4) an organization of the speech, (5) an organization plus supporting evidence, or, ideally, (6) a keen appreciation of the abstracting process that we have witnessed and that we have performed in listening.

1. THE INTRODUCTION. Those precious first seconds! How are you as public speakers to make them count? This question has no proper answer apart from your general or entire abstract. The speech is often conceived in a flash of insight, a twinkling of the eye, and is envisaged as a presentation to people. Frequently this abstract may not take into account the idiosyncrasies of audiences. This is left for that stage in which we shape the abstract: "I shall tell the story about . . . ," "I'll remind them of this unusual event," "I'll knock them off their chairs with this statement," "I'll remind them of this coincidence," "Maybe this analogy will bring home to them . . . ." There are no foolproof rules about how you gain the interest of your audience. You stay within the bounds of your abstract and good taste and do your utmost to gain interest with words. Both in the introduction and the subsequent de-velopment, you will employ the ideas you developed about the motiva-tion of listeners while reading Chap. 9.

2. THE CONCLUSION. You won! You held the attention of your audi-ence. They have heard you through to your conclusion, summary, exhortation—the final words before the applause. Those final seconds have a special value, too. They last, in that what is said then has the advantage of recency among your several contributions in the speech. Those moments are your last chance to correct misunderstanding. They permit you to "resay" your speech, if you have worked through the abstract thoroughly enough to be able to abstract the abstract pointedly.

SUMMARY

The ideas that we have explored in this chapter are principally these. Public address is personal address as contrasted to a report of materials from secondary sources. The speaker's knowledge and convictions are revealed in his discussion of his subject. This view leaves no room for such comments or questions after a speech as, " I wonder what he really thinks," "That was only a political speech that I made; I really believe . . . ," " I don't know anything about it; I only said what I read," etc.

A speech involves a topic that is of genuine interest to a speaker.

The same abstracting processes occur in impromptu and prepared speeches, in long and short speeches. The differences in the speeches occur in (1) amount of detail and (2) the amount of experience and knowledge that we abstract.

The speaker is always responsible for the fact that he is making the speech. With this choice on his part he accepts the obligations that attend responsible speaking. One obligation inherent in speaking is that the speaker attempt to be clear. He tries to achieve clarity with words and with such speaking aids as are feasible.

Projects for Practice

1. Include as part of a speech an explanation of an object or portion of an object that is no larger than a pocket watch.

2. Discuss the limitations and errors that may attend the representation of human activities by a set of lines, such as the organization chart. Suggestions: the chart is a "still" picture; there often seems to be no interaction between *top* and *bottom;* there is oversimplification, etc. Do the advantages outweigh the disadvantages? Draw the chart that is implied in the following account:[1]

> You readers of *at Denison* frequently surprise us by your reaction to our pieces. For example, the November issue that dealt with *We Have a Test Case* provoked more mail than any issue since the series on *Academic Freedom* and *Freedom of Speech on the Campus* a year ago. In addition, as we have met with alumni in various parts of the country, one of the first questions tossed at us is an inquiry as to what happened in *the automobile case.* In view of this curiosity we feel impelled to write a sequel to the November issue.

[1] A. Blair Knapp, "Test Case Is Settled; Problem Remains," *at Denison,* vol. 13, no. 6, 1953. Used by permission.

Let us remind you again that the issue in the test case was *not* the matter of automobiles for sophomores. The automobile question was simply the problem which created the issue. The real issue had to do with the interrelationship between trustees, administration, faculty, and students in the community government of the college. The crux of the matter was whether or not our developing tradition of community government had been violated when the Executive Council of the Faculty, acting alone, banned automobiles for sophomore men beginning in 1953, without consultation with student representatives and *without prior notice* to the students who would be affected. Was the question of automobiles one which should be settled by faculty and student joint action, by the President, or by the Board of Trustees? Who should determine jurisdiction in any problem which might arise?

Frankly, we can tell you now that the moment the issue was raised, when students protested the *unilateral* action, we knew what our answer to these questions had to be. *Certainly we were wrong.* We, of necessity, would have to admit it and rescind our action. But we did not want to do so at once because our students were concerning themselves with these questions of community government and their part in it to a far greater extent than usual. It was important for student and faculty discussion to continue so that a general understanding would result.

The Student-Faculty Council reviewed the whole matter at the request of the Student Senate. Very specific conclusions were reached. It was quickly agreed that the Board of Trustees is the source of all authority in the government of the college. It was further agreed that the Board at its discretion could delegate and has delegated some of its authority to the President in some areas and to the Faculty in others. It was also agreed that the Faculty, by specific authorization of the Board, could delegate and has delegated to student officers some jurisdiction, most of which is exercised jointly with faculty committees. It became clear, however, that while the delegations of the Board to the Faculty and to the President were clearly spelled out in official documents, such was not the case with respect to the re-delegations of authority by the Faculty to student officers. It seemed clear that this lack of formal and written declaration was at least partly responsible for what had occurred. As a consequence of these conclusions a specific statement of re-delegation of authority to student officers will be prepared in written form and published. Furthermore, the D Book, college handbook, will make clear in every case the source of the regulations which have been adopted for the government of the college.

Another question then arose: Who shall determine jurisdiction over a new problem which is not specifically enumerated in the written statements? Without much discussion the group unanimously agreed that the President would have to accept that responsibility because of his central position and close relationship to all elements in the college constituency. Thereupon the President made clear that he would expect any dissent from his ruling in such a matter to be proper basis for appeal to the Board of Trustees.

With these *constitutional* problems settled it was time for the President to inform students with respect to three matters:

1. What was to happen with respect to the rule adopted by the Executive Council of the Faculty;

2. What assignment of jurisdiction was to be made regarding the automobile problem; and

3. What was to be the procedure used in solving that problem.

At a regular Monday morning convocation with nearly all of the college community present these three items were discussed by the President. The ruling of the Executive Council of the Faculty was nullified on the grounds that it violated the tradition of campus government because of lack of notice and consultation with student officers and also on the grounds that the Executive Council of the Faculty itself lacked jurisdiction. This area of college government had never been delegated to the Faculty by the Board of Trustees. It was then ruled that the question of automobiles was a matter within the jurisdiction of the Board itself, which would decide the question upon recommendation from the President. Finally, it was made clear that the President's recommendation would be arrived at only after consultation with student leaders and that full notice of that recommendation would be given.

The problem remains, but our students will help to solve it. Our *test case* has resulted in a stronger community government and a wider student interest in the functions of student leaders. One student was overheard to say, "What I like about the whole thing is that Prexy showed us that he isn't afraid to admit a mistake."

3. Note exhaustively the visual aids that a television newscaster or informative lecturer employs in his program.

4. Reconcile the point of view that a speech is essentially a mental formulation with the implication that a speaker can employ visual aids advantageously.

5. Extend the enumerated reasons for public speeches. Is *to make money* the most obvious omission from the ones that are cited?

6. Compose a list of reasons for listening to public addresses. Cite examples in the instances of the reasons that have applied to you.

7. Discuss the following passages in relation to both (*a*) the reasons people make speeches and (*b*) other accounts in this book of the development of

speech. The three excerpts below are by the same author, De Laguna. She advocates the social-control theory as an explanation for the development of speech.[1] With the projects of Chap. II, this project is your third view of the origin of language. The supposition that language derived from the necessity for leadership, control, and coordination in society is popular among social scientists.

a. It is common enough to regard language, as distinguished from the act of speaking it, as a social phenomenon comparable to art or religion, and to study it by the historical and comparative methods of anthropology and philology. But the activity of speech has always been regarded as a phenomenon of individual life and treated from the standpoint of individual psychology. Yet it is evident that, while it is the individual who speaks, speech itself is as much a part of the organized life of society as is buying or selling or bearing arms. I have attempted in this book to investigate speech from this point of view, and to inquire first of all what specific function it performs in society, and how speaking as a social enterprise is related to other forms of group activity. In doing this it has been my hope that fresh light might be thrown on the vexed problem of the origin of speech, and that at the same time the way might be prepared for a more fruitful study of speech as a phenomenon of individual psychology.

The first part of the book, accordingly, deals with the social function of speech. It compares speech in this respect with the animal cry, and offers a tentative and partial theory of the evolution of the one from the other. . . . More specifically it is argued that the change from arboreal life to ground-dwelling must have made a more flexible type of group organization highly advantageous, if not indeed necessary, and that it was probably in serving this end that speech developed. . . .

b. That speech is used to influence the behavior of others is, of course, evident. That this is its essential function, and that the characteristic structure of language has evolved from the animal cry in order to meet the needs of expanding group life, it is our purpose to show in the succeeding pages. Here we shall only point out certain significant points of contrast between the type of social control exercised by speech and that exercised by the cry. For this purpose it will be convenient to consider separately the three fundamental forms of speech-response—or of language structure—the *declaration,* the *command,* and the *question.*

c. No attempt will be made to show how the further development of the structure of language—*e.g.,* the differentiation of gender, number, and case, or of voice, mood, and tense—has been influenced by the

[1] Grace Andrus de Laguna, *Speech: Its Function and Development,* pp. ix–x, 37, 118–120, Yale University Press, New Haven, Conn., 1927. Used by permission.

utility of language in social control. We have been concerned only with the essentials of explicit predication in the complete sentence, which are common to all languages whatever their morphological type. . . . Even so, although the conception of language as the instrument of social coordination does not provide a theory of the complex changes in structure and form which languages undergo, still, if our contention is sound, that this is the essential function of all language, no theory can hope for success which does not keep this conception clearly in view.

8. Write an enumeration for yourself: five public performances (sports, etc.), five speaking occasions, your best speech, your poorest speech, age, places you have lived, states you have seen, other countries you have visited, where you have worked, any difficulty you have had in speaking, what your stage fright is like, who makes speeches in your family, what your hobbies are, five books you have read, five that you never expect to read, five magazines that you would not want as a gift, five unusual foods that you have eaten, two odors that were unusual, your probable vocation, the organizations you hope or plan to join.

9. Study the relationship among the topics of (a) and (b) below and the relative merits of the four possibilities as subjects for classroom speeches.

   a. I like my class in literature.
      Everyone should know the folklore of his locality.
      Literature is our best history.
      Imagination is the feature of the human mind.
   b. My trip to Monticello
      Jefferson as an inventor
      The early inventors of America
      The patent laws are defensible
   c. Consider Herrick's speech of Appendix A to be fourth in a series like (a) or (b), and enumerate the appropriate three topics that would complete the series.

10. Discuss the relation between experience and subject in the instances of recent lecturers at your college or university.

11. Discuss the point of view presented by George Crane in his syndicated column "The Worry Clinic."

THE WORRY CLINIC[1]

George W. Crane

Case F-375: Lorna S., aged 33, is president of her Parent Teacher Club.

"Dr. Crane, I'm scared to death about making a speech," she con-

[1] George W. Crane, "The Worry Clinic." Used by permission.

fessed. "I didn't want this job, but they elected me over my protests. "Since I'm in it, however, I'd like to learn how to make a good talk. So can you please give me any helpful advice?"

Employ the "anecdotal formula," for that is a sure-fire recipe, whether you are a beginner or a professional.

Select the topic about which you wish to speak. Try to inject a few wise utterances or major principles.

Then document them immediately with concrete examples which clarify the laws even for a child's understanding.

Draw your examples preferably from the lives and homes of yourself or your audience, for it always arouses greater interest to hear how our neighbors live. That is probably the secret of gossip.

In short, make your speech a string of stories or narrative episodes that illustrate the general text you wish to present to the crowd.

Jesus used this anecdotal method in his parables. He would also cite current newspaper articles and even the comics if he were speaking from the modern platform, for Christ's parables were simply news stories that failed to be in print for lack of a printing press at that time.

Do readers prefer the long, descriptive paragraphs in a novel or the dialogue?

You know the answer. If they want to cover the book in a hurry, they ignore the lengthy paragraphs which lack quotation marks.

What the average readers prefer is dialogue, for quotation marks mean people, and people spell "human interest" and suspense values.

Clergymen should take a lesson from this fact and humanize their sermons by tactfully injecting names of parishioners. They should employ narratives drawn from contacts with the local town folk.

If you are a clergyman, don't indict gambling or alcoholism, in a dull, pedantic fashion. Use the "parallel comparison" method which Jesus often employed as in the Good Samaritan story.

Cite a local girl who is noted for her goodness and popularity. Cite another dissolute home town woman, and ask which one should make the better wife and mother. Then leave the decision to the audience.

Alternate your humor with some heart touching episodes or pathos, and if you wish to thrill the audience with a lofty emotional climax, use poetry to express the final thought, for people are emotionally conditioned to verse. Prose doesn't move an audience as rhythm does.

12. In Chap. 9 we paid particular attention to premises, the guiding and underlying principles from which our statements emerge. As our statements evolve from assumptions, so do our larger points of view as represented by subjects for speeches. All we need, frequently, is a reminder that will help us call to mind *what we believe* as a result of our experience and reading. Read

these statements, including the alternative wordings, slowly and say your belief, "Yes" or "No."

1. Honesty in matters of money (examination, statements) is presumed.
2. C (A, B, etc.) is a grade to be proud of (ashamed of).
3. Everyone (every male, every female) ought to earn his own living.
4. Gold (platinum, silver, diamond) is prettier than stainless steel (glass).
5. Fat people are jolly (healthy, happy, to be pitied).
6. One should mind his parents (teacher, elders, minister).
7. I could do more (run faster, make better grades, earn more) if I had to.
8. Husbands (wives) should handle the family bank account (drive the automobile, buy the tickets).
9. One should do his duty (to self, others, employer, class, church, city, family).
10. My country (state, college, automobile) is better than others.
11. The twentieth century is better for me than the seventeenth.
12. I pity (envy) my great grandparents.
13. Clothes (uniforms) today are sensible.
14. Shoes should be shined (hair groomed, weeds cut).
15. The country is going to the dogs.
16. If my country does not have the best planes, it will.
17. War is defensible (senseless).
18. Clubs (fraternities) are worth joining (to be avoided).
19. *Who's Who in America* lists the top Americans.
20. It's in print; therefore, believable.
21. Peasants are less intelligent than royalty.
22. Reading Thornton Wilder is more worthwhile than reading Plato.
23. I don't want to be seen in a coach (bus, truck).
24. A reputation is worthwhile.
25. Life in Alaska (Ohio, Maine, Alabama) would be dull (preferable to my present life).
26. My generation knows the answers.
27. An actor's (artist's, physician's, teacher's, traveling salesman's) life for me.
28. I can drive fast with safety.
29. I wouldn't really be killed.
30. College (graduate study) pays off (does not).
31. I must speak louder to a person who wears a hearing aid.
32. White people are smarter than others.
33. An expensive automobile is preferable to a less expensive one.

34. A person who makes $10,000 a year is on Easy Street.

35. If I do not earn as much money (high grades) as my brother, I am a failure.

36. Buying and selling stock (real estate, automobiles) is gambling.

37. No one should teach (marry, drive a tractor) after he is 65.

38. I ought to do (earn) more than I am doing (earning).

13. Particular cultures at various times have accepted the following tenets. Would you listen to expositions of these approvingly? Would you view the speakers as uncivilized?

1. Our leader will be the man who brings back the most scalps.

2. We shall take this cake to grandfather's grave.

3. The cow is sacred.

4. I do not have time to work.

5. The most handsome girl has the honor of jumping into the crater.

6. My great family is the oldest clan of thieves in the world.

7. Having failed, I must commit suicide.

14. Prepare a factual test of not less than 15 items over your next speech. Administer the test immediately after the speech.

15. Discuss these phrases: "a well-turned phrase," "four years in untraining a person to be a teacher," "glue the ideas to the mind," "a meeting of minds," "put his foot in his mouth," "came a cropper." Discuss these passages: "Stand at a window and practice throwing dollar bills away. If you like the feeling, then you may enjoy amateur photography." "The lens for that telescope would not lie in this room; the walls aren't far enough apart by two feet. If we could lay the lens here it would be a bit higher than my belt line."

16. Discuss the probable accuracy of this newspaper account. Is it consistent with a report that you would expect from such a meeting? How would you set about checking the validity of the report? Suppose that the story is wrong. How would you set about undoing the damage? Are the headline and the penultimate sentence consistent?

PROFS UPHOLD TEACHER'S FIRING. Philip Jones, 10171 Frank Ave., was dismissed from the college teaching staff May 20. Following a conference with the University President the dismissal was made permanent.

Dr. Roger Niles, president of the campus chapter of the faculty association, said that a study by a committee on tenure showed no violation in the method of dismissal.

"Our entire discussion was about procedure," Dr. Niles stressed. "We did not discuss whether Mr. Jones should have been fired or not. We found that the President had the right to remove him under the circumstances."

17. As you prepare your next speech, prepare its life story. Do you find this abstracting of your abstractions interesting? With what ideas did you start? How are these supplemented by specific inquiry, reading, and casual or deliberate observation?

18. How do you get *for* or *against* some idea? Cite some of your loyalties and oppositions. Do these change somewhat as you shape your abstracts for speeches? Have you changed sides completely in some instances?

19. Try to secure some edited pages of manuscript from a local speaker or writer. Alternatively, examine pictures of edited manuscripts. Give a plausible reason for each change that has been made.

20. List the instances of documentation in Yeager's speech in Appendix A.

21. Some plays have been published with alternative scenes or acts, as Tolstoy's *The Power of Darkness*, which has two entirely different final acts. Cite counterparts in public address. How does this relate to shaping the abstract?

22. Compare the probable processes of shaping the abstract in these two sectional programs of an annual meeting of the Speech Association of America.

Presiding: Paul D. Bagwell, Michigan State College.

General Theme: "Approaches to the Field of Speech."

"Address of Welcome." President Raymond Walters, University of Cincinnati.

"The Communication Approach to Speech." Elwood Murray, University of Denver.

"The Interpretation Approach to Speech." Gerald March, University of California.

"The Phonetic Approach to Speech." Malcolm S. Coxe, Brooklyn College.

"Differentiation of Speech Sounds by the Skin." Earl D. Schubert, State University of Iowa.

"Laryngeal Functioning in Voice Production." Paul Moore, Northwestern University.

"Spatial Localization in Isolated Binaural Stimulation." Gilbert C. Tolhurst, U.S. Naval School of Aviation Medicine, Pensacola, Florida.

"Ratings Given to Patterns of Voice by Judges Who Exemplify a Typical Vocal Pattern." Roy Tew, University of Florida.

"A Quantitative Approach to Assimilation." John V. Irwin and Keith St. Onge, University of Wisconsin.

"A Study of Meaning in Scrambled Messages." John Dreher, Ohio State University.

23. Fluency of speech is one of 27 topics treated by Stogdill in a summary of materials on leadership.[1] The cited correlations indicate that ability in speaking is not everything but that it contributes to leadership. Are these findings in keeping with what you would expect?

Baldwin reports a definite trend for leaders to be rated by their teachers as confident in tone of voice, while non-leaders tend to be rated as lacking in confidence as to tone of voice. A factor analysis of teachers' ratings of high school leaders reveals "pleasant voice" as one of the four factors found to be associated with leadership. Flemming reports a correlation of .28 between "pleasing voice" and leadership in high school students. Partridge reports that boy leaders can be reliably distinguished from non-leaders when taken into the presence of strange boys, but hidden from view so that judgments must be made on speech alone. However, Fay and Middleton, in repeating this experiment under somewhat similar conditions, found a correlation of only .08 between leadership ratings and degree of leadership as estimated by voice alone. Eichler also reports a correlation of—.112 between voice and leadership.

Talkativeness and leadership are reported by Tryon to be correlated to the extent of .41 and .31 for 12-year-old boys and girls respectively, while the correlation coefficients for 15-year-old boys and girls are .15 and .44 respectively. In Goodenough's study a correlation of .61 between talkativeness and leadership is found. Thurstone did not find highly paid administrators to surpass their lesser well paid associates in word fluency test scores but he did find a significant difference in linguistic ability test scores. Simpson also reports verbal ability to be correlated with capacity to influence others. The correlation coefficient is .45.

Chevaleva-Ianovskaia finds that child leaders are characterized by longer duration of verbal excitation. Terman reports that leaders are more fluent of speech, and Leib finds leaders to excel in speaking ability. The same skills are reported in adult leaders by Bernard and Merriam. Zeleny reports a correlation of .59 between leadership ratings and total remarks made in class. Interesting conversation and leadership are correlated .28 in Flemming's study. Further evidence is found in the studies of Burks and Malloy, who report that vividness and originality of expression and facility of conversation are associated with successful social relationships. Considering the size of the experimental groups, the competence of the experimental methods employed, and

[1] Ralph M. Stogdill, "Personal Factors Associated with Leadership: A Survey of the Literature," *Journal of Psychology*, vol. 25, pp. 43–44, 1948. Used by permission.

the positive nature of the evidence presented, it would appear that fluency of speech, if not tone of voice, is a factor to be considered in the study of leadership. It has long been recognized that effective leadership cannot be maintained in an organization without an adequate system of intercommunication. Thus it does not seem surprising that some of the most searching studies of leadership should reveal the capacity for ready communication as one of the skills associated with leadership status.

24. Compare the two points of view about the value of developing speaking skill as implied by A. Craig Baird and W. Hayes Yeager in their speeches in Appendix A.

Readings

Baird, A. Craig, *Argumentation, Discussion, and Debate*, McGraw-Hill Book Company, Inc., New York, 1950.
———, and Franklin H. Knower, *General Speech*, McGraw-Hill Book Company, Inc., New York, 1949.
Brigance, William Norwood, *Speech: Its Techniques and Disciplines in a Free Society*. Appleton-Century-Crofts, Inc., New York, 1952.
Crocker, Lionel, *Public Speaking for College Students*, American Book Company, New York, 1941.
Ewbank, H. L., and J. Jeffery Auer, *Discussion and Debate*, Appleton-Century-Crofts, Inc., New York, 1941.
Harding, Harold F., *The Age of Danger*, Random House, Inc., New York, 1952.
McBurney, James H., and Ernest J. Wrage, *The Art of Good Speech*, Prentice-Hall, Inc., New York, 1953.
Monroe, Alan H., *Principles and Types of Speech*, 3d ed., Scott, Foresman & Company, Chicago, 1949.
O'Neill, James, *Extemporaneous Speaking*, Harper & Brothers, New York, 1946.
Sanford, W. Paul, and W. Hayes Yeager, *Principles of Effective Speaking*, 5th ed., The Ronald Press Company, New York, 1950.
Thonssen, Lester, and A. Craig Baird, *Speech Criticism*, The Ronald Press Company, New York, 1948.

15

GROUP DISCUSSION

In a democratic society, individuals must communicate freely and openly with one another if their many diverse social and economic aims are to be made known, reconciled, and integrated. For the most part, this communication takes the form of face-to-face talk or discussion. Without such discussion the daily organization and promotion of our business life could hardly proceed. Without it, our cultural and intellectual advancement would be impossible. So essential to our democratic mode of life are the forms and methods of discussion that in recent years numerous books, monographs, pamphlets, and articles setting forth its techniques and examining its nature have appeared. In a word, so essential to democracy is discussion that discussion of discussion has occupied much of the time and attention of research psychologists, historians, social scientists, anthropologists, and even physicists and mathematicians. Without including the many excellent books on discussion by teachers of speech, the following brief list of works with their authors and their authors' professions will suggest the wide scope of interest in discussion and indicate the wide range of reading that a student of discussion should undertake:

The Discussion of Human Affairs, Charles A. Beard, historian
Resolving Social Conflicts, Kurt Lewin, psychologist
The Intelligent Individual and Society, P. W. Bridgman, physicist
The Human Use of Human Beings, Norbert Wiener, mathematician
Roads to Agreement, Stuart Chase, author, economist
Democracy through Discussion, Bruno Lasker, author, social researcher

It would appear from these and similar works and from numerous research monographs that discussion in human affairs has the important function of the perpetuation of discussion. And in order for discussion to be self-perpetuating, it must be refined and improved. Hence, much research has been concerned with the discovery and analysis of those forces in social groups which shut off discussion and which have disruptive and disintegrative effects upon groups. At the same time, it has been directed toward the formulation of hypotheses which will explain mature and efficient interaction among individuals within groups.

GROUP DYNAMICS

As a result of the repeated observations, measurements, and objective evaluations of groups, certain of the hypotheses regarding the interaction of individuals within groups have gained widespread acceptance. Of especial concern to the student of discussion are the generalizations concerning the dynamics of groups. Although the dynamic forces which affect group behavior are extremely complex and although they may be differently described as future research refines generalizations, still certain current principles may well serve to guide both participants and leaders in discussion groups.

1. GENERALIZED MOTIVES OF GROUPS. Any consideration of the dynamics of groups must start with the motives of individuals to become a part of a group. Why, for example, did you join a particular club, fraternity, or religious group? If you did not become a member of any outside group, why not? In general, human beings band together in groups because they feel that through membership in a particular group some individual need will be satisfied. The need, in some instances, may not even be conscious. It may be only the need to belong to some group which will accept and approve the individual. Most human beings, even criminals, experience pressure and dissatisfaction when isolated. On the other hand, the need for the group may be a complex one, such as drives to gain wealth or to introduce social reforms. When individuals perceive that grouping together will fulfill a need, they form a group. When one individual perceives that a group is not fulfilling a need, he withdraws from the group, unless other social pressures to remain are directed toward him.[1] Similarly, when a group perceives that an individual member is not helping it to achieve its general goal, it may reject him altogether. If, however, it feels that a nonconforming member may become an effective part of the group effort, it will increase and intensify its communication with him.

2. GENERAL PURPOSES OF GROUPS. Although the individual motives

[1] Leon Festinger and John Thibaut, "Interpersonal Communication in Small Groups," *Journal of Abnormal and Social Psychology*, vol. 46, p. 92, 1951.

for belonging to groups are varied, still the purpose to be achieved by a group may usually be considered as one of three general ends, or purposes, just as the numerous specific aims of a speaker have been grouped under four or five general ends, or purposes. First, the primary goal of a group may be to learn. The learning may take place first by means of pooling the information and knowledge of the individual member, or, second, it may be advanced by the cooperative formulation of relevant questions or lines of inquiry. These lines of investigation may be assigned to different individuals or may be left unassigned. In the latter case, the members may follow their inquiries as they are able. In some permanent learning groups the individuals report back to the group the results of their investigation. The group, then, through discussion selects and organizes the most reliable data into whatever system of knowledge the data belong. More and more in our highly technical fields such cooperative planning and critical evaluation precede and follow research. In graduate seminars, and even in some undergraduate courses, group discussion is basic to the advancement of learning.

A second general purpose of discussion is to formulate a plan or course of group action, to select a policy which will win the loyalty of the individual members of the group and lead to united action. The discovery and formulation of a policy that will be attractive to all or nearly all of a group are obviously difficult. In emergencies the discussion may stop as soon as a bare majority will support the policy, although such a decision endangers the cohesiveness of the group.

The third general purpose of group discussion, which in some instances is an end in itself and in others a means of achieving the second general purpose, is that of resolving tensions and conflicts between members of a group or between different groups. In many of our cities and even in some of our small towns and villages, the lines of communication between economic, racial, and religious groups are so completely broken that misunderstanding and open conflict flare up intermittently. This segmenting and splitting up of groups is, of course, a threat to peaceful democratic living. When individuals from these different social or economic groups come together in discussion groups, tensions appear. In many instances, group discussion, properly planned, has been a means of introducing some appreciation and tolerance of the beliefs and attitudes of other groups, even though complete reconciliation was not possible.[1]

[1] See Stuart Chase, *Roads To Agreement*, Harper & Brothers, New York, 1951.

The clarity of the discussion by the individual members of the group will depend largely upon the clearness with which they perceive the purpose for which the group is organized. The honesty and objectivity of their discussion will be influenced by how well they perceive their own motives and how openly they dare to discuss them. The functioning of the group, as well as its cohesiveness, will be affected by the extent to which diverse individual motives can be reduced and unified around a group formulation. It is, of course, at this crucial point that group discussions often break down. The psychological and cultural blockages to communication treated in Chap. 6 operate not only to prevent agreement but to stop further discussion. On the other hand, group cohesiveness is necessary for the perpetuation of the group. Still, if the demands for cohesion and uniformity are too strong, novel contributions from individuals tend to be stifled.

3. INTERACTION WITHIN DISCUSSION GROUPS. What effects upon individuals does participation in a discussion have? Are they more efficient or less? Do they reason more logically, solve problems with greater precision? Although the investigations are not altogether conclusive, still many point to the beneficial interaction of groups upon individuals.

In the first place, learning groups function more effectively than individuals working alone. After discussions individuals think more logically[1] and solve more mathematical problems.[2] They also have more accurate judgments of events in a legal situation.[3]

Whether the superiority of the product of group discussion is more than the result of pooling individual judgments has not been finally determined. Nevertheless, in tasks involving a number of logical steps, all of which must be in a correct order if the solution is to be reached, group discussion has real advantages over individual endeavor. The advantages are due to the rejection of incorrect suggestions, the check-

[1] Goodwin Watson, "Do Groups Think More Efficiently than Individuals?" *Journal of Abnormal and Social Psychology*, vol. 23, pp. 328–336, 1928.

[2] Marjorie Shaw, "A Comparison of Individuals and Small Groups in the Rational Solution of Complex Problems," *American Journal of Psychology*, vol. 44, pp. 491–504, 1932.

[3] John Dashiell, "Experimental Studies of the Influence of Social Situations on the Behavior of Individual Human Adults," *Handbook of Social Psychology*, Carl Murchison (ed.), pp. 1133–1140, Clark University Press, Worcester, Mass., 1935.

ing of individual errors by the group, and the greater range of suggestions and original ideas.[1]

On the other hand, certain restrictions to learning do appear in group discussions. Groups often reject correct answers submitted by unpopular members and accept incorrect ones, particularly when a leader maneuvers to have them approved. At times, learning is blocked because groups spend so much time on one problem that they forget information on other topics. In general, whenever tensions between members of a group arise, the superiority of the group product to that of the average individual is minimal. Certainly under such circumstances the product is less than that of the best individual of the group.[2] When no interpersonal tensions arise, groups learn faster and show less fatigue than do individuals.

In a group striving to formulate a course of action, discussion exerts a pronounced pressure in the direction of uniformity. When a wide diversity of opinions or motives prevails, communications tend to be directed toward those members at the extremes of the range, unless they are persons the group does not wish to retain. If most of the members of a group wish to be rid of the dissenters, they direct their communications away from the undesirable members, who thus become isolated from the discussion. If the dissenters talk, the other members ignore the content of the communication. In a contrary manner, members of the group increase their communication to individuals whose speech is relevant to the group's objectives. The reconciliation of divergent views expressed in a group will depend upon the intensity of the motives of diverging members to stay in the group and upon the group's need to retain them.[3]

Also, the psychological forces pressing group members in the direction of uniformity become greater as the opinions have little physical or objective validity and depend more and more upon social approval for their validity. For example, individual physical scientists who have made

---

[1] Mary Roseborough, "Experimental Studies of Small Groups," *Psychological Bulletin*, vol. 50, pp. 275–303, 1953.

[2] Howard Perlmutter and Germaine DeMontmollin, "Group Learning of Nonsense Syllables," *Journal of Abnormal and Social Psychology*, vol. 47, pp. 762–769, 1952.

[3] Leon Festinger, "Informal Social Communication," *Psychological Review*, vol. 57, pp. 271–282, 1950.

different measurements and have formed opposite opinions will face, in most discussion groups, less pressure to adopt the group's opinion than will social scientists who have formed contrary judgments. This tendency toward conformance with the majority opinion is checked in some instances by the beliefs which are anchored in other groups. For instance, an independent in politics will resist the pressures of a partisan political group to the extent that he perceives his beliefs are given approval by independent thinkers. He can face the threat of rejection by the particular group without feeling the threat of complete symbolic isolation.

The centripetal forces in group discussion, that is, those psychological factors pulling the individuals away from the fringes of group opinion and toward agreement at the center, increase as the cohesiveness of the group increases. Two factors which accelerate the cohesiveness of a group are, first, the feeling of its members that they are dependent upon the group and, second, their feeling that uniformity is essential to the attainment of a goal. Discussion tends to be aimed at showing how the group goal is related to individual goals and at how individuals will suffer if they diverge from the group.

It must be kept in mind, however, that factors other than fundamental differences over relevant issues may act to reduce cohesiveness and to force the disintegration of the group. Groups composed of members who are striving for prominence, who are suspicious, or who lack the special knowledge demanded by the situation lose friendliness, cohesiveness, and efficiency.[1] These factors are generally unconscious and are the cause of semantic blockages, such as those described in Chap. 6. With the breakdown of the lines of communication come increased segmentation of groups and accented threats to democratic living, since, without communication, there is no opportunity for reconciliation of either relevant or irrelevant conflicts.[2]

Still another factor which often threatens both group cohesiveness and individual satisfaction is the absence of any designated leader, with the attendant necessity of sharing leadership. Apparently members of

[1] William Haythorn, "The Influence of Individual Members on the Characteristics of Small Groups," *The Journal of Abnormal and Social Psychology*, vol. 48, pp. 276–284, 1953.

[2] John Thibaut and John Coules, "The Role of Communication in the Reduction of Interpersonal Hostility," *The Journal of Abnormal and Social Psychology*, vol. 47, p. 770, 1952.

many groups expect a role differentiating them from designated leaders. They believe that leaders and members possess distinguishing functions.[1] In groups without designated leaders, uncertainty of role may be followed by an aggressive drive for leadership which prevents the smooth and efficient working of a group. Some investigators have found that leaders who emerge in leaderless groups are more "authoritarian" than appointed leaders: the appointed leaders act as coordinators; the emergent leaders strongly support their own points of view in efforts to establish their status as leaders.[2]

A summary of the evidence related to the dynamics of groups reveals that although there are certain traits of personality which in general contribute to smoothly functioning discussion groups, there is no general quality which assures effective participation in all groups. Rather, effective group discussion must evolve from individual members who differ widely in temperament, in ways of thinking, in points of view, but who are striving to discover a common social good in a specific situation. What apparently is required of the student are specific preparation for highly specific groups and practice in applying what he knows of group dynamics and the principles of discussion. Skill in discussion does not consist of a few tricks and glibness in the use of a few principles. It requires broad education, insight, and scientific knowledge of human beings, as well as articulateness and adequacy in the evaluation of specific motives of different groups.

4. INTERACTION OF A DISCUSSION LEADER AND MEMBERS OF A GROUP. Numerous excellent books on discussion set forth the qualities possessed by a good group leader. Experimental studies likewise reveal that skillful leaders have a different type of interaction with members of a group from that shown by ineffective leaders. Students who desire to develop effective leadership should study carefully the following traits:

1. Leaders are superior to nonleaders and isolates in their ability to judge group opinion on familiar and relevant issues.[3]

[1] Leonard Berkowitz, "Sharing Leadership in Small, Decision Making Groups," *The Journal of Abnormal and Social Psychology*, vol. 48, pp. 231–238, 1953.

[2] Lannor Carter, William Haythorn, Beatrice Shriver, and John Lanzetta, "The Behavior of Leaders and Other Group Members," *The Journal of Abnormal and Social Psychology*, vol. 46, pp. 589–595, 1951.

[3] Kamla Chowdhry and Theodore Newcomb, "The Relative Abilities of Leaders and Non-leaders to Estimate Opinions of Their Own Groups," *The Journal of Abnormal and Social Psychology*, vol. 47, pp. 51–57, 1952.

2. Leaders excel in the ability to keep the lines of communication open between individuals in the group. They establish rapport quickly and easily with a wide variety of personalities.[1]

3. Leaders show greater adaptability than nonleaders. They adjust to the changing demands and size of groups.[2]

4. Leaders possess specific skills and qualities demanded by particular groups. Leaders of groups emerge because they possess more than such generalized qualities as affability, responsiveness, and adaptability. Leaders of different groups play their particular roles because they have the specific information, insight, or quality most demanded by their group. Their role depends upon the functional relation between their *individual* attributes and the specific goal of their group at any given moment.[3]

5. Effective leaders act as coordinators and employ nonauthoritarian methods to stimulate group discussion rather than to support their own opinions.[4]

Obviously any check list of leaders' traits will be incomplete. This one is meant to be suggestive of others that will stimulate critical observation and careful evaluation of self and others while playing the role of leader.

PATTERNS OF DISCUSSION

As we have seen, group discussion occurs when members of a group are seeking answers to a common question or are seeking to discover which of a number of courses of action will best satisfy a common need. The very first step in discussion, therefore, is the formulation of a question which is relevant to the group's need and which will stimulate the sharing of information and opinions. The framing of unanswerable questions leads to fruitless discussion that irritates and divides. To be answerable a question must (1) rest upon assumptions which can be stated clearly and which can be granted, (2) lead to the making of unbiased and accurate observations and measurments, and (3) require the clear reporting of observations and measurements.[5] Questions which

[1] Helen Jennings, *Leadership and Isolation*, pp. 164–166, Longmans, Green & Co., Inc., New York, 1943.

[2] John Hemphill, "Relations between the Size of the Group and Behavior of Superior Leaders," *Journal of Social Psychology*, vol. 32, pp. 11–22, 1950.

[3] Cecil Gibbs, "The Principles and Traits of Leadership," *The Journal of Abnormal and Social Psychology*, vol. 42, pp. 267–284, 1947.

[4] Carter, Haythorn, Shriver, and Lanzetta, *loc. cit.*

[5] See Percy Bridgman, *The Logic of Modern Physics*, pp. 28–32, The Macmillan Company, New York, 1928. Also Wendell Johnson, "How to Ask a Question," *Etc.*, vol. 5, pp. 113–118, 1948.

prompt speculation and the airing of diverse opinions may be entertaining, but they can hardly lead to smooth group functioning. If you will review Chap. 6, you will quickly see that questions which can be answered only by high-order abstractions are in fact unanswerable. In testing the validity of answers to answerable questions, the methods outlined in Chap. 7 will, of course, be applied.

After the question has been formulated in accordance with the purpose of the group and the requirements for asking answerable questions, skilled leaders and participants will follow an orderly pattern of thinking and talking in their efforts to discover a satisfactory answer. There are many different patterns of thinking, both for individuals and for groups. However, students just beginning their study of discussion will find the following three patterns well suited to the purpose of the group and still highly flexible.

1. DISCUSSION PATTERN IN LEARNING GROUPS.

1. Define and limit the area of investigation.

2. Pool the information and the assumptions of the members.

3. Organize the acceptable knowledge and inferences as definite answers to the question under discussion. (Some groups, such as students who are reviewing, may stop at this point.)

4. Locate the gaps in information and knowledge and formulate answerable questions which will direct observation.

5. Consider methods of investigation which will lead to discovering answers to the questions formulated.

Subsequent discussions for the purpose of considering reports on the investigations will begin with step 2.

2. DISCUSSION PATTERN IN POLICY FORMING GROUPS.

1. Analyze the areas of action included in the question.

2. Analyze the factors contributing to the dissatisfaction of the members of the group.

3. Survey possible courses of action designed to eliminate the disturbing factors.

4. Select the course of action that seems most likely to remove the sources of dissatisfaction.

3. DISCUSSION PATTERN IN GROUPS SEEKING TO RESOLVE CONFLICT. The culture in which we live accepts social, economic, and professional competition as healthy, vitalizing factors. The desires to excel in grades, to win a contest, to build a better product for less money activate and

sustain much of human endeavor. The wish to rise in the social and economic scale serves as a refining and culturalizing force. The point at which this healthy competition turns into social conflicts, which are characterized first of all by war with words and often by resort to physical force with or without weapons, is a vague and transitory one. Some groups accept competition without conflict. Other groups are set into open conflict upon the most casual contact. Racial feeling in some cities is so strong that military force is required to check open violence. Rivalry between schools becomes so great that all contests are canceled. The differences between fundamentalists and liberals have split church congregations and even destroyed churches.

To use discussion to prevent conflict or to reduce it once it has started requires not only skill in discussion but patience, tolerance, and understanding. At present, discussion seems the only way to restore peaceful if not amicable relations between conflicting groups. Even peace conferences following open warfare are filled with hours of talk before there is restoration of intergroup relations on a large scale. To say that discussion can always resolve conflicts, however, is to ignore the hidden motives, the rationalizations, and the use of talk to conceal, rather than to reveal, thoughts and desires. No claim can be made, therefore, for the efficacy of any methods of speech as long as fear, suspicion, and hate dominate the feelings of the participants.

On the other hand, certain speech methods seem better designed to resolve social conflicts than others, if they are sincerely used. They seem to be particularly valuable in dealing with those conflicts growing out of differences in high-order abstractions and generalized attitudes. These differences seem to be focalized upon symbols that have vague, ambiguous, and changing meanings.

One of the authors had, in a class experimenting with discussion, an Islam from Pakistan, a Buddhist from Burma, a Roman Catholic, a Lutheran, a Methodist, and a humanist. In a 2-hour panel on the topic "What I Believe About My Religion and Why," each talked and questioned the others according to the plan given below. Many of the terms used by all six speakers were the same. Some were different. Certainly no one was persuaded by any of the others. On the other hand, a new commonality of feeling was reported by all. They found that the points of agreement outweighed the points of disagreement, and they even reached agreement on the principal causes of their disagreement. The plan will not always be successful, since much will depend upon the spirit of the participants. However, while some procedures tend to lead to disagreement, the following plan tends to lead to greater degrees of agreement and to maintain a willingness to listen as well as to talk.

1. The first phase of the discussion is devoted to exploring the assumptions, facts, and inferences which are relevant to the problem and on which general agreement can be reached quickly. (a) The participants *describe*, but *do not defend*, their different social, economic, cultural, and political backgrounds. The participants seek to discover areas of agreement and disregard for the moment the areas of disagreement. (This is equivalent to finding a common ground.) (b) The participants explore their goals in the areas covered by the problem, in order to discover common purposes and objectives. (c) They explore the greatest obstacles which stand in the way of achieving their goals. They may discover those obstacles to be their own patterns of thinking.

2. The second phase is devoted to exploring the essential differences of opinion and the evaluational processes which underlie those differences. This involves such questions as the following: (a) Are the differences due to different information? (b) Are they due to different basic assumptions? (c) Are they due to confusions of terminology? (d) What are the evaluational factors tending to divide the group? (e) Can they agree on the causes of their disagreement?

3. The third phase is given to exploring possible solutions in the light of the common evaluations which have appeared.

4. In the fourth and final phase of the discussion proper, each participant gives a synthesizing speech in which he stresses: (a) the points of strongest agreement; (b) what seem to him the most generally accepted beliefs; (c) the principal reasons in support of them. The group, then, may select the solution or solutions which have the greatest appeal, or they may continue to work for still greater harmony of belief. Or, of course, they may fail to find mutual respect and understanding.

PARLIAMENTARY DISCUSSION

In many situations the forms of discussion which have been presented may not be appropriate or adequate. Organizations, legislative bodies, and temporary committees are pressed for time. Action must be taken before all differences are resolved. The body of rules governing discussion in such groups is called parliamentary law. Parliamentary law protects the rights of the minority and of the individual without permitting time-consuming abuse of privileges. The successful use of parliamentary law demands the same intelligent insight into group attitudes and relevant issues that good leadership requires. It also demands more than a

book knowledge of the conventions and practices of parliamentary
bodies. Such knowledge, however, may serve as a helpful start in the
use of parliamentary law. This chapter presents the barest essentials

1. ORDER OF BUSINESS. An aid in the efficient functioning of any
group is a definite order of business. The following outline is suggestive
At some meetings several of the items will probably be omitted.

1. Meeting called to order by presiding officer
2. Roll called by secretary
3. Minutes of last meeting read, corrected if necessary, and approved
4. Reports of officers
5. Announcements
6. Reports of standing committees
7. Reports of special committees
8. Unfinished business
9. New business
10. Program
11. Adjournment

2. STEPS IN CONSIDERING NEW BUSINESS. The steps in *introducing*
and in discussing the motions, preparatory to adopting or rejecting the
proposals involved, are as follows:

1. Obtaining the floor by rising and addressing the presiding officer by
title: Mr. President, Madam Chairman, etc. The chairman recognizes the
speaker by calling his name, or, if the speaker's name is unknown, by asking
the speaker to state it.

2. Making a motion: The correct form is to say, "I move that . . . " (not
"I make a motion").

3. Seconding a motion: The member seconding the motion need not rise
nor address the chair, but states, "I second the motion" (not "I support it").
No main motion may be considered until it has a second.

4. Stating the motion: The presiding officer should then state the question
by repeating the motion. After a motion has been stated by the presiding
officer, it cannot be withdrawn without the consent of the assembly. If the
mover wishes to withdraw his motion, he rises and says, "I ask permission to
withdraw my motion." The chairman states, "The member asks permission
to withdraw his motion. Is there any objection?—hearing none, the motion
is withdrawn."

5. Debating a proposal: Any main motion is debatable if any member
desires. In the debate on a proposal, the mover of the motion has the first right
to speak. *Debate must be limited to the merits of the pending question.* Filibusters

re not permitted. A member may speak twice to the same question and for
o minutes, but he should not be recognized the second time if a member who
has not spoken rises to debate.

6. Putting the question: The chair may not stop debate by putting the
question. If the discussion stops, the chair may ask, "Are there any further
remarks?" If there is none, the chair puts the question. An officer should not
prolong debate if there is no desire for it. Nor may the chair put the question
merely because someone cries, "Question, question." A member, if he wishes
to stop debate, must receive recognition by the chairman and say, "I move
the previous question." This motion is not debatable and must be carried by a
two-thirds vote of the members. When so carried, debate is stopped, and the
vote on the pending motion is taken.

In taking a vote, the chair should ask for the nays as well as for the ayes
except in cases of a complimentary motion.

3. CLASSIFICATIONS OF MOTIONS. The action that an assembly or
organization desires to consider is formulated as a *motion*. This proposi-
tion expressing the action to be taken (motions should always be stated
in the affirmative) is known as the *main motion*.

While the main motion is being considered, other motions to perfect,
modify, or dispose of the measure may be in order. These are *subsidiary
motions*. Still others that protect the privileges of all members may
likewise be in order during debate on the main motion. These are
privileged motions. The following outline gives the rank of these subsidiary and privileged motions which the student is most likely to use.
It does not give the complete list of motions.

RANK OF MOTIONS

I. Main (lowest in rank)	13th	Two main motions may not be pending simultaneously. The second main motion offered is out of order until the first has been disposed of. Subsidiary and privileged motions are in order, provided that one of higher rank has not been moved.	
II. Subsidiary	12th	Postpone indefinitely	Motions of higher rank
	11th	Amend	may be introduced
	10th	Commit	when other motions are
	9th	Postpone definitely	pending. They should
	8th	Limit debate	be introduced if discus-
	7th	Previous question	sion and action can be
	6th	Lay on table	clarified and sharpened.

III. Privileged   5th   Call for orders of the day
    (highest in   4th   Raise a question of privilege
     rank)   3rd   Take a recess
               2nd   Adjourn
               1st   Fix time at which to adjourn

CHARACTERISTICS OF MOTIONS

Main Motion

Main motion:

1. The purpose is to formulate action to be taken by the group.
2. It is the lowest in rank. It yields to all other motions.
3. It is debatable.
4. It is amendable.
5. A simple majority is required for passage. It can be reconsidered.

Subsidiary Motions

Motion to postpone indefinitely:

1. The purpose is to permit test vote by opponents of main motion without risking defeat.
2. It yields to all other subsidiary and privileged motions.
3. It is debatable. It reopens the main motion to debate. Hence one who has already spoken twice may speak to the motion to postpone.
4. A simple majority vote is required for passage.
5. If carried, the main motion is disposed of for the session in which it was introduced. The main motion cannot be reintroduced until the succeeding session.

Motion to amend:

One of the most important and most frequently used subsidiary motions is the motion to amend. It may be applied to other subsidiary motions as well as to the main motion.

1. Its purpose is to improve a motion by some change which must be pertinent to the motion.
2. It is in order while an amendable motion is pending or while a motion to postpone indefinitely is pending. It yields to all other higher ranking subsidiary motions and to privileged motions.
3. It is debatable. The *debate must be upon the amendment*, not on the motion amended.
4. It is sometimes amendable. Amendments are of two degrees: an amendment to the pending motion is of the first degree; an amendment to the

amendment is of the second degree. Not more than one amendment of the first degree and one of the second is in order at any one time. A motion may be amended as many times as desired, however, so long as the original subject is dealt with.

5. A simple majority is required for passage.

6. The pending motion is altered as specified in the amendment. It can be reconsidered.

An amendment may be expressed as (*a*) an addition or insertion, (*b*) a deletion, (*c*) a deletion and an insertion.

Examples:

Motion: "I move that the Sigma Chapter of Sigma Iota Theta have a benefit dance on the night of June 1."

1. "I move to amend the motion by deleting the word 'benefit' and inserting the words 'formal dinner' before the word 'dance.'"

2. "I move to amend the amendment by striking out the word 'formal.'"

At times, a speaker may wish to amend a motion by substituting a new motion. The following illustration shows how this is done.

"I move to amend the motion by substituting the motion that Sigma Chapter of Sigma Iota Theta invite all other fraternities to join with it in holding an interfraternity dance on June 3."

Motion to commit to a committee:

Frequently, in debating or discussing a motion, an assembly does not have information which is needed if a sensible decision is to be reached. In order to delay action until that information is received, the motion may be referred to a committee for study. If the question comes under the jurisdiction of a standing committee, it is referred to that committee. Otherwise, it is referred to a special committee created for the purpose of studying the question.

1. The purpose is to provide time and means of securing needed information.

2. It is of higher rank than a motion to postpone indefinitely and a motion to amend.

3. It is debatable; but discussion must be upon the need of referring.

4. It can be amended as to number on committee and manner of appointing.

5. A simple majority is required for passage.

6. If it passes, the committee is appointed, and action on the pending question is delayed until the committee reports.

Motion to postpone definitely:

1. Its purpose is to postpone action on the pending question to a definite time. Postponement may not be beyond the next meeting.

2. It takes precedence over motions to commit, to amend, and to postpone indefinitely.

3. It is debatable, but discussion must be on the necessity of postponing

4. It is amendable as to time.

5. A simple majority is required to pass.

6. If it passes, the pending question becomes the unfinished business for the next meeting, or the order for the specified time of the same meeting.

Motion to limit debate:

Not infrequently it is necessary to place some limit upon discussion. Members of an organization may become discursive and circuitous; time may be wasted. Again it may be necessary to extend the time of debate.

1. Its purpose is to decrease or increase the time for debate.

2. It is in order whenever a debatable motion is pending.

3. It is not debatable.

4. It can be amended in regard to the time limits set upon debate.

5. A two-thirds vote is required for passage.

6. If it passes, debate is limited on motion pending and on all motions subsidiary and incidental to the pending motion. It may be reconsidered.

7. There are three ways of stating the motion to limit debate:

   a. It may fix the hour for closing debate.

   b. It may limit the length of debate.

   c. It may reduce the number or the length of speeches or limit both the number and length of speeches.

Motion for the previous question:

1. The purpose is to stop debate on the pending motion or on all motions specified.

2. It takes precedence over motions to limit debate, to postpone definitely, to commit, to amend, and to postpone indefinitely.

3. It is not debatable.

4. It is not amendable.

5. A two-thirds vote is required for passage.

6. If carried, the pending motion and such subsidiary motions as may be specified must be voted upon at once.

Motion to lay on the table:

This motion makes it possible to put the pending question aside in favor of more urgent business. The majority may take up the business again at a more convenient time. The motion to lay on the table applies only to main motions. A motion laid on the table takes with it all pending subsidiary motions such as amendments. While a motion is on the table, no motion which affects it is in order.

1. Its purpose is to make way for more urgent business.

2. It has precedence over all subsidiary motions and such incidental motions as may be pending. It yields to privileged motions.

3. It is not debatable.

4. It cannot be amended.

5. A simple majority is required for passage.

6. If it carries, the pending motion is laid on the table until taken from the table by majority action or until the close of the next meeting. The pending motion is dead if not taken from the table by the close of the next meeting. It *cannot be reconsidered.*

Motion to take from the table:

1. A motion to take from the table makes it possible to take up the pending question that has been tabled.

2. It does not have precedence over any of the subsidiary or privileged motions, but it has priority over a new main motion, if it has not been stated by the chair.

Privileged Motions

Since privileged motions serve the purpose of treating an emergency which may arise, they take precedence over all subsidiary and incidental motions as well as over the main motion. They have a rank within their own class of privileged motions.

Motion to raise a question of privilege:

It is in order even when a member is speaking. A member moving this motion need not wait to be recognized, nor does the motion need a second. It is used chiefly when discomfort or annoyance interferes with the meeting.

It is usually stated as follows: "Mr. President, I rise to a question of privilege. Mr. President, the members in the rear should be seated. May not chairs be provided for them?"

It takes precedence over subsidiary, incidental, and main motions, but it yields to motions for recess, to adjourn, and to fix time to which to adjourn.

Motion to adjourn:

This motion is privileged, unless it is for the purpose of dissolving a mass meeting or a meeting to organize.

1. Its purpose is to close the meeting.
2. It has precedence over all motions except motion to fix time to which to adjourn.
3. It is not debatable.
4. It is not amendable.
5. A simple majority is required for passage.
6. If it carries, the meeting is declared adjourned.

Motion to fix time at which to adjourn:

If made when a motion is pending, it is a privileged motion. If made when no other business is pending, it is a main motion. If privileged, it takes precedence over all other motions, is not debatable, but may be amended as to time and place to adjourn. It is of importance only in meetings that have no permanent organization.

Incidental Motions

In addition to the subsidiary and privileged motions, there is a class of motions which arise from the conduction of business, and which must be decided before the question from which they arise can be completed. They have no particular rank, but generally they have precedence over subsidiary motions, except to lay on the table, and yield to all privileged motions. Incidental motions are in order even when another is speaking, *do not need recognition from the chair*, and *most do not require a second*.

Question of order:

A member may rise to a point of order to call attention to unparliamentary practice.
1. It takes precedence over the pending question out of which it has arisen.
2. It is not debatable.
3. It is not amendable.
4. No vote is taken. The chairman rules on whether the point is well taken.

Appeal from decision of chair:

1. The purpose is to object to the ruling of the chair on a point of order.
2. It can be made only at the time a ruling is made, before the other business is considered.
3. It is debatable.
4. It is not amendable.
5. A tie or majority vote sustains the chairman.
6. If it carries, the ruling of the chair is suspended.

Call for division of assembly:

If the vote on a motion is close and a member doubts the ruling of the chair on its passage or defeat, he may call for a division. No vote is taken on the call for a division, but a rising vote is at once taken on the motion of which the passage or defeat was in doubt.

The chart shown on page 352 will help the student to understand how the most frequently used subsidiary motions are applied and to what issue the remarks at each stage of discussion should be addressed.

Experience has taught that the beginning student of speech cannot hope to gain mastery of more than a few basic principles in a short time. These are presented in this section in the hope that they may be practiced conscientiously in campus clubs and fraternities as well as in class, for it is only through such repeated practice that they become an essential part of discussion techniques.

Projects for Practice

1. Play the role of leader in class discussions and elsewhere. College students who sooner or later will advance to positions of group leadership should prepare for that responsibility by playing the role of leader in student groups. By playing the role of effective leaders, students can strengthen their desirable traits and inhibit their resistance-provoking ones. In practice groups discussing questions which will come up in other classes, in fraternity meetings, and in religious groups, leaders-in-training should check one another on the following items:

    a. Did the leader encourage individual members to express their views?

    b. Did he safeguard the diverging members from isolation?

    c. Was he skillful in discovering and expressing the most relevant and most unifying desires of the group?

    d. Did he possess the specific knowledge demanded of a leader?

    e. Did he adapt his talk to the ebb and flow of contributions from individual members?

    f. Did he tactfully expose irrelevant, illogical, biased, or disintegrating statements?

    g. Did he contribute to the cohesiveness of the group without resorting to threats or warnings?

2. Organize within the class three or four learning groups. Let each choose one area in speech in which each member is interested and which is worthy of further study. Suggested topics are "Visible Speech," "Inflection and Meaning," "The Use of Socio-drama," "Literature and Life," "Logic, Semantics, and Truth." Each discussion group should meet outside of class, formulate relevant questions for investigation, and assign one to each member of the group. The group can then report the results of their investigation before the whole class.

A. MAIN MOTION: Purpose: group action; to get something done.

Rank: lowest; only one main motion at a time.

A number of subsidiary motions to refine group action on main motion are in order.

Example: I move that the speech class meet at 6:00 p.m. three weeks from Tuesday for dinner.

> Discussion Pro and Con on the Idea of a Dinner

B. 1st Order Amendment: Purpose: alter, refine, clarify main motion.

Example: I move that the motion be amended by adding the words "in the Union Ballroom".

> Discussion Pro and Con on Place of Dinner

C. 2nd Order Amendment:

Example: I move to amend the amendment by substituting "Grillroom" for "Ballroom".

> Discussion Pro and Con on Amendment of 2nd Order i.e. Grillroom vs. Ballroom

D. Motion to Refer to Committee: More information needed.

Example: I move that the problem of time and place of a speech dinner be referred to a committee to report at our next class meeting.

> Any discussion must pertain to the need to refer to a committee--not to the main motion.

Note: The votes are taken in this order:

1st D. If D carries, other motions are disposed of. The whole item becomes an order of business when the committee reports.

2d C. If D does not carry, vote on C. If C carries, B is reworded. Discussion continues on B as amended.

3d B. Vote on B. If B carries, discussion continues on main motion as amended. If B does not carry, discussion continues on A.

4th A. Main motion either carries or is lost.

3. Choose a question which is highly controversial. Let the class form two or three groups, each composed of members with different opinions. Let each group follow the pattern designed for resolving conflicts in a discussion before the class.

4. Organize the class into demonstration teams of five or six members each. Let each team demonstrate different parliamentary procedures to the rest of the class. Suggested team assignments follow:

Team A. Demonstrate the opening of a meeting, the taking up of new business, the making and seconding a motion, the orderly discussion of that motion and its disposal by voting.

Team B. Demonstrate the making of a motion, the amending of an amendment, and the orderly disposal of each action.

Team C. Demonstrate the making of a motion, the amending of the motion, the referring of the motion to a special committee, and the tabling of the motion.

Readings

Baird, A. Craig, *Discussion Principles and Types*, chaps. 1–3, 6–8, McGraw-Hill Book Company, Inc., New York, 1943.

Haiman, Franklyn S., *Group Leadership and Democratic Action*, chaps. 4–8, Houghton Mifflin Company, Boston, 1951.

Lasker, Bruno, *Democracy through Discussion*, chaps. 14–16, The H. W. Wilson Company, New York, 1949.

16

MICROPHONE SPEECH

We are old hands with microphones, all of us. Our generation of American culture has not known a system of communication that has depended solely upon the vocal power of the speaker and the natural hearing acuity of a listener to carry on. The extent to which our social patterns have been wrought by our telephones, radios, motion pictures, television, hearing aids, etc., can only be conjectured. We know the impact has been of revolutionary proportions. Yet even we are not far removed from the olden days of solely voice-powered sound waves in speech.

From the time that we associate with grandparents and extending backward to the thousands of years that are summarized in the Old Testament, for centuries of recorded history there was only direct transmission by air-borne sound waves from the talker to the listener. There was also unrecorded history, a tremendous span! The culture of ancient Greece that produced tragedies and comedies which have been replayed to theatergoers these 25 centuries had no electrical booster for the voice or the ailing ear. The sermons of Paul were spoken directly to listeners, as were the orations of Cicero. Indeed, much of the tragedy and romance that we read zestfully from our literary heritage derives some of its setting from the bold requirements of a pre-electronic-tube age; for example, "Carrying the News from Ghent to Aix," "Paul Revere's Ride," and "A Message to Garcia." We have read with humor of early sound control. Homer's hero Odysseus fashioned of beeswax the earliest-reported ear protectors. These were required not because of industrial noises but to protect his associates from the cries of the sirens. Homer's imagination encompassed sounds of great magnitude, but not electronically amplified ones that pass through a microphone and on to a loud-speaker or earphone. Alexander of Macedon allegedly constructed a gigantic horn as a military signaling device, but its output was neither affected by a battery nor amplified by an electronic tube.

In somewhat the same manner that the wireless of Marconi speeded and made common a kind of communication that had relied on the foot runner, gun blast, or smoke signals, the telephone of Alexander Graham Bell gave a scope to the sound waves of the voice that extended their distance of transmission from a few hundred yards to all habitable space. This extension has been in process for hardly a century.

The popular home radio, the conventional hearing aid, the talking movie, the high-fidelity voice recorder, and a public-address system as-a-matter-of-course are scarcely a quarter of a century old. Even so, we have taken recordings and phonographs for granted throughout the discussions and projects of this book.

Sound waves are preserved on phonograph records, motion-picture film, magnetic wire, tape, etc. An actor performs once, is recorded, and plays in the motion-picture theaters throughout the world; a radio announcer says of a program, "Presented from transcription"; or a traveling executive dictates his letters en route and mails a recording to his secretary for typing.

Much of our twentieth-century talking is microphone speech.

THE SOUND SYSTEM

Two terms are characteristic of all sound systems, *input* and *output*. These are typically such pairs as (1) microphone and loud-speaker, (2) phonograph needle and loud-speaker, (3) microphone and earphone, (4) microphone and headset, etc. These components are *end pieces*. Inserted between the two of them is usually at least one stage of amplification and frequently several stages. The amplifiers simply increase the level of the electrical signals that have dimensions proportional to the sound waves that "shaped" the electrical currents.

1. MICROPHONES. The most elementary sound system to include a "microphone" is a pair of tin cans, or such substitutes as are available, connected by a taut string or wire—a toy. The sound waves from the child's mouth "shake" or vibrate the end of one can. These movements are transferred through the string or wire longitudinally and shake the closed end of the second can. A listener can receive a message through this system if the cord is not too long, and possibly if he goes to some precaution not to hear the message through the ordinary air

channel. The tin can shown in Fig. 29 picks up the speech at the mouth and is a pseudo microphone.

a. Sound-powered Microphones. The sound-powered systems of wire communication are a bit more complex than the toy of the preceding paragraph. The principal differences lie in the addition of permanent magnets in the microphone and receiver and the requirement that the connecting line be an electrical conductor. Usually two wires connect the magnets of the microphone and the receiver, but one wire will suffice. A metal diaphragm is placed close to—but not touching—the poles of the magnet of the microphone. From your experience with horseshoe magnets as toys, you can appreciate that some of the mag-

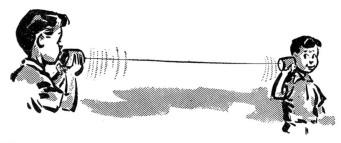

FIG. 29. The ends of the tin cans are serving as a transducer or microphone and as a receiver.

netic flux would travel from one pole to the other through the metal diaphragm in spite of the small gaps between the poles and the diaphragm. The flow is more and less as the diaphragm is closer and farther from the poles. As an imbalance occurs in this simple system, electromotive forces are generated in the line. This is the state of affairs when sound waves begin to impinge on the diaphragm of the transmitter or microphone. These waves vibrate the diaphragm and alter the distance between the magnet and the diaphragm. With each change in this distance, the amount of flow of magnetic flux changes and the current in the line to the receiver or listener's position is altered. The variations of current affect the flow of magnetic flux at the listener's diaphragm and the vibrations that are set up as this diaphragm is pulled more and less toward the poles of the listener's magnet correspond with the vibrations in the speaker's microphone. The vibrations at the receiver reestablish a pattern of sound waves in the adjacent air similar to the waves that impinged on the microphone. The amplitude of the waves at the output, however, is diminished. Some of the distinguishing irregularities of the sound wave are attenuated. The frequency of the fundamental is unaltered by the somewhat low-fidelity unit. This system resembles the one that was constructed by Alexander Graham Bell. Having no batteries, it has much to recommend it for some applications, particularly with distances under one-eighth of a mile. This sound-powered telephone is the principal unit for shipboard communication. As you might guess, a strong voice operates the telephone better than a weak voice. As you can see in Fig. 30, the microphone and the receiver are identical inside; either unit can be used for sending or receiving.

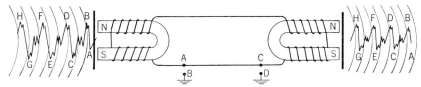

FIG. 30. The movement of the diaphragm of the microphone toward and away from the magnets alters the flow of magnetic flux and hence the flow of current in the line. Thus, the complexities of a sound wave are regenerated by the disturbances of the diaphragm in the listener's receiver.

b. The Crystal Microphone. The sound-powered microphone just described exemplifies those that seem to generate their own power. Particularly, they do not require an external source of power—for example, a battery. Another of this type is the popular crystal microphone. In this instance, advantage is taken of the fact that a crystal, for example Rochelle salts, will generate a voltage when "squeezed," and the amount of the voltage is proportional to the amount of the "squeeze." Quite simply, sound waves impinge upon the crystal, and the crystal generates voltage that is proportional to the instantaneous pressure of the sound wave. Thus, as the pressure varies from instant to instant in the saying of a speech sound, the voltage or pressure of the current varies. The changing current is amplified and fed to a loudspeaker or headset, and the loud-speaker sets up sound waves of rarefaction and condensation like those that "squeezed" the crystal microphone.

c. Moving-coil Microphone. Still a third type of microphone that is its own power system is the moving-coil or dynamic microphone. In this instance a magnet, wrapped with wire, is generating magnetic flux and hence current in a closed system. Advantage is taken of the fact that the magnetic field and electric flow are altered by the insertion of a wire or rod into the field across the lines of force, and of the further fact that this effect is proportional to the number of magnetic lines of force that are cut. Hence, a nonmetallic diaphragm lies in the path of the sound waves and moves to and fro in keeping with the pressure pattern of the waves. This diaphragm is attached to a wire or rod that cuts many or few magnetic lines of force, depending on the extent to which the sound pressure distends the diaphragm and pushes the rod into the magnetic field. Alternatively, the rod may be fixed in position and the coil move in keeping with the action of the diaphragm. The varying electrical current from the microphone is amplified and fed to an output, for example a loud-speaker.

d. Velocity Microphone. A somewhat similar effect to that of the dynamic microphone is achieved in the ribbon, or velocity, microphone. In this instance a thin metal ribbon, possibly one-quarter of an inch wide and two inches long, is facing the bars of the magnet and separated from them by about one-sixteenth of an inch. The movements of the ribbon across the lines of force of the magnet alter the current that is generated. This microphone allows the sound waves to impinge on the ribbon as though it were a diaphragm, but equally, or more importantly, the sound waves pass by the ribbon and set up varying degrees of a partial vacuum on the far side of the ribbon. This double action results in greater displacement of the ribbon and thus greater excursions of the "cutting agent" through the magnetic lines of force.

e. Carbon Microphone. There are also microphones that operate on a basis of primarily altering a flow of current through the microphone itself. The oldest of these is the carbon microphone, which is shown in Fig. 31. Of course the ultimate effect would be for the microphone to alter the current in the system too, but the reason for the variation is different. Whereas the crystal generates voltage, the carbon granules only vary the amount of voltage that passes through them. Thus, this microphone requires an external source of current such as a battery and the microphone itself is "dead" or "live." In the previous instance the microphone is always "live" whether the system is *off* or *on.*

Probably because of the importance of the carbon microphone in telephony and military communications, it is the one that you have used most. A flow of current is powered by batteries and flows around the system whenever the circuit is *closed.* This current passes through a small chamber of carbon granules. These granules conduct more current when they are pressed or tightly packed than when they are loose. This again may be remindful of the changing action of crystals when they are "squeezed." Possibly the change in the conductivity of the carbon granules is due to the fact that they have more interparticle contact when they are pressed together. In any event, the amount of flow of battery-supplied current is determined by the "pressing" action of the sound waves of speech upon the carbon particles. Obviously, the voice will be more effective in pressing the granules together when the carbon chamber is close to the speaker's mouth. The continuously varying current from the activated microphone is amplified and fed to an output, a receiver at a listener's ear, or a loud-speaker.

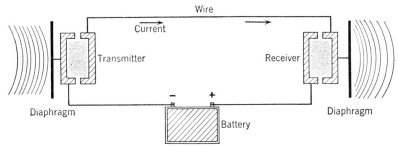

FIG. 31. Current flows continuously in the carbon system when the circuit is closed. The amount of the current that flows varies with the compactness of the carbon granules. Two wires may be used or one wire may be replaced by "ground," the earth completing the circuit.

f. The Condenser Mircophone. Finally, an important type of microphone, the condenser, was understood early in the development of telephony but had to await the vacuum tube before the principle was exploited and to await the miniature tube before the microphone became popular. This microphone is a little more difficult to explain in our layman's language. Technically, the microphone operates on the principle that the current through a condenser depends upon the capacitance and the rate of change of voltage. The microphone acts as a condenser; that is to say, when the microphone is fed a varying voltage, a varying current flows through the system. As sound waves impinge on a movable face of the condenser, a balanced or steady-state current in the line with the condenser is thrown into imbalance because of the change in the capacitance of the condenser. The microphone, when in use, might be viewed as continually seeking a state of balance.

As the capacitance is altered, however, a weak voltage emerges from the microphone. This varying voltage is fed to amplifiers. The microphone unit itself, the condenser, may be no longer than a drum that might be cut from a one-quarter-inch length of your fountain pen. However, the extremely small current that makes up the output of the microphone is amplified close to the microphone itself, and the same housing frequently includes both the microphone unit and an amplifying tube. Even so, the whole assembly may be no larger than a fountain pen. This microphone is often used as a standard in acoustical measurements. It is quiet in operation and transmits a wide range of frequencies faithfully.

g. Summary. The words "good" and "poor" are hardly applicable to a microphone apart from its application. Rather, the instrument is suitable or unsuitable. The application might require the highest possible fidelity, as in the instance of recording or transmitting a symphony orchestra. High fidelity means that, as nearly as possible, the microphone is responding linearly, or in amounts proportional to differences in the sound pressure level in the sound waves. Alternatively, if the microphone is partially insensitive to some bands of frequencies, this disparity must be corrected in the amplifying system. However, there may be situations in which ruggedness of the microphone is of prime importance. It must be able to withstand mechanical vibration and even accidental blows. This is no place for the delicate adjustments of a ribbon or diaphragm relative to a magnet, nor for a crystal that might crack. As the speaker's choice of microphone differs from one circumstance to another, so will his manner of using the microphone differ with the type he talks into. A comparison of some of the characteristics of the microphones is summarized in Table 2.

2. Receivers. Typically the speech that has been picked up by a microphone is delivered to a listener through an earpiece or a loudspeaker. The former category includes hearing-aid receivers, telephone receivers, and headsets or earphones. These receivers are similar to the microphones that were described above. Instead of responding to sound waves and setting up varying current, they respond to varying current and set up sound waves. The action is very similar. Obviously from Fig. 30, and as mentioned above, either end of the system could be employed as a microphone or a headset. Similarly, there are carbon receivers, crystal receivers, condenser receivers, moving-coil receivers, etc.

Table 2. Summary of Characteristics of Popular Varieties of Microphones and Suggestions About Operating Them

Type	Level of output	Frequency response	Directional	Talking distance	Impedance	Notes
Sound-powered	Low	Quite poor	Front only	Touching lips	Low	No batteries; sturdy; simple
Crystal	High	Fair	No	....	High	Avoid heat; avoid blows
Carbon	High	Poor	Front	Close to lips	Low	Noisy; sturdy; the granules sometimes "pack"; tap the microphone lightly against the hand.
Moving-coil	Medium	Good	Front	....	Low	Try using a moving-coil loudspeaker as a microphone; it will work.
Velocity	Low	Good	Front-back	Away from breath stream	Low	Do not use outdoors (wind noise)
Condenser	Very low	Very good	Not very directional	....	Low	Very satisfactory; relatively costly

The loud-speakers that we see in our phonographs, radios, and public-address systems are typically of the moving-coil type, and usually terminate in a paper-cone sound radiator. More powerful sound sources may lead to a horn. Either one serves to generate a sound wave with a "wave front" of considerable size. Interior applications are almost always of the paper-cone variety. These must be housed in a baffle. The cone moves in a pistonlike manner, except in the instance of high frequencies, in which instance the cone bends considerably. Without a baffle the displaced air tends to move around the edge of the cone to the rear, equalizing the pressure about the cone and reducing its qualities as a sound radiator. The baffle sets up a barrier to this movement and delays the arrival of the equalizing air at the back of the cone until the movement of the cone has been fully effective.

THE APPLICATIONS OF MICROPHONE SPEECH

There are few instances in which speech is singular to microphone usage. It simply extends normal speech (1) in daily conversation, (2) in entertainment, as in radio and television shows, (3) in public address and education, (4) in business, as from one office to another. The exceptions to the general rule are such instances as ship-to-shore, airplane-to-ground, and engine-to-caboose radio. In these instances, speech would not occur except for the presence of the microphone.

1. THE TELEPHONE. The telephone has provided your principal practice in the use of a microphone. Toy telephones probably came into your make-believe games as a child. Most students have used the home or office telephone as long as they can remember for business calls and social calls in point-to-point talking. The distances, of course, exceed the ones that can be reached by voice alone. You learned early to place the mouthpiece or microphone close to your mouth. This placement of the microphone or telephone transmitter in relation to the mouth used to be more critical than it is now, because the carbon-type microphones in the older telephone systems gave a weak signal and a relatively high noise. Moreover, the talker had freedom in getting his mouth to the transmitter and the receiver to his ear. As you know, telephones are engineered now to accommodate "talking close to the transmitter" through the one-piece construction of the transmitter and receiver.

The speech that is directed to telephones is essentially the speech of conversation, interview, query, and announcement. In special instances, though, there is an advantage in an "engineered language" over conventional language. First, a special language may assure shorter messages, and the "channel capacity" of the telephone system is thereby improved. This is an important consideration in military communication or with the radio messages at a busy airport. Essentially, several pilots are on a party line, although the airplanes may be miles apart. The line can carry only a single message at one time. The operational messages are given in a brief standardized wording with which all talkers and listeners are intimately familiar. Frequently they have been trained in saying these messages and have become practiced in hearing them even before being permitted to fly airplanes that are equipped with radios. Second, the routinized messages increase the likelihood of quick and accurate reception on the part of the listener, however bad the interfering noise may be. Consequently, both because of brevity of wording and insured reception, the line is tied up a minimum time with each transmission, and the channel capacity is accordingly increased. In ordinary telephone usage, however, channel capacity is given little thought, and a person who has the line assumes that his time is the factor that limits the length of a conversation. Possibly the busy signal that we hear as we try futilely to get through to a dormitory causes us to wish that the other person would give thought to channel capacity. Oddly, though, when we do get our party, we become the thoughtless offender.

2. THE PUBLIC-ADDRESS SYSTEM. The public-address system—often pronounced simply P.A.—enlarges public address in somewhat the manner that the telephone increases the distance over which conversation can be conducted. The P.A. system is simple—a microphone, an amplifier, and one or more loud-speakers. The talker is often in full view of the audience, and the illusion is created that ordinary face-to-face public speaking is in process. This is hardly the case. The speaker assumes the responsibility in ordinary public address for making himself heard to as many of his audience as possible. The larger the hall or the greater the circle of people around the speaker's stump, the louder the speaker's voice must be, a circumstance that doubtless contributed to some of the peculiar patterns of "public voice" of the premicrophone days. The announcer, for example, knows that the spectator in the most remote seat in a large stadium is *hearing* (1) who carried the ball on the last play and (2) how much ground he gained. Possibly for good measure the announcer adds gratuitously how this run affects the player's run average for the game and season. The

announcer may be on the side line, following the ball up and down the field. He may be soft-spoken as he talks into a portable microphone, held close to his mouth, or he may have an acoustically isolated station in an advantageously located press box and talk into a microphone like the one that is used in a ballroom P.A. system. The principal feature of the public-address system is that it amplifies and distributes the speaker's voice. Loud voice is not needed. One difference that it makes to the public speaker is that the responsibility for his being heard throughout the auditorium now to some extent falls on another's shoulders: the engineer. The engineer, in turn, is as frequently concerned with reducing the output level of the system as he is with increasing it.

a. Makeshift Systems. Public-address systems are qualitatively dissimilar. A temporary, portable installation is not fitted or "engineered" to the room in which it is used. It cannot be; this system must be useful in another room tomorrow night. The talker has long since learned to gauge proper loudness by the level of the side tone that comes back to him as he talks. We employ the same method as we hear the speech come to us directly from the loud-speakers and the sound that is reflected from the walls of the auditorium. This time we may encounter difficulty, particularly if the talker is some distance from the loud-speaker. In the short discussion of loud-speakers, we explained the need for a baffle in order that the movement of air around the edge of the cone-type loud-speaker would be impeded. In other words, a time delay was deliberately introduced into the mechanical operation of the loud-speaker. The public address in the auditorium may present a similar but somewhat longer time delay *at the speaker's* ear as he monitors his amplified output. If the reflection of the sound is from a sufficiently distant wall or loud-speaker, it may return to the speaker about the time he is preparing to utter the succeeding sound or syllable. If so, he has a frustrating experience as he blocks, repeats, and proceeds with continuing hesitancy in his speech. The loudness of the returning sound is less at fault than the fact that the preceding syllable—one that should be gone by now—has returned at the very instant that a succeeding syllable is ready for utterance.

b. Permanent Systems. A well-designed auditorium may have sound-treated walls with much absorption and little reflection of sound, and have irregular wall surfaces with 10-degree angles every 6 or 8 feet, giving the wall a zigzag effect. Thus, some sound from the loud-speakers is absorbed and some is diffracted. Less than a normal amount comes back to the talker. Moreover, there are several scattered loud-speakers, and each elevates the level of the sound by somewhat less than a normal amount. The sound level at any one spot in the room is considerably less than in the circumstance outlined above; but the sound is more evenly distributed throughout the room than would be the case if there were fewer loud-speakers. This "fitted" system gives the speaker a minimum of "room feedback," even though the listening condition is excellent for all the auditors. Some individuals, taken aback by their first experience with these optimum conditions, are concerned that the P.A. must be inoperative. They may proceed to speak inordinately loudly and to get closer and closer to the microphone. They strive to get the familiar side tone. Ironically, the excellent sound system becomes overloaded and may yield unintelligible speech in spite of its superior quality. The entire situation has its almost humorous side; the listeners see the consternation of the speaker, hear him raise his vocal level, and watch him do all but swallow the microphone.

c. Operation. As a rule, the talker (1) will speak 18 inches or 2 feet from the microphone, (2) will test the P.A. system *before* he gives his speech, and do this testing with the help of an observer who will assure him that all is well even though there is no substantial feedback, and (3) will speak in a manner appropriate for a face-to-face audience of the first 10 to 15 rows without a P.A. system and will let the system and the audio engineer take care of the rest.

3. THE SINGLE OUTPUT. The word microphone is usually associated first with mass communication. It brings to mind radio, television, and public-address systems. A relatively small number of amateurs use the microphones that lead to these three outputs, although of the three, the P.A. comes into our activities and experiences more frequently than do the other two. For the most part, we shall assume that use of mass radio and television as it affects you will occur under supervision and in keeping with the policies of the professional station. However, private use of radio, as from an automobile, airplane, or boat, is another matter. As soon as we bring telephones, dictating machines, and hearing aids into the discussion, our principal concern with microphones becomes apparent. These microphones simply lead to one listener, and it is a topic that has daily applications with all of us.

a. The Voice before a Microphone. The presence or absence of a microphone alone does not, on the average, affect speech. We had supposed differently. We were under the misapprehension that microphone speech was both louder and more understandable than speech of comparable circumstances that was not intended for a microphone. Two experimental approaches thus far have failed to reveal any difference. In both of them a microphone was placed 2 feet in front of a speaker for one-half of a speaking task and was absent during the other half of the exercises. In one instance, the material that was being read was the words of an intelligibility test, and the tests as read by several speakers were heard by a listening panel. The listeners were at different distances from the speaker, ranging upward to a distance of 80 feet. The speakers were of the same intelligibility whether there was a microphone present or not. In the second instance, short five-syllable phrases were read. Again a microphone was at the speaker's position one-half the time. However, there was a real microphone that was hidden from the reader's view. This microphone fed a meter that indicated graphically the level with which each phrase was read. There was no difference in vocal intensity between the two circumstances.

b. The Voice before Obstacles. There are characteristics of the microphone situation, however, that do affect speakers. The story is told of the university official who typically spoke loudly over the telephone. The summer day was warm, and the doors of the administration building were open. The voice boomed through the corridors; the president asked anxiously what the business officer was "up to" and got the answer, "Talking to Sacramento." The president replied, "Tell him to use the telephone!" The tendency to adjust the level of the voice in some manner commensurate with the distance through which we are talking seems to be common and to some extent is independent of the level of the speech that we hear from the other party. Researchers of the Bell Telephone Laboratories inserted a level meter into a set of long-distance lines and obtained measures of the intensity of speech when the circuits were employed in conversations that carried varying distances. The outcome, stated simply, was: The greater the distance between the speaker and the listener, the louder the speaker talked![1]

Another interesting pattern in response to a one-purpose microphone is the speaker's tendency to raise his voice level when he is talking with a person who wears a hearing aid. The speech is probably directed to a

[1] V. Subrizi, "A Speech Volume Survey on Telephone Message Circuits," *Bell Laboratories Record*, vol. 31, pp. 292–295, 1953.

hard-of-hearing *person*, and experience has taught us to talk up to such a listener. The speaker forgets that he is really talking to a microphone and an amplifier that feed a private loud-speaker that is worn in the ear canal. Obviously, the hearing-aid system is built to compensate for the wearer's hearing loss. The speaker who adds a second compensation through his unusually loud talking to the hard-of-hearing person only leads to the wearer's ear being blasted. The response is to turn down the amplifier control. Moments later, when Mr. Loud Voice turns to speak with a normal-hearing person, our wearer of the hearing aid has to readjust the amplifier upward if he is to stay in the conversation. The motivation to talk up to a hearing aid is so general that the story is told of one man who had no difficulty with his minor hearing loss because he wore a black button in his ear and allowed a string from the button to run beneath his coat as though to a hearing-aid control box. People spoke louder to the man with the "hearing aid," and he had no trouble hearing them.

STORED SPEECH

All the applications of microphone speech above include an output that feeds human ears directly. Some microphones lead to recorders, to analyzers, and meters. The recorder may be only a temporary storage device that will ultimately lead to human listeners, even many listeners, as a P.A. system does. The recording system offers several possibilities for the voice to be distorted, and the playback system adds further opportunity. Until an exception is found to be feasible, the rule should be that speech that is sufficiently important to call for storage is of a nature that requires high fidelity. Thus, it is advisable to take precautions to ensure that the equipment is of suitable fidelity and that it is operated in a manner to assure minimum distortion. First, the microphone to the recorder will pick up reflected speech as well as the speech that comes directly from the speaker. The reverberation of the room is recorded along with the voice. This would be all right except that when the recording is played back in a normal room, the reverberation of the second room will get into the sound as well, and the aural experience of the listener will include both reverberations. The suggestion is made that the original recording be made in a recording studio or dead room if possible. Second, the microphone to the recorder will pick up the noise that is present when the recording is made. Automobile horns, squeaking chairs, and class bells come back to haunt one when the recording is reproduceb. Hence, the original recording should be made under the best conditions of isolation that can be obtained. Third, there is inevitably noise in both a recording and playback system. This includes an inescapable circuit noise and, in the instance of disk equipment, the additional friction of groove noise. This noise need not be bothersome. Principally, the signal must be recorded at a sufficiently high level, so that when it is reproduced at an optimum level the noise is below audibility. Microphone placement is important here. Since the intensity of sound diminishes approximately with the square of the distance, the advantage that accrues from having the microphone close to the source of speech is apparent. This can be overdone, of course. The high-fidelity microphone should not be permitted to pick up the wind blast that accompanies speech. To an extent, a weak voice signal can be augmented by turning the amplification higher on the recorder. However, you have learned from operating phonographs that the circuit noise becomes distracting when the amplifiers are set at full gain.

The good-quality recording would be made in a sound-treated, sound-isolated room; the speaker would be approximately 2 feet from the microphone; and the level of recording would be high rather than low, but not so high as to suggest overrecording.

Similar precautions attend the feeding of speech to analyzers, for example, visible speech units. This kind of operation is usually in connection with studies that point toward new knowledge.

Nonreverberant radio studios give few clues that help the talker set his pace, and the absent audience yields no visible signs of approval. In this circumstance, although a friendly glance from the control room or through the window from an adjoining studio may be helpful, the reduction of uneasiness comes chiefly as the speaker becomes pre-occupied with his topic of the moment, with doing a satisfactory job, and with reviewing the relationship that applies to a speaker and his speech, in other words, the adjustment of the speaker.

MICROPHONE VOICE FROM THE LISTENER'S VIEW

The relative significance of fluency among microphone voices has not been determined. In the instance of radio, one can reason himself into the view that since the listeners have no visual clues of progress, the speaker must always demonstrate forward progress with his voice. This would seem to put a premium on fluency and absence of hesi-tations. Another reasonable view would be that since the radio listeners have no visual aid to determine meaning, they should be given the advantage of more than usual time to understand what they are hearing. However, a reliable solution of these questions will have to await thorough study. Meanwhile, we are probably safe to assume that *good voice is good voice*, whether it be in a living room, from a platform, or over a microphone, and that the aspect that is singular to microphone speech is that the talker must take special pains to keep the voice and the microphone in a fairly constant spatial relationship to each other, not separated by 2 feet now and by 4 feet a moment hence.

SUMMARY

The sound system may be variable or fixed in amplification. If it is variable, the operating engineer relieves the speaker of the need for much of the adjusting of the level of speech. The talker's responsibility lies with maintaining a fixed relationship in distance with the microphone. The system with fixed output, such as the telephone, leaves with the talker the task of maintaining at least the "normal" level of voice to which the instrument is adjusted.

Much microphone speech has no visible component for the listener. This imposes upon the talker the need for conveying all his animation by voice. A further requirement is that the speaker assure his listener that the speech is ongoing. Both vocal pitch and duration would seem to become relatively more important in these circumstances than in face-to-face talking.

Projects for Practice

1. "Paul Revere's Ride" and "Carrying the News from Ghent to Aix" were cited as instances of difficult person-to-person communication that have been treated in literature. Cite similar instances that would be handled today by telephone or radio.

2. Write a paper entitled "The Role of the Telephone in Dramatic Literature."

3. List a variety of situations that require a microphone. Explain why you would use a particular type of microphone in each instance.

4. Watch for microphones on telecasts and pictures of microphones in popular magazines, including those in general advertisements. Identify the types of these microphones by referring to advertisements in trade journals, etc.

5. If you are acquainted with microphones and your classmates are not, explain to them several connectors that may be used in microphone lines.

6. The microphone and loud-speaker of a public-address system may set up a condition of howling. This is attributable to acoustic feedback. Explain.

7. Some radio and television shows are almost completely "structured." The time of entrance of a particular character or feature can be predicted almost to the minute. Make note of the order and time of some scenes from your favorite programs to find to what extent they are the same in pattern.

8. Review and recount an experience of meeting or hearing in person a familiar professional radio, television, or motion-picture star. What were the surprises that you experienced?

9. A surprisingly convincing radio program can be enacted within a classroom, although an adjacent performance area is desirable. The participants work in a rear corner of the room. The audience occupies the front rows near the loud-speaker. The necessary equipment includes a microphone, amplifier, and loud-speaker. Submit programs and suggest participants to your instructor or a committee in charge. A varied program will be arranged from the suggestions.

10. Examine a phonograph record under a microscope. A sound wave that extends through 5 to 10 feet in air is stored in what distance? Make similar observations of the sound track of a sound film. Dip a segment of recorded tape in fine iron filings and repeat your observations. (Note: Do not use the tape after dipping it in filings.)

Readings

Abbot, Waldo, *Handbook of Broadcasting*, 3d ed., McGraw-Hill Book Company, Inc., New York, 1950.

Bender, James F., *NBC Handbook of Pronunciation*, Thomas Y. Crowell Company, New York, 1943.

Black, John W. (ed.), *Speech Monographs*, vol. 13, no. 2, 1946.

Ewbank, H. L., "A Classified Bibliography on Radio Speaking and Writing," *Quarterly Journal of Speech*, vol. 23, pp. 230–238, 1937.

Frayne, John G., and Halley Wolfe, *Elements of Sound Recording*, John Wiley & Sons, Inc., New York, 1949.

Lazarsfeld, Paul F., and Patricia L. Kendall, *Radio Listening in America: The People Look at Radio Again*, Prentice-Hall, Inc., New York, 1948.

Miller, George A., "Language Engineering," *Journal of the Acoustical Society of America*, vol. 22, pp. 720–725, 1950.

Nelson, H. E., "The Effect of Variation of Rate on the Recall by Radio Listeners of 'Straight' Newscasts," *Speech Monographs*, vol. 15, pp. 73–100, 1948.

Read, Oliver, *The Recording and Reproduction of Sound*, Howard Sams, Indianapolis, 1949.

Schramm, Wilbur (ed.), *Communications in Modern Society*, University of Illinois Press, Urbana, Ill., 1948.

APPENDIX A. SPEECHES FOR STUDY

Four compositions follow. They are selected to represent diversity in subject matter, point of view, and treatment of topics that fall within the interests of speech.

I. ARGUMENTATION AS A HUMANISTIC SUBJECT[1]

A. Craig Baird

The case for argumentation as a liberal course, although fairly clear, has been more or less forgotten in the hurly-burly of specialization. The subject, to be sure, has been recommended for mental discipline, but the practical character of argument has been chiefly stressed. It has been freely prescribed for teachers, clergymen, intercollegiate debaters, journalists, salesmen, and engineers. Too little, however, has been said about the function of argumentation as a medium for correlating and unifying the curriculum of the liberal college and for liberalizing the capacities that contribute to the college graduate's happiness and usefulness. Argument as a course in writing and speaking aims specifically to communicate ideas to the end of affecting the

[1] A. Craig Baird, "Argumentation As a Humanistic Subject," *Quarterly Journal of Speech Education*, vol. 10, pp. 258–264, 1924. Used by permission.

A. Craig Baird read this paper before a national meeting of teachers of speech in 1923. At the time, he was teaching at Bates College. Soon thereafter he moved to the State University of Iowa. He has written many books about speech, has been a leader among students of rhetoric, and has contributed importantly to international speaking by students, sometimes being called "the father of international debating." Baird's enthusiasm for humanistic learning pervades his teaching and counseling. Among the titles of his books are *College Readings on Current Problems* and *Essays and Addresses toward a Liberal Education*. The student should study the meaning of *humanism*, being sure not to confuse it with *humanitarianism*. With respect to education, *humanism* emphasizes the traditional subjects. The first objective lies in the development of the student through his reconciling and integrating literature, philosophy, and the history of mankind, and developing a personal philosophy.

judgment and action of an audience. Such purpose, however, from the point of view of education for Illumination or Reason, as Cardinal Newman calls it, as contrasted with Learning or Acquirement, presupposes a spiritual outlook and motive. No reason is there why the student of argument who is properly instructed should not be guided into a humanistic channel. He should survey broadly the field of controversial knowledge and develop something of associative and interpretative ability, even a philosophy of life. This purpose and result are one with the expressed aim of the liberal college. To establish, or reestablish the character of argumentation as a liberal subject should be one of the sound objectives of departments of speech.

Any solution of the problem assumes the validity of the humanistic or liberal ideal. With the repudiation of the rigid classical program and the substitution, more or less half-hearted, of the university ideal, the American college has moved with confessed indirection. The liberal arts school has continued officially to affirm this faith in the unity of knowledge; wherever the university spirit has overshadowed, however, the program has been based upon the multiplicity of knowledge. Specialization has won hands down. The growth of the social studies, the abandonment of education exclusively for the socially elect, and the application of science to practical affairs have undermined the liberal ideal. The result is that sometimes the collegian has dipped for four years into an educational melange. He has gone in for isolated fragments and has become, as Charles Evans Hughes says, an intellectual vagrant. He is in no sense a specialist, but he has often become the victim of the impasse between two educational conceptions.

The college of freedom needs what the discarded routine of the classics, pure mathematics, and moral philosophy undeniably yielded: a grasp of the problem as a whole and something of the disinterested passion for perfection. Our collegiate ancestors, although they placed a mistaken emphasis on dead tongues and tested modern life too sharply by the Hellenic pattern, never-the-less saw life steadily and whole. They lacked severe scientific training; but certainly they did synthesize knowledge and evolve a philosophy for approaching the riddle of the world. They did aim to create the type of man described by Plato as one "who has magnificence of mood and is the spectator of all time and all existence."

Back to the humanistic ideal even the most heterodox college administrators are returning. The group system, the Oxonian honor schools, the survey courses in civilization, the general examination at the end of the senior year, and similar departures express the trend. Courses, modern in content, yet those that invite a genuine analysis, that deal with the outstanding problems of life, that relate those problems in such way as to unify the field of knowledge, that give a consistent and spiritual explanation of life, must furnish a means for stemming the tide of purely utilitarian training. Departments of speech should provide such courses. Argumentation, I believe, naturally adapts itself to such fundamental aims.

Specifically argumentation as a humanistic subject provides a problem rather than an answer. This problem is usually one of wide social significance. Argumentation outlines the correct principles for analyzing the problem and for gathering available data; suggests logical methods for the solution and for expressing question and answer in terms that command attention and win assent. The subject thus provides a method; it does not offer a selected body of material to be appropriated. It sets the student's mind to work in ways that lead, or should lead, to greater elasticity of thought, power to state great issues, judgment in their solution, increased facility in the communication of those judgments, and, if the course has been thorough, some ability to resolve a complex world into a unit.

If argumentation is this liberalizing system, why has it failed to establish itself securely in the confidence of liberal educators? Partly because those who behold it are still divided in their counsels as to whether it is English, Public Speaking, or Economics; partly because it has all the attributes of a prelegal course, or at least those of a technical course in contest debating; further, because the material with which it deals is usually too limited to furnish that complete notion of things demanded of a fundamental subject; again, because the undergraduates in the course are often too immature in educational experience to correlate successfully ideas involving economic, governmental, educational, and other fields; finally, because those who direct such instruction are by training and temper, more likely than not, apathetic toward the cultural aim.

As to the first charge, that the true character of argumentation has thus far not been disclosed, we may content ourselves with a modest rejoinder that for our educational purpose we may claim the subject as the rightful property of the Department of Speech. To influence an audience by speech is its historical and characteristic function, whatever we may say about it as written composition.

For teachers of speech to allow argument to drift as a derelict unit of elective English has meant a distinct loss for argument and for speech. The antecedents or constituents have been philosophy, law, logic, composition, ancient rhetoric, psychology, and—shall we add?—economics, history, and sociology. But attempts to outline the subject from the point of view of any one of these sciences or arts have been abortive. Argumentation comprehends them all, or rather directs them to the specific task of moulding public opinion through logical reasoning. Such, I believe, must be the angle from which to begin an analysis of the content of argumentation.

Another reason for refusing to assign argument to the liberal group is the fact that it has been linked so closely with law and with that handmaiden of law, intercollegiate debating. The alliance between law and argument has been natural, for law, more than any other profession, has applied practically the art of persuasion. The college course has thus fallen heir to much of the legal formula for discussion. In the typical course much is said about the case, the plea, the burden of proof, tests of evidence, and so on. The brief with its twelve or fifteen rules is drafted directly from the court room.

Debating, a special application of courtroom procedure, has also made up much of the course. Argumentation, converted into a legal game of formal discussion under fixed rules, gains a certain attractiveness. Students may see at once the analogy with athletic competition. Even though writers of texts carefully disclaim such purpose, the course as outlined seems to aim largely at preparation for winning contest debates. Accordingly the teacher or writer begins with rules for contest propositions, and ends with suggestions about the content of the third negative speech or about Napoleonic strategy for annihilating the enemy. The major part of the advanced work usually consists of debates. Whoever completes the classroom exercises with credit is supposed to be armed with a technique calculated to overthrow all comers.

The union of the legal stream with that of the older rhetoric and oratory undoubtedly produced a better product of college teaching. Emphasis on evidence and detailed briefing have, in theory at least, stiffened and sharpened student wit in controversy. But this excessive legalism and this specialization in debate have given the subject a technical tone that in aim, method, and content is usually inconsistent with the cultural spirit of argumentation. My proposal is that argument shall be taught as a systematic attempt to discover and present the truth, whereas debating, although also having this purpose, shall continue to aim first of all at gaining a decision on definite issues by means of exact technique. Argument must continue to base its procedure on the sure foundation of logic and evidence. But a more just proportion is to be observed between Thought, Composition, and Delivery. Discussion will be substituted for formal debating; figures and citation of authorities will not submerge vital thought; individual expression will have freer scope than is usually the case in debate. These suggestions are admittedly fragmentary; they are intended only to point the general approach to argument. They are not to be regarded as a wholesale condemnation of debating, but rather as an attempt to classify it in its utilitarian character and to suggest that it belongs where most teachers of speech have officially placed it—in a unit distinct from argument.

This shifting of emphasis from the legal to the rhetorical and philosophical will logically lead to an enlargement of the field of discussion. The debater must rightly confine himself to a topic specific, well-balanced, capable of approximate proof, and sufficiently untechnical to appeal to an average audience. The range of topics is thus limited to current economic, political, and educational topics. Argument, on the contrary, will include the whole field of philosophy, science, literature and ethics. Such material furnishes current magazine articles and dormitory discussions. It is the free property of courses in English and in speech. If argumentation, the peculiar province of which is to deal with large issues, is to give students a detached survey of things, access to this broad field must not be denied. The student's reading in the course will include both the Congressional Record and Morley's Possible Utility of Error. The student will write and speak on such topics as government control of railroads, fundamentalism, law and justice, immorality, the scientific basis of optimism, art and decency, individualism, socialism, pacifism, Eugene O'Neill and recent drama, Walt Whitman, the World Court, and evolution. Considerable was lost when the colleges abandoned the literary society debates on such problems as, Was Shakespeare a greater poet than Milton? But care must be taken always that this content shall be significant, that sufficient analysis and discussion shall be conducted to assure an appreciation of the problem, both in its definite effects and in its larger relations. The course will thus provide the student with an instrument for an interpretation of the college curriculum as a whole.

Does not the importance that I have attached to range and type of material mean that content looms up as the chief end? Certainly that tendency must be avoided. But on the other hand, we are agreed that proper method cannot be dissociated from proper content. Strong argument must depend upon real thinking. Teachers of English composition have seized upon this principle and have made the most of it. It is significant that Greek and Roman rhetoricians passed into oblivion partly because their teaching came to concern itself with form to the neglect of content. I believe with Professor Wichelns that "For those who start from the concept of the unity of the human spirit, no enduring separation of method and content is possible."

If this course has the pretentious aim of going behind mere speaking to bring its members face to face with great questions and to inspire productive thinking, it is apparent that only those students who have a back-ground of two and preferably three years of college study are qualified for admission. Those enrolled will discuss the central problems of internationalism, economics, education, and literature in turn. Their technique as disputants will improve. And their fund of well-grounded opinion will ripen into a philosophy by which to bind together their educational experience.

Finally, my conception of argumentation as a liberal subject may best be clarified by considering the equipment and outlook of the instructor of the subject. With the movement for specialization in speech, it is inevitable that the ideal herein expressed should be regarded with misgivings. Does not such program threaten the definite and exact type of teaching? Will not the members of the course be in doubt as to whether their role for a semester is that of speakers, or philosophers who sit in state holding no form of educational creed but contemplating all? Will not the specific virtues of argument resulting from the severe discipline of brief-making and use of evidence vanish in thin air? The danger of such drift, I admit, must be faced. The course in argument must be in the hands only of a specialist fitted by training and interest to criticise and inform wisely his pupils concerning voice control, action, gesture, time, pitch, and the rest of the speech technique. Too little time has thus far been given in argument courses to the matter of delivery. The instructor, moreover, must teach argument as a problem in communication in which attention, interest, use of imagery, and other aspects of suggestion will be understood and applied. The teacher, moreover, must be in sympathy with the contributions of law and logic. Students must continue to work from an argumentative outline, and must express themselves tersely and logically. Further, he will fall short if he is not more or less of a specialist in English composition. Finally, it were well if this professor of argument were an investigator in at least one of the social sciences. His duty it is to have engaged in some productive work in economics, sociology, or politics. Almost fanciful, I admit, seems the range of ability and attainment demanded of this instructor. Nevertheless graduate departments of speech must attract and develop such high grade teachers.

One other qualification must be stated. Cultural education is always described in terms of personality. The test is one of an awakened spirit. Only one who has faith in character and life as an end rather than profession or attainment can perform this pedagogical service. Our teacher must be a man of liberal educational faith, whose students will catch the true spirit of inquiry and will measure life by those same cultural standards. Under the guidance of such a stimulating instructor the undergraduate will piece together the fragments of his world and will be able to explain with logic and conviction the meaning of it all.

2. Effective Speaking in Business[1]

W. Hayes Yeager

A few weeks ago I had luncheon with four men who are professors in our College of Commerce. The conversation turned to two students who might be said to be joint products of the College of Commerce and the Department of Speech, which is a part of our College of Arts and Sciences. Both boys took their undergraduate work in the College of Commerce, and along with their

[1] *Proceedings of the Fourth Annual Fire and Casualty Insurance Conference,* Mar. 22, 1948. Columbus (Ohio) College of Commerce Conference Series, no. C-52, pp. 20–30. Used by permission.

W. Hayes Yeager is chairman of the department of speech at The Ohio State University. Previously, he held a similar position for 16 years at George Washington

courses in business organization, economics, accounting, etc., each took courses in public speaking. In addition to courses in public speaking both boys represented the University for several years as members of our intercollegiate debating teams, in which activity they had a great deal of practice preparing and presenting speeches. Both became graduate students—one in Commerce and the other in Speech.

One of the professors in Commerce recently took both boys to a meeting of sales executives in St. Louis to put on a demonstration. So much knowledge did they display and so skillfully did they present it that they were offered more than twenty-five positions.

As we sat around the luncheon table, we agreed that those boys are destined to go far. One of the professors in Commerce aptly singled out the reason for our unanimous opinion when he said to me, "*There is no stopping a man who has both the knowledge we supply in Commerce and the skills in communication which you supply in Speech.*"

We have all heard and at times approved, or perhaps almost worshipped, the old saying, "Knowledge is power." We often see this statement carved on school buildings, for in education we have often deluded ourselves into believing that it is true. But knowledge alone, as basic and important as it is, is *not* power; it never *has* been power, and it's a safe bet that it never *will* be power. Knowledge, of course, is essential. We must have it. Without it we cannot understand the past history of the businesses with which we are associated, we cannot properly appraise what is happening in the business world today, and we cannot look with sureness into the future. Knowledge, therefore, is a vital need of everyone in business, but it is not power. Knowledge alone will not keep the wheels of industry turning, adjust labor-management disputes, sell insurance, or bring an increase in salary. Knowledge locked in men's brains or embalmed in annual and research reports is *not* power. Knowledge becomes power only when it is brought out of the many hidden recesses where it may be found and put to work. It is the *use* of knowledge that is power. The best which can be said of knowledge alone is that it is potential power. It becomes power only when it is put to work in a good cause.

University and prior to that taught for shorter periods at other universities. He has been a leader in professional organizations concerned with speech, serving in the highest elected and appointed positions. He is also a lecturer and man of practical affairs. Either as a lecturer, teacher, or consultant, he has been associated with many business firms and associations, and he is now consultant on communications at the headquarters of the United States Air Force. Among Yeager's several books—including ones of which he is coauthor—are *Effective Speaking for Every Occasion*, *Principles of Effective Speaking*, and *Practical Business Speaking*. Hence, the title of the speech that is reproduced here falls in a line of major interest to him. The speech presents the utilitarian view of the study of speech, a view that may predominate among undergraduate students of the subject.

A very large part of the average person's use of his knowledge is to *com*
municate it clearly, accurately, vividly, and (listeners also hope) briefly t
others. The knowledge of the executive is of little use either to himself or t
his organization if he can't communicate it effectively to both top manage
ment and employees down the line. The knowledge of a foreman or depar
ment manager has no value if he can't communicate it to those workin
under him in such fashion as to enable the unit to operate smoothly an
profitably and to communicate it to his superiors in such fashion as to give
clear understanding of his problems and needs. To have value, the knowledg
of the insurance salesman must be communicated effectively to prospects.

The importance of skill in communication, particularly in speaking, ha
long been recognized. "As a vessel is known by the sound whether it
cracked or not, so men are proved by their speeches whether they be wis
or foolish." So spoke Demosthenes, effective speaker, business-man, an
political leader of Athens more than 2,000 years ago. Shakespeare saic
"Mend your speech a little, lest it may mar your fortunes." Daniel Webste
usually regarded as the most effective speaker America has produced, onc
said, "If all my possessions and powers were to be taken from me with on
exception, and if I could choose that exception, I would choose to keep th
power of speech for by it I could soon recover all of the rest." Owen D. Youn
once asked a college graduating class, "Have you acquired adequate skill i
communication with others?" Then he added, "If you can't answer th
question satisfactorily, you will find it difficult to succeed." S. C. Allyr
president of the National Cash Register Company, in an article entitle
"Speech and Leadership in Business," which appeared in the February, 194
issue of the *Quarterly Journal of Speech*, official publication of the Speec
Association of America, says, "The lifeline of any business is its channels c
communication, and there are only two principal methods of conveyin
information from one person to another or from one group to another. On
is the written word; the other, the spoken word. There is no point in trying t
evaluate their relative importance, both play a vital role in the operation c
any business, for there can be no success where there is no understanding, an
there can be no understanding where there is not a free exchange of ideas.

Some years ago the Wharton School of Finance of the University of Penr
sylvania sent a questionnaire to its graduates. Among the questions aske
was, "If you had the opportunity to return and begin your work over agair
what courses would you take?" A large majority wrote that they would tak
all of the courses in writing and in speaking that they could get. They ha
discovered that they couldn't make the fullest use of their knowledge becaus
of lack of skills in communication. A similar questionnaire sent to the execu
tive staff of the United States Department of Agriculture brought a simila
response.

What attention have you ladies and gentlemen been giving to evaluating your methods of communication within your organizations and to improving the communication skills of your executives and salesmen? Frankly, I don't know the answer to that question. I suspect that some of you are giving a great deal of attention to these matters, and that others are giving very little.

President Allyn of the National Cash Register Company, in the article already referred to, said, "Ability to speak well no longer is a professional art to be mastered only by lawyers, preachers, teachers, and entertainers. The man preparing for leadership in business needs this ability too, because leadership expresses itself primarily through speech."

So my purpose today is to attempt to supply you with an introduction to the art of effective speaking in business. And let me emphasize that what I have selected to say to you is such a small part of the field of effective speaking in business and industry that it can be no more than an introduction.

Probably the first question an inexperienced speaker asks himself is, "Can I learn to make a speech?" Perhaps he has listened to Franklin D. Roosevelt, Winston Churchill, Walter S. Gifford, Owen D. Young, Charles F. Kettering, Eric Johnston, and Paul Hoffman, to name only a few, and exclaimed, "They are born speakers!" Of course, all effective speakers are born—nature not having provided any other way of bringing them into the world—just as lawyers, carpenters, doctors, teachers, and bricklayers are born. But no effective speaker in the entire history of the world ever attained the skill he possessed merely by reason of being born; to the mental and physical equipment which nature gave him, he had to add training—either in the class-room or by means of experience or both—because *only through training are effective speakers made*. Anyone who possesses the mental and physical equipment which enables one to speak can increase his effectiveness in communicating his ideas to others if he is willing to pay the price in time and effort.

However, if you are looking for a magic formula that will make you effective speakers on any and all occasions, almost overnight, with little or no effort on your part, you are doomed to disappointment. There is no magic formula; there are no "cuts" so "short" that mastery comes overnight; there is no "open sesame" to immediate success as a speaker. Why is it that so many people think that learning to speak effectively should be as easy as learning to breathe? Do men become effective lawyers, doctors, teachers, plumbers, mechanics, foremen, or insurance executives overnight, or in a week or a month? To become an effective speaker requires much hard work.

Then you ask, "How do speakers become effective?" Have you ever heard of anyone who became a great architect merely by reading books and listening to lectures on architecture? Have you ever heard of anyone who became a great portrait painter merely by reading books and listening to lectures on portrait painting? Have you ever heard of anyone who became a great news reporter merely by reading books and listening to lectures on news reporting? Have you ever heard of anyone who became a great insurance salesman merely by reading books and listening to lectures on insurance? Have you ever heard of anyone who became a great speaker merely by reading books and listening to lectures on speaking? It is a safe bet that you have not, for in developing skills, we learn principally by doing. Architects learn to design good buildings chiefly by designing buildings, portrait painters learn to paint good portraits chiefly by painting portraits; news reporters learn to write good news stories chiefly by writing news stories; insurance salesmen learn to handle their problems successfully chiefly by handling those problems; effective speakers learn to make good speeches chiefly by making speeches. To be sure, all of these persons will learn much that will be of value to them from books and lectures, but they will never get to first base as effective practitioners without speaking practice, and more practice. So not only read good books and listen to good talks on effective speaking, but get up on your feet and make speeches. Make your own contribution. Chiefly through the actual making of speeches will you attain greater skill in the art of effective speech making.

The first step in learning to speak more effectively is to understand clearly just what effective speaking is. What do we mean when we say that John Jones is an effective speaker, but Samuel Smith is not? The answer is that different people mean different things; they attach different meanings to the word *effective*. One man says that John Jones is effective because he projects his voice out to the audience and can be heard easily. Another says he is effective because he has a friendly and pleasing manner and because everybody likes him. Another says he is an effective speaker because he always has a good story to tell. Still another says that he is effective because he has a musical voice and pleasing gestures. And so we could go on and enumerate many other reasons, ranging from the cut of his clothes and the color of his hair to his choice of words and ideas, advanced by different people to explain their opinion that John Jones is an effective speaker.

Now let us examine Samuel Smith and see what different people mean when they say he is not an effective speaker. One man says that he does not like him because his voice is harsh and rasping. Another says he is not effective because he mumbles his words and it is hard to hear what he says. Another says he is not effective because his clothing doesn't fit him and he always looks like something "the cat dragged in." Another says that he is not effective because he is always expounding "crack-brained" ideas. And another says, "That silly grin on his face makes it impossible for me to take him seriously about anything." And so it goes; almost everyone has a somewhat different opinion about why Samuel Smith is as poor a speaker as he is.

We must, therefore, decide what we mean by effective speaking so that we can decide when other speakers are effective, and what is far more important, so that we can make our own speeches effective. Can we accept any of the miscellaneous tests expressed by our critics of John Jones and Samuel Smith? The answer is that not one of our critics has put his finger on the one vital point which, in the last analysis, must govern all speech effectiveness; they have not been able to "see the woods for the trees." Their eyes and ears have been so occupied with general impressions of sounds and sights they have lost sight of the speaker's message, whatever it may have been. "Ah," you say, "message! What has that to do with it? I just happen to like John Jones' voice and I think Samuel Smith's is terrible."

But let us ask ourselves this question: "Just what were those men up there for, anyway?" Did John Jones go up there just to project his voice out and make himself heard easily? Or did he do it just to let people know what a friendly and pleasing manner he had? Or was it so he would have a chance to throw in a good story? Or was he merely anxious to display his musical voice and pleasing gestures? If he spoke for any of these reasons, or others like them, he is either a conceited exhibitionist or a fool.

If our John Jones knew what he was doing, and if he is neither an exhibitionist nor a fool, he spoke because he had some object in view; he spoke because he wanted to influence the understanding, the belief, or the action of those who heard him, or he wanted to amuse them. How do you think he would feel if, after he had done his best to persuade you to believe that you should vote for his candidate for Congress, the only thing you can respond with is "That's a great voice you have there, John." If this is your comment and if he knows what he is doing, he will realize that his speech has been a failure because he failed to impress his objective or purpose upon you.

Effective speakers, therefore, are those who, having a definite objective or purpose in view, accomplish what they set out to do. The effectiveness of a speaker who attempts to explain anything is always determined by whether or not the members of the audience, at the end of the speech, have a clear understanding of the topic. If the audience does understand, the speech has been effective; if it does not, the speech has been a failure. The effectiveness of a speaker who attempts to persuade an audience to believe, or to do anything, is always determined by whether the members of the audience at the end of the speech believe or do. If they believe or do what the speaker asks, the speech has been effective; if they do not, the speech has been a failure.

"But," you say, "what about the things the critics have mentioned? Isn't it important for a speaker to be able to project his voice out and be easily heard, to have a pleasing and friendly manner, to be able to tell a good story, and to have a musical voice and pleasing gestures?" Yes, certainly;

these are some of the means effective speakers use to attain their objectives, but they are not the ends or objectives themselves. Do everything in your power to develop these and other qualities which will be real assets to you in your speaking, because by the use of these means you will be better able to reach your objectives.

Now that you understand what an effective speaker is, you are ready for the next step in learning how to speak more effectively. That step is: Be aware of your audience. Since an effective speaker is one who attains his objective or purpose, i.e., one who obtains the response he desires from the members of the audience, it follows that the audience is a rather important part of the speech situation. That consideration of the audience is important would seem to be a simple truth, yet often speakers disregard their audiences completely.

Audiences influence every step of the preparation and delivery of effective speeches. Any speaker who disregards his audience and who insists on speaking in terms of his own knowledge, experience, interests and wants, rather than in terms of the knowledge, experience, interest, and wants of the members of his audience, is doomed to failure. He is always just short of success and he is always wondering why his speeches fail to "click."

Not only must we analyze our audiences, but we must understand the influence of a speaker's personality in his speech success and failure. Whether or not the members of the audience like the speaker as a person has the very greatest effect on speech success and failure. Many speakers, because the members of their audiences have formed bad opinions of them in their previous contacts or through what they have read or heard, are defeated before they have opened their mouths and uttered a word. What happens when the members of the audience have a bad opinion of the speaker? Immediately they become far more critical of everything the speaker says and does. Because they dislike the speaker, they erect mythical Chinese walls around themselves to keep the speaker's ideas from finding any permanent lodging. In effect, they say to him, "Your ideas can't enter here. I'll have none of them!" When they dislike the speaker, they tend to discount everything he says. Test yourself. The next time you listen to a speaker you do not like, notice how you resent what he says and how critical you become.

On the other hand, what happens when the members of the audience like the speaker? If they have a good opinion of him, they tend to accept what he says as true. A speaker on a controversial subject who is well liked by his audience, finds that his assertions and opinions are accepted with much less proof, or supporting material, than those of a speaker who is disliked. Can there be any question about the persuasive power of speakers' personalities? Can there be any question that speakers' personalities either assist them in attaining their goals or make reaching those objectives more difficult? Who has listened to Franklin D. Roosevelt or Winston Churchill without being impressed by the tremendous importance of personality in speech success?

Speakers win audience approval of themselves primarily through the appeal of their virtues and accomplishments—through their character, their popularity, their expert knowledge of the subject, their intimate knowledge of the audience, their enthusiasm, sincerity, earnestness, use of tact, confidence in themselves, ability to think clearly, and through their speaking ability.

The next step is to carefully plan what you want to say. Too often speakers get up to speak without having any clear notion of what they want to accomplish, talk aimlessly until they run out of ideas, and then sit down. Very frequently, also, speakers know what they want to accomplish by their talks, but they give no thought to ways and means of attaining their objectives. They ramble over their subjects and by pure chance they may hit upon a few ideas which bear directly on the accomplishment of their purposes; but while they are doing that, they are also discussing many ideas which are irrelevant. The result is that the members of the audience are confused and do not get a clear impression of the speaker's objectives and his supporting material. These speakers have not learned the importance of "marching ideas into the minds of listeners single file." Again, many speakers know what they want to accomplish by their speeches and they know how to select the main ideas which will help them to attain those objectives, but they give no thought to making their ideas attractive; they fail to appeal to the interests and wants of their listeners.

There can be no question that a very large part of the success of any speech is due to careful planning. Speakers who trust to the "spur of the moment" to carry them safely through the difficult task of speechmaking, usually find that, when the moment arrives, "it has no spur." They fail to hit the "bull's-eye" because they don't know what, or where, the target is; because they don't know how to hold the "gun" or sight it; and because they are not even sure the gun is loaded. Speakers who know what targets they wish to hit, and who see that their speeches are loaded with the kind of material that will, when directed toward the audience in effective delivery, hit those targets, will go far. Those who fail to plan carefully usually will meet defeat.

In planning our speeches, we must clearly formulate specific statements of our purposes; select main ideas and speech details; plan introductions to catch attention; plan conclusions to summarize, to appeal for belief or action. Plan to make use of visual aids. Mastery of these steps in speech planning will make it possible for you to compose your speeches effectively.

Having carefully planned a speech and outlined it, the next step is to put enough glue on your ideas, through how you state them, to make them stick in the minds of your listeners—to make them remembered. Speakers put glue on their ideas by making them vital, familiar, striking, and specific. The insurance salesman who can present his message in terms of his listener's wants and ideas, makes it vital. The foreman who can compare a new procedure which he wants followed, to one already understood by a worker makes it familiar. The department manager who states his needs to a superior in a striking or unusual way, gets attention. The sales manager who gives specific directions about how to sell a product, gets results.

Charles G. Dawes at one time was director of the Federal Bureau of the Budget. On one occasion he addressed the President, the members of the Cabinet, and the heads of all departments, bureaus and agencies on "The Business Organization of the Government." Early in the speech he wanted to impress on the audience that the budget bureau had nothing to do with policy making but merely carried out the policies determined by the Congress. He said, "Again I say, we have nothing to do with policy. Much as we love the President, if Congress passed a law that garbage should be put on the White House steps, it would be our regrettable duty as a bureau, in an impartial, nonpolitical way, to advise as to how the largest amount of garbage could be spread in the most expeditious and economical manner." That is one way of putting glue on ideas.

If our speeches are to get results, we must understand our audiences, we must recognize that our personalities help or hinder us. We must prepare carefully, and we must put glue on our ideas to get them remembered.

Insurance executives, and most other executives, to do their job properly should be able to make almost every kind of speech. They should be able to pay tribute to employees, to make speeches of introduction, presentation and welcome. They should be able to make speeches celebrating achievements in their organization, speeches explaining policies and procedures to employees, speeches to create good will among employees, speeches to inspire employees to greater effort and higher achievement, and speeches to persuade employees to adopt new attitudes toward management and to approve and carry out new policies. Each of these speech types requires a somewhat different plan and procedure. In addition to speechmaking before audiences of both sexes, executives should be effective speakers in interviews and small group discussions.

Insurance executives, of course, vary a great deal in their ability to handle their jobs successfully, as do people in every profession and vocation. It would be interesting to discover whether the best insurance executives are strong in their ability to communicate. I can't at the moment prove this to be true, but I believe it is.

Houser Associates reports a recent employee-attitude survey which throws some light on the general problem. This survey was concerned with measuring employee attitudes in a number of separate units of the same company, each under its own manager. The separate units were almost identical in size location, type of work, pay, hours, and working conditions. The survey measured the variability of the performance of the managers, each of whom had his own methods of handling his people, and his own ways of presenting and interpreting company policies and operating methods.

The survey results showed the usual wide differences in employee attitude and morale from unit to unit. Here, in summary form, is a comparison of employees' answers to seven questions in the unit that liked the company best and in the unit that liked the company least.

	Unit "A" best	Unit "B" least	Difference
This is a better-than-average company to work for.....................	95%	65%	30%
This company treats its employees better than most other companies do.........	77	43	34
I am proud of working for this company	86	39	47
The morale of the people here is fairly high, or very high..................	91	26	65
When I am corrected or have my work criticized, this is usually, or always, done in a friendly and helpful way.....	100	43	57
When I do some unusually good work, I usually, or always, get recognition or praise for it.....................	91	13	78
As a person to work with, my boss is better than average, or one of the very best	100	36	74

Employees in both of these units were working for the same company, under the same policies, doing the same types of work for the same pay, following the same methods. Only the bosses and their methods of administration were different.

These figures reveal where both the best and the worst jobs of communication were being done, and they probably reveal also where there is full knowledge of the business and its operations, and where that knowledge is largely lacking.

In addition to staff and equipment space, two things are necessary in the operation of any business if it is to function smoothly and perform its best service—knowledge and the ability to use it effectively. The executive must know his work and his organization inside out, and equally important, he must be able to communicate his knowledge to both employees and top management. A considerable part of his communication to both employees and top management should be in the form of speeches. A good speech saves time.

It may reach hundreds or thousands of employees, while a personal interview reaches only one. Think how long it would take to give the same information contained in a half-hour speech to 500 employees in personal interviews. Also, when a personnel director has the ability to make effective speeches, he does not have to depend upon subordinates who often are weak in their ability to communicate, to get his company's story to the rank and file. When the business executive is an effective speaker, he can tell the story himself and be sure that it reaches employees in the form he wishes.

If there is need for training in the making of effective speakers in your organizations, there is no reason for delay. Highly competent teachers of effective public speaking are available in almost all sections of the country.

"Have you acquired adequate skill in communication with others?" asked Owen D. Young. "If not," he added, "you will find it difficult to succeed."

All of my study and experience leads me to believe that there is no stopping the man who has both knowledge and the ability to communicate it through speech.

3. MOULDING THE GOLDEN SPOON[1]

Robert T. S. Lowell, Jr.

Reposing among the stunted Massachusetts hills is a rambling slate-covered building. Forever it mellows with increasing ivy and additional cloisters. At one end a small slate-roofed and ivy-buried chapel juts out; at the other, the useful magnificence of a field house, camouflaged with cloisters and vaunting through its open doors expensive panelling and expensive memorial portraits. A mammoth pea-green water tower stupidly stares down on these monastic precincts,—a sentry of the brutal, boisterous, outer world. Entering you meet a life-like lion in bronze, this is the lion of Saint Mark. This is St. Mark's Boarding School. A motto is carved on the cement shield above the gate-way, *Age Quod Agis.* "Do What You Do."

Here two hundred rich boys are educated. Here the many mansions of Tuxedo Park and Long Island send the flower of their youth. The name is legion: St. Mark's, Milton, St. George's, Noble and Greenough, Groton, St. Paul's.

---

[1] Robert T. S. Lowell, "Moulding the Golden Spoon," *Hika*, vol. 6, no. 8, p. 8, 1940. Used by permission.

This speech was given in 1940 in a formal oratory contest among undergraduates. The autobiographical aspects of the speech contributed to the high good humor and uproarious laughter that was generated in the "packed house." Lowell gave the speech with considerable "steam." There was complete unity among speaker, topic, language, and delivery. Only 7 years after the date of this speech Lowell was awarded both the Academy of Arts and Letters and the Pulitzer prizes for poetry.

But why on earth speak of the rich? Are we not familiar with that visionary maxim: "Look after the poor and the rich will take care of themselves"? Here, surely, is no crying need. The patrons of America have no need of our charity. And others of you who are not taken by specious, eastern glitter will ask: "Why lug your little New England boarding schools into this great Middle West? If you must speak to us, you must speak to us on everyman's problems. You must speak on national problems."

Yet you must not say this. You are the voices of chaos or the voices of the optimist's outrageous aplomb, chanting: "To hell with the rich. To hell with the rich." The rich will *not* take care of themselves and reform that does not sabotage our entire social machinery must, perforce, begin at the top and is high falutin' only when it stops there. In so far as the eastern rich are detached from the rest of their country, this *is* a national problem. A responsible economy demands the investigation of so monstrous an anomaly. In so far as the eastern rich are not detached, an acquaintance with their habits is indispensible to everyone. And this is the reality. Eastern aristocracy is the pattern of all contemporary, American aristocracies. In manners, in occupations, in education, and in ethics the East has set the pace. Also, all who rise in the industrial world are affected by the set at the top and Lazarus is shackled to Dives. If Dives' education is brutal and inefficient, all Americans suffer, from the President of the United States and the mayor of Cleveland down to the underpaid scholar and the much publicized but still starving worker out of "relief."

And yet the speaker would be wildly childish who offered any startling or immediate reforms. I am going to give you a picture of St. Mark's Boarding School. For us, this is very apropos. In rapping the rich and in criticizing their schools, few speak with intimacy. Oh no! I am not singling out that ignorance which cannot imagine what it lashes; I am speaking of those who do imagine the schools of American wealth and yet cannot know how these poor uneducated patricians feel. How great are their temptations to sin, how few their chances, how little their encouragement, how dead they are to any passion for improvement! We may only insinuate that their education is responsible but not modern, literate but not enlightened, reasonable but not brotherly. And my qualifications? I am a St. Marker. Ages ago and for three years, my great-grandfather was an egregiously nondescript head-master.

I must wander. Lucretius, in a passage familiar to Latin students, sang, that as a children's doctor smearing his bitter pills in honey, he had embellished his serious and arid philosophical poem with all the beauties of style—that the medicinal truth might be consumed unawares. The practice of preparing truth in honey is generally distasteful. It is the adulteration of art and science. Yet, baldly, I am drawing an analogy, not to apologize for proposing an important social question in terms of my picturesque boarding school—the contagious implications of St. Mark's are sufficiently obvious—I am drawing an analogy to bring home to you the perfect gentleman. He captures all truth. To dispense this truth he smears it in elegance and altruism. This is the goal of an aristocratic school, a preparation with which to endow aristocratic scholars. Trust me, I am not parodying the "Sweetness and Light" of the eloquent humanist poet of Oxford. A gentleman is a questionable superfluity, the insect perpetuating its subtle furniture; and yet, he may survive in a modern society if he is efficient, humane, and cultured.

Let us attack the successful St. Marker. He enters Harvard. He is drafted for one of three quite snobbish clubs. He ascends into life as a banker, a member of the "exchange," a high-class lawyer, a financier, or a director of some great manufacturing industry. Alas, our aristocracy is scandalously effete. Numbers never rise to their own aspirations or their school's. Some cannot stay at Harvard but emigrate to Williams or Yale or one of Ohio's one hundred and one colleges, outposts of higher education. Others, successful at first, eventually flee reality. You have seen them, school teachers, sculptors, curators. To treat on these would be to waste time . . . *Non ragionem di lor.* They are severed and despised.

But to criticize the successful? The man who succeeds in what he undertakes, who is preëminent in a career disputed and envied by thousands? Among the theoretical Greeks, this saying was rife: "Criticism is easy, action is hard." By this they meant no very remarkable talents are required for sane criticism. Supported by Greek example, I may safely proceed to vivisect the education of the successful St. Marker.

An anachronistic property of St. Mark's and other eastern boarding schools is that they are Episcopal church schools. As a social convention the Episcopal Church is not an anachronism. But in our age of free-thinking its doctrines are disregarded. Absolute wisdom, truth are irrelevant among students who assume the stupendous practical failure of Christianity and encounter dogmas with a mortifying indifference. I remember, at a time of Confirmation, naively asking many of my classmates: "Do you believe in God, the immortality of the soul, and the salvation of Christ?" "No," they said. "What's the importance?" This state is not scandalous. The Church is the student's gospel of moral training. He does not take his Church seriously; as a result he never receives the salutary and practical authority of a systematic ethic.

In place of Christ the God of St. Mark's is the discobolus. The poor chapel and magnificent fieldhouse are real symbols of the relative status. Of course the discus thrower, here, is not that hyper-hygienic German figure of your art books. He is a casual, luxurious creature, sprinting in flannels, a disciple of teamwork and football. Athletics as a religion originated at Harrow and, in many ways, the cult is a good thing. It is spirited, strenuous, and healthy.

But when it is the one activity worshipped by a decent number of students; when it utterly swamps religion and knowledge; when, "You must plug through life just as against Groton!" is the most inspiring exhortation the student hears; and mausoleums, in the form of virgin-pine-panelled parlors and field houses, are raised for dead athletes, the result is bathos. Bathos is harmless and desirable until in college and "out in life" this religion of Harrow is impractical, puerile, and hideous.

Studies designed as a preparation for college are a transient stage in a man's education. I must note certain faculties which they do not bestow and which are never attained. On the cultural side one art is taught, literature. In the modern languages this study is dilatory; the student never learns to speak the language; he reads, if at all, its classics without taste. Latin and Greek are better taught than at other schools but even at that with incomparably less discipline than in the last century. English is studied without enthusiasm or perception. After six uncomfortable years, the student, still bordering on illiteracy, has no notion of literature's urgency and value. This is, for nearly all, the final stage; the other arts are a closed door. Sciences are well enough taught, but are injured by an over-emphasis on the humanities. History is pedestrian, sociology and economics voluntary. Ethics, as I have observed, are incidental, and, being limited to an aristocratic class-universe, are ultimately detached and selfish. In addition all advanced courses are paralyzed, relegated to scrap-work for Harvard entrance examinations. Examinations, doubtless, quicken study but they force appreciation to be accidental. If a brilliant radical professor came to St. Mark's, he would never be debarred from teaching; the occasion would never arise for him to speak the unconventional.

Perhaps the feature of a St. Mark's education is its isolation. Its fashionable religion—I must specify that all Episcopalians are not as fashionable as these—its savage athletic code, and its highbrow learning—I must specify again that among professionals this learning is neither scholarly nor modern; all these contribute to isolation. Intellectuals, other classes, other sections, and foreign nations are alike foreign. No wonder, in his dealings with such, the St. Marker is embarrassed, short-sighted, and provincial; the St. Marker whose hand reaches, reaches—ah how vicariously, every magnate and small-town storekeeper from, say, Hollywood to Newport, Rhode Island; and when New York sends her sons to New England for their schooling she persists in a custom. But customs are not a culture. Boston is no longer Athens. I am emphasizing a glaring problem: our aristocracy, and by this term I mean all American aristocracy—in my figure of St. Mark's and the green water tower I made only a specious contrast—our aristocracy has special advantages but no superior way of life. Its manners are the automatic accident of wealth.

Think of the motto of St. Mark's: *Age Quod Agis*. Unlike most mottoes,

Do What You Do, is insanely accurate. *Do* in our American idiom means to *do* one's job, and more, to plug and sweat at one's job. Do What You Do; this is a fine utilitarian prescription for man and master. A scholar before a scholarly audience, I hesitate to invoke as my symbol our great, ox-eyed Statue of Liberty, Liberty brandishing her cyclopean incandescent torch; but as runners in a great race, it is our pleasant and devout ambition—not merely to Do What We Do, not run with a painted stick—but to hand on a torch. And so it is with aristocracies, they must have aspirations. For you all know that as the Philistines and Goths proceed in their spiritless way to dismember civilization, they will come to all the golden palaces of learning, they will come at last to Milton, Groton, St. Paul's, and St. Mark's and there, the students who are neither efficient nor humane nor cultured will be doing what they are doing. And the indignant Goths and Philistines will turn these poor drones out of the hive, and there will be no old limbs for the new blood, and the world will revert to its unwearied cycles of retrogression, advance, and repetition.

4. A Neurologist Makes Up His Mind[1]

C. Judson Herrick

I

A septuagenarian having reached the age appropriately characterized as his anecdotage may be expected to have made up his mind about some things. He likes to ventilate these matured opinions and to support them with anecdotes selected from his experience. If these experiences include a life-long study of the brain, its evolution, development and normal functions, his interest may go beyond the particular opinions about which he has made up his mind to the larger questions, How does one make up his mind about anything? What kind of stuff is a mind made of and where does this mindstuff come from? This is our present theme, and incidental to it some beliefs will be expressed about minds in general and their relations to many other things that come within our experience.

[1] C. Judson Herrick, "A Neurologist Makes Up His Mind," *The Scientific Monthly*, vol. 49, pp. 99–110, 1939. Used by permission.
C. Judson Herrick had retired from active teaching before he delivered "A Neurologist Makes Up His Mind" at the University of Pittsburgh in 1939. Herrick earned his successive academic degrees at three universities and was subsequently awarded honorary degrees from all of them. He served as editor of the *Journal of Comparative Neurology* from 1894 to 1950, was a member of learned scientific societies in six countries, and served as professor of neurology at the University of Chicago for 30 years. This speech might be viewed as an integration and interpretation of a mass of details that the speaker had worked with closely during a scholarly career.

At the outset I shall avail myself of the privileges of anecdotage, for this must be a personal record, based primarily upon what I find in my own mind. This mind is the only one that I know anything about at first hand. In this domain my own experience is the ultimate court of appeal.

I have made up my mind that this mind of mine is something that I myself have made. It has grown up with me. It is part of me as truly as is my body. It is not something added to my body to make it go. It is not something that I have. It is something that I am. It is an active part of me, something that I am doing. There are no mental states, only mental acts. What the psychologists call the content of my mind is the pattern of this performance of mental work by bodily organs. Thinking is real work as you know very well if you ever tried it. It makes you tired, and it is your body that is tired because it is the body that is doing the work, as has been proved by the Benedicts with their calorimeter.

Our minds, then, are not given to us by kindly fairies or handed down to us ready-made in the genes or by tradition in social heredity. However we may be influenced by hereditary organization, by social pressure or mob-psychology, it remains true that every mind inheres in a single person; it is something that the individual has made and that he alone can use. It is this personal, this solipsistic, attribute of mind that makes us so jealous of it.

II

As a neurologist I am a naturalist, and what we are undertaking here is a scientific approach to our theme, an inquiry into the natural history of mind. We should, then, try to make clear what we are talking about, what we mean by mind.

There are as many definitions of mind as there are schools of psychology and philosophy. Our minds bother us. Our most serious troubles are mental, and many problems of practical life and of science would be simplified if the mind were given a holiday. Many people do this more or less deliberately with results not always fortunate. Some objective psychologists have done their best to lay the ghost, but it will not down. It does not do any good to try to solve a difficult problem by ignoring the troublesome factors or by identifying mind with every sort of nervous action, with adaptation or with all totalizing or integrative functions. And panpsychism is a speculative excursion of more interest to metaphysics than to science.

For our present purpose the traditional usage is adequate: My mind is my awareness of what is going on. I shall not try to define this; I don't have to, because I experience it, and so do you; but I do have to accept it as a natural phenomenon, and as a naturalist I can, therefore, claim a legitimate scientific interest in it. The possibility of scientific treatment of the subjective has been denied, I know, but this denial is based on erroneous assumptions, that is, on the traditional doctrine that my mind is a ghost and not an organic part of me.

The aim of natural science is generalization and the method is a survey and comparison of particular things or events which have come within experience and abstraction from them of some general characteristics common to all of them. Science can do nothing with an isolated fact. How, then, can we investigate scientifically anything so intimately personal, so unique and detached, as the idea or the emotion that has just flashed through my mind?

This is the naturalist's dilemma, which is resolved very simply by the transcendentalists, who say there is no problem here because the mind belongs in a spiritual realm which is not bound by the rules of the natural order. This is the tradition of the New England Protestant orthodoxy in which I was brought up and of such teaching of psychology and philosophy as was offered in my early schooling. But it does not square with my experience as a neurologist or in the common affairs of adjustment to things and people in the daily routine of life.

Common observation shows—if it shows anything at all about human nature and conduct—that my conscious motives, what I want, what I work for, and my ideas about it, are actually caused by previous events, some of which are conscious and some are unconscious, some inside my own body and some outside. All these are natural events, and no one of them is an isolated event. Even our most intimately private mental experiences have discoverable relationships with other things and events. They can, therefore, be investigated scientifically, for the study of relationships is the basic scientific method. All that we know about anything is its relationships; in fact, the thing is defined by these relationships. This holds for everything in our natural cosmos from electrons to faith, hope and charity.

If I make up my mind to sell my house and move my family to a hotel, this decision is the result of countless things that have happened before— changes in the physical and social environment, increase in taxes, the state of my health or perhaps the desire for ready cash to finance a speculation. The relation between these previous events, both the objective and the subjective, and my present motive is a true cause-and-effect sequence by all the rules of scientific evidence that we commonly apply in other fields of inquiry.

From the other angle my motive in advertising my house for sale, which is of course a conscious act, is also a real cause of some later events. If I find a purchaser and invest the proceeds in a wildcat speculation, the loss of my fortune affects all the rest of my life and the lives of my children. Here we have a mental or "spiritual" event actually having material consequences, and nobody would challenge it as a cause-and-effect sequence if it were not for a preconception or taboo rooted in mysticism and mythology.

It should not be necessary to labor the point that mind and body form an organic unity. We have no experience at all of any mentality apart from bodily organs. This is the opinion of the business executive when he pays a large salary to "a man with brains." Here is a case where the popular idea stands up under the most searching scientific criticism better than the sophistries and dogmas of the schoolmen. Yet even those of us who are biologically trained are apt to give only lip-service to this sound scientific conclusion. The tradition of the pre-scientific mythologies is so deeply implanted that we often fail to recognize its influence. Most people still cherish some modern version of those primitive demonolatries which split the human personality up into physical and spiritual components.

But my mind is not something detached or detachable from my body and so capable of dallying at large independently of the rest of me. Whatever may be acceptable in theology and metaphysics, the biologist as biologist can not be a dualist, a trinitarian, a hydra or any of the other fabulous chimaeras of our mythologies. All nature as he knows it is an orderly unit, and anything outside of this integrated and law-abiding system of things and events is unnatural and therefore out of reach by the method of natural science. Our present interest is to see how far we can go in the exploration of the mental life without overstepping the boundaries of the natural order.

It is obvious that even in the field of medical practice the ghosts of traditional spiritism have not yet been exorcised. The average physician is apt to neglect the mental attitudes of his patients, forgetting Osler's teaching that mental therapy—he called it "faith"—is the most potent remedy of his pharmacopoeia. Even the surgeon should not neglect it. The late Dr. Billings, toward the end of his distinguished career as an internist, underwent a major surgical operation, after which he is reported to have said that every surgeon before being permitted to perform an operation should be required to submit to one himself. This, no doubt, is asking too much. Nothing so drastic has ever been tried, except perhaps by the psychoanalysts.

In psychiatry a methodological barrier has been set up between so-called "organic" and "functional" diseases. The treatments required in the two cases are indeed radically different. If a toxic goitre is diagnosed as a cause of mental disturbance, the surgeon may effect a cure. But our most distressing cases of mental disease are as yet known only symptomatically, that is, as mental disorder. Knowing nothing of the colligated bodily disorders, we apply mental therapy, often with gratifying results. Functional disorders may be treated by functional therapy; but where this fails, as alas! it does too often, we are thrown back upon a search for causes, and, as we have seen, the causal complex of any mental process is a web of structure-function relationships which must be seen in its entirety before we can hope for complete understanding. The exclusively mentalistic systems of some psychiatries are rooted in transcendental philosophy. They have, accordingly, an internal consistency and in some cases good practical results, for our mental life is normally orderly and some of the laws of this order are obvious within the domain of introspective experience alone. Yet this type of medical practice at its best has serious limitations which can not be wholly overcome by the most scrupulous care on the part of the psychiatrist in referring his patients to other specialists for diagnosis and treatment of possible organic complications. For the psyche has no existence apart from the soma, and the psychiatrist, like every other physician, must treat his patient as a whole and not some disembodied complex of symptoms.

Do not misunderstand me. It is not recommended that mental therapy be abandoned and replaced by organic therapy. That would be a blunder far more serious than the neglect of organic therapy by a psychiatrist. Organic therapy and mental therapy must converge upon the patient. The practice of mental medicine must employ its own armamentarium of principles and technique which are as different from those of other specialties as surgery is from hydrotherapy. But the psychiatrist as truly as the surgeon must be first a physician and then a specialist. This is fortunately now fully appreciated by progressive psychiatrists, as typified, for instance, by Adolf Meyer's psychobiological approach to mental disease.

III

Having now decided that my mind, that is, my awareness, is a vital function, we come to the nub of the question—How is my mentality related with other vital processes, what is the apparatus employed in thinking, and how does it work?

There are two traditional formulations of this problem. First, How does a body make a mind? and, second, How does a mind make a body? These questions in one form or another have been debated for centuries, and we are no nearer the answer to-day than was Democritus or Plato. I am convinced that the question formulated in either of these ways, that is, in terms of either traditional materialism or traditional idealism, is insoluble.

Those dualistic philosophies which segregate the physical and the spiritual in two parallel but independent and incommensurable realms of being are incompatible with any kind of natural science. And those traditional monistic systems which postulate either matter or mind as the primary or ultimate reality and the other as secondary or even illusory are equally sterile and misleading in the domain of natural science.

Things and their properties, mechanisms and what they do, organs and their functions, human bodies and human experience, can not be divorced in this way. What nature has joined together, let not man by artifice of logical or metaphysical analysis tear asunder. These things do not exist separately.

To abstract one from the other is to annihilate both. Count Korzybski in his "Science and Sanity" has exposed the futility of these elementalistic systems. His definition of structure is dynamic, in terms of relations. Bodily structure, accordingly, is not one element, its function another, and its mental experience a third, for these can exist and be defined only in their relations one with another and with the surrounding world with which they are in adjustment.

Of course, we experience these things differently, for we do not live in a world of pure experience. We live relativistically, and our finite experience can not hope to encompass ultimate reality or any of the other absolutes of the metaphysicians. "For now we know in part, and we prophesy in part," and the human mind can not hope ever to attain "that which is perfect." Neither the Apostle Paul nor any other philosopher has ever succeeded in encompassing the infinite within the three-pint capacity of a human brain.

If now you demand specific and detailed answers to the questions, first, What are the bodily organs of the mental processes? and second, Exactly how do these organs operate in the performance of mental work? the neurologist can supply a great deal of information about the first topic. The right answer to the second question is that we do not know. The knowledge already available about the bodily apparatus employed in mental processes and recent developments of new methods and instruments of precision encourage the hope that this second question is not insoluble.

It is possible to find out what parts of the body are actively engaged when we perceive a flash of light, when we are hungry or angry or when we imagine a muscular movement without actually executing it. We do not yet know all about any of these processes, but it is a great gain to have identified some of the organs involved and to be able to record quantitative measurements of some of their activities. We are beginning to know just where to look for other essential facts.

One general statement may now be made with complete assurance. The search for some particular localized organ of consciousness in general or of any particular conscious experience is as futile as was Descartes' identification of the pineal gland as the seat of the soul.

If at night I am looking at the sky, recognize one of the stars as our nearest neighbor, Alpha Centauri, and am steering a boat by the light of that celestial beacon, then the bodily organs involved in this mental act include eye and brain and muscle, all acting in reciprocal interplay. Indeed, the dynamic system operating is more far-reaching than this, for the star is also an essential component. It follows that the causal complex of which my conscious control of the course of the boat is one component embraces, not only an intricately linked series of very diversified bodily activities, but also events which took place 25 million million miles away and nearly five years ago, for Alpha Centauri is distant 4.35 light-years from the earth.

If we attempt to view this causal situation in its entirety, we recognize a number of things and events which are localized in space and time and which are locally segregated as organs with specific functions such as sense organs, groups of cooperating muscles, reflex arcs, and so on. Each of these "partial patterns," as Coghill calls them, has a certain measure of unity and individuality. These local and partial patterns are woven together into larger "total patterns" which involve integrated activity of the organism as a whole or major parts of it.

Now, thinking is a total pattern. It is not performed by any linkage of particular nerve cells or centers in fixed and stable combination, like the arrangement postulated in the traditional diagrams of the reflex arcs. The search for localized cortical centers which perform the functions of perception, ideation, imagination or volition is vain. These, it is true, are acts performed by the body and specifically by the cerebral cortex in a restricted sense; but no one of these acts is ever exactly repeated, the set-up of conditions is never twice the same, and the cortical apparatus at each successive moment of the ceaseless ebb and flow of nervous impulses through its inconceivable web of nervous pathways is under the influence of outside events on both the sensory and the motor side. The sensory systems play upon the cortex at every moment of waking and sleeping life and all motor activities are reported back to the cortex and in turn influence subsequent cortical adjustments.

Our awareness of what is going on, the content of consciousness, is elaborated (we know not how) from these sensorimotor experiences. These may be recombined in new patterns in imagination, fantasy and abstraction, but even invention and creative artistic inspiration can not go far beyond the domain of sensory experience. The most inspired genius can conceive no glories that are other than kaleidoscopic recombinations of what he already has sometime sensed. A scientific hypothesis is old facts reset and redirected, and the heaven of apocalyptic vision has gates of pearl, streets of gold and diadems of jewels of earthly form.

IV

Now we come back to the original question, What kinds of stuff are minds made out of? The answer seems to be that mindstuff is bodystuff. This does not mean that mind is matter or that matter is mind. Neither matter nor mind is inert structure. A structural psychology is to-day outmoded as completely as is the atomic physics of a generation ago. Matter is not something passively acted upon; it is a very lively thing and its activity is inherent in its structure. The biologist is driven to the conclusion that some special patterns of material structure exhibit the properties (that is, the activities) of life. This living substance we call protoplasm. Following the same line of evidence further, the conclusion is equally unavoidable that some special structural arrangements of protoplasm exhibit the properties of mind, that is, an awareness of some components of the flowing network of process which is characteristic of this particular kind of structure.

Life is still a mystery. We have not yet found a scientific formula for it. Mind is still more mysterious. But the preceding statements seem to rest on the safe ground of well-validated scientific evidence. The mystery of mind will probably remain, for if mind is a manifestation of the activity of structure, the mind can not know itself as awareness and at the same time have *direct* knowledge of the structural apparatus that performs the function of knowing.

This seems to be an inherent limitation of our nature as finite beings. Our awareness is a process patterned in the four dimensions of space-time. The apparently static structural patterns of naive experience seem like objectified cross-sections of the process, pictured as arrested motion like a single frame of a moving picture film. The temporal dimension is eliminated. But temporal relations are essential features of mentality. There are no mental states, only mental acts.

All our knowledge of structure is indirect, and must be so. From this it does not follow that material structure is illusion or less real than mind. The naturalist must be a practical realist—and so must everybody else, for if we do not adjust our conduct to the realities of the objective world we quickly perish.

Just as we have learned to use subjective experience as a token or representation of things and events of the outer world to which we must adjust and also of the operation of certain bodily mechanisms (as yet very imperfectly understood), so conversely we may use the behavior and bodily structure of other men and animal kind as objective tokens or indicators of what they are probably experiencing. This indirect evidence about other minds than my own is more reliable the closer the resemblance between these other patterns of behavior and bodily organization and those which I myself exhibit. I feel, for instance, that I understand my wife's mind better than I do that of my dog and I am sure that my understanding of both of them leaves much to be desired.

Since the organ and its function are inseparable, once we have discovered this relationship we can safely infer the presence of the organ if the function is manifested and the presence of the function wherever the organ is found. A competent zoologist can tell a great deal about the habits even of an extinct dinosaur from a study of its skeleton. We use in this way not only bodily structure, but evidences of animal handicraft, beehives, beaver dams, and the like. So also the archeologist may reconstruct and evaluate an extinct human culture, correlating utensils, works of art and dwellings with skeletal remains, cranial capacity and cephalic index.

Because this indirect evidence is all that we have, we must make the most of it. This method is serviceable in proportion as our knowledge of both structure and function is complete and reliable. So we study comparative anatomy, comparative physiology and the comparative embryology of both structure and behavior. But the most comprehensive knowledge of these things will never take us to the desired goal unless all the facts are actually brought together and converged upon the particular individual whose vital processes are under investigation.

For an adequate understanding of the actual relationship between bodily structure and performance it is necessary to know the past life of the individual, both his personal development and his ancestral or evolutionary history. We look for sources, for beginnings, and then follow the steps of subsequent development and differentiation. By way of illustration let us now summarize briefly two programs of research into the origin and early development of behavioral capacity of the individual.

We owe to the insight, skill and indefatigable industry of Coghill the demonstration of the importance and the practicability of this correlation of development of patterns of behavior with the organs which actually execute the behavior. He selected for intensive study a primitive and generalized animal where the essentials of the problem are reduced to simplest terms, the salamander, Amblystoma. This was a fortunate choice, for during the span of the forty years of his labor this animal has proved to be the most serviceable type for a wide range of researches upon fundamental biological problems.

Dr. Coghill's first step was the determination upon statistically adequate numbers of specimens of the actual sequence of development of patterns of overt behavior which are characteristic of this species. He then took a series of specimens, each of which was known by test to have reached a specific stage in this physiological scale, and subjected every one of them to detailed microscopical study, thus revealing the corresponding series of structural changes. It has been my recent good fortune to repeat many of Coghill's observations on a different series of specimens prepared by methods different from his, with full confirmation of his findings. These studies have stimulated many others, so that we now have comparable observations upon a wide range of animal species.

It is already clear that the sequence of events in the process of maturation of the action system may be very different in the various kinds of animals. Amblystoma, which may hatch from the egg before the twentieth day and thereafter swims actively, shows from the start a different pattern from that of the toadfish, whose yolk-laden eggs develop more slowly. It is unsafe to carry over generalizations from one species of animal to another without actual control by critical observation and experiment. As the late W. K. Brooks used to say, "The only way to know is to find out."

Some men have been described as rats, but no rats are men. The course of human prenatal development does not run exactly parallel with that of any of the other animals whose fetal behavior is now under investigation. Yet the difficulties in the way of successful prosecution of studies of human prenatal behavior are very numerous and baffling. Fortunately several investigators have to varying degrees overcome these obstacles. The pioneer was Minkowski. The most completely documented and systematic observations are those of Hooker. Parallel with the accumulation of these records of behavior, anatomical studies of the accompanying changes in structural development are in process. These researches yield a wealth of facts which can now replace speculation about many features of early human development which are of fundamental value in fields as diverse as embryology, physiology, anthropology, psychology and medical practice.

These studies of embryological origins and subsequent differentiation do not go back to the beginning, for every individual is endowed by his ancestors with a characteristic hereditary organization. This is his working capital as he begins his career as a separate person. These inherited potentialities and limitations must be known and carefully invoiced and appraised. Neither nature nor the natural man can make something out of nothing or perform any other miracle. It follows that the entire evolutionary history of the race must be surveyed to learn as much as possible about the genetic composition of the fertilized egg, for this tiny fleck of protoplasm has somehow concealed within it all the potencies which are transmitted to the germ from countless generations.

My own attack upon the problem of the sources and growth of the apparatus of our mental capacities is directed toward a search for evolutionary origins. Trained as a comparative anatomist and structurally minded, as an anatomist must be, I fortunately was taught when very young that structure has no meaning apart from what it does. There is general agreement that the human cerebral cortex is the master tissue in the control of our conduct. It is equally clear that this cortex has been elaborated in the course of many million years of intense evolutionary struggle for survival from a simpler and more primitive sort of nervous tissue which is not cortex as we define it. It may help us to understand the still unsolved mysteries of cortical activity to inquire where the cortex came from. Fishes have no cortex, though the rest of the brain is organized on much the same plan as our own. Can we trace the emergence of cortex from primordial tissue which is not cortex, and can we discover the agencies operative in effecting this transformation?

Our knowledge of the texture of the brains of fishes and of representatives of all groups of animals from fish to man is very extensive. We know the fossils of these various types of animals from early Silurian times until now, and from their skull casts we can restore the forms of their nervous systems and write a fairly accurate history of the evolution of the brain.

From the assemblage of all available evidence it is obvious that when some primitive ganoid fishes developed lungs and were able to emerge from the water as air-breathers these revolutionary changes in the mode of life were reflected in the structure of the nervous system. This transition from primitive amphibian fishes to true amphibians was effected perhaps three hundred million years ago, and fortunately we still have with us living representatives of some of these transitional forms. These are the critical species for investigation of early stages in the emergence of cerebral cortex from its primordial matrix in the cerebral hemispheres. I have, accordingly, for now nearly fifty years devoted myself to the study of the minute structure of these amphibian brains, with especial attention to Amblystoma, the same salamander which Coghill employed in his classical researches.

Even a brief summary of these investigations and similar studies by other comparative neurologists would require a thick volume of very technical neurological description. It is possible to recognize in fishes and salamanders and frogs, which have no cortex, the parts of the forebrain within which cortex emerges in reptiles and to discern some of the physiological agencies there operative which prepare the field for cortical differentiation.

In the more primitive amphibian species most of the activities are generalized mass-movements. Their brains, accordingly, possess few sharply localized reflex arcs, but the entire nervous fabric is woven together by an intricate feltwork of very fine and widely branched nerve fibers. This tissue we call neuropil. It seems to be the chief apparatus of integration of behavior and of those totalizing activities which the gestalt psychologists have brought to light and which can not be fitted into the stimulus-response formula. It is also probable that it is employed in conditioning of reflexes—a learning process—and many other forms of modifiable behavior. This neuropil, together with its derivatives in higher brains, such as the reticular formation, is the parent tissue from which all the more highly elaborated organs of integration and totalizing functions have been differentiated. This nonspecific and labile tissue and many complex cerebral organs derived from it may be regarded as an equilibrated dynamic system which operates more or less as a whole and in constantly fluctuating patterns depending on the sensorimotor activities at the moment in process in the more sharply localized tracts and centers of the analytic systems. The further differentiation of this tissue culminates in the emergence of cerebral cortex within particular fields of the cerebral hemispheres, and the early chapters of the history of this critical period in the evolution of brains can now be written.

We can also trace the progressive complication of the texture of the cortex in the series of animals from serpents to men and so arrive at some conclusions as to the difference between the wisdom of the serpent and the wisdom of man. For, as Dr. Cannon has graphically shown, there is a wisdom of the body and, as I maintain, there is no other kind of wisdom.

V

The human brain is the most complicated structural apparatus known to science. If all the equipment of the telegraph, telephone and radio of the North American Continent could be squeezed into a half-gallon cup, it would be less intricate than the three pints of brains that fill your skull and mine. More than half of this brain tissue is cerebral cortex and parts immediately dependent upon it. The most ungifted normal man has twice as much of this master tissue as the most highly educated chimpanzee.

This cortex is a sheet of grayish jelly spread over the convolutions of the cerebral hemispheres within which are embedded ten thousand million nerve cells. It is a conservative estimate that each of these cells is in anatomical and (potential) physiological relation with at least a hundred other cells by means of an interwoven fabric of nerve fibers of inconceivable complexity. The possibilities of functional patterns of interconnection among these nervous elements are practically infinite. These arrangements are not haphazard; they are orderly; and it is the neurologist's task to discover the laws of this order.

Good progress in this program is already recorded, and the immediate future offers promise of still more rapid advance, for we have new points of view and new instruments of precision. I have ventured the prediction that the recently developed electrical methods of recording nervous impulses by means of the oscillograph and radio tube amplifiers will enlarge the field of nervous physiology as fruitfully as the science of anatomy was revolutionized by the invention of the compound microscope.

Examination of the brains of animals from low to high in the scale and of mankind from early fetal stages to the adult reveals differences in texture which are directly correlated with patterns of behavior and presumptively with types of experience. This presumption can be tested in the case of the human brain, where correlated studies in clinical neurology and neuropathology reveal numberless clear demonstrations of the relations between particular cerebral organs and various sorts of conscious experience.

It is possible to trace, in the course of vertebrate evolution and in human embryological development the progressive maturation and complication of cerebral tissue, first in the older stem portion of the brain and later in the cortical fields, and to correlate these changes with the gradual transfer of control of behavior from brainstem to cortex. The more stereotyped reflex and instinctive types of behavior have their central adjusters in the primitive brain-stem. The maturation and elaboration of the cortex comes later, and with it greater capacity for learning by personal experience and all the higher mental process which make this possible. These two kinds of control of behavior—that is, the relatively stereotyped innate reflex and instinctive as contrasted with the more plastic individually learned—have a common origin in the adaptability of all living substance. They are not sharply separated, and every human activity is a blend of both of them. Yet the distinction between them is of great practical significance, and increasingly so as we pass from lower to higher species of animals. The nervous apparatus employed in the primitive subcortical types of adjustment is recognizably different from that of the cortical adjusters and the enlargement of our knowledge of these differences is now at the focus of interest, for this is the key-problem of physiological psychology.

VI

In my own experience the feature which seems most characteristic of the higher mental processes is the ability to use mental symbols of one sort or another as tools of thought. These symbols evidently have grown up by abstraction from many particulars of something which is common to all of them; thus all squares differ from all circles in easily definable ways, and for these differences the words are symbols. Language is, of course, the chief vehicle of these symbols, but it is not the only one.

The symbolisms of language, mathematics, pictorial art, and so forth are consciously employed. Ability to use abstractions of this sort has grown up very gradually in the life of the individual and the history of the race. In its more primitive forms it may be, so far as we know, entirely unconscious. All plants and all animals show some capacity to adjust their behavior to the uniformities of their natural surroundings. In racial experience these common features have been abstracted from the heterogeneous environment and by natural selection or other biological agencies woven into the hereditary texture of their bodies so that they make these adaptive adjustments to the alternations of day and night, change of seasons, and so on quite "naturally." Here we see on the most elementary biological plane an abstraction from mixed experience of some general features which enable the animal to adjust himself in advance to future events before they happen, as when the fur thickens in preparation for winter and a bee, wasp or beaver lays by his store of food in a skillfully constructed dwelling.

This "animal faith," as Santayana calls it, may be exercised blindly and unwittingly, but it seems to be the germ from which all higher types of abstraction and symbolism have grown. When a rat is taught to discriminate between a square and a triangle, regardless of size, illumination or arrangement of the test objects, we are dealing with a higher grade of abstraction which must be individually learned, for this ability is not part of the rat's hereditary endowment. If this sort of learning has any intelligent control, it is of rather low order, though even in rats Dr. Norman R. F. Maier, of the University of Michigan, has objective experimental evidence of types of performance which fundamentally are indistinguishable from human rational behavior.

The progressive enlargement of this capacity for abstraction can be tested in terms of objective behavior. Experiments with monkeys by Kluever and Bucy are now in process which show that destruction of certain definite cortical structures may cause a mental disorder (agnosia, asymbolia) comparable with the simpler types of human aphasia. The acquisition of symbols for abstractions provides a useful objective index of the growth of intelligence, whether the symbol is expressed as gesture or a spoken word.

Parallel with these studies of the development of patterns of behavior and comparative psychology, we have a series of anatomical descriptions which show a close correlation between the grade of performance which an animal (or a child) can exhibit and the structural differentiation of the nervous system. These details are intricate and technical, but I wish to make it clear that we are not merely guessing when we say that it is possible to cite a wealth of facts about the location, structure and physiological properties of the bodily organs employed in making mental symbols and in all those higher rational processes which employ them—in short, the semantic functions.

I have elsewhere suggested a biological classification of the kinds or grades of learning under three heads: First, organismic or protoplasmic learning, that modifiability by use or practice which is a general characteristic of all living substance, for all protoplasm can learn. Second, sensori-motor or neural learning, whose exercise requires a differentiated nervous system. This is typified by a rat's ability to learn to make an errorless run through a maze. Third, semantic or cortical learning which works with ideas and mental symbols of various grades of abstraction. This kind of learning can not go far without the aid of language and is a token of our humanity. It is distinctly a cortical function.

The transfer in higher mammals of the dominant control of conduct and of the course of conscious experience from brain-stem to cortex and from physiological to psychological technique has momentous consequences. The mental symbols elaborated in some unknown way by the integrative apparatus of the human cortex give to mankind new tools of adjustment which have extended the reach of his control from the present into the future. The human brain, as Sherrington aptly expresses it, is "fraught with a germ of futurity."

Mental symbols and their objective signs in language, mathematics and so forth are the indispensable tools of the life of reason. With the help of these tools mankind can preserve and profit by the past experience of the race as recorded in tradition and literature and by imagination and invention enlarge his understanding and control of the inorganic, organic and human agencies of production and enjoyment. And, of far more importance, he can predict the future and lay out his present course of action in the light of probable future consequences of the present act. The most intelligent brute lives mainly in the present. Men attentively bind the past and the future into their present and thereby become as gods, knowing good and evil.

This capacity for "time-binding," as Count Korzybski phrases it, is perhaps our most distinctive human characteristic. The ability to select from among several possible courses of action the one which intelligent foresight indicates will at some future time yield the satisfaction desired provides the key which opens doors of opportunity which are closed to all the brute creation. We are free to make choices in the light of past experience and to make up our minds about what we propose to do about it in rational judgment. This free voluntary choice sets the musty problem of the freedom of the will in a natural frame unobscured by any fog of mysticism, because this life of reason is part of our natural lives as sentient beings.

It is this which makes it possible for every individual to lay out an intelligently planned program of self-culture which shapes the course of his own growth in competence and the achievement of higher satisfactions. It is part of our apparatus of regulatory control, and it carries with it a personal responsibility for character building and for all the conduct manifested by the characters which we have built. Our natural freedom involves an equally natural responsibility. And this becomes, by definition, a moral responsibility as soon as a social component enters into the intelligent analysis of situations requiring the exercise of voluntary choice.

This is what our brains are good for, and the salvage of our civilization from its present peril of reversal to barbarism depends on our capacity by educational and other means to cultivate in all our people a more intelligent appraisal of the values sought and ability to curb irrational passion and selfish greed for wealth or power in the interest of those social values which make civilization possible. At the present stage of human culture a stable social organization is absolutely essential to personal welfare. This implies a proper balance between personal profit and the public good, and this is what we mean by moral conduct. We have, in fact, reached a stage of cultural evolution where some of the moral values have actual survival value. Without them our civilization perishes and we perish with it.

It follows that a natural system of practical morals can be elaborated from this simple principle: That social stability upon which the survival and comfort of the individual depend and that moral satisfaction upon which his equanimity, poise and stability of character depend arise from the maintenance of right relations with our fellow men. The right relations are those which are mutually advantageous.

APPENDIX B. INTELLIGIBILITY TESTS

MULTIPLE-CHOICE TESTS[1]

The 24 lists of Figs. 32, 33, 34, and 35 should be reproduced by the instructor in two sets of 12 lists each. None of the words would be underlined or italicized. Lists 1 to 12 should be designated "Form C," and lists 13 to 24, "Form D." These comprise *answer forms*.

The underlined words in the following 24 lists are test items and should be extracted from the lists and typed on 5- by 7-inch cards in the manner of Fig. 36. The lines (1) "Speaker Test 1" and (2) "I am Speaker One" and the 27 test items differ from card to card. Alternatively, the instructor may make full explanations and ask each student to write in Fig. 37 the words that he will say and to read from the textbook.

Students in groups of 12 are supplied with identical answer forms, either Form C or D. If the students have Form C, they are also supplied individually with Speaker Tests 1 to 12. If the students have Form D, they are supplied with Speaker Tests 13 to 24.

The following instructions assume that the instructor is using the material as a multiple-choice test. He always has the alternative of employing the material as a write-down test. In this event, however, the write-down tests, later in the Appendix, are recommended, for the words therein are read singly and the score is less affected by the memory span of the listeners.

[1] John W. Black, *Multiple-choice Intelligibility Tests*, U.S. Naval School of Aviation Medicine and The Ohio State University Research Foundation, Project NM 001 064.01.17, Joint Project Report 17, 1953.

Speaker 1 is ———————

1.
groove	modern	**vice**
drew	moderate	fight
crew	modesty	mice
grew	**modest**	bite

2.
say	forbade	**chink**
stay	pervade	kink
stayed	surveyed	check
spade	survey	chin

3.
stung	drunk	**intent**
stun	**grunt**	intend
sun	brunt	content
stunned	runt	intense

4.
quench	busy	wade
went	physics	waves
whence	**physic**	**wave**
when	visit	way

5.
pass	clearly	**fine**
past	weary	find
cast	quarry	sign
task	**query**	kind

6.
popular	nurse	**get**
poplar	first	gap
hopper	birth	guess
opera	**burst**	guest

7.
immense	named	only
commence	**name**	woman
emit	main	pullman
cement	knave	omen

8.
latter	**last**	swain
ladder	lash	**slain**
lattice	laugh	flame
rabbit	glass	plain

9.
crash	gold	pail
crab	bowl	poor
craft	cold	polo
crack	**bold**	palace

Speaker 2 is ....

1.
ninety	drum	**harrow**
nineteen	**rung**	peril
nightly	**rum**	herald
nine	run	arrow

2.
ran	putter	need
rank	tucker	lead
rang	pocket	**lean**
rag	**pucker**	leave

3.
kick	see	depot
tick	**seed**	people
pick	siege	equal
hick	seize	decoy

4.
shower	**earthen**	**bath**
scholar	earthly	bat
sour	urban	bad
scour	bourbon	back

5.
berry	spring	**listless**
carry	pray	mistress
bearing	**spray**	restless
very	spread	blissful

6.
mouse	Saturn	fog
mouth	sat	bar
now	second	**bog**
mount	**satin**	bug

7.
quarter	felt	horrible
fortress	**belt**	orchid
portrait	dealt	**orphan**
porter	bell	organ

8.
heavy	did	dollar
happen	live	jealous
package	led	**zealous**
happy	**lid**	develop

9.
hamper	**tendon**	**pond**
pamper	tender	on
panther	pendant	hound
pamphlet	pendulum	pawn

Speaker 3 is ....

1.
apply	gift	lamp
supply	**if**	**lance**
amply	hit	glance
fly	it	land

2.
bust	handle	**free**
fuss	anvil	freeze
but	amble	freed
bus	**ample**	tree

3.
airy	fed	laugh
hairy	stead	glad
arid	spend	**lash**
carry	**sped**	flash

4.
throw	low	rod
froze	rose	brown
prose	**loathsome**	**brow**
probe	lonesome	proud

5.
desk	stance	science
depth	stand	**silent**
dead	**stamp**	sound
death	spent	silence

6.
broke	code	begun
growth	told	**begot**
throat	**cold**	forgot
wrote	coal	deduct

7.
sister	hulk	**mild**
system	**halt**	mile
cistern	pulp	miles
pistol	fault	mine

8.
strike	limp	town
spite	**limb**	**townsman**
fight	lend	townsmen
spike	lent	count

9.
paid	cute	**fell**
page	**cunning**	spell
age	honey	felled
haze	**puny**	bell

Speaker 4 is ....

1.
much	uplift	**cypress**
mud	**uproot**	cipher
month	approve	siphon
monk	group	sightless

2.
twelve	mind	blister
well	mild	**blissful**
dwell	**mine**	listful
weld	line	wistful

3.
wren	barter	found
went	**barker**	crown
rent	sparkle	cloud
lent	parker	**clown**

4.
guide	lively	love
die	widen	**lull**
died	wisely	low
dive	**widely**	lag

5.
stove	amiss	equipped
sold	omit	**acquit**
stole	**amid**	equip
soul	emit	quit

6.
reverse	sired	simple
traverse	siren	**dimple**
perverse	fire	pimple
pervert	**sire**	temple

7.
drove	**warrant**	dog
stroke	one	gone
strode	warm	**don**
strove	warn	darn

8.
fire	stale	evil
hire	jail	easel
tired	**dale**	**measles**
tire	gale	needle

9.
gaily	barn	lip
fail	**bark**	**lift**
daily	bought	lisp
five	spark	list

Speaker 5 is ....

1.
crash	least	wouldn't
drag	**lease**	wood
trash	niece	**wooden**
thrash	leaf	**wooded**

2.
pillow	**peg**	loosely
pillar	keg	gruesome
killer	egg	**loosen**
filler	pay	nuisance

3.
lava	wait	hour
loud	which	how
lock	wake	howl
robber	**wig**	**owl**

4.
glad	fable	part
lad	**tablet**	**art**
laugh	habit	heart
lag	cattle	arch

5.
puncture	sigh	bake
teacher	size	bait
tincture	**side**	**fate**
picture	scythe	faith

6.
tempt	green	seller
tense	**cream**	solemn
tent	tree	solid
hemp	creed	**sullen**

7.
youth	allege	muster
you	away	lusty
use	allayed	bluster
mute	**allay**	**luster**

8.
tight	birds	chat
pike	bird	cap
height	birth	check
hike	**burden**	**chap**

9.
devise	chaff	Ed
defy	**shaft**	head
divide	chap	add
beside	shack	**ebb**

Speaker 6 is ———————

1.
feel	fruit	pelvis
deal	true	elder
steal	troop	elbow
veal	**truth**	**eldest**

2.
tasty	sheep	add
hasty	shield	ask
hasten	**she**	**as**
pastry	sheath	has

3.
wrist	depth	fortune
risk	**death**	fort
rip	deaf	**important**
list	guest	**forty**

4.
shoe	defense	**hamper**
choose	**methinks**	tamper
too	repent	hampered
chew	bethinks	hamburg

5.
led	palace	stow
red	**palate**	stole
ledge	talent	stowed
leg	pilot	**stove**

6.
butter	heat	tick
flutter	hate	chicken
flood	paint	**ticket**
fluttered	**ink**	picket

7.
thumb	coy	auto
from	**toy**	bottom
come	tore	often
sum	torque	**autumn**

8.
bower	fast	**sit**
borrow	fact	six
flower	**fat**	sick
power	that	sift

9.
deceive	cars	heard
precede	**carve**	verge
concede	card	**urge**
receive	car	herb

Scoring boxes: 1, 2, 3, 4, 5, 6, 7, 8, 9, 10, 11, 12

FIG. 32. Reproduction of Answer Form C, lists 1 to 6, with the correct responses (items) underlined.

406

Speaker 7 is ....

providence	worse	pledge
1 problem	work	sled
promise	**worst**	**sledge**
province	worth	sleigh
row	wearing	stomach
2 throw	**wearer**	**staunch**
grove	wary	stark
grow	wear	starch
suffer	scram	**grandsire**
3 zipper	swing	grandstand
supper	slam	transpire
zephyr	**swam**	grandchild
bathe	reverse	anew
4 save	invert	**unused**
space	divert	amuse
spade	**revert**	unuse
depth	dangling	bristle
5 deck	sandy	**brittle**
death	sandwich	ripple
debt	**sanguine**	riddle
attend	bold	**steward**
6 **akin**	fold	sewer
attempt	**bowl**	stool
again	hole	Stewart
break	spurt	increase
7 rate	**stirrup**	entreat
rape	sterile	retreat
rake	syrup	intrigue
tack	souse	mystery
8 **tax**	**south**	mystic
facts	sound	mischief
tact	sack	**misty**
anew	**bake**	rhythm
9 balloon	date	written
aloof	bait	**ridden**
allude	fake	ribbon

Speaker 8 is ....

eighty	trump	irk
1 acre	front	hurt
aching	truck	**earth**
eight	**trunk**	heard
delude	head	gauge
2 remove	**edge**	**gaze**
elude	hedge	gave
renew	egg	gay
can't	arm	flatter
3 **scant**	armed	climate
scamp	**on**	**planet**
scan	odd	plant
find	purse	fitness
4 **bind**	burst	**thickness**
vine	hurt	sickness
fine	**first**	picnic
dumb	bedroom	royal
5 gum	reverend	**broil**
dump	brother	broiled
done	**brethern**	boil
snout	**wide**	afford
6 smelt	why	**abhor**
snub	wise	accord
snap	ride	afore
stead	**price**	bury
7 dead	Christ	barely
sped	fight	**fairly**
bed	strike	fairy
white	**gown**	error
8 poison	down	**errand**
hoist	gam	barren
voice	gauze	Arab
next	racket	drab
9 nets	**blacken**	**draft**
mix	blackened	graft
neck	black	grab

Speaker 9 is ....

bite	abhor	**pulse**
1 bike	applause	fault
vice	applaud	pulp
fight	apply	false
apace	runny	**goose**
2 attain	rubbish	noose
face	ready	use
aface	**ruddy**	deuce
bruise	by	rather
3 brood	spy	letter
brew	fire	lever
cruise	**five**	**leather**
bramble	love	**hence**
4 scramble	mark	tense
gravel	large	tent
ramble	**lark**	hint
stain	**patron**	train
5 stink	patient	crane
sting	hasten	brain
sing	paper	**frame**
groom	cub	listen
6 prune	tug	**christen**
broom	tough	Christmas
room	**tub**	prison
handsome	parcel	fear
7 cancer	hardly	**peer**
camphor	partly	hear
cancel	**parsley**	tear
suit	cotton	neither
8 soon	coffin	**meter**
soothe	**coffee**	meager
sue	copy	leader
steam	hump	**exalt**
9 seen	hunt	result
speed	**pump**	gulf
esteem	punk	exhaust

Speaker 10 is ....

artist	vesper	**knoll**
1 harness	**fester**	known
harvest	pester	no
orchid	festive	mold
simple	bomb	Boston
2 **sinful**	bound	**frosty**
summon	**bond**	frosting
stomach	barn	cross
litter	wrestle	pope
3 little	rascal	**hope**
glitter	rapture	oak
liquor	raffle	post
main	twelve	march
4 mink	welt	**margin**
make	wealth	marching
mate	**twelfth**	Martin
lengthen	geese	rain
5 ointment	east	wing
Lincoln	meat	green
link	**yeast**	**ring**
bud	rough	hearing
6 bus	drunk	hairy
bust	**rump**	carry
but	rum	herring
pleasant	**widen**	**saint**
7 **pheasant**	wide	safe
peasant	wife	faint
present	wagon	sink
winter	model	log
8 **winner**	**marvel**	**lawn**
where	marvelous	blond
woman	marble	long
lose	**itself**	mash
9 **loose**	excel	gnash
loot	sell	smash
blue	himself	nag

Speaker 11 is ....

toward	feeling	**dome**
1 forge	dealer	don't
ford	fever	zone
board	**feeler**	stone
destroy	girl	**flicker**
2 deprive	pearl	clipper
defraud	curled	liquor
defrost	**curl**	quicker
chart	frightful	sultry
3 short	rifle	culprit
shark	greatful	sculpture
sharp	**rightful**	**sculptor**
native	pearl	calf
4 navy	**crow**	cad
naked	throw	**calves**
nature	grow	cab
lathe	candy	ink
5 **lay**	pantry	pinch
laid	**pansy**	**inch**
leg	handy	hint
thus	**legend**	hit
6 bust	ledger	**fist**
duck	leaden	this
dust	lesson	kiss
bulb	cut	**net**
7 bulge	carpet	met
bald	**cotton**	neck
ball	copper	nest
breast	Capital	glass
8 friend	**hapless**	lad
breath	hatless	**blast**
bread	happen	black
harbor	soft	hood
9 **harder**	sought	**could**
ardor	**salt**	put
artist	sulk	good

Speaker 12 is ....

needle	large	**haven**
1 evil	**lodge**	heaven
meal	lie	even
neither	live	able
dimple	interest	cast
2 gentle	penguin	**past**
devil	**hindrance**	pass
dental	kindred	path
armload	pen	wooden
3 armholed	**ten**	**woody**
armhole	tend	wood
armful	tent	witty
gem	**glaze**	creeping
4 gent	play	**greeting**
gin	blade	greedy
gym	blaze	reading
flush	**size**	waitful
5 pledge	sigh	wake
fresh	scythe	wasteful
flesh	side	**wakeful**
auburn	astride	dial
6 often	**ascribe**	guile
author	prescribe	vial
autumn	describe	guide
nest	rug	harrow
7 **mess**	love	**herald**
meant	rough	arrow
met	**rub**	peril
grain	bench	**nuptial**
8 raise	theft	nocturnal
raid	**fetch**	nutshell
rage	thatch	neptune
flapper	stole	wallet
9 **leopard**	stone	swallow
leper	school	wall
letter	**scold**	wallow

Fig. 33. Reproduction of Answer Form C, lists 7 to 12, with the correct responses (items) underlined.

Speaker 13 is _____

1. virtue / blend / fort
   merchant / land / dwarf
   <u>virgin</u> / when / <u>thwart</u>
   burden / <u>lend</u> / quart

2. birth / casual / bud
   first / passion / bug
   <u>verse</u> / peasant / <u>budge</u>
   burst / pageant / <u>fudge</u>

3. wench / caught / bottle
   <u>quench</u> / pot / <u>vomit</u>
   clinch / <u>hot</u> / bomber
   went / fox / bonnet

4. <u>pious</u> / beat / loop
   highest / beef / <u>root</u>
   bias / eat / loose
   higher / <u>deep</u> / roof

5. deface / bridle / beach
   debate / <u>vital</u> / seed
   base / rifle / see
   <u>debase</u> / Bible / <u>siege</u>

6. flare / pose / <u>left</u>
   fire / <u>hose</u> / laugh
   fighter / cold / let
   <u>player</u> / hold / lamp

7. stun / peppy / bring
   <u>stung</u> / heavy / break
   sun / <u>petty</u> / <u>brink</u>
   sung / penny / drink

8. <u>frankness</u> / foil / callous
   Franklin / boil / <u>palace</u>
   practice / <u>toil</u> / pilot
   frankly / coil / palate

9. craze / <u>limit</u> / third
   phrase / women / thoroughly
   <u>praise</u> / linen / heard
   pray / lemon / bird

Speaker 14 is _____

1. mouse / drink / towel
   mountain / <u>bring</u> / Holland
   <u>mount</u> / brink / tallow
   mouth / spring / <u>hallow</u>

2. quarter / dove / cook
   porter / dope / approach
   order / <u>dough</u> / <u>croak</u>
   <u>border</u> / dull / broke

3. dull / detect / hinge
   gulf / effect / <u>tinge</u>
   <u>gull</u> / deflect / pin
   dog / <u>defect</u> / king

4. effect / goat / hash
   <u>infect</u> / <u>scope</u> / add
   inspect / spoke / ask
   confess / stake / <u>ash</u>

5. root / <u>wash</u> / doubtless
   <u>group</u> / watch / thoughtless
   droop / why / <u>dauntless</u>
   roof / walk / darkness

6. shell / try / <u>staple</u>
   chow / cry / table
   <u>shall</u> / <u>fry</u> / stable
   child / pry / spacious

7. <u>sudden</u> / front / <u>gauze</u>
   sun / punch / cause
   seven / punt / guard
   southern / <u>hunt</u> / dog

8. cuss / green / razor
   put / dream / <u>raisin</u>
   <u>puss</u> / greed / reason
   push / <u>grieve</u> / brazen

9. talk / happy / repress
   toss / after / depress
   <u>taught</u> / happily / regret
   hat / athlete / request

Speaker 15 is _____

1. urge / envy / cobweb
   heard / engine / <u>cobbler</u>
   <u>purge</u> / <u>ending</u> / problem
   courage / pending / copper

2. <u>scallop</u> / gild / <u>fog</u>
   scholar / fill / five
   scout / hill / bog
   gallop / <u>ill</u> / by

3. bless / often / perish
   <u>less</u> / <u>author</u> / parent
   left / auto / carrot
   last / offer / <u>parrot</u>

4. bridge / downing / grace
   rich / doubt / brake
   <u>ridge</u> / <u>downy</u> / <u>brace</u>
   rig / down / great

5. even / fear / deluge
   beacon / beer / elude
   deacon / <u>beard</u> / delude
   <u>deepen</u> / dear / village

6. <u>settle</u> / list / gallon
   subtle / <u>lisp</u> / <u>gallop</u>
   settled / left / galley
   seven / lip / gallant

7. hung / listful / day
   <u>hum</u> / <u>wistful</u> / bay
   tongue / whisper / days
   come / wishful / <u>bathe</u>

8. <u>meager</u> / kill / brook
   maker / <u>till</u> / <u>rook</u>
   meter / fill / cook
   eager / pill / roof

9. caught / bring / <u>repute</u>
   <u>talk</u> / grin / refuse
   taught / <u>brim</u> / refute
   trough / grim / compute

Speaker 16 is _____

1. decides / hate / <u>pamper</u>
   <u>besides</u> / taste / tamper
   beside / <u>haste</u> / hamper
   decide / paste / pamphlet

2. spinach / all / dozed
   clinic / fog / dove
   senate / <u>fall</u> / goes
   <u>cynic</u> / hall / <u>doze</u>

3. litter / fat / mouth
   <u>lizard</u> / back / moss
   whether / <u>spat</u> / moth
   blizzard / stack / <u>malt</u>

4. in / rubbish / hate
   <u>hinge</u> / radish / <u>take</u>
   pin / <u>reddish</u> / cake
   king / ready / intake

5. scared / <u>aid</u> / lava
   secret / aim / Florida
   safety / paid / <u>larva</u>
   <u>sacred</u> / age / larger

6. plant / Farley / cloth
   slam / barley / fall
   <u>slant</u> / <u>parley</u> / flog
   plan / Harley / <u>flaw</u>

7. passing / foundry / crawled
   <u>after</u> / <u>founder</u> / craw
   apple / bounder / frog
   <u>acid</u> / flounder / <u>crawl</u>

8. content / Dick / rapid
   contest / <u>dig</u> / rattle
   contact / gig / <u>wrapper</u>
   <u>convent</u> / big / grapple

9. <u>cause</u> / atom / <u>toward</u>
   poise / <u>abbot</u> / torn
   pause / habit / tore
   car / avid / board

Speaker 17 is _____

1. lurch / faces / shuffle
   work / baker / shudder
   <u>lurk</u> / basic / <u>shutter</u>
   alert / <u>basis</u> / shuttle

2. sought / muster / hard
   <u>sock</u> / <u>rustic</u> / <u>card</u>
   sun / rusty / tard
   stop / rustle / car

3. only / <u>horn</u> / fruit
   <u>olden</u> / corn / root
   older / form / <u>brute</u>
   golden / thorn / group

4. island / flange / <u>shelf</u>
   <u>highland</u> / <u>plan</u> / shout
   pilot / clam / shelve
   pylon / planned / shell

5. bondage / ten / blimp
   abandon / pen / <u>blink</u>
   <u>bandit</u> / <u>pin</u> / bleak
   bandits / pinned / link

6. <u>cat</u> / line / theft
   hat / <u>lying</u> / heck
   cap / flying / <u>peck</u>
   catch / lion / pet

7. rim / <u>gobble</u> / <u>cleft</u>
   brim / goblet / theft
   <u>grim</u> / goggle / crept
   grin / gobbled / slept

8. bed / <u>spill</u> / counting
   did / still / bounty
   dead / spilled / country
   <u>bid</u> / fill / <u>county</u>

9. mail / <u>earl</u> / horn
   <u>maiden</u> / pearl / <u>torn</u>
   neighbor / burrow / thorn
   maybe / girl / corn

Speaker 18 is _____

1. summer / man / bun
   <u>summon</u> / <u>mass</u> / <u>fun</u>
   summit / mask / front
   summons / mad / fund

2. lighter / <u>roller</u> / none
   spider / rolling / mountain
   <u>fighter</u> / roll / now
   piker / roar / <u>numb</u>

3. <u>verbal</u> / breeze / eat
   burble / greed / <u>heat</u>
   gurgle / <u>breathe</u> / feet
   purple / grieve / peak

4. fried / <u>plus</u> / child
   try / flood / childish
   tribe / bust / <u>childless</u>
   <u>tried</u> / pluck / childhood

5. we / retold / guess
   read / refold / <u>guest</u>
   <u>weed</u> / <u>threefold</u> / gas
   weave / repose / get

6. <u>sofa</u> / hate / <u>best</u>
   soap / cape / bet
   silver / <u>cake</u> / desk
   sober / case / theft

7. lung / hurt / pardon
   love / turn / hardly
   drunk / <u>turf</u> / <u>harden</u>
   <u>lump</u> / Turk / hard

8. <u>shilling</u> / falcon / mark
   chilling / <u>pulpit</u> / <u>mock</u>
   chilly / culprit / lock
   killing / poker / mop

9. gag / nap / allow
   <u>gad</u> / <u>nest</u> / <u>aloft</u>
   gas / mess / lock
   gab / net / allot

Answer columns: 1 2 3 4 5 6 7 8 9 10 11 12

Fɪɢ. 34. Reproduction of Answer Form D, lists 13 to 18, with the correct responses (items) underlined.

408

Speaker 19 is ....

1. pleasing / wolf / chap
   easy / wolves / chaff
   <u>fleecy</u> / wore / <u>chat</u>
   sleepy / <u>wool</u> / check
2. yule / noise / <u>hem</u>
   fuel / snow / hemp
   new / <u>snowy</u> / pen
   <u>mule</u> / snowing / hemmed
3. field / woodland / curse
   deal / wooden / hearse
   heel / wouldn't / <u>purse</u>
   <u>feel</u> / <u>woodman</u> / perch
4. farm / heel / <u>tighten</u>
   <u>harm</u> / feel / type
   pawn / yield / tight
   arm / <u>eel</u> / title
5. mouthful / palm / <u>lip</u>
   <u>mirthful</u> / <u>calm</u> / lick
   Myrtle / pound / lift
   merciful / come / lit
6. shaky / <u>face</u> / glow
   <u>shady</u> / fate / <u>blow</u>
   shade / faith / slow
   shaving / base / flow
7. raw / buy / enjoying
   drawl / <u>bought</u> / <u>enjoin</u>
   <u>brawl</u> / box / enjoyment
   draw / fought / enjoy
8. <u>hairy</u> / kind / paid
   fairy / mind / hey
   carriage / <u>pine</u> / <u>pay</u>
   carry / time / key
9. soothe / whence / sweep
   <u>sue</u> / <u>glimpse</u> / <u>sweeten</u>
   suit / bliss / sweet
   soon / blimp / sweetened

Speaker 20 is ....

1. scout / weed / rider
   spouse / <u>weave</u> / lighter
   bout / reed / <u>writer</u>
   <u>spout</u> / leave / writing
2. needy / <u>put</u> / clean
   meeting / foot / please
   easy / book / <u>plead</u>
   need / cook / flea
3. pick / snuck / naive
   detect / snub / name
   <u>depict</u> / snow / maid
   eclipse / <u>snuff</u> / <u>nave</u>
4. fold / logic / string
   cold / logging / <u>strain</u>
   <u>hold</u> / <u>lodging</u> / strange
   hole / Roger / drain
5. brazen / <u>brought</u> / scald
   break / broad / gull
   great / drop / stall
   raisin / drought / <u>skull</u>
6. hot / course / tenant
   not / <u>force</u> / <u>penance</u>
   <u>pot</u> / horse / pennant
   plot / forest / tennis
7. mission / <u>troll</u> / doomed
   vision / toll / dune
   fisher / told / do
   <u>bishop</u> / crawl / <u>doom</u>
8. soft / barren / court
   sought / bear / courts
   <u>sauce</u> / <u>bearer</u> / <u>corpse</u>
   saw / barrel / torch
9. fill / <u>defile</u> / wreck
   built / file / wrench
   guild / defy / <u>wretch</u>
   <u>bill</u> / devise / rest

Speaker 21 is ....

1. far / want / late
   barn / one / like
   <u>farm</u> / <u>wanton</u> / <u>light</u>
   arm / wanted / right
2. <u>unstained</u> / wasp / dog
   insane / watch / <u>dull</u>
   unseen / lost / gull
   unstain / what / doll
3. vowel / hammer / elf
   bow / hemlock / held
   vow / cannon / elm
   <u>valve</u> / <u>hammock</u> / elves
4. spouse / cost / platter
   astound / <u>cross</u> / <u>planter</u>
   <u>espouse</u> / frost / planted
   espoused / fraud / lantern
5. <u>tongue</u> / <u>tall</u> / viper
   hung / called / piper
   hum / call / lighter
   ton / solve / vital
6. wet / time / icing
   west / <u>ton</u> / <u>icy</u>
   <u>wept</u> / come / ice
   weapon / tongue / item
7. author / <u>vest</u> / <u>thought</u>
   <u>offer</u> / best / box
   often / theft / fox
   office / desk / fought
8. prune / mouth / reduce
   crude / month / review
   true / mumps / refute
   prove / <u>monk</u> / <u>rebuke</u>
9. <u>fuse</u> / pity / saved
   feud / city / <u>save</u>
   hue / tippy / say
   few / fitting / sage

Speaker 22 is ....

1. jig / right / lay
   gate / <u>brighten</u> / blade
   dig / frighten / <u>blaze</u>
   <u>gig</u> / bright / glaze
2. safer / worn / lift
   savor / one / <u>lick</u>
   favor / <u>wand</u> / lit
   <u>saber</u> / blend / lip
3. decay / <u>gross</u> / smile
   debate / growth / <u>smart</u>
   efface / group / smock
   <u>deface</u> / broke / mock
4. wool / blast / village
   <u>woe</u> / glad / visit
   wove / <u>glass</u> / busy
   low / black / <u>vivid</u>
5. plain / room / gold
   playmate / loom / go
   plainly / move / dull
   <u>plainness</u> / <u>moon</u> / dough
6. rigid / lion / <u>bit</u>
   bridges / why / fit
   <u>frigid</u> / wind / disc
   tribute / <u>wine</u> / dip
7. mortar / flood / <u>press</u>
   warble / luck / crept
   <u>mortal</u> / blunt / crest
   morbid / <u>bluff</u> / pressed
8. does / bend / resort
   bud / gem / export
   <u>buzz</u> / <u>dim</u> / absorb
   bug / den / <u>exhort</u>
9. lesson / <u>bug</u> / <u>sold</u>
   glisten / bug / so
   <u>blessing</u> / buzz / scold
   blessed / budge / sole

Speaker 23 is ....

1. long / ask / <u>vulture</u>
   round / act / bolster
   loud / hat / also
   <u>lounge</u> / <u>ax</u> / vulgar
2. puzzle / might / able
   huddle / nice / <u>table</u>
   cuddle / <u>knife</u> / fable
   <u>puddle</u> / night / cable
3. <u>ounce</u> / <u>bless</u> / earthly
   out / less / virtue
   house / bled / virgin
   bounce / blessed / <u>urgent</u>
4. omit / <u>flow</u> / jade
   <u>commit</u> / slow / jail
   commence / blow / <u>jay</u>
   permit / glow / jig
5. tiny / bran / blunder
   <u>kindly</u> / <u>brand</u> / plunger
   hang / grand / <u>plunder</u>
   timing / brass / thunder
6. purpose / <u>string</u> / keeper
   <u>propose</u> / strength / <u>caper</u>
   oppose / strain / taper
   suppose / strange / paper
7. frighten / <u>guise</u> / tremble
   <u>brightness</u> / guide / several
   greatness / dies / trouble
   breakfast / dive / <u>treble</u>
8. bland / hem / smithy
   land / hand / Smitty
   plan / <u>end</u> / <u>smitten</u>
   <u>gland</u> / hen / Smith
9. flack / gaze / <u>merit</u>
   <u>flat</u> / gain / match
   black / <u>gave</u> / marriage
   blast / gay / marry

Speaker 24 is ....

1. wax / <u>herb</u> / <u>glance</u>
   waxing / hurt / glass
   waxy / urge / gland
   <u>waxen</u> / heard / glands
2. home / <u>and</u> / speaker
   roam / end / teacher
   <u>own</u> / an / <u>feature</u>
   old / hand / Beecher
3. screen / lying / love
   free / line / <u>log</u>
   <u>spree</u> / lion / lost
   spring / <u>lining</u> / loud
4. length / bank / whiskey
   <u>link</u> / <u>thank</u> / trip
   leak / sank / drifting
   blink / think / <u>thrifty</u>
5. <u>yea</u> / <u>basin</u> / move
   gave / hasten / <u>mood</u>
   gale / basement / lewd
   gay / basic / smooth
6. follow / stuffed / brought
   folly / <u>stuff</u> / <u>wrought</u>
   bother / stop / rock
   <u>father</u> / stuck / rocked
7. <u>intrude</u> / <u>brass</u> / paint
   confess / drag / ink
   improve / grass / <u>pink</u>
   intrigue / grasp / peak
8. loss / bathe / stomach
   block / spade / summon
   lost / fade / <u>summit</u>
   <u>gloss</u> / <u>phase</u> / summer
9. grip / address / frock
   drift / regress / crock
   rip / regret / <u>crop</u>
   <u>drip</u> / <u>redress</u> / prop

FIG. 35. Reproduction of Answer Form D, lists 19 to 24, with the correct responses (items) underlined.

409

SPEAKER TEST 1
When called upon by the instructor
READ FROM THIS CARD
In reading the test, remember to pause after
each line of test items.

I am Speaker One. I say again, I am Speaker One.
My name is (last name and initials).
   Number 1 grew modest vice
   Number 2 stay pervade chink
   Number 3 stun grunt intent
   Number 4 whence physic wave
   Number 5 pass query fine
   Number 6 poplar burst get
   Number 7 immense name omen
   Number 8 lattice last slain
   Number 9 craft bolt polo

FIG. 36. A sample speaker list prepared for Speaker 1, Form C in multiple-choice intelligibility testing.

The following explanation is on the back of the Speaker Test card and is facing *up* when the student first sees the card.

Read These Instructions Carefully

This is a test of your ability to be intelligible, that is, to be heard correctly. Your rating as a speaker depends upon the number of times the words that you speak are recorded correctly by your listeners. It is important that you read the test exactly as it is printed on the opposite side of this card.

Speakers will read in the order of assigned seat numbers; the student in Seat 1 will speak first, Seat 2 second, and so on. When it is your turn to read, identify yourself as indicated on the opposite side of this card; then read the test words, being certain always to use the phrase "Number 1 _____," "Number 2 _____," etc. Pause for about two seconds after each group of test words. This will give your listeners time to record what you say. Please reread this paragraph.

When you are not speaking, you will draw a line through the words that you hear and that are on your answer sheet. Record each speaker's number and name. The front cover of your answer sheet shows you how to cross out what you hear.[1] Your instructor will give further instructions and will answer any questions.

[Instructions like the following ones are given orally and informally. They are altered to suit your circumstances. For example, you may have no sweep-hand timer. Substitute the saying of a phrase that requires one or two seconds.

[1] Presumably the answer sheets are given a cover page that resembles Fig. 38.

SPEAKER TEST _____
When called upon by the instructor
READ FROM THIS CARD
In reading the test, remember to pause after
each line of test items.

I am Speaker _____. I say again, I am Speaker_____.
My name is (last name and initials).
　　　Number 1
　　　Number 2
　　　Number 3
　　　Number 4
　　　Number 5
　　　Number 6
　　　Number 7
　　　Number 8
　　　Number 9

FIG. 37. A form in which a student may write the mssing words and from which he may read in administrations of multiple-choice intelligibility tests. Forms C and D.

For example, "After each line, say silently 'one hundred one, one hundred two' and then read the next line aloud."]

You have two papers on your desk. These are materials for an intelligibility test.

This test will prove interesting to you. It will demonstrate to each of you, and to the remainder of the group who are to serve as your listeners, how efficient you are as a speaker under conditions of (describe conditions, i.e., 75 db of electric-fan noise, 110–114 db of recorded aircraft noise, classroom quiet, etc.). The words you speak are to be read from the small card ($5'' \times 7''$) that is on your desk. As an illustration, suppose your card contained the following words, "I am Speaker One. I say again, I am Speaker One. My name is Doe, J. G. Number 1 mortar shut assist. Number 2 blimp injure knob. Number 3 gliding battle ignite." You would read it as I did. You may have noticed that I said the identifying information, speaker number and name, without attention to the clock (sweep-hand timer). Then I waited until the hand pointed to 12 to read "Number 1 mortar shut assist." The hand goes around in six seconds. When it hit 12 again, I said, "Number 2, etc." The next time it passed 12, "Number 3, etc." This pacing of the lines allows the listeners time to respond. You may have noticed also that I read "Number 1 mortar shut assist" as a unit, a phrase, as if the words were a sentence and made sense. They usually don't, but read them as though they do, as a group, all in one breath. This permits you to read each line with the natural speech patterns of ordinary sentences. Remember: (1) read from the card; (2) say the introductory material when it is your turn to talk; then watch the clock and when the hand reaches 12 start with "Number 1 . . . " Wait until the clock is at 12 again; then "Number 2 . . . "; (3) read naturally with each group of three words—and the words *number* and (a digit) that preceded the three words—said as a single phrase as though the line made sense, all on one breath. (Questions are called for; if none, an informal summary of the instructions is repeated.)

The following instructions are given to the listeners, probably the same people who are talkers. A convenient answer sheet can be reproduced in quantity with a cover somewhat like the one of Fig. 38. The cover should emphasize listening, should not use examples that are drawn from the test itself.

Now look at the listeners' answer form.

As listeners you are going to hear a series of groups of three words. From your responses we can measure both the intelligibility of the individual(s) who read the words and your efficiency as a listener in this communication system (the particular listening environment is then described). Let's look at the front cover of your answer form. You will hear:

> I am Speaker 1; I say again, I am Speaker 1. My
> name is Doe, J. G. (pause) number 1 mortar shut assist
> (pause) number 2 blimp injure knob (pause) number 3
> gliding battle ignite.

You will notice that for each word I read there are four possible choices on the cover of your answer form. You heard me say, "Number 1 mortar shut assist." The first word after "Number 1" was *mortar* and this appears in the first, or left-hand, group of four words. Put a line through mortar (not under the word but through it, please). The second word *shut* is found in the second group of four words of *Number 1*, and the third word *assist* is found in the third group of four words of *Number 1*. Your response is to draw a line *through* the word you hear, making one mark in each group of four words. Erasures are permitted. (Repeat the explanation for examples *Numbers 2* and *3*. Questions are called for.) Each speaker will read nine groups of three words. Write the speaker's name in the space above the list he reads. Remember, draw a line *through* the words you hear, or think you hear.

A principal advantage of the multiple-choice form is that it provides an opportunity for the preparation of a scoring template and for rapid scoring. Simply cut the correct responses from one answer form and lay the remainder of the page over each student's answer form. Draw a red line where the student has not marked. The intelligibility score may be retained as (1) number of errors, or (2) number of right responses, or (3) per cent right, $1 - \dfrac{\text{No. of errors}}{27}$. (With some electric calculating machines this answer is

P.O.S. Form **C**

YOUR NAME .... DATE ....

CLASS & WING .... POSITION ....

WHEN YOU HEAR....

Number 1
MORTAR   SHUT   ASSIST

Number 2
BLIMP   INJURE   KNOB

Number 3
GLIDING   BATTLE   IGNITE

MARK YOUR PAPER LIKE THIS..

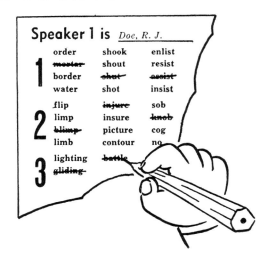

Speaker 1 is *Doe, R. J.*

1
order   shook   enlist
mortar   shout   resist
border   shut   assist
water   shot   insist

2
flip   injure   sob
limp   insure   knob
blimp   picture   cog
limb   contour   no

3
lighting   battle
gliding

FIG. 38. A cover design that is helpful in explaining how to respond to a multiple-choice intelligibility test. The design emphasizes the role of the listener, includes an identification of the listener and his listening position, and shows how he responds to test items.

obtained directly by entering the reciprocal of 27 on the keyboard and multiplying by the number of errors, using *negative multiplication* key.)

WRITE-DOWN TESTS[1]

The following lists of words may be reproduced on 5- by 7-inch cards in much the manner described above for the multiple-choice tests or, alternatively, may be read directly from the textbook. Each line contains but one test word, and this would be preceded by a carrier phrase, such as "Number 1" or "I am saying" or "You will write." The instructions may be adapted from the ones above and are, of course, much simpler.

To the readers: Read the card one line at a time and pause 2 seconds between lines or pause long enough between lines to say silently, "One hundred one, one hundred two."

To the listeners: Write down the words you hear, using a separate paper for each reader.

The instructor at the end of the test will give all the answer sheets that pertain to the same speaker to that speaker and ask him to bring his score to the next class meeting. Errors in spelling do not count as errors if the right word was obviously intended (right number, tense, etc.). With a panel of 12 students, the speaker's score will be

$$1 - \frac{\text{total no. of errors}}{11 \times 24} = \text{right score in per cent}$$

24-ITEM INTELLIGIBILITY TESTS

List 1	*List 2*	*List 3*	*List 4*
rupture	menace	zero	mute
behold	pun	royal	city
transfer	half	converge	iris
habit	salad	sixteen	shiftless
replace	navy	daily	quack
peanut	keyboard	propose	in
finance	owl	urgent	gallant
journal	dismay	entry	visit
jar	made	jail	bishop
garden	southeast	flicker	ampere

[1] C. Hess Haagen, *Intelligibility Measurement: Techniques and Procedures Used by the Voice Communication Laboratory,* The Psychological Corporation, New York, OSRD Report 3748, 1944.

List 1	*List* 2	*List* 3	*List* 4
option	measure	candy	western
discard	darken	felt	income
horror	headache	year	perfume
function	journey	binding	ransom
gang	rich	knuckle	faithful
naval	lady	goat	wicked
startle	world	fable	quiver
maiden	preserve	disgust	tonight
fence	woolen	beef	air
us	beware	envy	double
acorn	beaver	junction	held
tiger	galore	late	odd
concern	end	entrust	common
find	pulp	pad	rubber

List 5	*List* 6	*List* 7	*List* 8
outline	nasal	arrest	hip
uncle	verse	hardly	got
improve	suspend	thirteen	lash
oblige	heel	excite	merry
icebox	arrow	became	lanky
virtue	bill	across	impulse
pressure	beg	speed	pause
divide	goal	arch	rabble
nature	partner	neutral	misuse
author	farflung	hungry	unit
sweet	grenade	traitor	ablaze
volley	robust	project	manner
opal	ice	epic	design
recent	living	rub	inland
hall	gamble	sitting	up
irk	former	medal	acute
vacant	help	usage	oppose
distract	forego	race	reform
minute	prevail	eve	earthquake
deafen	weather	pace	upright
laundry	inquire	wallet	fourteen
pebble	guilty	odor	jawbone
blow	quaint	ego	content
fact	art	infect	firm

24-ITEM INTELLIGIBILITY TESTS

List 9	List 10	List 11	List 12
forbid	ocean	hotel	airport
rabbit	prow	forget	only
perfect	mar	hello	fifteen
raider	hit	autumn	enroll
bird	decent	rigid	conclude
join	fasten	elm	invite
earmark	salt	lemon	ramp
helpful	motion	useless	endorse
young	himself	issue	swear
purge	each	yonder	calm
relief	proud	copy	belief
vacuum	wine	beneath	profit
plate	carbon	leave	narrow
chapter	icebound	behalf	scatter
often	enclose	possess	wheat
rusty	yet	vain	throb
dot	target	seaside	mood
thimble	engage	thorn	keystone
vermin	old	eldest	juice
leaf	yellow	noon	moss
address	fair	joyful	elsewhere
crowd	absent	vibrate	joke
wife	nonsense	ask	nation
hive	outlet	case	keep

List 13	List 14	List 15	List 16
lame	surprise	massive	key
quart	abrupt	thud	zoom
errand	hope	itch	escape
jobber	fishing	dental	meaning
profess	secure	ceiling	offend
tropic	lumber	ox	faint
zone	obstruct	gracious	fashion
money	man	mad	trifle
tomb	ride	precede	parlor
feast	quarter	law	timid
enjoy	zigzag	halfback	unclean
garage	quit	bright	brutal

List 13	*List* 14	*List* 15	*List* 16
profane	hate	achieve	thousand
willow	blunder	damp	room
yard	talent	resume	killer
shipping	gain	you	wade
glide	sustain	below	valley
quarrel	license	iceman	cannon
younger	threat	ready	transcribe
row	tassel	out	open
unload	born	wood	question
hazel	shoot	good	jockey
deduct	daisy	lifelike	accent
bat	oral	tender	oath

List 17	*List* 18	*List* 19	*List* 20
obey	screech	worship	knitting
without	dance	stampede	native
final	this	silver	herald
acquaint	maker	trapeze	pain
ugly	ark	call	kennel
lamp	dainty	uphill	swoop
hangar	crop	urge	district
wallet	nothing	gather	rummage
banquet	raid	lava	grasping
heading	induce	enough	acre
shut	beyond	kiss	culture
captain	legion	temper	traffic
cabin	persist	valve	recline
harvest	darling	germ	anger
doe	treasure	pardon	oval
manage	withhold	storage	rumor
glimmer	jumbo	at	abroad
heat	wise	keel	bombard
drab	reverse	fault	detail
zinc	direct	morn	walking
wool	figure	observe	hurdle
banner	occur	junior	index
campaign	handcuff	molest	abound
robe	vote	nap	boast

24-ITEM INTELLIGIBILITY TESTS

List 21	*List* 22
broken	vast
week	shudder
foreclose	eighty
extreme	crook
change	justice
upon	mankind
driven	napkin
able	practice
gold	complete
ignite	soldier
untold	panic
slaughter	tackle
gearshift	kodak
victor	nature
class	kingdom
describe	wall
foremost	lament
afraid	tack
gage	import
census	canteen
north	pistol
union	needy
distance	orphan
salute	quake

INDEX